Heart Advice

Essential Instructions on the
Path of Liberation

Younge Khachab Rinpoche

Edited by Gregory Patenaude

YOUNGE DRODUL LING

Copyright © 2019 by Younge Khachab Rinpoche

All rights reserved. Thank you for buying an authorized edition of this book and for complying with copyright laws by not reproducing, scanning, or distributing any part of it in any form without permission.

ISBN-13: 9781796539998

Cover Design by DilleyDesign

BUDDHA SHAKYAMUNI

CONTENTS

Editor's Preface	ix
Introduction	1

PART ONE: FIRST TURNING OF THE WHEEL OF DHARMA

1	**The Basis**	15
	The four noble truths	15
	Examining ignorance, the root cause of all suffering	16
	Self-grasping	18
	Five skandhas	20
2	**The Path**	31
	General presentation	31
	Specific presentation	35
	Differences between the sravakas and the pratyekabuddhas	41
3	**A Concise Presentation of the Practice**	43
	Hinayana	43
	Mahayana view of the skandhas	47
	Tantric view of the skandhas	48
	Summary	52

PART TWO: SECOND TURNING OF THE WHEEL OF DHARMA

4	**The Basis**	55
	Lineage history	55
	Why is emptiness important?	61
	In pursuit of emptiness	63
	How to develop the wisdom of emptiness	64
	The view of emptiness with five features	72
	Concise presentation of the middle way at the level of the basis	79
5	**The Path**	82
	Method and wisdom	82
	Union of shamatha and vipasyana	85
	The actual path	89
6	**A Concise Presentation of the Practice**	99
	Daily practice of the path Middle Way	99

PART THREE: THIRD TURNING OF THE WHEEL OF DHARMA

7	**The Tathagatagarbha**	107
	Why the tathagatagarbha is taught	108
	The sutras and shastras on buddha nature	111
	The ten natures and nine metaphors of buddha nature	113
8	**Presentations on Buddhanature**	121
	Buddha nature in the Indian traditions	121
	Buddha nature in Tibet	124
9	**Carrying Buddhanature into Our Own Practice**	129
	A seven-point summary	130

PART FOUR: PRAJNAPARAMITA, THE PERFECTION OF WISDOM

10	**Prajnaparamita, the Perfection of Wisdom**	157
	The meaning of prajnaparamita	157
	History of the prajnaparamita lineage	159
	The heart of the Buddha's teachings	164
	Subdivisions of the perfection of wisdom	168
	The hidden meaning of the perfection of wisdom	170
	Maitreya's *Ornament of Clear Realization*	175
	Prajnaparamita: the essence of the three baskets	180
11	**Carrying the Prajnaparamita Teachings into Practice**	182
	Ground perfection of wisdom	183
	Mahayana potential	185
	Path perfection of wisdom	191
	Path of meditation	198
	Practicing the six perfections in meditation	204
	Mind training as an enhancement practice	206
	Dedicate the merit	207

PART FIVE: THE RESULTANT VEHICLES OF THE VAJRAYANA

12	**Essence of Tantra**	211
	Meaning of "mantra"	211
	History of tantra	212
	Hindu tantra and Buddhist tantra	219
	Tantra and the three baskets	225
	Essential meaning of the ripening initiation and liberating instructions	234
	The guru—the root of the path	239

	The three continuums	245
	Generation and completion stages	254
	Summary	262
13	**Essence of Mahamudra**	264
	Brief history of the Kagyu tradition	264
	Mahamudra in India and Tibet	270
	Differences between Mahamudra and Dzogchen	272
	Path of method- the Six Yogas of Naropa	273
	The path of liberation- Mahamudra	284
	Uncommon Mahamudra instruction and enhancement practices for eliminating errors in meditation	290
	How to carry the practice of Mahamudra into one meditative session	291
	Closing Advice	294

Notes — 295

About Younge Khachab Rinpoche — 301

YOUNGE KHACHAB RINPOCHE

EDITOR'S PREFACE

It is an honor to write this preface to Younge Khachab Rinpoche's breakthrough book that distills the depth of the Dharma and the various Buddhist traditions, making them accessible and practical to our own life and mind. Rinpoche offered these teachings in 2011 with the intention to present the three vehicles of the Hinayana, Mahayana, and Vajrayana in their essential form so that we can have a working basis for our own study, contemplation and meditation.

In this book, Rinpoche condensed the most essential elements of the teachings, the ones we must know, to practice the path. He then presents these teachings in a format that is accessible to Westerners. Rinpoche has a remarkable ability to see how all the teachings are connected in our own practice. He teaches us how to carry these various practice traditions onto our own path by understanding all of the Buddha's teachings as instructions for practice.

It would be very difficult to understand a work of this magnitude by simply reading through the book. You must work over these teachings, contemplate them, meditate on them, and allow them to stir the depths of your own wisdom. This in-depth study and contemplation will help you discover their meaning manifesting in your life in unexpected ways. These teachings have been an immense benefit in my own practice, and I find myself returning again and again to reexamine sections or to build connections with new material that I am studying.

As a brief overview, we can start by understanding that all of the Buddha's teachings are contained within the three turnings of the wheel of dharma. Throughout this book, Rinpoche makes reference to the basis, path and result of each of the three turnings. 'Basis' refers to the view, or understanding of the nature of the person and of reality. 'Path' refers to the practice that grows out of that view and understanding. The 'result' refers to the resultant state that is achieved after having practiced the path. It is not the case that each turning rejects the view of the other; instead, the view and understanding becomes more subtle and profound as we progress from one turning to the next.

In Part One, Rinpoche focuses on the teachings of the first turning of the wheel of dharma, where the Buddha presents the four noble truths and dependent origination as the foundation of his teachings. Rinpoche takes an in-depth look at how the five skandhas, or psychophysical aggregates, serve as the basis for our dissatisfaction and suffering in this life. By examining the five skandhas we become experts in understanding the nature of the human condition and come to fully understand the first noble truth, the nature of suffering in this life. Understanding the skandhas reveals how we can uproot ignorance to break free from the cycle of suffering and forms the basis for the practice of the first turning of the wheel. By understanding suffering and what gives rise to suffering, we meditate on the nature of the self and give rise to the wisdom of selflessness. Rinpoche gives a concise presentation on how to carry these teachings into our own practice in order to actualize the resultant state of cessation.

Part Two focuses on the teachings of the second turning of the wheel of dharma, where the Buddha presents the principles of the Prajnaparamita sutras and the Middle Way view of emptiness. In the first turning of the wheel of dharma, the wisdom of selflessness was realized by understanding the five skandhas. In the second turning, that wisdom becomes more subtle and profound by relying on the two truths as presented by Nagarjuna. These two truths, relative and ultimate, serve to eliminate ignorance and grasping to self and phenomena. Rinpoche explains how we can carry this view of emptiness into our own life through the practice of shamatha and vipasyana. Step by step he guides us along the path to arrive at the view of emptiness free from extremes, culminating in how to experience the mind itself as the union of the two truths. Rinpoche concludes this section with how we can carry the Mahayana's profound understanding of method and wisdom into our own daily life through the practice of the six perfections.

In Part Three, Rinpoche summarizes the teachings of the third turning of the wheel of dharma, where the Buddha introduced the tathagatagarbha, or buddha nature. These teachings on buddha nature develop from the understanding of the nature of the mind introduced in the second turning, and form the basis for the practice of Mahayana sutra, Tantra, Mahamudra and Dzogchen. Rinpoche gives an extensive explanation on how the tathagatagarbha is present and how our practice serves to reveal our naturally present buddha nature. Based on his extensive knowledge and understanding of the various practice traditions in Tibet, Rinpoche explains the different perspectives on buddha nature and concludes with a concise summary on how to carry these teachings into our own practice.

Part Four reviews the Prajnaparamita literature that was revealed during the second turning of the wheel of dharma. Having gained some understanding of the second and third turnings of the wheel of dharma, Rinpoche provides a detailed review of the hidden meaning of the prajnaparamita teachings and gives us elaborate instructions on how to progress along the bodhisattva path. Presenting the path of the bodhisattvas in both an extensive and concise form, Rinpoche reveals how we can carry these teachings into our daily life.

Part Five focuses on the resultant vehicles of the Vajrayana, specifically tantra and Mahamudra. These traditions grow out of the Mahayana sutra understanding of the tathagatagarbha, but take the resultant state as the very path itself. Rinpoche generously explains critical aspects of Buddhist tantra, such as the role of the teacher, empowerment and samaya- concepts that are often foreign to the Western audience. Then he moves on to presents the tantric path and the role of the generation and completion stages in actualizing buddhahood in this very lifetime.

Rinpoche concludes this section by describing the practice of Mahamudra as it evolved in Tibet. Rinpoche presents the history of Mahamudra and some critical distinctions between Mahamudra and Dzogchen. Rinpoche then describes how the Mahamudra tradition came down to us today as the path of method and the path of liberation, including some essential practice instructions for the practice of Mahamudra. Rinpoche concludes with a concise presentation of Mahamudra and how to carry these profound teachings into a single practice session.

As Vajrayana practitioners, it is important that we do not make the mistake of looking down on or neglecting the foundational teachings of the Buddha. All of the Buddha's teachings are relevant to our own practice. Studying and contemplating all of the Buddha's teachings is not simply information gathering for the sake of conceptual knowledge. It is through our experience that we realize the profound wisdom and impact of these teachings in our own life.

Notably left out of this presentation of the path of liberation is Dzogchen, or the Great Perfection. When Rinpoche gave these teachings he spent an entire year focusing on the material that would become this present book, and another year devotedly entirely to Dzogchen. We are currently working on publishing Rinpoche's masterful presentation of Dzogchen, and understanding the teachings and path presented in this book will prepare the ground for our practice and realization of Dzogchen.

ACKNOWLEDGEMENT

Work on this book began many years ago and has relied on the efforts and generosity of many people. Members of the Samye Translation Committee worked closely with Rinpoche, carefully reviewing the text with him and making many clarifications and revisions. Committee members involved many volunteers to whom we are most grateful.

When Rinpoche taught these teachings in 2011, it was the effort and careful attention of the translator Tenzin Bhuchung that helped bring these profound instructions to the world. Jane Braaten and I first transcribed these teachings and worked on the original manuscript. Jane was instrumental in providing reference materials and footnotes throughout the text. Jenya Antonova served as the project manager and was involved in editing the book during the final stages. Trisha Lamb was extremely generous with her suggestions and completed the copy editing. Throughout the process I worked extensively with Rinpoche to clarify difficult sections and to ensure that we were presenting these teachings correctly.

We could not have completed this effort without the generous support of our Kyilkhor sponsors, who provided the financial support necessary to undertake such a project. These are all the best of Dharma friends and companions and I am forever grateful to share this journey with them.

HEART ADVICE

The material for this book has served as coursework for all students of the Younge Drodul Ling Sangha in order to build a foundation for practice and to provide context for understanding all of the Buddha's teachings. Jon Dilley and I led a number of classes on each section of the book to students who eagerly read and discussed the material. Their insights, questions, and feedback helped us clarify some sections of the book.

Lastly, thank you to Younge Khachab Rinpoche, for your kindness, patience and wisdom. Your persistence and encouragement motivated all of us to keep doing the hard work of making these teachings available for the benefit of all. Your expansive view is truly a gift for all of us who follow in your footsteps, as we too strive to hold all of the Buddha's teachings free of contradiction, carrying their essence into our own practice. You continually show us through your example that heartfelt connection is not a part of the spiritual path to awakening, it is the path itself.

Gregory Patenaude
Seattle, Washington

YOUNGE KHACHAB RINPOCHE

INTRODUCTION

I would like to thank all those who are reading *Heart Advice*. Some of you are my longtime students and friends, and others may be new to the dharma. We should all rejoice in the opportunity to study and reflect on these teachings. I personally impart these teachings with great joy and confidence.

Ours are times of tremendous change, both in the external environment and in our inner lives, in the way we live and work. At the same time, the Buddha's teachings are flourishing. My wish is that we all see how the Buddha's teachings can be directly relevant to our lives – our own mind and body, but especially our mind. My intention is to provide the entirety of the Buddhist teachings in their essential form. I will highlight their essence, so that we can directly see their relevance and benefits.

I focus on the essence of the Buddhist path because Westerners do not have adequate time to follow the traditional six-year training of daily study, contemplation, and meditation. I will present the essence of the traditional curriculum, so that my students have a practical basis for their own study, contemplation, and meditation. That is my primary goal.

With these teachings, I hope to help you understand the essence of all of the Buddha's teachings, from Hinayana to Vajrayana. Because I am going straight to the essence, studying this material will be almost like having undertaken a six-year study. I am confident that, when it comes to actual practice, my approach will be as beneficial as the traditional course of study.

The Buddha's teachings are vast and profound, but if we understand the essence, we can easily grasp what is most meaningful and beneficial to our mind and body. Another benefit of studying the essence is that we can become able to easily navigate the material. Even if it is lengthy and complex, we will know how to approach the subject matter, without getting confused by the details. If we apprehend the essential content of the subject matter, then we are able to appreciate the unique qualities of a book.

Many Western academic programs are geared toward intellectual study, mostly of the sutra teachings, and are usually based on a particular text. Each text can be taught for several years, with much commentary and analysis. My goal is to present the teachings in their essential form, so that in a short time we can cover a lot of material and apply it directly to our own practice.

Presenting these teachings on the three turnings of the wheel of Dharma will prepare your mind for the practice and realization of Dzogchen, or the Great Perfection. If we look to the Dzogchen masters of the past, we find accomplished masters who had a comprehensive understanding of all the Buddha's teachings. We find early masters like Manjushrimitra, Shri Singha and Jnanasutra, who were all learned in both the sutras and tantras. In Tibet, we find great masters like Vimalamitra and Longchenpa, both who wrote extensively on Dzogchen, but also had many commentaries on the Mahayana sutras and tantras.

In Dzogchen, we find all the teachings contained in the nine yanas, or vehicles. These nine yanas are based on the capacity of the student, with the higher yanas being supported by the lower yanas. As Dzogchen practitioners, our view may be vast, but none of the teachings of the lower yanas are rejected. It is important that we can see how all of the yanas are connected and support each other, and that the path can be gradual or sudden based on the capacity of the student. We cannot speak of an instantaneous or sudden path if we ourselves are unable to comprehend the essence of all teachings in a single instant.

This book presents a practical, step by step summary of the teachings. The Buddha's teachings are vast and profound, but we don't need to make them complicated. What I present here is a very clear and practical guide in order to build that foundation for our own practice.

In Dzogchen, we often find people using very high words like rigpa and rainbow body, or talking about non-duality. Those are just concepts. The reality is that when we look at our own mind and examine our experience, we have many dualistic thoughts. Looking at our own mind, we can develop knowledge and understanding, gaining a direct experience and inner conviction of the Buddha's teachings. In this way, we can use the teachings that best suit our mind in order to come to the realization of Dzogchen, the natural Great Perfection. By understanding our own natural condition and the vast teachings of the nine yanas, we can truly benefit others by meeting them where they are at, in a way that is most beneficial to them.

HOW TO USE DHARMA TEACHINGS

We must remember the preciousness of this opportunity to study the Dharma. We have attained this precious human embodiment with its freedoms and resources, have come into contact with the teachings of the Buddha, and have met a spiritual friend of the Mahayana. Having these three advantages – a human embodiment, having encountered the Dharma, and having met a spiritual guide – we should be delighted at the opportunity to study the Dharma.

All of the 84,000 teachings of the Dharma come down to one point: the transformation of our own mind. This point is made by Nagarjuna in his *Letter to a Friend*. He ends the letter by saying:

> Oh King, all of what I have said before,
> you should take the main point of this to be
> to take the Dharma and use it to transform your mind.
> This is your main practice.

The Dharma is more than just what we have studied and heard. We need to know how to integrate these teachings into our own lives and how to apply them to our own mind.

The Three Jewels are very important in Buddhism. As Buddhists, we take refuge in the Three Jewels. Of the Three Jewels, the Dharma is most important to us, especially at first. Why is that? What makes the jewel of Dharma present or not present in our lives? The jewel of the Dharma is present for us when we are using it transform our mind; when the teachings are transforming us. When this happens, we gain trusting confidence and faith in the Dharma. If we do not use the Dharma to transform our own mind, the Dharma jewel is not present for us and we do not gain any confidence. If we do manage to use the Dharma to transform our minds, even to a small degree, then the Dharma jewel is present, and we gain confidence and faith in it. As a result, simply by the power of our faith in the Dharma, we also gain faith in the jewels of the Buddha and the Sangha.

The jewel of the Dharma is very important. If we have taken authentic refuge in the Dharma jewel, the Dharma is present in our mind and is transforming our mind. Through the trust and confidence that we have in the Dharma, we gain faith in the community that supports these teachings, as well as in the teacher, or the Buddha, who has made them available to us. This means that the Dharma jewel is not just a bunch of books. It is not the writing in the books or the words that we hear in talks. It is the way in which we use our learning or understanding to transform our mind. It means that on a daily basis, we are using the teachings to reduce the negative aspects of our mind and cultivate the positive ones. Even if the benefit is only temporary, it is the Dharma that improves our mind, eliminating its faults and developing its positive qualities.

To ensure that the Dharma jewel is present within our minds, we first need to understand that our mind can be transformed. If we do not believe that our mind can be transformed, then obviously the Dharma will have no effect on us. Thus, to make the Dharma jewel present in our lives and to gain faith in it, we must see its efficacy and how it works.

By investigating the nature of the mind, we can discern whether the mind is, in fact, capable of transformation, and if so, how it can be transformed. The more we investigate the mind, the more the Dharma can transform it. In this way, we deepen our faith not only in the Dharma, but also in the Buddha and the Sangha. If we are taking refuge in the Three Jewels only based on the pictures and books that we see, or because we are moved by the peaceful monks that teach the Dharma, then we might as well not take refuge at all.

Here I have emphasized the Dharma as the most important of the Three Jewels. However, this is not to downplay the importance of the community, or Sangha. The Sangha is also very important. To be able to effectively implement the Dharma and to transform our mind, we need a field of positive merit, from which to gain positive mental energy. For this, we need to have a community with whom to interact. Through that interaction, by practicing generosity and so on, we are able to gain the positive mental energy that enables our mind to be transformed by the Dharma jewel. In this way, the Sangha jewel is very important.

Occasionally, we face obstacles in our practice. Some of these can be external, such as lacking the material support, such as food or shelter, that enable our practice. There are also internal obstacles, which can be just as devastating and problematic as the external ones.

In the context of a community, we tend to experience the internal obstacles – the negative mental states present in us since beginningless time. The flaring up of internal obstacles can impede our Dharma practice by making it difficult to interact with others in our community. The negative mental states of jealousy and competitiveness can be especially blinding and constraining to us.

It is very important for us to recognize that, as ordinary persons, we are going to experience these negative mental states. When negative mental states are present, we need to very clearly recognize them, along with the problems or obstacles they create for our practice. We should also recognize and rejoice in the times when we experience reverence and respect for other members of the community. Furthermore, we should strive to cultivate reverence and respect towards others as an antidote to jealousy and competitiveness.

In my personal opinion, the Western, and especially American, culture suffers from a substantial problem: people are taught that an individual must possess certain qualities to be a worthy person, but these qualities include a very strong sense of independence in a prideful way. This self-centered image of what it means to be an individual encourages negative mental states, implying that no one needs to listen to anyone; that no-one can tell him or her what to do. As a result, Westerners may have difficulty following some Dharma principles, such as revering their teacher and showing a deep respect towards all sangha members. To practice the Dharma, it is very important to adjust some of our Western cultural assumptions about what it means to be an individual, and to eliminate the false notion of complete independence from everyone, the notion that 'you are your own boss.' Unless Westerners make this cultural adjustment, the Dharma is not going to be effective in transforming the mind.

Sometimes Westerners feel discouraged on their journeys on the Dharma path, and some even become depressed. It may seem paradoxical, but the depression and discouragement stem from this prideful individualism. It is because people perceive themselves as self-contained, independent individuals, who are entitled to do whatever they want, that they feel depressed, worthless, and discouraged when they fail in their attempts. This depression and discouragement feels like self-deprecation, but these feelings are actually a reflection of pridefulness or conceit.

I am not suggesting that it is a mistake to have a sense of pride if things are going well. When we develop positive mental states, we should rejoice in them so that we can develop them even further. What I mean is that when Westerners are dealing with negative mental states, and either the lama or a community member gives them advice, they tend to reject the idea that there is something wrong with them. Instead, they think that the fault lies with someone else. It is really hard to give advice to people with this kind of mentality. The recipients of advice may even smile while the lama or sangha member is speaking, but they are not really listening to the feedback or advice that is being offered. When there is a problem within us or our families or communities, we each need to take responsibility and determine the extent to which we are contributing to this problem.

Sometimes people criticize us or point out our faults. Our family members, other sangha members, or the teacher may recognize our negative behavior and try to offer solutions. When this happens, we need to recognize this as an opportunity to look clearly at our mind and determine whether what they are talking about is the case or not. Then, if we see some truth in what they have to say and recognize the problem, we need to take their feedback to heart and try to work with it and do something about it. Otherwise, if we know deep in our hearts that we have a problem, but respond by blaming others or denying the problem, then we will become very frustrated.

A prideful attitude contradicts the Dharma and creates obstacles for Dharma practice. This problem is not unique to Americans. We Tibetans have this problem too, although it may be less obvious than it is in Americans. Whenever I receive criticism, I sincerely examine myself to determine whether, and how, it applies to me.

We should always investigate whether our Dharma practice is changing our mind as well as our activities. We are receiving teachings on tantric practices, Mahamudra, and Dzogchen from the highest traditions. If on the one hand, we receive these incredible teachings that have the power to transform our mind, and on the other hand, our behavior - the actions of our body, speech, and mind - actually worsens, then something is clearly wrong.

I encourage those of you who are Dharma practitioners to strengthen your good qualities and your ability to behave well. The problems begin when we start handing over our responsibility to others or worrying about whether we can control others. We need to have an open heart and open mind. We need to sincerely wish to act, and act, with the intent to help others.

World peace starts in our own mind. It branches out into our local community, and then outwards to the larger world. This is the way we build world peace. If we have peace in our own community, then it can grow outwards.

May your body, speech, and mind conform to the Dharma. May you be humble, kind, positive-minded, and willing to look into yourself to determine how you can improve. I encourage you to use the Dharma to transform your body, speech, and mind.

PRACTICE OF THE MIND

We should always speak of the Dharma in relation to attaining happiness and rejecting suffering. Our well-being depends on our environment. And our environment, even on the large scale, depends on the minds of sentient beings, specifically of humans. For the Earth to be healthy and well-maintained, the minds of humans must be used to promote happiness and eliminate suffering. The only effective means for generating such a mental attitude is the Dharma.

When speaking about eliminating suffering and promoting happiness, we should not simply pay lip service to the idea, but rather actually investigate the basis for happiness and suffering. What are the causes and conditions that produce suffering and happiness? As human beings, we must look into these things carefully.

To maintain our intent to attain happiness and eliminate suffering, we must maintain our enthusiasm and positive mental energy. For that, we need to realize that all of us equally have the right and the potential to attain happiness and eliminate suffering. Such positive thinking can encourage us to engage in practice. Once we have realized that we have this potential, we can speak about the benefits of the Dharma, based not on blind faith, but on logic and reasoning.

We should rationally investigate our current situation; the causes and conditions present in our lives. For example, how can we explain the differences between those who read this book and those who do not? One way to distinguish readers from non-readers is by recognizing that the readers have sufficient merit, or positive mental energy, to approach and study this book. That is the kind of reasoning we can use.

When considering merit, we can start by thinking on a large scale. We should recall that there are more than 7 billion people living in this world, but only a small percentage of them are interested in the Dharma. Most people care about external issues – their appearance, their jobs, and so on. Relatively few care about spiritual issues – what to do or avoid doing in order to attain happiness and eliminate suffering.

Tibetan Buddhism arrived in the United States more than forty years ago, but many Tibetans who came to the United States have forgotten about the Dharma. However, some Americans – just a small number so far – became interested in Tibetan Buddhism. These are people who have positive mental energy, or merit. So, it is not cultural background or genetics, but merit, that allows people to connect with the Dharma.

Given the cultural environment here in the West, where even Tibetans tend to forget about the Dharma, you are especially fortunate to find yourself reading this book. In this cultural environment, you have nonetheless taken a strong interest in the Dharma and engaged in it. I feel delighted to know that some of you have taken up the Dharma with such enthusiasm.

One important point to note: even though we have the positive merit to take up the study of the Dharma, we must make sure to continue our practice. Sometimes people encounter the Dharma based on their good merit, but they fail to practice continuously. Their

Dharma practice is a 'flash in the pan,' their positive mental energy directs them towards the Dharma, and their interest is very intense for a little while, but then it burns out. Instead, we need to persevere over a long period of time; month by month, year by year, we should continue studying the Dharma, contemplating what we have studied, and putting what we have contemplated into practice. This sequence – learning, contemplating, meditating, and practicing – is very important for implementing the Dharma in our life. We must maintain a long-term view and not expect immediate results; such expectations often lead to burnout.

In discussions of the Dharma, we often talk about certainty. We often understand certainty in the context of studying something until we understand it. We develop an 'external' or intellectual certainty when we are reading books. However, within our Dharma practice, we must search for internal certainty as well as intellectual understanding. In particular, you need to develop certainty in regard to your own mind. We should be studying our own mind: how it works, what its propensities are, and what happens when the mind engages our body and speech. Inner certainty related to these kinds of issues is very important. Therefore, we should develop not only external understanding, based on reading books and listening to teachings, but also internal certainty with regard to our mind.

The focus on the mind is what defines us as Buddhists. The Tibetan language has two terms that literally mean "insider" and "outsider." "Insider" signifies a Buddhist, and "outsider" refers to a non-Buddhist. I personally understand these terms slightly differently. All three vehicles of Buddhism – Hinayana, Mahayana, and Vajrayana – agree that the mind is the central and most important thing to understand. It is the object of transformation in our practice. I understand an insider as someone who focuses his or her attention on the mind and sees its transformation as their main personal practice and responsibility. In contrast, outsiders, in my view, are those who are concerned with something outside of themselves: the external world, a deity, a god. Outsiders direct their spiritual energy outside of themselves, toward an external object of focus. Therefore, from the standpoint of conviction the most important concern is internal. Our mind should be the main focal point of practice.

We can understand the importance of the mind if we recognize that it is what creates both our happiness and our misery. We all want to be happy, but often we feel the opposite. We all want to avoid suffering, but somehow, we always find ourselves in unfortunate circumstances, feeling uncomfortable and suffering. What causes these situations to arise? They arise primarily because of our mental attitude or way of looking at things. For example, we find ourselves avoiding someone who we used to consider a good friend. Conversely, we embrace someone who we used to consider a bad friend, or even a rival. Clearly, our attitudes towards people change continuously, and this is why we should not take our current thinking too seriously. However, what does become a problem is our inability to distinguish good friends from bad friends. Such confusion leads us into suffering, away from happiness.

Each of the world's religious traditions – Christianity, Hinduism, Buddhism, and so on – offer all kinds of magnificence: splendid places of worship and learning, grand monuments, beautiful buildings, great texts written by great authors, and great speakers, admired by their audience. Each of these traditions has many followers who have a lot of faith in certain people and in things. However, when we take a closer look, we can see a fundamental flaw in this kind of faith. Any faith in an external object or person, even the lamas dressed in fine robes, is fundamentally false. This kind of faith relies on an external refuge, which is deceptive.

Upon close examination, we find that outwardly-focused faith is driven by our own self-cherishing. It is our own desire and self-centeredness that orient us towards external greatness – things or people – in the hope of somehow satisfying this self-cherishing. Self-cherishing is always projecting outward to satisfy our internal craving. Therefore, as long as self-cherishing fuels our external faith, our refuge will remain false. Instead of happiness, this false faith will always lead us to suffering. Although we are always looking for happiness, we are going to suffer if we continue relying on external faith and false refuge.

To be clear, I am not criticizing your coming to Dharma centers and practicing as a group; this is not what I mean. I am not saying that there is no benefit in these activities. There is a lot of benefit in practicing the Dharma together with other sangha members. Contrary to discouraging this, I often remind my students that they belong to a group of practitioners. And as a member of a center, they need to cherish it. But our primary focus should always be on the mind. Do not externalize your faith; internalize it.

At all times and in all contexts, we must examine our mind by using our mindfulness and discriminating awareness. As we are exposed to our own faults, we should eliminate them. As we begin to see the four positive qualities, we should cultivate them further.

If we do not accustom ourselves to the internal practice of looking for our own faults, then we might find ourselves getting pulled further and further into self-cherishing. Based on their external faith, some people may even start setting themselves apart from others, in a special social position. By doing so they further boost their self-cherishing, self-centeredness, and self-righteousness, telling themselves that they are special because they have received special teachings, obtained special knowledge, received special empowerments, or engaged in special practices. On that basis, husband and wife may not get along. All kinds of conflicts will arise due to such self-cherishing.

I am not saying that we must eliminate our self-centeredness all at once. This is a long-term, gradual practice. The aim here, and what we find among the great practitioners of India and Tibet, is to make self-investigation a general bodhisattva practice. We must see the faults in ourselves, be critical of ourselves in an honest way, and we must see the positive qualities in others. This is a basic, fundamental, bodhisattva practice we must follow.

Shantideva said that if we do not guard our mind, there is no point in doing any of the other practices. If we sincerely engage our discriminating awareness and mindfulness to guard our mind, our practice will gradually improve. We will come closer to authentic wisdom, our community and environment will improve, and we will find ourselves and the people around us better and happier. There are many great benefits to be gained from the practice of guarding the mind. Alternatively, if we do not guard our mind, then we will not be able to advance in our practice.

Guarding our mind is important not only for seeing our faults, but also for maintaining a positive mental attitude. Occasionally, in the context of our practice, we may find ourselves losing our enthusiasm; we may become discouraged and think that things are not going well. During such times, we should remind ourselves that the mind of every being, including ourselves, is a treasury of good qualities and we cannot lose this treasury. With this reminder, we will continue to develop additional good qualities and won't lose the ones we have gained. When things are not going well, we should remember that our mind still has infinite potential. Such positive thinking can help us overcome depressive feelings and internal and external obstacles, bringing forth the energetic state that allows us to practice effectively.

Since beginningless time we have maintained an inauthentic view of ourselves, which leads to suffering. With this spurious view, we have been self-centeredly fixated on our erroneously-conceived qualities, thinking them good. Instead of this we can adopt an authentic and proper view, focus on cultivating the good qualities of our mind, and praise ourselves for practice or study. This positive state of mind can be very beneficial for our practice.

Thinking about burning out or losing enthusiasm for practice reminds me of how gradual and lifelong Dharma practice really is. We should not get 'hyped-up' about practice and plunge into it too enthusiastically, forcing ourselves to practice all of the time. We should develop our practice gradually, making sure it remains stable and strong. Practicing this way, we will not burn out.

OVERVIEW OF THE ESSENCE OF THE PATH

To gain the state of liberation, we need to understand three things: the basis, the path, and the result. In the first turning of the Wheel of Dharma, Buddha presented the basis, which is nirvana. The second turning focused on the actual path, including the three doors of liberation. The second turning taught the antidotes that enable us to eliminate the ignorance that was discussed in the first turning. The third turning of the Wheel of Dharma focused on the irreversible resultant state, our innate buddha nature.

Teachings on each of the turnings of the Wheel of Dharma have their own subject matter, suitable for disciples of a specific mental capacity. Each of the turnings has its own basis, path, and result, and these differences in subject matter reflect the differences in capacity of the disciples. The first turning targets disciples with a narrow mental scope, and so emptiness of self is presented at a very gross level. In the second turning, the disciples' mental scope is greater, and the teachings are more subtle than those of the first turning. In the third turning, the disciples' mental scope is extremely vast, and so the teachings are extremely subtle. These nuances are important to understand, because a lot of people think that the Buddha taught the same thing again and again. Instead, he emphasized different points at different times, based on the mental capacity of the students who were there with him at that time.

Younge Khachab Rinpoche
Madison, Wisconsin

PART ONE

THE FIRST TURNING OF THE
WHEEL OF DHARMA

YOUNGE KHACHAB RINPOCHE

1

THE BASIS

THE FOUR NOBLE TRUTHS

From our own experience, we know that at this moment, we are not free from suffering. We are subject to conditions that have resulted from our past actions or karma, and to negative emotions resulting from unskillful actions that will lead to more unskillful actions.

Our goal is to be free from suffering. In order to reach this goal, we need to rely on the guidance of someone who has eliminated karma and the negative emotions – one who has followed the path, perfected it, and obtained freedom from suffering. It is important that this person has also experienced the influence of karma and negative emotions and then trained in the path to achieve the result. Only such a guide can teach from his or her own experience. There is no shared basis on which a divine creator, or someone with magical powers, can help us with our own situation as ordinary human beings. Any teacher who is in a position to help us must have experienced the same conditions him- or herself.

In his first teaching after attaining complete awakening,[1] the Buddha introduced four fundamental truths concerning reality – the four noble truths, the principal teachings of the first turning of the wheel of Dharma. The first truth, the truth of suffering, teaches that despite seeking happiness, we do not find it, and instead we experience suffering and discontentment. The second truth reveals that suffering has a cause, which is ignorance. The third truth tells us that we can end suffering, and for that we need to follow the guidance and example of an enlightened person. That guidance is given as the fourth truth, the truth of the path. Anyone with sincere motivation, whether a Buddhist or not, can listen to and benefit from these teachings.

In the first turning of the wheel of Dharma, the Buddha introduced the root cause of all suffering, which is ignorance or confusion. Ignorance is not some sort of independent thing or being in the world; it is nothing more than perceiving things wrongly, not as they truly are. When a mind of ignorance perceives an object, it is confused regarding its reality. It is confused by accumulated habitual patterns of thought and perception, which are activated by the circumstances – 'causes and conditions' – that arise. As a result, we perceive things incorrectly, in a way that is confused. We call that state of confusion 'ignorance.'

Ignorance depends upon many internal and external conditions. Confused perceptions result from a combination of internal sensory, cognitive, and psychological factors interacting with external material conditions. All of these factors together generate confused motivation and karmic actions, which result in suffering. Therefore, ignorance is not something separate from these various contributing conditions, something that gives rise to suffering all by itself. As a result of past actions, the imprint of ignorance is carried over into the present at the most basic level of consciousness, and this imprint comes together with many internal and external conditions as the cause of suffering. Without these other conditions, the imprint alone cannot give rise to suffering. If the imprint of ignorance is not activated by conditions, then the confused state is not produced. Consciousness itself and the imprints carried over within it do not have the power to give rise to suffering.

EXAMINING IGNORANCE, THE ROOT CAUSE OF ALL SUFFERING

The nature of ignorance is essentially self-grasping, or grasping at self-identity. Self-grasping occurs in two forms: innate and conceptually-produced. We are all born with innate self-grasping. Innate self-grasping is the root of samsara, or cyclic existence. This is the imprint on basic consciousness that has been with us from beginningless time. Conceptually-produced self-grasping, on the other hand, results from our attachment to ideas or concepts, such as philosophical and religious views.

Because ignorance is produced by wrongly-perceiving conditions and is not something that exists in its own right, it is possible to eliminate ignorance, to become enlightened. This is done by understanding its nature. We gain this understanding by accumulating wisdom via study, contemplation, and meditation.

In the first turning of the wheel of Dharma, the Buddha taught that we can accumulate wisdom through study of and meditation on how we and the worlds that we experience are put together, the basic constitution of our being. The basic constituents of our being and experience are called *skandhas* in Sanskrit ('skandhas' translates as 'aggregates' or 'heaps' in English). The *ayatanas*, or 'sense generators,' and *dhatus*, or 'sources', are another two complementary ways of categorizing what we are made of, for understanding some of our faculties and powers.[2] On the basis of this study and meditation, we gain insight into causality – how things, such as our bodies, our feelings and perceptions, and our actions, arise through a process of dependent origination.

In the first turning, the Buddha explains self-grasping, or ignorance, in terms of the five skandhas (and in a supplementary way, the twelve ayatanas, and eighteen dhatus). In his first teachings, he advised us to become experts in understanding the aggregates, though 'expert' here does not imply intellectual understanding. Instead, we need to understand the confused and unconfused states through our own practice and experience. Thorough understanding of the nature of the five skandhas, twelve ayatanas, and eighteen dhatus undermines the root cause of suffering, which is innate self-grasping. If we understand the skandhas, then we also understand that self-grasping is a confused state.

By analogy, if we perceive a rope lying in the dark as a snake, we react with sudden fear. This fear will not subside until we realize that it is just a rope. When we see the rope for what it is, we are freed from the state of fear and confusion. Just as directly perceiving the rope as a rope dispels ignorance and fear, the correct understanding of the skandhas eliminates the ignorance of self-grasping, and the suffering that results from it. It is for this reason that the Buddha taught the five skandhas.

The most important thing to understand about the skandhas, ayatanas, and dhatus is that they are the things that we grasp at – the objects of self-grasping. Grasping at the skandhas, etc. as self is the root cause of samsara. The five skandhas (our bodies, feelings, beliefs, motives, and consciousness) are the direct objects of grasping at self. The twelve ayatanas are a bit less direct as objects of grasping than the skandhas. The eighteen dhatus are most indirect objects of grasping.

When the Buddha first gave the teachings on the four noble truths, the truth of suffering and the cause of suffering were explained in terms of the skandhas, ayatanas and dhatus. The five skandhas are suffering and the cause of suffering, because they are the objects of self-grasping. Somewhat indirectly, the twelve ayatanas and eighteen dhatus also comprise suffering, the cause of suffering, and the objects of self-grasping.

Without understanding the five aggregates, the twelve sense generators, and the eighteen dhatus – in other words, without understanding how we are put together – it is not possible to practice any of the vehicles, whether Hinayana, sutric Mahayana, or even the tantric Vajrayana. Even in the ancient Nyingma school of Tibet, there is no way we can carry out the practice of the nine vehicles without understanding the skandhas, ayatanas, and dhatus. Therefore, if we are to take our practice seriously, we have to devote ourselves to studying and contemplating the nature of the human condition.

In summary, the skandhas, ayatanas, and dhatus together comprise the basis of the Hinayana vehicle, the vehicle of the first turning. The Hinayana path is realizing the four noble truths, and the result is the state of an arhathood, or cessation.

SELF-GRASPING

For as long as we have been reborn as karmic beings in samsara, we have lived in a state of confusion and ignorance, which manifests as self-grasping.

Self-grasping has three characteristics. First, we see the self as a unitary, independently existing entity. However, by studying the skandhas we find that we are aggregates or temporary collections of external and internal factors, not a unitary self-existent entity.

Second, we take the self to be a unitary subject of experience, seeing ourselves, the 'experiencers,' as separate or independent of what we experience. However, in studying the ayatanas we find that the subject of experience is a composite, produced from multiple interdependent factors.

The third characteristic of self-grasping is that we think of the self as a prime mover, agent, or cause of our thoughts and actions. But when we study the eighteen dhatus, we find that our movements originate from multiple factors. Coming to such an understanding of self-grasping undermines attachment to the existence of self, and we no longer engage in karmic actions based on attachment. As a result, we do not accumulate negative karma.

Let us look at the three characteristics of self-grasping in detail. The first characteristic of self-grasping is grasping at the existence of a unitary and independently-existing entity. When we look for such an entity, we find nothing more than the aggregates: material form (most importantly, our own body), feeling (good, bad, and neutral), perception (discerning experience), mental formations (particular features of those objects), and consciousness (of sensory objects and mental objects). If we look closely and systematically for the self, we find nothing that is not dependent on these five skandhas, or aggregates. Our bodies or body parts, feelings, beliefs, and states of consciousness are not 'self.' Eventually we realize that there is no such entity, and we are no longer confused about the way the self exists. If we can understand this at an experiential level, we can let go of our strong sense of self, which is produced by grasping at the five aggregates. We can gain this experiential understanding by observing the way in which this sense of a unitary, independently-existing self is produced.

If we look at the confused state of self-grasping mind, we find that it begins when our mind and faculties come into contact with material form. This initial contact with something gives rise to feelings. The aggregate of feeling gives rise to discrimination, or perception, which identifies the material form as a desirable or undesirable object. Further judgments and motives (mental factors) shape the perception into a motivation or 'agenda' and the resultant state of consciousness. In this way, each aggregate depends on the others, impelled by grasping at an intrinsically-existing self. The resulting state of consciousness is confused, because it is a product of grasping at an identity in the aggregates.

We should analyze the five skandhas by looking at our own experience. The aggregates are not metaphysical constructs, something to be analyzed in the abstract. Rather, we should use these teachings to learn how to understand our own samsaric experience at a very practical level.

The second characteristic of self-grasping is attachment to the self as a subject that takes in experiences, but that is somewhat independent of what he or she experiences. To understand and eliminate this type of self-grasping, the Buddha taught the twelve ayatanas or 'sense generators.' Our perceptions depend on a combination of two components of experience: an internal sense generator (or in the case of the mental generator, the mind), and an external sense object (including the mental objects of the mind). For example, the 'conscious self' that experiences sound is possible only when the ear, or capacity for hearing, and the auditory consciousness meet with sound, something that is capable of being heard. We can only have a visual experience when the eye and the visual consciousness come into contact with a visible form, something that can be seen. It means that the 'visually experiencing self,' the 'me' who sees something, is possible only in dependence on a sense generator and some visible form. If we are admiring a beautiful flower, the consciousness or "self" that experiences that admiration is not possible if there is no flower. Understanding these twelve ayatanas undermines the notion that there is a truly existing self that is the basis of all experience.

Finally, the third characteristic of self-grasping is grasping at a self as the primary agent. To eliminate this level of ignorance, the Buddha taught the eighteen dhatus.

The eighteen dhatus comprise the six external sense objects, the six sense faculties, and the six consciousnesses corresponding to those faculties. The six external objects – visible forms, sounds, smells, tastes, tangible objects, and mental objects – become the objects of the six consciousnesses based on the six faculties. For example, a visual experience comprises (1) the visual consciousness coming together with (2) the visible object presented to (3) the faculty of vision. For consciousness to arise, the presence of both the sense object and the sense faculty is necessary. The six consciousnesses depend on these sense objects and sense faculties, therefore a single consciousness, or self, cannot be a principal agent.

Of these three characteristics of self-grasping, the most important is the first – conceiving of a self that is unitary and independent. This type of innate self-grasping is the root of samsara. To eliminate this attachment to a unitary self in the form of one or more of the skandhas, we have to study the teachings on the five skandhas. The skandhas are the basis of imputation, or direct object, of self-grasping.

A basic understanding of the five aggregates, twelve ayatanas, and eighteen dhatus is very important for practice. Without it, we will not be able to practice the path that is taught in the first turning of the wheel of Dharma. While great depth and subtlety of understanding may not be necessary, we need to have some general understanding of these principles. Otherwise, it is not possible to explain and understand the practices. This book provides a general introduction of the principles behind the five aggregates, twelve ayatanas, and eighteen dhatus. Then, it is up to you to come to understand them through contemplation and analytical meditation.

FIVE SKANDHAS

The root of all suffering is ignorance, which manifests as self-grasping. Each of the three turnings of the wheel of Dharma explain self-grasping differently, describing 'self' with deepening degrees of subtlety. However, at its core, self-grasping involves two different objects of grasping: the self (the subject) and the other (the object).

First, the mind grasps at a self. The grasping mind imputes a self, based on the aggregates (skandhas). There is actually nothing there other than the aggregates to take hold of. Usually, self-grasping mind identifies the self with our own body (material form aggregate), but it could also identify it as a sensation (feeling aggregate), a judgment or reaction (perception aggregate), an attitude (mental factors aggregate), or the thinking subject (consciousness aggregate). As such, the mind imputes a self as something that truly exists from the side of the subject.

Second, the self-grasping mind imputes something 'other,' namely the object that it is perceiving or thinking about. The object is also nothing other than an aggregate, a heap of fleeting appearances. Nevertheless, the mind perceives the object as truly existent from its own side. Just like the self, the object is purely fictional.

When we see what is going on in the act of self-grasping – when we catch ourselves in the act – we can see the confusion that is its nature. When we talk about being trapped in samsara or attaining to nirvana, the one bound in samsara and the one who gains liberation are the same – the self.

To completely take apart this self-grasping mind and understand what we are doing when we impute the existence of a self, we need to understand the basis on which the self is imputed. The aggregates form this basis. In the confused state, our mind can label any of the five aggregates as a truly-existing self. Therefore, we need to understand what it is that our mind is labeling in the process of self-grasping. For that, the Buddha taught the aggregates, and this is why we should understand them.

Rupa Skandha

Skandha, meaning 'heap' or 'aggregate,' literally refers to a pile of something, in this case our six sense faculties, their six external objects, and the six consciousnesses. The first aggregate taught by Buddha is the aggregate of material form, or *rupa skandha*. The material form skandha is the 'heap' of everything material in our experience. It includes the five sense objects (visible things, sounds, smells, tastes, and tactile sensations), and the five sense organs. The material-form skandha encompasses all matter, including our own bodies, other people's bodies and the physical environment.

For practical reasons, we discuss the material-form skandha through the example of our own karmic bodies. We have our bodies as a result of our past actions. Because our own bodies are the most karmically significant part of our physical experience, we focus on them when we discuss the material-form aggregate. The karmic body represents a 'heap' because it consists of many impermanent parts and substances, though we often think of it as a permanent unitary entity.

The form, or rupa, skandha includes two types of material form, distinguished by their relation to karma: karmically-propelled form and matter that is not karmically propelled. The karmically-propelled form depends on our karma – the consequences of our past actions. The non-karmically-propelled matter does not depend on our own karma. Our bodies and the bodies of others who are karmically linked to us are examples of karmically-propelled form. Some material form, such as insensate objects like our furniture and automobiles, are not karmically-propelled.

Karmically-propelled material form is further distinguished by gross and subtle aspects. The gross aspect is our body of flesh and bones. The subtle aspect is the subtle body of the channels, winds, and drops.

As long as we have attachment to karmically-propelled form, we will experience suffering. If we possess form, there will be a consciousness residing in it. The two mutually reinforce each other. They reinforce the idea of self, which generates self-grasping. Therefore, we cannot escape suffering as long as we have attachment to form. Even if we take care of our bodies, we still experience suffering and deteriorating health because of our self-grasping. I am not suggesting that health and taking care of our bodies and not important, but this is the reality of attachment to form.

The Buddha taught the material-form aggregate first because of its significance for understanding the first two truths, the truth of suffering and the truth of the origin of suffering. The karmic body, being the result of past actions and suffering, is also the medium through which we experience suffering. At the same time, it is the cause of suffering and the result of suffering. Through our bodies, we experience pleasant and unpleasant feelings, which lead to attachment and aversion. By recognizing the nature of our physical being as the result of, the medium for, and the cause of suffering, we can appreciate and understand the truths of suffering and origin of suffering at a very intimate level.

Besides being directly linked to suffering, the material-form skandha (like all of the skandhas) is impermanent. The body and other physical objects seem to be permanent, but in fact their existence is as fleeting as that of a water bubble. When we cling to impermanent things like the body as if they were permanent, we experience suffering.

According to the Hinayana tradition, our karmic body is created by ignorance, which manifests because of clinging to the idea of a self. Ignorance is the root cause in the chain of the twelve links of dependent origination. Ignorance, or self-grasping mind, leaves an imprint on the sixth consciousness, the mental consciousness. When this imprint is activated, it manifests, in a way that is linked to the elements – the five external elements and the five internal, or subtle, elements. Because of that, the physical body is formed from the union of activated imprints with the elements. Self-grasping comes into contact with the elements through the twelve links of dependent origination. That is how our consciousness unites with our parents' ovum and sperm to form an embryo.

Now that we have this body, composed of the five elements, we cling to it as a self. In doing so, we are clinging to something that does not last. The elements of our body continuously deteriorate, and we experience decay, old age, sickness, and death. Even though the cycle of deterioration just repeats itself, our grasping is relentless, and we continue to create and experience suffering.

We are tremendously attached to our karmic bodies. A story of the daughter of a rich sea captain can illustrate the power of this attachment. She was very beautiful and well aware of her own beauty. She was so attached to her beauty that she would always have three or four mirrors placed around the deck so that she could behold herself at any time. One day the ship sank, and everyone on board died. When she died, she took rebirth as a sea snake. The snake found her bones lying on the sea bottom and kept swimming around and between them – because of her strong attachment.

We need to use antidotes to eliminate the strong attachment to our form that binds us to samsara. The method of this practice involves seeing all physical forms as impermanent and fleeting. We should also remember that our karmic body serves as the vehicle of our current suffering and the cause of future suffering. Because of self-grasping, we cling to the body as if it were a permanent and independently-existing self. As an antidote to clinging, the Buddha taught the practice of seeing all material form as momentary and fleeting, like a water bubble. By practicing this way, we can let go of the attachment to our physical body. Some people might think that these practices are needed only by the Hinayana practitioners. However, the reality is that we all have a strong attachment to our body. Even if we call ourselves tantric, Mahamudra, or Dzogchen practitioners, we have to deal with our attachment to our bodies. Although there are many practices that can counteract this attachment, the practice of seeing material form as impermanent and fleeting is the most important one.

The Buddha emphasized attachment to the body and the antidotes for this attachment because, as humans, we live in the desire realm. Unlike the (nonmaterial) form and formless realms, the desire realm is characterized by a strong attachment to material form – to our bodies and sense objects. Among all aggregates, the aggregate of material form is the coarsest and most tangible one, and the one most resistant to change.

The predominant emotions of the desire realm – desire and anger – are very gross as well. Gross emotions exert a very powerful influence over us, which gives rise to unskillful actions that end up causing suffering. It is relatively easy for us to cause ourselves suffering in the desire realm because of the grossness of the aggregates we experience here. This is why practitioners strive to eliminate desire and anger.

We can see how difficult it is to counteract these negative emotions in our meditation. It is very difficult to cultivate stability and clarity in our meditation practice because strong negative emotions and coarse conceptual thoughts are always disrupting it. This is happening because of the winds that course through our gross channels. The gross vital energies or winds are impure, because the psychophysical aggregates that we are attached to are gross and contaminated. Because of the grossness of the impure channels and winds, the mind is easily distracted, disrupting the stability and clarity of our meditation.

Even though this momentary and impure material-form skandha results from and causes suffering, it is still of great value. Despite all of the faults of clinging to the material-form skandha, this precious human birth presents a rare opportunity. Certainly, we should not think that cultivating non-attachment means that we are supposed to stop caring about our bodies. Without the material-form aggregate, we would not have consciousness. The body is the medium through which mind experiences itself, and so taking care of the body is extremely important. In the tantric context, as we traverse the path to enlightenment, the body is transformed from an impure to a pure body, from gross to subtle. Then, in the enlightened state, the mind and the body become inseparable. Although the teachings on the first turning of the wheel of Dharma do not discuss the skandhas in the same way as they are presented in tantra, we need to be aware of the big picture. The Vajrayana and Dzogchen vehicles also teach us how to use our current body on our Dharma path.

The main reason that the Buddha emphasized the negative aspects of material form was to inspire us to eliminate our attachment to our own bodies. Without eliminating this attachment, we are not able to understand or experience the natural condition of the body and the mind. Because we fail to understand the body's actual mode of existence, we experience suffering as a result of our attachment to it. Attachment to the body "solidifies" it, which creates further suffering. This is why the Buddha taught that we need to let go of our attachment to the body if we want to free ourselves from suffering.

We need to view our karmic body in a balanced way and see its negative and positive aspects. Although the karmic body is a result and cause of suffering, without it we would not have a human mind capable of eliminating negative qualities and of cultivating positive ones, even qualities that were not present before. In the Hinayana tradition, the monastic sangha focuses on the negative aspects of the body and remains silent about the positive aspects. In the words of the Buddha in scripture, however, both aspects are emphasized. There is no contradiction. This is why we need to understand both the positive and the negative aspects of the body, and why I refer to the Buddha's instruction that we should become experts in the five skandhas.

Understanding the skandhas, especially the form skandha, is critical to understanding our experiences of suffering and happiness. Although studying the skandhas may feel like a merely intellectual exercise, understanding them helps us realize how they relate to our experience of suffering. Once we have this direct experiential understanding, we will realize the significance of the teachings.

The material-form aggregate is significant because it is the foremost object of self-grasping. The second and third aggregates, feeling and perception, are important to understand because they are the primary inducers of negative emotions. The other skandhas also give rise to negative emotions, but they are not the primary causes.

Vedana Skandha

Feelings drive conflict, and therefore create suffering. We enter into disputes and conflicts because we seek good feelings, or relief from bad feelings. We fight over resources that we associate with good feelings and fight against people or things that we associate with bad feelings. Because of our fixation on our feelings, we scheme and manipulate to protect them. Feelings conjoined with perceptions or judgments cause ideological conflict. As a result, people disagree about and even fight over political, philosophical, religious, and sectarian views. Feelings and perceptions comprise a major part of human communal life. Business and politics are largely based on people's feelings and perceptions.

This is why the Buddha pointed to feelings and perceptions as the main causes of conflict within the human society. Feelings of happiness and suffering are the main causes of conflict. Fights over resources and social issues grow from feelings. To help us eliminate attachment to the feelings, the Buddha taught us to view them as akin to foam or water bubbles. Feelings may seem real, but they are impermanent: for a moment they are very vivid, but in the next moment they are gone. Similarly, we should view our perceptions as like a mirage. What seems very real from a distance disappears on close investigation.

The sensation aggregate, or vedana skandha, arises when our mind comes into contact with what is appearing to it. Just as the body is a 'heap' of many sense generators and sense objects, the vedana skandha is a 'heap' of the sensations that arise when our mind comes across something. It is how our mind first experiences everything it comes into contact with.

Our sensations of pleasant, unpleasant and neutral play a critical role in inducing suffering, because they influence how we experience everything as good, bad, or neutral. For example, we experience material forms as objects of pain or pleasure. We have responses to sensations like, 'My body is in pain; I am uncomfortable,' or 'This texture is soft; it feels pleasant.' These sensations then generate judgments of good or bad, which lead to desires and aversions.

If all of the conflict in the world is really about feelings, then conflict probably never makes much sense. We fight over our feelings as though they were something essential, but all feelings are ephemeral, like a dream. They come and go. There is nothing lasting whatsoever, nothing worth fighting over. We should see feelings as like foam bubbles and understand that all conflict is meaningless. It is only the ignorance of self-grasping that drives us to hold onto our feelings and fight for them.

As long as we have this karmic body, we are bound to have sensations or feelings. Sensations and feelings depend on discrimination, and therefore on whether we see things correctly or incorrectly. Then, sensations and feeling induce attachment and aversion. Even though it is self-grasping that is the root cause of negative emotions, sensation enables and intensifies this grasping, leading to emotions such as jealousy, aggression, and so forth. When self-grasping manifests as sensations, it is like pouring fuel onto a fire.

Like the other skandhas, sensations have no independent existence. They are momentary and caused by temporary conditions. When these conditions pass, so do the feelings. The measure of success in our practice should not be based on how we feel. If we become attached to our practice when we feel good, or if we doubt our practice when we feel bad, our practice is not strong. Feelings are an unreliable measure. We should judge our practice based on self-awareness and discriminating wisdom, not on how we feel in the moment.

Samjna Skandha

The third aggregate is the *samjna skandha,* the aggregate of perception. In perception, an external object comes together with the internal sense faculty observing it, and the consciousness that arises from this contact. This consciousness recognizes the object as an object of a certain kind. Perception is a mental factor or "secondary mind" that is able to appreciate and discriminate between different objects and their features. It is perception that discriminates between good and bad, long and short, mine and yours, etc. Another term for this aggregate is discernment or discrimination, which how it translates into Tibetan.

This skandha contributes to suffering in its own unique way. For example, it induces attachment, aversion, and ignorance by discriminating between objects of perception as friends, enemies, or strangers. The skandha of perception is a confused state because these objects have no inherent nature that makes them one thing as opposed to another, such as friends or enemies. There is no basis for these distinctions in reality. Perceptions are similar to a mirage that appears as a body of water on the horizon of a desert. Even though there is no such thing as friends or enemies, we perceive them as such, and this perception induces attachment and aversion.

Americans have the view that they are 'number one' in the world – this is a collectively-shared perception here. Tibetans collectively share a perception that they are very poor, and nobody supports them. When open-minded people transcend distinctions between us and them, friends and enemies, this also happens through perception or discernment. In the latter case, perception has a unifying function rather than a divisive one.

The perception skandha plays a significant role in our meditation practice. At the beginning of our meditation session, the mind is either agitated or dull. Both of these states are produced by perception. Gross perception, or coarse discernment, induces gross thoughts, which arise in the form of agitation or dullness. The goal of meditation is to experience stability and clarity, both of which can eliminate gross thoughts. In practical terms, gross thoughts hinder us from experiencing the natural condition of the mind. What we are accustomed to calling "perception" is actually gross perception, not true or valid perception.

The quality of perception depends on the one who perceives. Refined practitioners have subtle, pure, and virtuous perceptions, whereas unsophisticated practitioners experience crude, impure and non-virtuous perceptions. The desire, form, and formless realms each allow for different levels of subtlety in perception.

The Hinayana tradition teaches that the desire realm allows for only limited perceptions, because of attachment to material things. Form-realm beings, who are immaterial, do not experience the same attachment to objects that we do. Form-realm beings view attachment to material form as an inferior mental state, something to be abandoned. When we take rebirth in the form realms, we do not experience the attachment to material objects that predominates in the desire realm. Likewise, beings in the formless realms perceive the mental states of form-realm beings as inferior. Therefore, the perception of beings in the formless realm is much more profound or vast than the perception of beings in the desire realm.

For practitioners, it is useful to understand the differences in the perception of beings in the desire, form, and formless realms. However, it is much more important than that to understand whether our own perceptions are subtle or gross. In the context of Hinayana practice, we engage in meditation to eliminate gross feelings and perceptions. The more successful we are at eliminating gross mental states, the more we will experience subtle levels of feeling and perception.

Gross perception refers to discrimination between people and things that we encounter in daily life; for example, friends, enemies, and strangers. This discrimination induces feelings of attachment, aversion, and indifference. When we investigate these feelings, we find that they are like a distant mirage or illusion. When a thirsty person experiences a mirage, he or she goes after it with great determination but never finds it. We react to our perceptions of friends and enemies similarly. We pursue gratification, but when we really get down to it, we find no gratification because there is no one who is intrinsically a friend or an enemy. For a practitioner, it is useful to understand and view all perceptions as being like a mirage. Such understanding assists us in renouncing gross discrimination and attachment.

The first turning of the wheel of Dharma teaches renunciation of the causes of suffering as the fundamental practice. To generate renunciation, we eliminate attachment to feelings and perceptions. The teachings say that when we are attached to feelings, we engage in endless activities to distract ourselves from dissatisfaction. But all of these activities only result in further suffering. Attachment to feeling is itself a form of suffering. Therefore, the actual practice of renunciation entails renouncing attachment to feelings and perceptions as well as the activities driven by that attachment.

In summary, the Hinayana teaches that most of our ordinary activities are a waste of time, because we pursue them for the sake of pleasant or happy feelings. We act mostly on the basis of our feelings. However, feelings are like bubbles – they simply don't have the reality that we want them to have. By pursuing meaningless mundane activities, we neglect the opportunities present in this precious human life for the sake of something no more substantial than a bubble. Why do we do this? Why do we so tirelessly engage in activities whose nature is suffering?

Samskara Skandha

The fourth aggregate is the *samskara skandha*, the aggregate of mental formations or 'mental factors.' Feeling and perception are also mental factors present in every cognition, but because of their primacy in causing attachment and aversion, they are designated as aggregates in their own right. All other mental factors – attitudes, emotions, judgments, and volitions – are grouped together in the samskara skandha.

Traditionally, there are between forty-six and fifty-one principal mental factors, though there are many more particular ones, and infinitely many possible combinations in a single consciousness. Some are present in all cognition (such as volition and attention), some are virtuous (like faith), some are non-virtuous (like resentment), and some are indeterminate, that is, they are either good, bad, or neutral (like regret).

Mental formations constitute the potential of consciousness to engage with and respond to objects in very specific, conceptually elaborated ways. With mental formations, the mind engages with objects conceptually on an abstract level. Mental formations include all of our emotions, reactions, and ulterior motives, both virtuous and non-virtuous. This aggregate includes all the different ways we react to feelings and perceptions. Because of our past conditioning and the many other causal factors that come together to produce a moment of consciousness, our minds react very strongly to the things and people that we perceive.

The factors involved in developing wisdom, such as mindfulness, faith, diligence, concentration, and discriminating wisdom (*prajna*) itself, along with the mental functions that give rise to non-virtuous mental states and negative emotions, mostly belong to the samskara skandha. Mental factors belonging to the mental formations aggregate are virtuous and non-virtuous, and so they are cultivated or eliminated accordingly. For this reason, it is important to learn how to recognize the various mental factors and which aggregate they belong to when we are experiencing them.

Vijnana Skandha

The fifth aggregate is the *vijnana skandha*, or the aggregate of consciousness. Whereas material form is the least subtle of the aggregates, consciousness is the most subtle. In the first turning of the wheel of Dharma, six types of consciousness are taught, one corresponding to each of the five senses, which cognize sense objects, and the mental consciousness, which cognizes mental objects. Consciousness is simply the ability or potential to have an object of consciousness. It is the capacity to engage with an object. It is also referred to as the 'primary mind,' because it is simple awareness of there being an object of experience. It does not itself discriminate between good and bad or adopt an attitude. These are the actions of mental factors or 'secondary minds.' For example, the visual consciousness simply cognizes visible form as visible form. It does not interpret or judge that form, nor does it cognize sound, smell, taste, touch, or a mental object.

In the first turning, the sixth consciousness is important because it carries the weight of karmic imprints and thus is the primary causal agent of the skandhas, ayatanas, and dhatus. Because it carries these karmic imprints, it is the material cause of the negative emotions. In the second turning, the Cittamatra or Mind-Only schools recognize eight consciousnesses. The eighth consciousness, the *alayavijnana* or foundational consciousness, is the basis for the storing of imprints that later ripen in the afflicted mind, which is the seventh consciousness. The division into eight consciousnesses becomes significant in the Tantrayana.

According to the Hinayana tradition, if we analyze who it is that experiences samsara and achieves liberation, it is not consciousness but rather the continuum of all the skandhas together. That continuum is what experiences suffering in samsara and then, having eliminated gross feelings, perceptions, and thoughts, experiences liberation.

2

THE PATH

In this chapter, I will first give a general presentation of the teachings on the Hinayana path, in terms of basis, path, and result. Then I will cover specific points about how basis, path and result are practiced on the path. As this presentation of the path relates to the first turning of the wheel of Dharma, the natural audience would be practitioners in the Hinayana tradition, or common vehicle.

GENERAL PRESENTATION

As it is understood in the first turning, 'path' refers to understanding and realizing the four noble truths. The path has a method aspect and a wisdom aspect. The method aspect of the Hinayana path is renunciation, which stems from meditating on the first and second noble truths, the truth of suffering and the truth of the origin. The wisdom aspect of the path, which becomes the foundation for meditation practice, comprises sixteen 'moments of insight' into the four noble truths, four for each truth, by which the causes of suffering are abandoned.[3] The wisdom aspect, or realization of the sixteen moments, is enhanced by the method aspect of contemplating suffering and practicing renunciation.

In the context of the Hinayana, liberation is gained by apprehending selflessness and destroying self-grasping. In order to cultivate and sustain the view of selflessness, we practice calm abiding (shamatha) and insight (vipasyana) meditation. Continuously sustaining this meditation requires renunciation, so we first give rise to renunciation by meditating on the negative aspects of the first and second noble truths (the skandhas). If we have not genuinely cultivated renunciation, then our meditation is quickly overcome by worldly desires and coarse feelings and perceptions. If we are subject to coarse desires, it's very difficult to sustain meditation on emptiness and selflessness. It is through renunciation based on the understanding of suffering in samsara – the first and second noble truths – that we become inspired to continue to sustain meditation on selflessness.

We often take a negative view of renunciation, but understood correctly, it is more like an inspiration to seek liberation than a need to give something up. Renunciation serves as an antidote to suffering and sadness. However, if we do not know how to practice it correctly, we might think of it as resignation to a depressing, hopeless existence. In actuality, it is the recognition that suffering can be left behind. In order to practice renunciation correctly, we need the support of insight or discriminating wisdom. Discriminating wisdom gives us the means to practice renunciation as part of the process of liberation, which then becomes a way to inspire joy and the intent to accomplish liberation.

The purpose of renunciation is to inspire us to gain freedom from the suffering of the five skandhas, but if we do not understand this, then the opposite can happen. Without the aid of the wisdom aspect, the practice of renunciation can become the cause of unhappiness. In the traditional monasteries of Tibet, young monks would sometimes dwell on suffering and the causes of suffering without placing it in the proper context. They would become very narrow-minded, sad, and hopeless. They would have a very difficult time communicating with other people because they would see everything as a source of suffering. However, if we are practicing renunciation correctly, our mind will become more expansive, bringing it closer to the ultimate nature of mind, which is freedom. Thus, meditation on suffering needs to be coupled with the wisdom aspect through insight meditation (vipasyana) on selflessness.

What is renounced?

When we generate renunciation, the first thing we need to understand is what it is that is being renounced, or the basis of renunciation. What we are renouncing is attachment to our own skandhas, which are the product of karmic suffering and afflictive emotions. We renounce our attachment to coarse feelings, perceptions, and mental formations. If we renounce these attachments, then the result is the state of cessation, the state of an arhat.

It is important to understand that renunciation pertains to our own skandhas, not something external to us. It is our own continuum of the five aggregates that is bound by karma and negative emotions, and which experiences suffering. We've established that the basis of renunciation is our own skandhas, but then who is it that generates renunciation? The answer is you, yourself. It is that simple. To be bound in samsara is simply to be attached to the five skandhas. Without renouncing the skandhas, we cannot reach liberation.

Let's take a close look at the reasons to practice renunciation.

Without it, we are attached to our own form skandha. We see what is impure to be pure, and then we generate attachment. Without renunciation, we are attached to our own feelings; we keep seeing everything that has the nature of suffering as having the nature of happiness. Without renunciation, we become attached to temporary pleasures that we confuse with ultimate joy, but which actually turn out to be suffering in the long run. Without renunciation, we confuse our perceptions and discriminations with valid and true observations, when they are actually incorrect or biased. By not understanding mental formations, we view something that is a composite of mental factors as being authentic and real. By not understanding the skandha of consciousness, we remain stuck in a state of confusion and cannot awaken primordial wisdom. Due to this confusion, we cycle in samsara through the twelve links of dependent origination, unable to find a way out. But by contemplating and coming to understand the aggregates, we begin to generate renunciation.

We especially need to contemplate the skandha of consciousness. At this time, we have no access to ultimate wisdom. We only have access to a very coarse consciousness that is in a state of confusion. Our current coarse confused consciousness is under the sway of our strong feelings and perceptions, which generate attachment and aversion. Because of attachment and aversion, consciousness reinforces the sense of self and remains in a confused state, and a confused consciousness cannot engage in refining itself, thereby denying us access to primordial wisdom.

Right now, we inhabit the desire realm. The desire realm comprises the six realms: gods, demi-gods, humans, animals, hungry ghosts, and hell beings. The consciousness of beings in the desire realm is coarser than the consciousness of beings in the form realms, who experience a more subtle level of desire. In the formless realms, consciousness is even more subtle.[4] These differences in subtlety of consciousness are contained within the skandha of consciousness, but the differences are not incidental; they arise based on different conditions. The relatively coarse nature of human desire-realm consciousness is due to the coarseness of our physical form, which produces coarse feelings, perceptions, mental formations and finally coarse consciousness. In a nutshell, our consciousness is related to the medium of consciousness, which is the physical body. Since the body is rather coarse, our consciousness is coarse relative to that of the form and formless realms where there is little or no attachment to physical form.

We need to understand the relationship between consciousness and the basis of the consciousness, which is the body. When we understand the interdependent relationship between these two, then we also can understand the consciousnesses of the different realms. Without this understanding, it is very difficult for us to apprehend why we cannot access consciousness in its more subtle forms.

In the Hinayana tradition, the ultimate state of cessation, arhathood, is achieved from within the continuum of the aggregate of consciousness. It is a mental state. This refined mental state happens in our own mind. Because cessation is achieved on a very subtle level of mind, we have to understand how to get there from our current state of mind. The way we get there is by relying on single-pointed concentration in a sequence of meditations that gradually eliminate the coarser feelings and perceptions and give access to more subtle forms of consciousness and realization. It is through this refining process of consciousness that we begin to experience more subtle levels of feeling and perception. The ultimate goal is to completely exhaust all grasping to the consciousness skandha and with that, all five skandhas. The extinction of all grasping is the attainment of arhathood.

Eliminating grasping to our own psycho-physical aggregates is not an easy thing to accomplish, however. We need to have a firm understanding of the basis, the path, and the resultant stage, and we need to understand how to enhance our practice on the path.

Since the ultimate goal is to bring the continuum of the contaminated skandhas to an end, we must look at the root cause of the negative emotions. The skandhas are of the nature of suffering, and are caused by karma and negative emotions. The root cause of these is the self-grasping mind, this mind of ours that grasps at a notion of self. Earlier we discussed how the self-grasping mind does not arise without depending on other contributing factors. We experience an object, and our perception of that object induces feelings of attachment or aversion. Based on these feelings of good and bad, we generate a perception or discriminatory mind that accepts what is good and rejects what is bad. The stronger our perception skandha, which is induced by feelings, the stronger our mental formations become. Recall that mental formations refer to mental reactions in the form of negative emotions and afflictions, and these formations are directly related to the strength of our perceptions and discrimination. When we have very strong mental formations, the experience of bondage becomes much stronger. The obscurations that we experience become thicker and thicker, and it becomes more difficult to perceive the true nature of mind. We can verify this in our own experience – when we meditate and the mind settles down to a certain degree, in that settled state it is easier to see our own natural state of clarity, and there is less negative emotion. When we are caught in a state of gross feelings and discrimination, it is much easier to generate negative emotions and much harder to see the clarity of our mind.

The reason that I have explained this process of cutting through coarse feelings and perceptions in the meditative state is to emphasize that it is not enough to just meditate on emptiness and selflessness. We need to understand that the goal is freedom from suffering. The intensity of our self-grasping depends on the intensity of our feelings and perceptions. When our feelings and perceptions are gross, this induces a stronger state of self-grasping, which leads to more confused appearances. This in turn induces a greater degree of suffering. When we fully understand this process, then we will see that meditation on our feelings as impermanent and selfless helps us gain freedom from conflicting thoughts and emotions.

SPECIFIC PRESENTATION

The Basis

The actual path is itself introduced in terms of the basis, path, and result. The basis introduces the wisdom of emptiness and selflessness through understanding the skandhas, ayatanas and dhatus. At the level of the basis, we need to understand our idea of a personal self is nothing but something that we conceptually impute or superimpose onto the five skandhas. The basis of imputation – that to which self is imputed – is the five skandhas. It is from this imputation that we develop a false notion of the self. However, when we closely examine this imputation and each of the five skandhas one by one, we find no self in any of them. We never find an independent self. We must understand this point. When we actually understand that we will not find a self no matter how closely we look, we will realize that the basis of labeling (the skandhas) and the label (the self) are actually of one nature.

There are two steps to this meditation on self. First, there is analytical meditation, for coming to a conceptual understanding of selflessness. Second, once we gain conviction about how the self exists and how it does not, then we sustain that conviction single-pointedly in shamatha meditation. That is the correct way to use these two forms of meditation, analytical and shamatha (calm-abiding).

To practice analytical meditation on the self and its relationship to the five skandhas, investigate each of the skandhas one by one to find a self. When a self is not found, eliminate that skandha and move on to the next. After a thorough analysis of the form skandha, we can move to feelings, perceptions, mental formations, and consciousness and find that in each a truly existing self does not exist. We will find that in the end they are all eliminated, and a self has not been found. This conclusion does not mean that there is no self at all; rather it means that we understand the actual manner in which the self exists, its natural condition. When we do not find an independently existing self, the result is not that there is no self at all, but that it doesn't exist in the way we thought it did. We thought that we knew what this self is, and that we should have been able to find it, but when we do not, we come to understand what the self actually is.

The purpose of engaging in this type of analytical meditation is that when we experience different mental states such as depression, extreme joy, or pride, this meditation on selflessness can be very useful. Through this process of analysis, we can destroy the mistaken sense of self and gain more equanimity. This a great method for calming the mind, because equanimity is one of the strongest antidotes to the three poisons that there is.

When I was young, I used to do this type of meditation and found it very useful. For instance, if I was experiencing fear, I would engage in this type of meditation, looking for the one who is afraid and what that one is afraid of. I would find that there is no self that is experiencing this fear – no 'one who is afraid.' Recognizing this brought with it a great sense of freedom from fear. I could see the pointlessness of it. When we are able to loosen up our strong sense of self-grasping in this way, then we also loosen up our bondage.

When we feel trapped, we are actually bound not by something outside us but by our own self-grasping. We can loosen these very strong bonds with analytical meditation on the way the self exists. When we employ the logical process of elimination on the skandhas and self to cultivate the wisdom of selflessness, eventually we generate a firm conviction that is beyond logic and reasoning.

The way to combine this analytical meditation with stabilizing shamatha meditation involves first realizing that the self is not to be found and then sustaining that state of not-finding single-pointedly in meditation. Sustain the recognition of selflessness for as long as possible, depending on your prior training. If your shamatha practice is very solid, then you will be able to sustain it for as long as you want to. If you do not have a good foundation in shamatha, then perhaps you will be able to sustain it for a minute or two. It is not possible to sustain a deep understanding without shamatha or stability.

Once you have gained conviction in your understanding of selflessness through stabilizing shamatha meditation, you can practice vipasyana (insight meditation) to directly perceive emptiness of self or selflessness. From a deep state of shamatha, when your mind has become very subtle and calm, you can dwell on the meaning of selflessness using a very subtle mindfulness that does not waver from calm abiding.

In the training of the basis, the view of selflessness is first cultivated by analytical meditation and then sustained through stabilizing or shamatha meditation. This meditation practice constitutes the wisdom aspect of the path. The wisdom aspect is enhanced by the method aspect of the path, which is renunciation. By renouncing the five skandhas, you should be able to increase and enhance the practice of wisdom.

In the presentation of the basis, we covered the first two truths, the truth of suffering and the cause of suffering. We reflected on renunciation and the five skandhas as they pertain to the truth of suffering, and we reflected on the causes of suffering, namely negative emotions and self-grasping. This forms the basis, and now we will look at the path.

The Path

The noble truth of the path refers to the path that enables us to directly perceive all sixteen aspects of the four noble truths. Two things happen when we meditate on the wisdom that directly perceives these sixteen features. First, in the post-meditative state, we contemplate the gross and subtle aspects of the four noble truths. Then, in the state of meditative absorption, we meditate without differentiating between selflessness and the basis of selflessness (that which is selfless).

This path, on which we cultivate the wisdom directly apprehending the sixteen aspects, has five stages, called 'the five paths': accumulation, preparation, seeing, meditation, and no more learning. In the Hinayana tradition, the sravakas and pratyekabuddhas each have their own presentation of the five paths. Both types of practitioner hold the view of the selflessness of the person – that the self is devoid of substantial existence – though the understanding of the pratyekabuddhas is more subtle than that of sravakas.

The common vehicle or Hinayana starts with the path of accumulation. At this stage, the practitioner is introduced to emptiness or selflessness and engages in the accumulation of merit. A principal focus is the practice of discipline. The main components of basic discipline are waking up early, going to bed early, eating appropriate food, and sustaining the body energetically. The practice of discipline entails practicing restraint in the conduct of body, speech and mind, so that ultimately one can maintain continuous mindfulness of body, speech, and mind.

On the path of preparation, we have gained an understanding of reality based on the four noble truths. At this stage, we understand the view of selflessness and emptiness and carry that understanding deeply into our meditation by practicing the four types of mindfulness (body, feelings, mind and phenomena). The path of preparation requires strong effort in order to continuously meditate using the four mindfulnesses and so forth. This is why it is called the path of preparation.

The four mindfulnesses are those of body, feelings, mind, and mental phenomena. Mindfulness of the body and mindfulness of feelings are predominantly practiced on the path of accumulation. Mindfulness of mind and mindfulness of mental phenomena are practiced on the path of preparation. Mindfulness of the mind refers to being mindful of the reality of the sixteen aspects, such as impermanence and selflessness.

The path of preparation has four distinct phases: warmth, peak, patience, and supreme dharma. In the warmth phase, we are able to conceptually understand emptiness. It is called the warmth phase because it is similar to being very close to a fire: we can feel its warmth radiating. In this phase, we still suffer from the fear of meditating on selflessness and emptiness, fearing insignificance. In the peak phase, we no longer generate fear of emptiness. In the phase of patience, we are able to continuously dwell in meditation on selflessness without any sense of conflict.

There are subtle differences between each of these phases in the conceptual understanding of emptiness. Whatever is not very clear in the warmth phase becomes clear in the peak phase and transforms into a direct understanding in the supreme-dharma stage. 'Conceptual understanding' does not refer to analytical meditation here. When we engage in gross conceptual analysis, we have not even entered the path of accumulation. Here, in the path of preparation, 'conceptual understanding' is understood in the context of single-pointed concentration on a conceptual understanding of selflessness.

As we are meditating in a deep single-pointed meditative absorption during the path of preparation, the stage of supreme dharma unfolds when the duality between meditator and the object of meditation, or the duality between observer and observed, disappears. When this duality dissolves, we transition to the phase of supreme dharma. As that stage becomes more subtle, we no longer need to rely on a concept, at which point there is a transition to the path of seeing wherein there is the direct perception of selflessness.

This direct perception of selflessness or emptiness happens during single-pointed meditative absorption, not in the post-meditative state. In the state of meditative absorption, most aspects of the mind are focusing on the sixteen aspects of the four noble truths, but within that deep absorption there is a subtle awareness that apprehends the ultimate reality of the four noble truths. Therefore, we can speak of this as 'the union of shamatha and vipasyana.' There is still one mind, but the features are different; there is a very subtle awareness within meditative absorption that directly apprehends emptiness. It is important to understand, however, that we are conceptually explaining an experience that is utterly beyond concepts. We are explaining that in the meditative absorption there is a part of mind that is absorbed, but also a part that cognizes. To the practitioner, though, all such duality has subsided.

The path of seeing refers to the stage where we directly apprehend not just the four noble truths, but also their sixteen features. At this point, we are directly seeing them. The meditator on the path of seeing is not making the distinction, 'Now I am meditating on selflessness; now the four noble truths.' There are no distinctions to be made in the state of meditative absorption. It is a real danger if we are separating our meditation like that. It sounds like we are talking about sitting in the center and seeing the four noble truths as these four pillars, but it is not like that. Ultimate reality is of one taste; there is no difference.

The meditator on the path of seeing is also not saying, 'This is the noble truth of suffering, something to be abandoned.' He or she is no longer engaging in such conceptual thinking. We think like this when we are training, but in meditative absorption this kind of dualism does not manifest.

Sometimes we have strange ideas about the five paths. We think of the path of accumulation as being very busy gathering lots of stuff. Then, on the path of preparation, suddenly we see things more clearly. On the path of meditation, we don't do anything but space out. On the path of no more learning, we disappear into the state of emptiness, becoming nonfunctional like a statue. That is actually how some people think.

Therefore, we need to make a clear distinction between how we imagine the five paths and what they actually are. To see the nature of reality, it is not sufficient to have an intellectual understanding; we need to walk the path and experience it ourselves.

On the path of meditation, we need to continuously sustain the ultimate reality of the four noble truths. In this process, all the grosser forms of perceptions and feelings disappear, and we gain access to a very subtle consciousness. Using that consciousness, we meditate very deeply on the four noble truths.

It is important to recognize the difference between this type of meditation and worldly meditation. In worldly meditation, we speak of the nine dhyanas or absorptions, such as the samadhi of no thought, no discrimination, and so on.[5] This type of meditative absorption does not maintain mindfulness on the ultimate nature of reality but sustains some of the gross and subtle aspects of thought dissolving. There is a very important distinction between the subsiding of thoughts and sustaining concentration on the true nature of reality.

In the worldly meditative absorptions, we can temporarily stop the arising of gross thoughts and feelings. However, as soon as the initial absorption is exhausted, we are plunged back into a state of confusion – because we have not eliminated the root, which is self-grasping. We can temporarily block gross thoughts and feelings, and in that state we are no longer accumulating karma, making it possible to take rebirth in the god realms and the form and formless realms. However, as soon as the meditative power of that absorption wanes, we give rise to grasping. This is very different from the path of meditation, because while we also cut off the arising of gross thoughts and feelings, we dwell on the ultimate meaning of selflessness, which eradicates self-grasping, the very root of negative emotions. We have to appreciate the difference between temporarily suppressing and completely uprooting the cause of suffering. Nagarjuna says that even though Indra is a god, once his power is exhausted, he will be reborn in lower realms.[6]

> Having become an Indra, fit to be honored by the world,
> You fall back again upon the earth through the power of karma.
> Even having changed to the status of a universal chakravartin king,
> You transform into someone with the rank of a servant in samsaric states.

It is important that we understand the fundamental differences between practitioners who practice the nine dhyanas, or worldly meditative absorptions, and those who practice the dharma according to the Buddha's teachings. The first and most important difference of all is in the intention. On the paths of seeing and meditation, the intention is to renounce samsara and gain liberation from it altogether. Practicing the wisdom of selflessness, when we attain the path of seeing and the path of meditation, we will never fall back into samsaric states. In contrast, practitioners of worldly meditation seek the bliss and peace of the desire, form, and formless realms Their intention is to take rebirth in the form or formless realms, both of which are still within samsara. Their meditation is not a subtle awareness of emptiness, but rather a meditation on consciousness as it becomes more and more subtle. They attain a very subtle consciousness, gaining access to subtle feelings that give rise to the form and formless realms. Because these still have a cause, they are temporary, and these practitioners will eventually fall back into samsara. It is not within the scope of this book to fully explain all of the details here, but I think if we examine these states in our meditation, we can appreciate the differences.

For the practitioner on the paths of seeing and meditation, there comes a point where not only grosser thoughts and feelings are exhausted, but the five skandhas dissolve or are exhausted into the basic space of selflessness, the dharmadhatu. This is very much like clouds that appear in the sky dissolving back into space. Through repeated meditation, the practitioner is able to exhaust all karma into the basic space of selflessness. It is said that there is a time when the practitioner has attained the state of an arhat but has not yet exhausted the karmic body. We call such persons 'arhats with remainder' because they have total cessation inside, total inner freedom, but they still have the remaining aggregates karmically propelled from their past lives.

Is it possible to dissolve the skandhas completely into the space of the dharmadhatu on the path of no more learning? It is possible, because with repeated practice on selflessness we can dissolve even the samskara skandha, or mental formations, the most difficult to bring to exhaustion. Once we are able to dissolve the mental formations, it is relatively easy to exhaust the other skandhas. That state, in which we have achieved the total exhaustion of all skandhas into the dharmadhatu, is called the "state of total cessation."

DIFFERENCES BETWEEN THE SRAVAKAS AND THE PRATYEKABUDDHAS

There are two vehicles within the Hinayana: the vehicle of the sravakas and the vehicle of the pratyekabuddhas. These two are very similar in their understanding of the selflessness of the person. They are also similar in that they meditate on renunciation as part of the method aspect of training, and they meditate on the four noble truths on the path.

There is, however, a difference in the subtlety and depth of their practice. Pratyekabuddhas have a subtler and deeper understanding of emptiness than sravakas; they understand not only the emptiness of self but also, to some extent, the emptiness of phenomena. They are able to abandon grasping at phenomena as well as grasping at a self. Their manner of teaching is also different: pratyekabuddhas do not have to rely on speech to give teachings on emptiness. All of these differences are taught in Maitreya's *Ornament of Clear Realization*.[7]

There is also a difference between the conduct of sravakas and that of the pratyekabuddhas. The sravakas aspire to live in communities, give teachings, and interact with the community. The pratyekabuddhas live a life of solitude and give teachings through symbols. There is no difference between the five paths of the sravakas and those of the pratyekabuddhas.

To summarize the difference between the sravakas and pratyekabuddhas, it is sufficient to understand that they share a common view and path, but there is a slight difference in terms of the subtlety of the view. The pratyekabuddhas not only understand the emptiness of the self but also, to a degree, the emptiness of phenomena. The pratyekabuddhas have a deeper understanding of dependent origination than sravakas, and in their conduct, pratyekabuddhas engage in solitary meditation practice.

3

CONCISE PRESENTATION OF THE PRACTICE

HINAYANA

In this chapter, I am going to give a very concise presentation of Hinayana meditation practice. I will describe the way that the Hinayana teachings are practiced, in terms of three kinds of meditation object – outer, inner, and secret.

Outer

To practice the outer object of meditation, we sit in a relaxed posture and meditate on the form skandha. For that, we look at our own physical body and how attachment to our body becomes the cause of suffering. This way, we realize how the body is the medium for the suffering. We contemplate the impermanence of the body and our strong attachment to it as being permanent.

To meditate on the skandha of sensation, we see all our experiences as water bubbles that come and go. Seeing their momentary nature eliminates our attachment or grasping to them, manifested as habitual views of our experiences as good, bad, or neutral.

We meditate on the skandha of perception by looking at how we perceive people and things. Within this practice, we see them as insubstantial and impermanent. There really is no reality to them; they come and go in an illusory manner. We meditate analytically in this way.

Within our meditation on the skandha of mental formations, we see all composite phenomena – our physical body, feelings, thoughts, and motivations – as composites of factors without any inherent existence. They seem very real and concrete, but they are just a product of dependently arising factors without intrinsic reality.

The meditation on the skandha of consciousness deals with the confused mind, which is also like an illusion. Here, we see that the consciousness that we take to be real is not real, but an illusion arising from confusion. Both the confused mind and its objects are illusory. Through this analytical meditation on the illusory nature of the self, our grasping at what we label as 'self,' and the very process of labeling, start to come apart.

There are several ways to do these meditation practices. One way is to meditate on the negative aspects and the positive aspects of each skandha. A temporary benefit of meditating in this way is that we are able to decrease our fixation and attachment to the body. As a result, we are able to decrease the obstacles that engender sickness. Because they are related to the degree of grasping, the more we grasp at the body, the more obstacles arise in the form of sickness.

These meditation practices are called outer because we focus our mind on the skandhas, which are external relative to mind.

Inner

Meditating on inner objects involves the mind looking at itself. Here we analyze our most prominent mental state, the one that keeps arising in our mind when we practice shamatha. Is it anger, desire, ignorance, jealousy or pride that predominates our mind? Do we have too many conceptual thoughts?

This type of meditation is unique to each individual. We have to understand our mental state through our practice, by observing whatever arises. During meditation, we may find that, again and again, our meditation is interrupted by desire, therefore we need to use a method to counteract it. The antidote to desire is to meditate on the impurity and illusory nature of things.

When we find that our meditation is continuously interrupted by anger or aversion, we counteract that with loving kindness and compassion. As soon as we begin meditating on loving kindness, we can overcome anger and aversion. This is not the same as eliminating the root of aversion, but it will help temporarily. As soon as we find that the overwhelming sense of anger is gone, we sustain that feeling of loving kindness as long as possible.

A predominance of ignorance expresses itself as dullness, or being spaced-out. Meditation on dependent origination is the antidote to dullness. Ignorance predominates when we fail to understand that everything is interconnected. In reality, both suffering and happiness are a product of dependent origination, of many independent factors coming together. As long as we do not recognize this, we remain in the state of ignorance and suffer. Happiness and suffering both result from causes and conditions, therefore, to eliminate ignorance, we need to meditate on dependent origination.

If we find that gross conceptual thoughts (another name for agitation) predominate in our meditation, we rely on the yoga of breathing as the antidote. Breath practice can calm down or completely eliminate gross conceptual thoughts.

Secret

The third technique is meditating on a secret object, the breath. Pranayama, or breathing meditation, is directly linked to both the mind and the body, but especially the body. In this meditation we visualize the body as made of light and energetic wind. Visually it appears as light, but energetically it feels as wind. One cycle of exhaling and inhaling is one round of breath. Within this practice, we count up to ten rounds and then count in reverse. With our eyes closed, we are perfectly aware of our breath. It is very important to breathe naturally and gently. If we force the breath or retain the breath inside too long, it can bring negative physical and mental effects.

When doing this practice, it is very important to see our body as being made of light, not as a solid body of flesh and bones. In the beginning, we spend a couple minutes visualizing ourselves as a body of light. Once we can sustain this visualization, we start focusing on counting the rounds of breath up to ten. If we can do this meditation for fifteen minutes, we will experience a calm and clear mind. Once our mind has calmed down and stabilized, we focus on the emptiness of self for fifteen minutes without focusing on the breath. Then we return to the breath-based meditation, rotating back and forth like this.

During the first week, we meditate in fifteen-minute increments. During the second week, we increase the breath-based meditation sessions to thirty minutes, alternating with the fifteen-minute sessions focusing on the emptiness of self. In the third week, we do only breath-based meditation for four three-hour sessions. When we start these three-hour sessions, we experience an influx of difficulties and obstacles. You might start to feel itchy or impatient or face other obstacles. The antidote for these situations is to change the object of meditation slightly, such as by lengthening the breath or gently holding the breath beneath the navel. These techniques are used not only in tantric practices, but they are also taught in the sutras. They are very profound if you practice them purposefully and correctly.

The secret meditation practice is profound because in the breath-based meditation we work with all five skandhas simultaneously. We are aware of the body because our breath is linked to it through physical sensation. When we are mindful of the breath, we experience sensations and watch them arise and fade away. We are aware of our perception skandha because when we experience feelings, we automatically interpret them, either liking or disliking them. We experience the skandha of mental formations because so many impressions (compositional or mental factors) are coming together at each moment. As for the skandha of consciousness, we are aware that we are being conscious, and our capacity to be mindful of all of the skandhas.

Another way to perform this type of meditation is to scan the entire body, a forearm's length at a time. Breath energy (prana) pervades the entire body from the crown of the head to the soles of the feet. Staying mindful of the breath, we bring mindfulness to the entire body one segment at a time. When we meditate in this way, aware of the movement of breath energy in the body, we sometimes experience obstacles in the form of physical pain or sickness. It is possible that a massive headache or nausea might arise because some previously-dormant karmic imprints have been being activated. When we have pain in a particular part of the body, we can eliminate it while maintaining mindfulness by sending a ray of light, like an arrow, from the tip of the nose to the affected area. We can visualize this light as nectar that soothes the pain. Whenever we feel great pain in the body, our consciousness will naturally go there; by intentionally bringing mindfulness to it, we can eliminate this kind of obstacle in our meditation practice.

It is important to be careful with this type of meditation and to learn it from a qualified master. If done incorrectly for a long time, this practice can create problems. If the mental focus or the breathing is too intense, it can actually cause wind disorders. 'Intensity' here refers to how we are breathing and holding the breath. If we hold the breath too deep or too long, it can induce wind disorders in the heart channel, which will also affect the mind. Also, breathing too gently can induce dullness, meaning that the mind is not alert and sharp. If we practice this meditation correctly, without being too forceful or too relaxed, we will start experiencing positive signs. For example, during the third or fourth week of the practice, our body begins feeling slightly lighter than usual.

After the meditation session, it is very important to dedicate the merit accumulated from practice. Do not get attached to it, otherwise it will be no different from non-Buddhist pranayama practice. We need to maintain the view of the basis, and we should never grasp at or cling to our feelings or experiences. Conduct is also very important for this type of practice. You should maintain a nutritious vegetarian diet and refrain from eating garlic, onions, and meat. Also, this practice requires refraining from sex. Adhering to wholesome, virtuous conduct is important for training in the physical discipline of the Hinayana. When we follow the meditation instructions carefully and abide by the precepts of correct conduct, then we will experience inner realization. If we combine the Hinayana practice with tantric practices, the Hinayana practice becomes an ornament of the tantric practice, and we experience further inner realization.

This concludes the presentation on the essence of the first turning of the wheel of Dharma. We have described the path of the Hinayana vehicle in three ways, including concise practice instructions. I will conclude this part by describing how the teachings of the first turning on the nature of reality are seen from the Mahayana and tantric perspectives.

MAHAYANA VIEW OF THE SKANDHAS

The Mahayana sutric definitions of the skandhas are the same as the Hinayana definition. However, unlike the Hinayana view that the skandhas, ayatanas, and dhatus all exist substantially from their own side as identifiable entities, the Mahayana view is that they do not intrinsically exist from their own side. In fact, they do not truly exist at all. That is the fundamental difference in the view of the basis.

On the Mahayana sutra path, we meditate on the skandhas, ayatanas, and dhatus in the context of three levels of dependent origination – outer, inner, and secret. The Mahayana divides phenomena into (1) external dependently-arising phenomena in the world around us, (2) internal dependently-arising phenomena, which are our own aggregates, sense generators, and dhatus, and (3) secret dependently-arising phenomena, which comprise our own mind and mental factors and their interdependence. From the Mahayana perspective, none of these three types of dependently-arising phenomena intrinsically exist. Rather, they exist in the way that illusions exist.

According to the Mahayana view, all external dependently-arising phenomena result from many factors coming together: the five elements, and the karma and merit of sentient beings.

With respect to the internal dependently-arising phenomena of our own skandhas, ayantanas, and dhatus, the Mahayana view is that they all result from the activation of karmic imprints on consciousness. There is no truly existing external reality and no intrinsic reality of our own skandhas, ayatanas, and dhatus. Our visions are unique to each of us, depending on our own imprints. The experience we have of the universe, the sounds we hear, these are all expressions of our karmic imprints. As the illusory play of dependent origination, various forms and sounds appear to us, but apart from that they have no inherent existence. Phenomena exist simply as illusory appearances.

With respect to secret dependent-arising phenomena – the movements of mind and mental factors – the Mahayana perspective is that they are momentary and ephemeral, not coming from a point of origin or going anywhere in particular. They are all simply the play of illusion; that is their only mode of existence.

The primary technique of Mahayana meditation practice is to eliminate the grosser aspects of the movements of mind and gain access to the subtler aspects of mind. Through this process, we are gradually able to actualize the true nature of mind. Applying ourselves to different types of meditation, we are eventually able to gain access to the true nature of mind, free from any mental fabrication.

While we are still in the domain of gross thoughts, we see things as existing in their own right. Then, because we are confused about the way things exist, we have no way to see the ultimate nature of mind. It is obscured by our fabrications. We need to eliminate these mental fabrications, and the way to do that is to see the subtle interdependent nature of all phenomena. Our primary goal is to pacify these fabrications, these thoughts and concepts. When we are able to do so, we are able to directly perceive the ultimate nature of all phenomena, which is the unity of emptiness and dependent arising. Even though things do not truly exist, even though the skandhas, ayatanas, and dhatus do not exist at all, they appear to us as a result of many causal factors. An example of this is a moon that is reflected in water. Even though there is no moon in the water, when the conditions – the moon in the sky and clear water on the ground – come together, we are able to perceive the reflection of the moon in the water. Likewise, even though there are no truly-existing skandhas, we experience them because many factors come together. This is how we should train in the non-duality of emptiness and dependent origination.

Unlike Hinayana, the Mahayana has no specific meditation practices for each individual skandhas. When we are able to meditate on the dependently-arising nature of all phenomena, while at the same time recognizing their empty nature, that alone is sufficient for understanding the skandhas, ayatanas, and dhatus.

TANTRIC VIEW OF THE SKANDHAS

Now we come to the tantric perspective on the skandhas, dhatus, and ayatanas. The tantric scriptures very clearly describe how to practice the five skandhas in order to transform them.

The tantric path is called 'the path of transformation,' meaning the path on which we transform the ordinary impure aggregates into pure aggregates. The practice of tantra is unlike both the Hinayana practice of mindfulness of the skandhas one by one, and the Mahayana sutra practice of seeing all phenomena as both dependently-arisen and empty. Tantra uses the exceptional method of purifying ordinary aggregates into pure aggregates. Here I will briefly explain this method.

It is very important for tantric practitioners to see all phenomena as the dynamic display of the mind. The Sarma (New School) tantras say that without understanding emptiness, we cannot possibly engage with the tantric path. Therefore, we cultivate the ability to see that all phenomena are an expression of our own mind, which we can easily blend into our daily lives. The skandhas, ayatanas, and dhatus are all expressions, or display, of mind. When we understand this, then transformation becomes possible.

When we are able to see all appearances as expressions of the mind, then we are ready to practice tantric transformation. When we see all experiences as aspects of mind, we are seeing the emptiness or lack of intrinsic existence of everything that appears. And when we directly experience form as empty, it becomes easy to engage in generation stage practice. Then once we are able to generate the deity, we become able to transform the body, arising as an illusory body in the completion stage practice. If we understand that form is primordially empty, then it becomes easy to transform empty forms into divine forms. The completion stage yogas for transforming our own ordinary body into divine forms is made possible by seeing everything as the display of mind.

The Mahayana sutras say form is emptiness and emptiness is also form. Apart from that understanding of empty form, there is no exceptional method of transformation. This is something that is only available in tantric practice. The yogis and yoginis have to directly see all forms as empty, all sounds as echoes, all feelings and judgments as like water bubbles. If the yogin or yogini actually experiences this, then it becomes very easy to engage in the generation-stage yogas. And as generation becomes more and more subtle, it becomes increasingly easy to engage in the completion stage.

What I said earlier about seeing that all phenomena are the energetic display of mind is the foundation of tantric practice. We are not talking about pure or impure, but rather simply seeing every experience – whether pure or impure – as the expression of the mind. This is foundational for every tantra, whether lower or higher. We often refer to the tantra vehicle as Mantrayana, because the mantra signifies protecting the mind from clinging to ordinary experiences. By engaging in deity yoga practices, we protect the mind from clinging to the ordinary body, speech, and mind. If, however, we persist in believing in our ordinary self as separate from the deity, then transformation will be impossible. 'Transformation' becomes a mere word and not something we are able to actualize.

In tantric practice, we have to be able to experience and understand empty form. In the Mahayana sutras, it is said that form is emptiness and emptiness is form, but how do we carry that "emptiness is form" into the practice? The Mahayana sutra does not offer a method for that. In tantra, the view from the beginning is that all phenomena are the appearance or energetic display of the mind. Mind itself is primordially pure, and this primordial purity is the basis of all phenomena, the source of all phenomena, because all phenomena are the display of mind. When we are able to access the primordial purity of mind, we will find that it is beyond emptiness or non-emptiness. We can be introduced to the mind's primordial purity through initiation, especially through the word initiation. This is the importance of receiving initiation.

Having established the fundamental purity of the mind, the subtlest mind, we are also able to realize the purity of the subtlest wind, on which the subtlest mind 'rides'. The subtlest wind is also primordially pure. And if the subtlest wind is primordially pure by nature, then all of the elements are primordially pure. As the elements become more gross, they give rise to the skandhas, but by nature, the skandhas are primordially pure. Once we understand that the skandhas are primordially pure, they become the basis for transformation. That is what we mean by transformation. It is not some magical thing, but it can only happen when we understand the purity of the basis.

However, simply saying that the subtlest mind, subtlest wind, and the aggregates are pure is not going to help us with the transformation process. We have to gain understanding of the primordial purity of these three on the basis of our own meditation experience, and then we can use that purity of the basis as the starting point for the transformation process. The main reason we are unable to perceive the skandhas as being primordially pure is the present condition of our own mind. In order to transform the skandhas, it is necessary to engage in deity yoga practice to purify and cleanse the mind. Through the practice of the generation stage, we can purify the gross, subtle, and subtlest obscurations and then engage in the completion stage yogas. Within the context of the completion stage, we are finally able to see the primordial purity of the aggregates.

That is why we say that the purified aspect of the five skandhas is transformed into the five Buddha families. The skandha of form is transformed into Vairocana, sensation – into Ratnasambhava, perception – into Amitabha, mental formation – into Amogasiddhi, and consciousness – into Akshobhya. It is not enough to meditate on emptiness like we do on the sutra path; simply purifying the aggregates through emptiness is not sufficient. We need to engage in the yoga of profundity and clarity. The generation and completion stages are the means by which we approach the mandala of the deity. The generation stage is fairly gross. Initially, we visualize the deity and mandala as very large, and then we refine the visualization into a very subtle drop, in which we can see the entire deity mandala. This is the subtle level of the generation stage. When we are able to visualize the entire mandala in that way, our mind has become very subtle, but we are still relying on very subtle concepts. From there, we enter into the completion stage yogas, where even the subtlest concepts subside and primordial wisdom is awakened. This is the wisdom of the dharmadhatu, the basic space of phenomena. That is how we transform the five skandhas into the five Buddha families and the five poisons into the five wisdoms.

The tantras outline special methods to actualize the rupakaya or form body of a Buddha. These techniques are not available in the Mahayana sutra practices, which rely on the purity of the subtlest mind, wind, and aggregates. Only tantra relies on the method of transforming the aggregates and five poisons into the five Buddha families and the five wisdoms of an enlightened being.

This tantric 'alchemy' is likened to the transformation of ordinary iron into gold. It is possible to effect this transformation when we know the primordial purity of iron and gold. In other words, we understand that there is no intrinsically existing iron and no intrinsically existing gold. Understanding the primordially pure basis enables us to engage in alchemy. Likewise, if the aggregates were not primordially pure, then we could not bring about their transformation. It is because they are primordially pure and without intrinsic existence that we can transform them.

Although Mahayana sutras mentions the rupakaya of an enlightened being, they provide no technique to actualize it. Because no practices are based on understanding the primordial purity of the mind and wind, there is no technique for perceiving everything as being primordially pure.

At the level of subtlest wind and mind, we are talking about a very subtle level of dependent origination that is beyond ordinary concepts. It is difficult to imagine the basis of transformation that allows us to transform the skandhas, which at present are the basis of our suffering. When we actually see the primordial purity of the subtlest mind and wind, then we start to see how the transformation of the basis can take place.

When I was being trained, a lot of teachers and scriptures would talk about visualization and recitation without focusing very much on the basis of the path, which is this primordially pure mind and wind. If we do not focus on this vital point, however, then we cannot gain any conviction regarding the path of transformation.

SUMMARY

This concludes the teachings on the essence of the first turning of the wheel of Dharma, with some additional comparisons to how Mahayana sutra and tantra understand the skandhas. Now, I will provide a brief summary.

I want to stress the importance of understanding the skandhas, ayatanas, and dhatus in terms of their relevance to practice, whether at the level of the Hinayana, Mahayana, Tantra, or Dzogchen. In Hinayana, the basis for practicing the four noble truths is the skandhas, ayatanas, and dhatus. For Mahayana practitioners, there is no way to understand dependent arising and emptiness without investigating the dependent arising and emptiness of the skandhas. In tantra, the transformation and deity practices start with insight into the purity of the skandhas and the elements. In Dzogchen, we focus on the primordial wind; especially in tögal we use the primordial wind, light rays, appearances, and visions connected to the skandhas, ayatanas, and dhatus. I personally think that understanding the skandhas, ayatanas, and dhatus is very important from the Hinayana up through Dzogchen. That is why I chose this topic, because it is relevant to our practice.

Sometimes tantric and Dzogchen practitioners tend to look down on these teachings, but in terms of actual practice they are very relevant. It is important to understand how to carry these teachings into our own practice experience. Otherwise studying the skandhas is nothing more than collecting information. We need to try to see how these teachings are relevant to our own experience by putting them into practice.

PART TWO

THE SECOND TURNING OF THE
WHEEL OF DHARMA

4

THE BASIS

The Buddha taught according to the particular aptitude or capacity of whoever was present and presented his teachings within the three wheel of Dharma. The teachings of the second turning were given for disciples of great aptitude. These teachings have two 'sides': (1) the profound teachings on the view of emptiness and (2) the extensive teachings on conduct, which assist in understanding the view. The teachings on emptiness provide the basis, and the teachings on conduct present the grounds and paths, or levels of realization, on the path of the Great Vehicle or Mahayana.

LINEAGE HISTORY

Although Shakyamuni Buddha presented all three turnings of the wheel of Dharma, they further branched into specific teachings by various lineage masters. The Mahayana has been propagated in three principal teaching lineages. The three principal lineages are (1) the profound lineage of the view of emptiness, (2) the extensive lineage of conduct, and (3) the practice lineage of blessings. The direct subject matter of the second turning teachings is the profound view of emptiness. The indirect subject matter is conduct or the method aspect, the bodhisattva grounds and paths. The blessing or practice lineage is the lineage of the mahasiddhas.[8]

It is important to be acquainted with and appreciate the lineages and lineage masters that passed on the Buddha's teachings. The view was passed from the Buddha to Manjushri, then to Nagarjuna, Aryadeva, and Chandrakirti in India, and to the Nyingma masters of Tibet. The translator Rinchen Zangpo and other masters carried this lineage further to the New Translation schools, or Sarma schools. We should appreciate that the teachings we receive today were preserved and transmitted as authentic teachings by successive generations of lineage masters.

The familiarity with the lineages and lineage masters helps our practice because it gives us confidence that our study, learning, and teaching will genuinely benefit ourselves and others. It helps us become certain of the authenticity of the teachings. If we are unaware of the lineage, then we cannot be clear about the authenticity of the teachings. For example, if we study medicine, we want to know for certain that the teachers are recognized as qualified authorities on medicine. The same applies to yoga teachers and others. If we have no guarantee that a teacher is qualified as an authority, the benefit of their teaching is doubtful. Certainty about authenticity is even more important for the of teaching about how to develop the mind than any non-Buddhist teachings.

In our study of the lineages, it is also helpful to learn about the 'chariot leaders' – the masters who founded each of the philosophical schools.[9] The role of chariot leaders is often described through an analogy of a field path. When a field path falls into disuse, it becomes overgrown; similarly, when no living practitioner teaches or practices specific teachings, they may become forgotten. A chariot leader is someone who retraces and reopens it, making a clear path that others can follow. For example, the Buddha taught extensively on emptiness: the eight types of emptiness, the eighteen or twenty types of emptiness, and so on. However, with time these teachings were lost, obscured, or misunderstood. As the Buddha had prophesied, the chariot leader Nagarjuna came along and re-revealed the teachings on emptiness once again. Nagarjuna reopened the path by returning to the original teachings of the second turning and presenting them as a course of logical reasoning. The Mahayana tradition considers two chariot leaders as two principal founders – Nagarjuna, the founder of the lineage of the profound teachings on emptiness, and Asanga, the founder of the lineage of the extensive teachings on conduct. Below, I will briefly outline Nagarjuna's biography and his contributions to the Mahayana school.

The second turning teachings directly reveal the profound view of emptiness, which the Buddha taught from his own experience to his high-level bodhisattva disciples. Because these teachings could only be understood by bodhisattvas, Nagarjuna faced the challenge of presenting these teachings to ordinary human beings. Always referring back to and quoting from the Buddha's words in the sutras, he found a way to present these teachings in a way that is accessible to ordinary people. This quality – the ability to reveal the teachings in a way understandable by the audience – uniquely characterizes a chariot leader, a founder, or a revealer.

The Buddha's teachings on emptiness employ negation rather than assertion, avoiding any implication that emptiness is an object or a property of objects ('this object is empty'). We find in the sutras of the second turning, such as the *Heart Sutra*, such lines as, 'There is no obscuration, no afflictive emotion, no eye, no ear, no nose, no tongue.' The *Heart Sutra* is spoken from the point of view of emptiness itself, by means of negation. It is spoken from the point of view of the Buddha's direct experience of the actual mode of abiding. The language of negation is difficult to understand, and the direct experience of the mode of abiding hard to imagine.

Nagarjuna presented the view of emptiness in two ways: from the point of view of practice and also philosophically, as part of the tradition of commentary on the view. For example, Nagarjuna wrote six texts on logic that reveal the view of emptiness through philosophical reasoning and debate. The principal root text of Madhyamaka, the *Mulamadhyamakakarika* ('Root Stanzas of the Middle Way') is one example from the great tradition of commentary.[10]

The Buddha taught the second turning from the point of view of his own meditative experience: what his meditation revealed, such as the non-existence of the skandhas of form, feeling, and so on. Because the Buddha taught based on his own experience from the point of view of ultimate reality, his discourses are difficult to follow for people who relate entirely to conventional reality. Nagarjuna contributed greatly to the transmission of the Buddha's teachings by explaining and contextualizing them for ordinary people. For example, he explained what the Buddha meant when he said 'there are no skandhas.' For those who do not appreciate intellectual elaboration or theorizing, Nagarjuna taught simply and concisely from experience. For those who like intellectual elaboration, he offered the logical-philosophical presentation.

In Nagarjuna's time, the predominant philosophical school was the Cittamatra or Mind-Only school. Cittamatra holds that other than mind itself, which does exist, everything is dependently arisen and does not truly exist. Nagarjuna composed the *Mulamadhyamakakarika* in response to the Cittamatra as well as to the early Buddhist schools, challenging its view of existence. He did not create a new philosophy, but rather wrote in accordance with what the Buddha himself taught.

The *Heart Sutra* says, 'there is no ignorance, no consciousness.' This is a subtler understanding of emptiness than is found in the Cittamatra. It is easier to understand the emptiness of objects than it is to understand the emptiness of the mind itself.

The Buddha's words may seem to contradict what we think we know from our own experience. For example, the statement 'there is no form' contradicts what we can see in ordinary experience. 'There is no ignorance' also contradicts experience; ignorance is the reason we suffer in samsara. Nagarjuna's job was to explain what the Buddha meant by saying 'there is no form' and 'there is no ignorance,' and he did it by clarifying the doctrine of the two truths, relative and ultimate.

For people who are actually seeking liberation from samsara, the doctrine of two truths is very significant, because to understand them is to gain liberation. One can only understand the two truths if one understands the ultimate truth, emptiness of inherent existence. So these teachings on emptiness are very important for anyone who is really determined to gain liberation. They are not merely academic topics for refined conversation; they are the way to realize the Middle Way.

Since the ultimate view of emptiness is non-conceptual and free from conceptual elaboration, Nagarjuna had no choice but to negate all of the conceptual elaborations of relative truth at once. This format of exhaustive negation of elaboration (theory, speculation) is not easy to digest. But it was not undertaken for the sake of intellectual showmanship. It uses reasoning to direct our mind, against the flow of rational habit, between the extremes of existence and non-existence.

Nagarjuna is regarded as the founder and chariot leader of the Madhyamaka school because he showed that the teachings of the second turning are free from the two extremes – existence and non-existence, or eternalism and nihilism – and free from conceptual elaboration. They are the Middle Way, or Madhyamaka, between the extremes.

This manner of understanding the Middle Way was preserved and transmitted by Nagarjuna's student Aryadeva. Nagarjuna and Aryadeva's teachings are considered the foundational teachings of all Madhyamaka schools, or the Great Madhyamaka.

As the Madhyamaka teachings continued to be transmitted after Nagarjuna and Aryadeva, there were ongoing debates about the essence of these teachings. After Nagarjuna and Aryadeva, we have Buddhapalita and Chandrakirti, the chariot leaders of the Prasangika Madhyamaka school. Some scholars speak of Buddhapalita as the actual founder, because he instigated the debate that brought about the division into the two main Madhyamaka schools, Prasangika and Svatantrika. Buddhapalita was debating Bhavaviveka's understanding of the Madhyamaka, which became known as Svatantrika Madhyamaka. Later, Chandrakirti presented the Prasangika view with even greater clarity, and thus most scholars speak of Chandrakirti as the real revealer. Chandrakirti also is regarded as the main sustainer or preserver of Prasangika. Bhavaviveka became recognized as the founder of Svatantrika Madhyamaka.

From these two schools – Svatantrika Madhyamaka and Prasangika Madhyamaka – further divisions arose from debate. The Svatantrika

Madhyamaka subdivided into the Sautrantika-Svatantrika Madhyamaka and the Yogachara-Svatantrika Madhyamaka. Of course, these debates were not mere competitive games. At the very heart of the matter was the need to understand the Middle Way, to experience the natural state for oneself, free of obscurations and fixation on appearances. However, the process of ascertaining the correct understanding and experience of emptiness is very subtle and profound. It is due to the very subtlety of the teachings on emptiness that the different schools evolved.

The Buddha taught emptiness in the second turning, with sayings like 'there is no form' and 'there is no ignorance,' in order to eliminate ignorance and confusion. The trouble is that we are attached to conventional appearances, which leads to a state of confusion. From within this state of confusion, we cannot see the actual mode of abiding, the way things truly exist. The Buddha gave the teachings on emptiness to eliminate this confusion.

It is helpful, in the middle of these debates, to remember that the teachings of the Middle Way are supposed to be understood at the most basic practical level as well. In our daily lives, taking care of ourselves - choosing what to eat, and so on - is not easy because our minds are not healthy. For example, one glass of wine is good for our mind and heart, but if we drink two or three glasses, that is a bad habit. If we use the Middle Way in daily life to bring moderation in our actions, it is very useful.

More essentially but still at a practical level, the purpose of the second turning teachings is the elimination of grasping or attachment. Attachment gives rise to cycles of agitation and disappointment, which prevent us from sustaining the natural state. For having figured this out, the Buddha can be recognized as a scientist – there is actually no greater scientist of the mind than the Buddha. Nowadays, people have a lot more appreciation for the Buddha's teachings, and scientists are taking a greater interest in them because of their scientific nature.

The teachings on emptiness are very complex, because they are also teachings on dependent arising. The Buddha did not make it complex; it is complex at the level of the way things are in conventional reality, as dependently-arisen. For example, without external objects we do not have the conditions that give rise to confusion. Without those conditions, there are no appearances, and without appearances or objects of perception, there is no object to get attached to, no object of grasping. Dependent arising was not created by the Buddha; it is real. At the level of reality, things exist as an intricate web of interdependent causes and conditions.

This is how Madhyamaka explains suffering. Grasping generates confused thoughts and opinions based on attachment or aversion. We accept and reject things because we are attached to the self-existence of objects. But since things and people are empty (do not have inherent existence), our attachments are unsuccessful in making us happy, instead leading to dissatisfaction and suffering.

This is connected to why we have the different philosophical schools. Philosophical ideas and positions are also external objects – objects of thought, not sensory perceptions – that are accepted and rejected. The higher schools reject positions held by the lower schools. The Vaibhashikas and Sautrantikas believe that material objects truly exist, that they exist outside of mind. At a higher level, this belief can be recognized as a form of grasping. The Cittamatra school says that only mind exists, and that external objects are nothing more than expressions of the mind. Then the Madhyamaka school comes along and says that if you think mind truly exists, you are wrong. The schools' challenges to each others' positions are essentially a form of grasping – grasping at the existence of inherently existing metaphysical positions. Acceptance and rejection, dispute and division, follow each other.

The Buddha taught in the *Heart Sutra,* and the second turning teachings in general, that 'there is no form, no feeling,' and so on. He taught this in order to eliminate our strong attachment to externally existing phenomena. He was not negating the conventional existence of form and feeling. The problem is that we do not understand how things exist – we think they truly exist. The Buddha taught the way that they actually exist, their actual mode of existence. When we understand this, attachment is eliminated. If we can eliminate attachment, then we can eliminate suffering.

The Buddha not only taught that sense objects do not exist inherently, he also taught that the mind that perceives them does not exist inherently. In the 'Heart Sutra,' he even says that ignorance does not exist. But what does this mean? Ignorance is the root of samsara. All of the teachings of the Buddha were given to gain freedom from conditioned existence, but the root of conditioned existence in samsara is ignorance. Thus, the teachings are there to eliminate ignorance. However, if ignorance does not exist, what is the point of eliminating it? In fact, we do experience ignorance and its results, but we do not understand the way in which it exists, and it is essential to understand this.

This is why we call these teachings on emptiness the 'profound teachings.' They are difficult to comprehend, difficult to put into practice, and it is difficult to give rise to realization.

The reason that the teachings are difficult to understand can be illustrated by analogy. If we try to teach a crazy person about his craziness, it will be difficult for him to understand. If we try to teach the downfalls of drinking to someone who is drunk, her intoxication makes it difficult for her to understand. When we are in a state of confusion, it is difficult to understand teachings that are meant to eliminate that confusion. That is why these teachings are difficult to understand. The teachings themselves are not complicated, but our mind is confused and complicated and the need to untangle the mind complicates the teachings.

The Buddha saw that beings are propelled in cyclic existence by confusion. The profound teachings on emptiness were given because he was moved by great compassion to eliminate the root of suffering, which is ignorance of emptiness. To help beings realize emptiness, he used many different methods, utilizing the many different kinds of phenomena, from external material objects to different kinds of conceptual and mental objects. All of these explanations were given in order to illustrate emptiness. If he could simply have said that all phenomena are by nature empty, then there would have been no need for further elaboration and debate, or for the many different philosophical schools that developed.

WHY IS EMPTINESS IMPORTANT?

In this second section, I will explain the reasons given in the sutras and commentaries for giving the emptiness teachings, and why we need to understand the meaning of emptiness.

One of the Buddha's disciples once asked, 'Why do you give teachings on the profound view of emptiness?' The Buddha replied that because sentient beings are under the influence of karma and negative emotions, they are helplessly propelled within samsara. The reason for their helplessness is that they do not understand the meaning of emptiness, pacification, and non-arising. Therefore, he gave the teachings on emptiness and sublime peace in order to liberate them.

Aryadeva explains in his *Four-Hundred-Verses*,[11] a commentary on Nagarjuna's 'Root Stanzas,' that the root of suffering is ignorance, and that if we do not eliminate ignorance, we will never attain freedom from all forms of suffering. To eliminate the root of all suffering and all of its variations, we need to understand emptiness and apply that understanding to our own practice.

These passages from th Buddha's and Aryadeva's words are two of many in the sutras, shastras, and even the tantras which show that the teachings on emptiness were given to eliminate ignorance and end suffering. Many other sources confirm that the purpose of understanding emptiness is to end suffering by eliminating ignorance.

The Buddha gave teachings for those who are intent on liberation from samsara, not for those seeking temporary benefits in their business or daily activities. We need to keep that fundamental motivation and determination in mind. For practitioners, it is very important to generate the intention to seek liberation from conditioned existence and samsara. This intention may be difficult to give rise by someone living in a prosperous country, but we have to be honest with ourselves about our real intentions, and renounce pointless attachments. Renunciation, based on insight into the nature and cause of suffering, is the heart of sustaining the intention to gain liberation.

We do not have to look far to discover the reason to cultivate the wisdom of emptiness. Every day we can see that there is tremendous suffering despite great prosperity and relatively good education. Prosperity and education do little to reduce the suffering that pervades our lives. At the very least therefore, it should be clear that there is a reason to be motivated to understand the source of this suffering and to find a way to eliminate it. This kind of motivation is the basis of renunciation, which is a minimum requirement for approaching the teachings.

We cannot hide from suffering, and denying it does not help. So first we have to be able to acknowledge it. Second, we need to recognize that in order to solve the suffering that is inside us, relying on something outside ourselves, such as material possessions or substances, will not bring benefit. Lastly, for the teachings on emptiness to be practical and beneficial, we should not treat them as an external object of knowledge but rather apply the meaning of emptiness to our own mind. These three points are very important to keep in mind.

When we begin to understand the teachings on emptiness, we see that it is not about making something substantial into something empty. Things are already, and always have been, empty. Instead we come to understand the difference between the actual mode of existence and the way things appear to us. When we understand that key point, we also understand emptiness.

In summary, to benefit from the emptiness teachings, it helps to remember why they were given – to eliminate ignorance and grasping. Grasping is what gives rise to anxiety, fear, loneliness, and depression, and the teachings on emptiness directly address grasping. If we understand emptiness as a sort of theory about the non-existence of things, then we are missing the key point of the wisdom of emptiness. We need to understand how the teachings directly apply to our own experience.

IN PURSUIT OF EMPTINESS

Once we are aware of the benefit of understanding emptiness, the next step is to gain that understanding for ourselves. The way to do this is to enter the Middle Way. The doorway onto the path of the Middle Way is understanding the two truths – relative truth and ultimate truth. We will explain the two truths in this chapter by looking at the Middle Way on three levels: at the level of the basis, at the level of the path, and at the level of the result. Now we are looking at it from the level of the basis.

Understanding the two truths at the level of the basis is the same as understanding the basis of the Middle Way. One of the main sutric references for the presentation of the two truths at the level of the basis is the *Sutra of the Meeting of Father and Son*.[12] This sutra is one of the most relevant sutras for understanding the two truths at this level.

There is a difference between the way things appear to us, which is the relative truth, and the way things actually exist, which is the ultimate truth. Things appear in the way that they do because, under the influence of ignorance, perceptions and their objects arise in a dualistic way, separated into an imputed subject and object. The dualistic character of appearances is important to understand because it provokes grasping. Appearances are not themselves the thing to negate, but rather grasping at those appearances and perceptions. As Tilopa said to Naropa, "Son, it is not appearances that bind us; it is grasping at those appearances that binds us. So Naropa, cut through your grasping." We seek the wisdom of emptiness in order to overcome grasping at appearances and perceptions.

We can see the ways that we grasp at material growth and technological development as if these were the solutions to all of our problems. We are carried away by our perceptions and our attachment to them. We have no leisure; we are always busy, propelled by hopes and fears. We suffer from anxiety because we put our faith in external appearances, which are ephemeral and, in reality, illusory. The more we put our faith in material gain as the source of happiness, the more we engage in activities that only bring us more confusion and anxiety.

We sometimes respond to television shows and advertisements in quite comical ways. We know that commercials are not real, and having heard teachings on emptiness, we 'know' that the self does not exist. Even so, we have thoughts like, 'I must have that amazing new device!' Even though we know that marketing is manipulative, we still go out and buy stuff. This reveals the actual intensity of our grasping at objects. Overcoming this powerful force is the fundamental reason the Buddha taught the emptiness of external objects.

In our contemporary context, it is helpful to recognize the great faith we put in the material world. Relative truth is this relationship between our attachment and the external world, which takes a certain materialistic cultural form for us. By coming to understand this relationship, we begin to see the emptiness of external objects, and gain insight into the relative and ultimate truths at the level of the basis.

Eliminating our grasping at things and people as though they truly existed does not happen all at once. We are not ascetics. We have a lot of daily activities and responsibilities for which we need to make use of material objects and interact with people. We also need to understand, however, that beyond their practical use or purpose, strong attachment to anything or anyone gives rise to suffering instead of happiness. It is very important to recognize the internal contradiction between grasping and freedom from suffering.

The wisdom of emptiness is disclosed within our own experience, by looking at and analyzing our own mind. By contemplating our own experience, we come to see that when we can let go of grasping, by recognizing the emptiness of real existence of things, it results in greater happiness. When you have seen this for yourself, it will motivate you to pursue the study and contemplation of emptiness with greater determination.

This seems to be the best method. The traditional approach is extremely elaborate and lengthy. First, you need to study and contemplate the teachings for years, and only after that engage in renunciation and the path. Our approach should be to start right now, applying the meaning of emptiness to our own experience in our own contemporary setting. We do not necessarily need to follow traditional courses of study. The Buddha himself gave a variety of teachings, in a variety of times and places, to a variety of students.

HOW TO DEVELOP THE WISDOM OF EMPTINESS

To cultivate the realization of the wisdom of emptiness, we undertake training. The nature of the training depends on the capacity of the disciple. When we refer to the capacity of disciples, we are referring to the external circumstances as well as internal dispositions of the student, and whether or not these conditions are supportive of the practice of the path. A disciple's capacity for practice can be of three types: small, middling or great.

Training disciples of the highest capacity

Disciples with great capacity are those who have great intelligence, and whose external circumstances and internal dispositions are very conducive to study and contemplation. Such a person should first find a qualified teacher, one who has mastered both the sutra and tantra teachings, especially the philosophy of the Middle Way, as understood in all five traditions, including the Bon tradition. The teacher's training should include not only intellectual understanding but actual experience.

The proper way to receive teachings from a qualified teacher is to receive teachings on one Madhyamaka sutra, such as the *Heart Sutra*, and from one shastra or commentary, such as the *Root Stanzas of the Middle Way* (*Mulamadhyamaka-karika*), the root text of Madhyamaka philosophy. It is best to rely on one commentary to begin your training. You first engage in study and learning, or what is called 'hearing,' then in contemplation of the meaning, and finally in meditation. If you follow this systematic approach, you will gain a meaningful understanding of the philosophy of the Middle Way.

At the level of hearing, you engage in extensive study with your teacher. 'Extensive study' here means studying the teachings of the Buddha, how the Middle Way became obscured over time, and how Nagarjuna revealed the essential teachings as the chariot leader of the lineage.

Then one studies how those teachings were clarified by Aryadeva and later debated in different ways by masters like Chandrakirti, Buddhapalita, and Bhavaviveka. It is important to understand how the Madhyamaka split into two branches, not due to differences about the view of emptiness, but rather to different ways of explaining conventional reality. The Svatantrika and Prasangika differ in their presentation of conventional reality, not that of ultimate reality. Within the Svatantrika school, we also have a further subdivision into the Yogacara-Svatantrika and Sautrantika-Svatantrika. The Yogacara-Svatantrika school accords with the Mind-Only (Cittamatra) school in its account of conventional reality. The Sautrantika-Svatantrika school emphasizes objects external to mind, so its depiction of conventional reality is more in accord with the Sautrantika view.

The sixth century master Bhavaviveka's interpretation of Nagarjuna's work forms the foundation of the Svatantrika Madhyamaka, again not on the basis of a different interpretation of the ultimate view of emptiness, but of a different way of explaining conventional reality. The sixth- and seventh-century masters Buddhapalita and Chandrakirti held a position on the Middle Way that came to be called the Prasangika Madhyamaka.

Bhavaviveka raised the question, 'If we interpret everything as mentally imputed so that nothing exists on the side of the object (as in

Prasangika), then how do we explain the way conventional reality exists?' Bhavaviveka argued that the wisdom of emptiness would be difficult to carry into practice if there were no basis for conventional reality. He held that conventional reality has to exist in some sense; we cannot regard everything as merely imputed. This question became the point of differentiation between the Prasangika and Svatantrika Madhyamaka.

This is a question about the nature of the 'basis of emptiness.' The basis of emptiness is the thing that is empty, or that to which emptiness is attributed. The question of how this thing, which is empty, does exist or does not exist is a difficult and subtle question. The differences between these two schools arise from the difficulty of understanding the basis of the subtlest ignorance, or subtlest grasping, in terms of conventional reality. In conventional reality, when there is confusion, there is some kind of identifiable basis of the confusion. But the basis of the subtlest confusion or obscuration – that which prevents us from understanding emptiness - is conventional reality itself. The two Madhyamaka schools interpret the nature of subtlest ignorance differently.

Our subtlest grasping at a truly existing reality is extremely difficult to eliminate, because we are always relating to objects. This is why we have to investigate the ways that we relate to them. Because it is a difficult and subtle business, there are different proposals for how to undertake this investigation. The Prasangika says that ultimately there is no object; nothing exists from the side of the object; the object is merely imputed. The Svatantrika finds this hard to accept. If the object does not exist from its own side, then what is it that we are relating to and grasping at?

The Buddha himself taught that nothing exists from the side of the object and that everything is conceptually imputed. Even though there is a basis for imputing an object (something there to label), if you examine that basis, the object cannot be found. In the absence of analysis, the object seems to exist from its own side, because there is something there that we're labeling, right? This is the basis of imputation. But when we analyze this thing, we find that it can not actually be found. It 'comes apart' under analysis. The differences in understanding this point, which we find in analytical meditation, give rise to the divergence of these two schools. Both schools are asking the same question, 'What is the fundamental cause of the subtlest grasping at reality?' Depending on how you answer it, you side with one school or the other. The differences between the Prasangika and Svatantrika actually come from practice – the practice of analytical meditation. These debates are not mere intellectual swordplay.

Both of the Madhyamaka schools are trying to find the same thing – the root cause of grasping at intrinsic reality, which is the basis of our confusion and misunderstanding of appearances. They both examine the subtle degrees of grasping. For example, what we experience in daily waking life is coarse grasping at intrinsic existence. We experience subtle grasping in the dream state. The subtlest grasping at intrinsic reality is experienced in the bardo, or intermediate state. The debate between the schools is about the subtlest ignorance and how to eliminate it. This is not a mere conceptual problem; it is directly related to our own liberation. As Chandrakirti says in his *Introduction to the Middle Way*, the reason to engage in debate is not attachment to our own philosophical view but attainment of liberation.[13]

Our basic, core motivation for studying the Middle Way philosophy has to be the intention to gain liberation. The main obstacle to realizing the wisdom of emptiness is grasping at things as intrinsically existing. It is difficult to identify grasping since it has no form or shape. It is difficult to eliminate grasping because it is not material but mental. It has to do with how things appear to us and how we cling to those appearances. If we know that this is happening and our goal is to attain liberation, then the more we study, the more our own wisdom expands.

The education of the disciple of great capacity includes extensive learning of the history of Mahayana, and the debates that shaped the various schools. These debates have persisted into the present in Tibet, where there is some disagreement with the standard view that Prasangika Madhaymaka represents Madhyamaka's highest form. Understanding the overall history of these debates helps to illustrate the extent of refinement required of the view of emptiness, and the caliber of training undertaken by these disciples.

In India, the Mahayana comprises Cittamatra and the two branches of the Madhyamaka, or Middle Way. The Madhyamaka teachings were transplanted to Tibet, first in the form of what we call the ancient Nyingma tradition, and then as the New or Sarma tradition. There were basically three schools of Madhyamaka in Tibet. At the time of King Trisong Detsen in the eighth century, they speak of the Madhyamaka view of emptiness as that of Nagarjuna, because there was as of yet no distinction between Svatantrika and Prasangika. The method or conduct aspect came from the early Buddhist Mulasarvastivadin system of monastic discipline, which provides the basis for our practice of the vinaya. After the eighth century, we begin to see the classification into the Svatantrika and Prasangika Madhyamaka, with the further subdivision of the Svatantrika Madhyamaka into the Yogachara-Svatantrika and Sautrantika-Svatantrika Madhyamaka. Around that time, still rooted in the ancient Nyingma tradition, practice in Tibet was primarily based on the Yogachara-Svatantrika Madhyamaka as taught by Indian teacher, Shantarakshita. This school of thought is still very relevant in Tibetan Buddhism, more so than other Madhyamaka schools, because it emphasizes the emptiness of the mind rather than the emptiness of all phenomena. Because of its emphasis on mind, it is intimately linked to tantric and Dzogchen practices.

Later, around the time of Atisha, Rinchen Zangpo translated Chandrakirti's *Introduction to the Middle Way*, thereby presenting the Prasangika view as Chandrakirti's ultimate intent. This is how Prasangika Madhyamaka became dominant in Tibet at the time of the new translations. It came to be held that the Prasangika is more profound than the Svatantrika view (reflecting Chandrakirti's intent), so the Prasangika replaced the Nyingma tradition's emphasis on Yogacara-Svatantrika Madhyamaka. Following Rinchen Zangpo, the Sakya school further explained and emphasized the Prasangika view. Following the Sakya tradition, Tsongkhapa clarified the Prasangika view even further, establishing the Gelugpa tradition. When you hear Gelugpa teachers explaining Madhyamaka, they are explaining Prasangika Madhyamaka.

At the time of the ancient Nyingma tradition, under the influence of Shantarakshita, the Tibetans mostly held the Yogacara-Svatantrika Madhyamaka view. Then the emphasis was on practice, so the main question concerned what kind of view was better from the point of view of practice. The position that Prasangika is higher than Yogacara developed in Tibet as a result of scholastic and debating practices that intellectualized the view. This position is primarily intellectual or academic and may not reflect what is actually most beneficial to our own practice.

In the Sakya and Gelug traditions, it is said that the difference between the Svatantrika and Prasangika Madhyamaka is as vast as the difference between the earth and the sky. Even today, you come across this view in commentaries. In the ancient or Nyingma tradition, however, neither Mipham nor Longchenpa differentiate between Prasangika and Svatantrika in their explanations of emptiness, because both positions are the Middle Way, free from the extremes of nihilism and eternalism. In that sense, there is no difference. The only differences are in how the subtle level of conventional reality is explained.

Furthermore, both Longchenpa and Mipham say that for a beginner, it is actually easier to digest the Svatantrika Madhyamaka position because it talks about the way in which objects exist from their own side. Some could interpret this as a claim that there is an intrinsically real external reality, but here we are really only talking about how objects exist in a conventional sense. If the beginner can provisionally accept that the object conventionally exists, it is easier to digest, and he or she avoids falling into a nihilistic position. Longchenpa and others have said it is more difficult to comprehend the Prasangika position, because there is a greater danger of nihilism when it is said that nothing whatsoever exists from the side of the object and that everything is mentally imputed.

However, the Nyingma tradition never mentions either position as being higher or lower. Each position is explained from the point of view of how the teachings are experienced as they apply to oneself. I prefer this approach because here they are not treated as mere conceptual content.

When we examine self-grasping in analytic meditation, we begin with more obvious, coarse levels of grasping at the aggregates, such as to the body and feelings. Looking for the actual basis of attachment, we take the analysis of grasper and object grasped to subtler and subtler levels. The differences between the Svatantrika and Prasangika Madhyamaka views occur at the subtlest level of analysis of conventional reality. There is no difference in the view of the ultimate, which is beyond analysis.

It is actually quite helpful for our purposes to clearly understand the difference between the Svatantrika and Prasangika Madhyamaka. At the ultimate level, both state that nothing exists from the side of the object. But when we try to communicate such a view to someone else it becomes difficult to comprehend. When we're immersed in grasping at an intrinsic reality, saying that there's no object to grasp sounds like nihilism, a view that there's nothing. The reason we slip toward nihilism is that we are unable to experience the emptiness of our mind. In addition, we are unable to see how phenomena dependently arise from the ground of emptiness.

For example, when we see the reflection of the moon in water and leave it as it is, we simply see the reflection in the water. That is the conventional mode of existence. If we are not content with this conventional mode of appearance, we look for something that truly exists in the water. We try to touch the reflection, but only get our hands wet. So we then analyze the water itself — what is the water really? We look for something concrete to explain the reflection, but we never find what we are looking for, the essential 'thing.' It does not really matter if we are Prasangika or Svatantrika. What is really happening is that we are so habituated to thinking that things actually exist that we cling to them. When we do not find the object, it becomes problematic to us because we are not used to that. The Svatantrika response to this problem seems less nihilistic than the Prasangika response.

If we actually understand the Prasangika view, that nothing can be said about existence from the side of the object, it is pretty profound. If we only understand it as a non-affirming negation (a negation that does not imply that something else is true), as they do among the Gelug and Sakya, then it is not so profound. Our view has to become baseless and free from concepts, with nothing to cling to. Then we can find the actual mode of reality through the Prasangika method. It comes very close to the Dzogchen view of rigpa, where we also talk about baselessness. Then it becomes very beneficial.

When we say 'baseless' in the Prasangika Madhyamaka, what we mean is that when we try to find the object of our thought, the object of our conceptual grasping, we do not . There is no identifiable, unitary object there. Finding that there's nothing really there is alone what it means to recognize baselessness. Nothing exists from the side of the object except through mental designation. The objects of our mental grasping have no basis in reality. The way things are is baseless in the sense that it's not there in the object. When we talk about baselessness is Dzogchen, we are talking about the baselessness of rigpa, which is beyond mind. I am not saying that Prasangika and Dzogchen are the same thing, but there is a relationship there. If we have a correct Prasangika view, it can help us with our Dzogchen practice.

As for the contemporary approach to understanding reality, we tend to think for example that conditions such as depression can only be genuinely explained on the basis of scientific research. When we ask scientists of the mind about this, they refer to the neurophysiology of the brain or to genetics. They want to explain everything from the point of view of matter. But the cause is not only the brain – we also have to consider the evolution of the mind. Depression or feeling overwhelmed or anxious is actually symptomatic of subtle, difficult-to-recognize self-grasping. The opposite of grasping is the wisdom of emptiness. When we begin to see the emptiness of form and sound and so on, we see all conventional objects as like the reflections of the moon in water, appearing but not truly existing.

In summary, the way to engage in study and practice for a person of great capacity is to study the texts of the Indian tradition, then those of the ancient and new traditions in Tibet. We can also contemplate the Madhyamaka teachings in the context of modern psychology, neurology, etc. It is not enough to come to the conclusion that 'everything is empty.' We need to see how everything is interdependent. This will lead us to the wisdom of emptiness. This is how someone of the highest capacity should engage in the teachings.

HEART ADVICE

Training disciples of middling capacity

For those of middling capacity, the method of engaging with the Madhyamaka does not involve the study of all of the great Indian and Tibetan philosophers. Rather, one relies on a qualified teacher and studies one text such as the *Heart Sutra*. After studying and learning from a qualified teacher, one engages in analysis and contemplation in order to eliminate all doubts with regard to the teachings of the Middle Way.

Training disciples of limited capacity

For disciples of lesser capacity, the Middle Way is studied as the two truths. It is especially important to understand the two truths as they apply to our own mind, and not as truths about relative or ultimate things that are outside ourselves. Even though we experience appearances as independent events and objects, they are actually interdependent products of causes and conditions. When we can begin to see them as being dependently arisen and empty by nature, then we have begun to apprehend the two truths. For example, when there is a reflection of the moon in water, it can be seen to be empty of true existence. But emptiness does not mean non-existence. In the analogy of the moon reflected in water, the moon definitely appears but it is empty of true existence. We can understand the key points of the Middle Way without relying on much intellectual elaboration if we rely on profound instructions from our teachers and then carry them into practice. This is how a person of lesser capacity should engage in the study and practice of the Middle Way.

The ultimate truth is the emptiness of our own mind. Within the emptiness of our own mind, all of our perceptions are relative truth. This is how conventional reality exists – in our own mind. Cultivating this realization is how we carry the two truths into practice.

I have explained the three ways of understanding, learning, and practicing the Middle Way philosophy for those of the three capacities, but it is important for you to find the best method for yourself, and then use that method. You do not need to use all three. Whatever is the best method for yourself is what you should practice.

If you want to follow the intellectual discussions, there are many distinctions and terms in the Middle Way, including 'emptiness in the sutric tradition,' 'emptiness in the tantric tradition,' *rangtong* (or 'self-emptiness'), and *shentong* (or 'other emptiness'). You may have come across such terms in books. For example, Jamgon Kongtrul's *Treasury of Knowledge*[14] discusses the rangtong and shentong views of emptiness.

The important thing to understand is that all of these discussions are meant to transform our own mind. The point is to apply these teachings, to identify our own dualistic thoughts and grasping and eliminate them. If we do not understand this critical point, then the discussions are nothing more than intellectual exercises. This is a problem that is very much a part of the Tibetan culture. All of the great masters of the past, such as Chandrakirti and Tsongkhapa, clearly mention that the purpose of analysis is not to support intellectual debate but rather to give rise to liberation. If we engage in debate, we should do it with tremendous respect.

Now we come to the actual teachings of the basis of the second turning of the wheel of Dharma. I will present these teachings in a condensed form; if you want a more condensed form I can say that everything is empty by nature and leave it at that.

THE VIEW OF EMPTINESS WITH FIVE FEATURES

As practitioners, we endeavor to gain the benefit of the Middle Way view of emptiness in this very lifetime. As I mentioned earlier, the Buddha taught different types of emptiness – the eighteen types of emptiness, the twenty types, the emptiness of external and internal objects, and so forth. Ultimately, however, the essence of the Middle Way teachings on emptiness – in other words, all of the Buddha's teachings, the commentaries, and the commentaries on commentaries – is the 'view of emptiness with the five features.'

When the Buddha gained complete enlightenment, he sat silent for forty-nine days. He said that he had found the truth in his own meditation experience, but that this nectar-like teaching would not be understood by others, so he would remain silent in isolation. Then in response to requests from Brahma and Indra, he described the nectar he had found as having five features: it was profound, peaceful, free from elaboration, had luminous clarity, and was uncompounded.

> Profound, peaceful, free of elaboration, luminous and uncompounded-
> A truth that is like nectar, I have found.
> Yet if I teach it to others, they will not understand,
> So in the jungle, silent, I shall remain.[15]

The Buddha described the truth he experienced as nectar, or *amrita*, which in Sanskrit means 'one medicine that can cure all disease.' Realization of emptiness is likened to amrita; the sickness is the ignorance of grasping at an intrinsic self. All sickness springs forth from the same thing - ignorance. All we need to eliminate any sickness is the nectar of the wisdom of emptiness.

When the Buddha used the word 'amrita,' he was identifying the appropriate recipient of the teachings as someone of the highest capacity. Such a practitioner needs three qualities: a sharp intellect, compassion, and the ability to put a lot of effort into practice. The Buddha was really describing how difficult it is to find a recipient of the teachings. He was not saying that no one at all would understand them. We are also aware that some people say that listening to the teachings on emptiness and selflessness gives rise to fear. In addition, most people are bored by the method-aspect teachings on impermanence and renunciation. They are not interested in renouncing anything.

We know that the Buddha's teachings are correct, but we can also see how difficult it is to find a proper receptacle for them. Even in China, India, and Tibet, people react negatively to the teachings on selflessness, acknowledging their truth but finding their practice impossible. They are better at practicing the preliminaries and the rituals. In the West, people are too frightened to put selflessness into practice; they need to start like babies with a lot of coddling and hand-holding.

When Aryadeva talked about the qualities of the appropriate recipient of teachings on emptiness, he said that objectivity, or the capacity to be unbiased, is very important. Chandrakirti said that if someone feels fear or aversion upon listening to the teachings on emptiness, then it is not the right time to give those teachings to that person. If someone responds with great joy, their hair standing on end, then that is a sign the person is a proper recipient. Joy upon hearing the teachings shows there is some potential or seed. If there is no capacity, giving the teachings is just like pouring water on a rock. As Chandrakirti states in chapter six of his *Introduction to the Middle Way*:[16]

> Certain simple, ordinary people,
> When they hear of emptiness, will feel
> A joy that leaps and surges in their hearts.
> Their eyes will fill with tears, the hairs upon their skin stand up.
> Such people are the vessels for the teaching;
> They have the seed of wisdom, perfect buddhahood.
> The final truth should be revealed to them,
> In whom ensuing qualities will come to birth.

The ultimate goal of studying Middle Way philosophy is to apply the wisdom of emptiness to our own practice and eliminate the ignorance of self-grasping. So we need to know how the Middle Way philosophy can be carried into practice. Carrying the emptiness teachings into practice mainly entails focusing on the mind as empty of intrinsic reality. We apply the view of emptiness with the five features to our own mind – the five features are qualities of the emptiness of our own mind, not something outside us.

The basis of emptiness with five features is our own mind, which is primordially pure and empty. It is like a mirror that can reflect anything in it. All phenomena of samsara and nirvana arise in our own mind. This mind, which has no true origin, is therefore primordially empty. This is the basis on which to understand the five features.

According to the Middle Way, things are empty by nature. There are two ways of understanding this expression 'empty by nature.' The first is through intellectual analysis of how we cling to perceptions and appearances; the second is through meditative absorption. With regard to the first, if we examine the actual object of our clinging, we will not find any truly existing object. That is how we come to the conceptual conclusion that it is empty by nature. This not finding any object at all, or 'non-affirming' emptiness, is the product of conceptual analysis; it is conceptually induced. There is a lack of affirmation or resistance; only in that sense is it like space.

To engage in non-affirming emptiness meditation, we analyze the nature of our mind by looking at the way in which it actually exists. We need to understand the way in which the mind exists and the way in which it does not exist. Generally, we think that there must be an intrinsically existing mind, something substantial. If we look at our memories, past and present experiences, hopes and fears for the future – if we analyze the mind with regard to the three times in this way – we will not reach a point where we can say, 'This is mind.' Not finding anything we can call 'mind' induces a sense of emptiness. Coming to the conclusion that no mind can be found does not affirm that something else can be found. It does not even imply that 'there is no mind.' That is what is meant by 'non-affirming emptiness.' According to the ancient tradition, non-affirming emptiness is not ultimate emptiness. It is referred to as the 'nominal ultimate reality.' But in the New Translation schools, non-affirming emptiness is considered as the ultimate understanding of emptiness.

From the point of view of the ancient tradition, this method of analyzing the mind in the three times – past, present and future – and not finding anything substantial, is still a conceptual construct. The understanding is still within the domain of mental fabrication. That is why it is referred to as the 'nominal ultimate' and not the actual natural state. The tradition does not say this is bad, as it is very helpful in gaining understanding, but it is still within the domain of mental fabrication. This non-affirming emptiness is therefore not yet the non-nominal ultimate. It does not have the first of the five features: profundity.

Profound

According to the ancient tradition, ultimate reality cannot be found or touched by logical analysis. The actual mode of being of phenomena can only be realized in meditative absorption. When the wisdom of emptiness is derived from deep meditative absorption, then it is free from contamination by mind and mental factors. Because it is free of mind and mental factors, the wisdom of emptiness is profound. It is beyond conceptualization and conventional understanding. Realization of emptiness is inconceivable; therefore it is profound.

Having engaged in conceptual analysis of the mind, if we do not then explore beyond conceptual understanding in meditative experience, then our attachment to concepts interferes with the direct realization of emptiness, the ultimate way of being. Because the nominal ultimate is a conceptual product of intellectual analysis, concepts continue to arise, hindering realization. Habits of gross and subtle grasping at intrinsic reality, that form as a result of analytic thought, obscure us from directly perceiving ultimate reality. Therefore, instead of relying solely on analysis, we have to bring the insight gained from conceptual analysis into shamatha, or calm-abiding, meditation. In shamatha, from the center of deep meditative experience, we realize emptiness free from concepts and language. We experience it directly. This method results in the direct realization of emptiness; it is non-nominal. Because the direct realization of emptiness is beyond analysis, we call it 'profound.'

Scholars have never been able to directly apprehend ultimate reality through intellectual debate and analysis. They are, of course, able to entertain a conceptual understanding of emptiness, but they are never able to directly apprehend emptiness through conceptual analysis alone. Attachment to philosophical positions actually prevents us from understanding emptiness. For example, the Gelug and Sakya monks hold debates on various positions on a yearly basis, but if we do not apply the teachings on emptiness to our own minds, then we really do not understand emptiness. The philosophical positions of the Svatantrikas and Prasangikas are irrelevant if they are not applied to our own mind. I spent a lot of time doing this myself, debating people, showing the intellectual prowess of one person or the next. However, even when our Prasangika philosophical view is very high, if we do not apply the teachings on emptiness to our own mind, then it is not going to benefit us.

Another reason that we speak of the wisdom of emptiness as profound is that freedom from the two extremes, eternalism and nihilism, is very difficult to attain. If we think that the objects and appearances we perceive actually exist, and do not realize their actual mode of existence, then we cling to them, falling into the eternalist view that things have intrinsic existence. On the other hand, we can fall into the nihilistic view that there is nothing whatsoever. We are not able to maintain the mind free from the two extremes because we are prone to the coarse distractions of excitement and agitation on the one hand and disappointment and dullness on the other. We are constantly under the sway of negative emotions. A symptom of this condition is that we cannot abide in a state free of the extremes. First it is difficult to identify negative emotions, second to suppress them, and lastly to uproot them. Freedom from extremes is thus difficult to attain, and therefore it is profound.

When we say that the wisdom of emptiness is profound, we do not mean it is somewhere outside us, found only in a faraway, amazing place. The wisdom of emptiness has always been with us; we have not yet encountered it only because it is so profound. This is why the Buddha found the nectar of the wisdom of emptiness in meditation, and not in his debates with non-Buddhists.

It may seem disconcerting if we first tell you that you have to engage in analytic meditation on emptiness, but then we deny that realization is possible by this means. There is a danger of losing confidence in the endeavor, but we should not lose heart. If we look at the history of the teachings, we can see that when the Buddha first taught emptiness, many people failed to understand it. Nagarjuna had to clarify and reinterpret the teachings. Again and again, throughout the ages, people have had to explain these teachings because of their profundity, and this has given rise to many different branches of interpretation. Emptiness is profound and subtle; it is very difficult to understand.

The message for practitioners to keep in mind is that if we understand the profundity of the teachings, then we see that the root cause of suffering is ignorance, which clings to intrinsic existence. The antidote to ignorance is the wisdom of emptiness, but conceptual understanding of emptiness is insufficient. We need to come to a direct realization through meditation.

Peaceful

The second feature of the Middle Way view of emptiness is

pacification, the view that it is peaceful. This refers to the fact that because it is empty, our own mind is primordially free from conceptual elaboration. For example, if we can meditate for even a couple of minutes in a state where we are not chasing thoughts and concepts, we will experience at least a temporary sense of relative calm and peace. However, when we directly apprehend emptiness, then we gain the state of tranquility and peace born from the cessation of *all* gross and subtle thoughts. That is why it is called 'peaceful.' Here we see the truth of the cessation of suffering.

If we can sustain this view of emptiness in meditation for days, months, and years, then we will gain freedom from distracting conceptual thoughts and indeed from all karma and negative emotions. As a result, we will experience a state of complete tranquility and peace. The main reason that we do not experience this now is the constant conflict within our minds that is induced by conceptual thought.

As long as we have not gained freedom from the bondage of karma and negative emotions, we will not experience the state of peace. It is possible, by progressing through the nine stages of shamatha, to eliminate gross thoughts and concepts, suppress negative emotions from arising, and give rise to relative calm and peace. However, this relative peace is not the subtle and permanent experience of the pacification of all thought that is referred to by the Buddha's 'peaceful.' In order to have that experience, we need to eliminate the root of negative emotions, which is subtle grasping. The antidote to subtle grasping is the direct realization of emptiness.

Grasping is very dangerous, both in meditation as well as outside it. If we do not know how to carry the view of emptiness into practice, then grasping is inexhaustible. We will grasp at philosophical positions, meditative experiences, and states of realization. It is important to cultivate skill and competence in carrying emptiness into our practice.

Our meditation should result in the elimination of layer upon layer of attachment and grasping. If we are not able to do this, or if we find we are grasping at realizations and experiences, then it means we are either not maintaining a correct view of emptiness or are not practicing the view of emptiness correctly.

Nagarjuna says that when those of lesser capacity fail to properly understand and practice emptiness, the danger of downfall is very great. In the beginning, we may have a relatively coarse understanding of self-grasping as negative. Then, if our meditation on emptiness induces inner experiences of joy and we cling to those experiences, that grasping becomes very difficult to undo. We are actually grasping at a more subtle state. It is said that grasping at the view of emptiness is the most dangerous form of grasping.

Nagarjuna uses an analogy to illustrate this danger in the *Root Stanzas of the Middle Way*:[17]

Because their view of voidness is inept,
Those with little wisdom are brought low.
It is as if they grasped a snake ineptly
Or ineptly cast a magic spell.

The snake charmers of India can control snakes through the power of mantra, but if they do not recite the mantra correctly the snake will bite and kill them. Likewise, it is important to understand and correctly apply the view of emptiness. Because of the danger of grasping at our own experience of emptiness, the Buddha taught the fourth of the eighteen types of emptiness – the emptiness of emptiness – to counteract attachment to the view.[18] Therefore, when we engage in meditation, we have to make sure we do not get attached to any realization we might experience. We should be instead like a snake shedding its own skin.

Free of Elaboration

The third feature of the Middle Way view of emptiness is freedom from conceptual elaboration. The emptiness of our own mind is free from elaboration because it is primordial. It is not created by the blessings of the Buddhas nor can it be changed by the conceptual elaborations of ordinary people. The primordial emptiness of our own mind is free from concepts, free from words, language, and ideas. It is like a perfectly clear sky that allows the sun's rays to pervade it.

Luminous

The fourth feature is luminous clarity. The mind is not simply empty, a state free from intrinsic reality. It also has the nature of luminous clarity, because any phenomenon in samsara and nirvana can be reflected in it. Clarity is what makes appearances possible. Although the mind's nature is empty, phenomena nonetheless appear, arising interdependently.

Uncompounded

The fifth feature of the view of emptiness is that it is uncompounded or unproduced. The primordially empty mind, which is the union of clarity and emptiness, is not impermanent. It is beyond time; it does not transition or change; it does not age. Therefore, it is unproduced and uncompounded.

This view of the emptiness of our own mind with these five features is the essence of the Middle Way at the level of the basis. Understanding the Middle Way at the level of the basis *is* understanding our own mind as empty with these five features. Whether we are engaged in learning, contemplating, or meditation, we have to rely on this basis.

This Middle Way view with five features was practiced by the Indian yogis and masters who gained realization. Zen masters in China and yogis in Tibet also gained realizations from practicing the Middle Way view. This meditation on our own mind as empty with the five features is direct. It is direct because it gives rise to realization, whereas mentally created, conceptually fabricated ideas of emptiness do not. This direct view of emptiness is the essence of the Middle Way, and it is the essence of the *Prajnaparamita Sutras*. It should also be the essence of your own practice.

The traditional process of affirming and negating positions in debate is actually meant to be capable of eventually inducing this state with the five features. In the absence of that, it has no purpose. If the direct perception of emptiness is not the end result, then you should not be engaging in debate. That is why I chose to present the emptiness of our own mind with these five features as the essence of the Middle Way.

CONCISE PRESENTATION OF THE MIDDLE WAY AT THE LEVEL OF THE BASIS

Earlier I summarized the union of the two truths at the level of the basis from a philosophical point of view. We can also approach the union of the two truths from the point of view of our own experience. It is helpful to think of the appearances of the mind (phenomena) as relative truth and the mind itself as ultimate truth. If we think of the mind in this way, it is easier for beginners to carry the two truths into their experience. Another way we can approach the union of the two truths is to see all apparent phenomena as relative truth and their ultimate nature as the ultimate truth. Phenomena are apparent yet empty; form is emptiness. They are empty, yet they appear; emptiness is form. Whatever is easier, use that. It is important not to follow the literal meaning of the words but to emphasize the meaning in our practice. Do not get caught up in the concepts themselves.

The Middle Way wisdom of emptiness is free from the two extremes of eternalism and nihilism. In cultivating freedom from the extremes at the level of the basis, it may be more practical to see the mind free of extremes itself as the basis or ground. Practicing the mind free of extremes as the ground may come more naturally. We see how the mind has highs and lows; it gets very excited, very agitated sometimes, and other times we are discouraged. We can readily see that cultivating the mind free from extremes is beneficial.

When we are able to abide in the Middle Way in meditation, sustaining the mind free from eternalism and nihilism, we will experience the temporary benefit of being free from disappointment and restlessness in a state of great equanimity. A long-term benefit of 'leaving the mind in the middle' is that it grows much more powerful and develops the capacity to achieve realization. That is why the Buddha went to great lengths to teach this basic level of practice. The great yogis of India and Tibet also regard the basis-level Middle Way practice as very profound.

The main reason to learn to let the mind abide in the Middle Way is the very heavy conditioning that inclines us to fall into eternalism and nihilism as a result of craving and aversion. The result of abiding in the Middle Way is the state of peace that is free from extremes and from the forces of craving and aversion. How to accomplish this freedom? First, one engages in analytical meditation to conceptually eliminate the two extremes. Then, the conviction gained from analysis is stabilized at a more subtle level in shamatha, which is how we carry the Middle Way free from extremes at the level of the path.

The essence of the second turning at the level of the basis is the experience of our own mind free from the two extremes of eternalism and nihilism. If we can understand this point, then we understand the essential practice of the Middle Way and of the second turning. If we understand and take this as the essence of our practice, it is sufficient, and we do not need to engage in elaborate intellectual discourse.

The great Nyingma master Dza Patrul Rinpoche says that one should establish the ultimate by analyzing the conventional. 'Conventional' here refers to the appearances of the mind, including how we perceive those appearances, and how we get attached to them. By analyzing the things that we perceive, and how they appear to us, we can establish the ultimate. What happens is that we become able to experience how apparent phenomena arise from the ground of the ultimate. When the mind abides 'in the Middle Way,' without falling into the two extremes, we can see from this point of view how the conventional world of apparent phenomena and grasping arises.

This concludes the teachings on the basis of the Middle Way. The second level of the Middle Way is the path. Here, we start with the premise that we are able to identify emptiness at the level of the basis;

now we need to know how to carry that into practice. This is accomplished by understanding the application of the two truths at the level of the path.

5

THE PATH

METHOD AND WISDOM

I will explain the path level of the Middle Way following the approach of the ancient Nyingma tradition. "Path Middle Way" refers to the union of method and wisdom, or the union of compassion and emptiness. The Buddha taught that the essence of the Mahayana teachings is the union of compassion and emptiness. This is the path that the great yogis of the past practiced. The teachings of the Mahayana are profound and extensive, but if we extract their essence, the heart of the practice is this union of compassion and emptiness, method and wisdom.

When we study the vast and profound practices of the Mahayana, we find root practices, branch practices, practices at the level of the basis, practices at the level of the path, and practices at the level of the resultant state. There are also numerous enhancement practices. But the essence of all of these is the union of method and wisdom, or the union of compassion and emptiness. This is the root of Mahayana practice.

The reason that the union of wisdom and method is the essence of Mahayana practice is that the realization of emptiness wisdom prevents us from falling into the extreme of samsara, and the practice of compassion prevents us from falling into the extreme of peaceful nirvana. On the path, merit and wisdom are accumulated through the practice of compassion and emptiness. Practicing their union ensures that we perfect these two accumulations, giving rise to the resultant state.

In his *Introduction to the Middle Way*, Chandrakirti says that just as a bird needs two wings to fly across the ocean to the far shore, we need the two 'wings' of the relative and the ultimate to cross the ocean of samsara to the state of enlightenment. This is why we practice the union of compassion and emptiness, relative and ultimate. In order to eliminate the extreme of samsara, we need the wing of emptiness wisdom, the ultimate truth. In order to eliminate[1] the extreme of the individual peace of nirvana and instead gain complete enlightenment, we need the wing of compassion. Once we have these two wings of emptiness and compassion, then we are able to cross the ocean of samsara and eliminate both temporary and ultimate suffering. As Chandrakirti states in the *Introduction to the Middle Way*:[19]

> And like the king of swans, ahead of lesser birds they soar,
> On broad white wings of relative and ultimate full spread.
> And on the strength of virtue's mighty wind they fly
> To gain the far and supreme shore, the oceanic qualities of victory.

The Mahayana teachings are vast and profound, but we can extract their essence by learning to identify, and practicing, the union of compassion and the wisdom of emptiness. Learning to identify how they are united is very important, as then we can practice compassion with the view of emptiness. The compassion we're talking about here is not limited or sentimental. We are talking about taking on the responsibility for delivering all beings from samsara. This is a very powerful mind, one that is determined and dedicated to delivering not only oneself but all sentient beings across the great ocean of samsara.

If our intention is not grounded in both the method of compassion and the wisdom of emptiness, then this intention would seem impossibly over-reaching. It would seem stupid to even entertain such an intention. No one who has not cultivated the compassion of a bodhisattva can conceive of the bodhisattva's wisdom and conduct. Our minds are very narrow relatively speaking, and the mind of a bodhisattva is extremely vast. Our radiance is like that of a firefly compared to the radiance of a bodhisattva's compassion, which is like the radiance of the sun. If we have not cultivated bodhicitta, we cannot begin to conceive of the intent of a bodhisattva.

The other reason why we undertake practicing the unity of method and wisdom has to do with how the mind of awakening is accomplished. We may wonder, 'If you cultivate the wisdom of emptiness at the level of the basis, why is not this enough to practice as the path that delivers us from suffering? Why do we need to carry compassion on the path?' The reason is that our understanding of emptiness has to be enhanced, intensified, and strengthened. In order to accomplish this, our mind needs to be opened so that it becomes unbiased, expansive, and powerful. The best method to open the mind and empower it to benefit others is the practice of bodhicitta. Our meditation on emptiness has to be enhanced and supported by this practice, or it does not fully develop. To actually cultivate the wisdom of emptiness, it has to be complemented by this superior method. This is why we practice the union of emptiness and compassion.

In my own experience, meditation on emptiness by itself fails to give the mind the necessary power and confidence to remain in that state, if we lack compassion and bodhicitta. We may experience clarity and wisdom for a while, but in the post-meditative state we are easily unbalanced by conditions that induce negative mental states. Meditating on the wisdom of emptiness without putting equal emphasis on the method aspect of the path – the practice of compassion and loving kindness – cannot develop the mind's power.

It is very important to understand loving kindness and compassion. We are not talking about superficial qualities like being affectionate or sweet. Compassion is very deep and stable; it does not have expectations or agendas. This may be something you have not yet experienced, and so it would be beneficial to make this part of your practice. I mention this because I know for sure that I need this practice myself, and I think you need this practice in your lives as well. Of course, if you do not want this in your life, then there is nothing I can do about it.

If we have practiced tantra and Dzogchen for many years and our mind has not changed; if we still have a big ego or feel jealousy, that shows something about our practice. I am not referring to realization. The wisdom aspect is not that difficult, and all of you are smart, but it is very difficult to give rise to deep compassion and kindness. Also, without compassion, it is difficult to practice mindfulness. The reason the mind wanders outward, getting caught up in distractions, is a lack of compassion. When we have compassion, our mind is grounded and stable, and mindfulness becomes easier. Once we have been able to identify and recognize the base Middle Way, the view of the basis, and we enhance our understanding of the view with the practice of bodhicitta, we have the very essence of the second turning of the wheel of Dharma.

So, how do we carry the union of method and wisdom into practice in our daily lives? First of all, we need to understand that all phenomena – ourselves, other people and things - are empty of a truly-existing self and then meditate on that emptiness and selflessness. We then train the mind to contemplate that even though on an ultimate level all phenomena are empty, our failure to recognize this causes confusion, and both we and others suffer. This gives rise to compassion.

This is how we practice the union of emptiness and compassion. When we say 'union,' we do not mean that two things are being made into one. That would be impossible. Instead, what happens is that the cultivation of the wisdom of emptiness transforms ordinary compassion, when we see that sentient beings suffer because they are unable to abide in the actual, ultimate nature of reality.

For example, in a state of meditation we are relatively relaxed and at peace, but if people nearby are involved in a conflict, we can see that they do not have that peace. For this reason, we can empathize because everybody wants to experience peace, but out of confusion and negative emotions they are not able to enjoy it.

The benefit of engaging in the union of method and wisdom is that we are able to make the mind more powerful and expansive. Ultimately, we are able to complete the two accumulations of merit and wisdom, and by perfecting the two accumulations, achieve the resultant state.

UNION OF SHAMATHA AND VIPASYANA

Suppose we have become able to identify the base Middle Way, the view of emptiness, and have even engaged in the practice of bodhicitta. Even so, our mind is still very prone to distraction. It fluctuates constantly, like a candle left out in the open, vulnerable to flickering and being extinguished by the wind. The purpose of the candle is to illuminate darkness, but if the wind is too strong, it is very difficult to light it and to keep it lit. The candle in the wind is a common analogy that we use.

The mind is also likened to a crazy elephant that we need to tame and subdue through meditation. Historically, it is said that Shakyamuni Buddha subdued a mad elephant. The elephant was so mad that no one could approach it. It is said that the Buddha was able to subdue and tame it through the power of his concentration and meditation on loving kindness and emptiness. Therefore, if we are able to tame our own crazy mind, it will be easy to tame the craziness of others. The way to eliminate our mad-elephant-like craziness is through the power of concentration. The Buddha's ability to subdue the mad elephant was not based on the power of mantra or medicine but on the power of his samadhi.

There are two basic types of meditation, *vipasyana*, or special insight, and *shamatha*, or calm abiding. In general, 'calm abiding' refers to the mind's ability to stabilize, and 'special insight' refers to the clarity aspect of the mind. Calm abiding is the ability to allow the mind to settle into a concentrated state. When we achieve stability, we are able to experience the clarity of the mind. The clarity of the mind is special insight. There are also gross and subtle levels of each type of meditation.

The union of calm abiding and special insight focusing on emptiness is very difficult to understand and experience. Before we come to that, we need to be familiar with the general, mundane understanding of this union.

First, I will give a very brief introduction to the general meanings of 'vipasyana,' 'shamatha,' and their union, the union of calm abiding and special insight.

Vipasyana

When we first engage in the analytical meditation on selflessness, on the gross level, we ask ourselves why we should accept the absence of the self when we clearly experience it in our day-to-day lives. In investigating this question, we contemplate why the Buddha taught selflessness and how we can give rise to the state of liberation through the practice of selflessness alone.

On the subtle level of our investigative practice, we try to identify how we experience self, what it feels like, and where it belongs among the skandhas. Therefore, we examine the skandhas. We can also examine whether the self is separate from the skandhas or is one and the same with one or all of them.

In the analytical meditation, we try to determine whether, and how, the meditator exists. Remember that the purpose of our meditation is to address the overwhelming self-grasping, which causes us suffering. We are bound by self-grasping and negative emotions, which leave us no freedom over birth and death. We have no freedom to choose the time of death, no freedom in the bardo state, and no freedom from rebirth. This is our real condition; we are 'bound' in this sense. I am not trying to make you depressed; we have to be able to see where we are.

The analytical meditation allows us to discover that grasping at self is the root of all negative emotions. This is the ultimate goal of analytical meditation. This is how we carry the Middle Way into the practice; in fact, there is no other way to practice the Middle Way. The point of this analysis is not to make us feel bad about our self-grasping. If our practice is causing negative feelings, it means that we do not quite know what we are doing with this analysis, we do not understand its real significance. The point of analyzing selflessness is to generate the firm conviction that the root of all negative emotions is self-grasping. Generating this conviction is very healthy.

The 'Middle Way' means 'an unbiased path, the true path.' It is helpful to understand that the Middle Way is not like a physical path we can point to and travel from point A to B. Sometimes we may expect it to be something like that. But we actually find the Middle Way when we ask the questions, 'Who is meditating?' or 'Who is it that is feeling this anger?' and experience not finding the self. I can tell you that the path of the Middle Way is profound, but that experience comes from our own practice.

When we find that there is no self, then we try to sustain the conviction that the self is not to be found. When, through this practice, we have actually directly experienced the natural state of being, we need to recognize and sustain that state. If we continue on by with the analysis, looking for some sort of conclusion, we will find that it never comes to an end. Instead, we should practice focused, deep analytic meditation two or three times, looking for the meditator, the self. When we do not find the meditator, then we just leave it there. Not finding the self should induce a great sense of emptiness. We then sustain that conviction, leaving the mind with this sense of emptiness. We can rely on shamatha to sustain that state. Analysis gives rise to the insight of emptiness, and calm abiding sustains that for as long as possible. That is the union of vipasyana and shamatha.

The goal of analytical meditation is to generate a firm conviction of selflessness. You may wonder why we need to do that if we can simply demonstrate that there is no self through reasoning. The answer to that is that without analyzing our own belief in self again and again, we cannot break down the strong conditioning of clinging to it.

Even though analytical meditation generates a very strong conviction, this conviction needs to be further sustained by calm abiding. Through analysis alone we might be able to suppress self-grasping and see the confused state, but we will not be able to uproot it. For this, we need a powerful shamatha practice. Using calm abiding, we sustain our insight single-pointedly for as long as possible, uniting deep stability with strong clarity. Ultimately, that is how we uproot self-grasping.

Common Shamatha

It is difficult to focus on emptiness right from the beginning. It is best to start with the mundane understanding of calm abiding as a mind that is settled and stable, and of special insight as the clarity aspect of the mind. It is relatively easy to understand the meaning of emptiness conceptually. In order to experience emptiness directly, we need to make that conceptual understanding more and more subtle, until it eventually approaches a direct experience. For this it is essential that we cultivate stability or calm abiding, because this is the way to eliminate gross concepts and attachments. If we do not have the experience of suppressing and eliminating gross thoughts and feelings through the practice of calm abiding, then we will not be able to experience the emptiness of the mind, which is very subtle. When we can sustain the experience of emptiness in meditation, then we have brought stability and clarity together, in the union of shamatha and vipasyana.

In the beginning of our practice, we need to eliminate gross concepts, thoughts, and distractions using the common shamatha technique. To train in the common shamatha technique, we traverse the nine stages of meditative absorption. There are many sources that can help us with this practice, for example, Kamalashila's middle-length *Stages of Meditation,* Tsongkhapa's *Lam Rim Chenmo,* and the Ninth Karmapa's *Ocean of Definitive Meaning.* All of these explain the nine stages of meditative absorption. Within the first step of shamatha find an object of meditation such as an image of a buddha, or our breath. Next, we apply mindfulness and mental vigilance as antidotes to the flaws of meditation: gross and subtle agitation and dullness. The most important things to abandon on the path are conceptual distractions, dullness, and agitation, and we counteract these with mindfulness and vigilance.

The first step is called *jogpa,* placing the mind. We place the mind on an internal object such as the breath, and we sustain mindfulness of this object, monitoring our state of concentration through mental vigilance. The role of *drenpa* or mindfulness is to sustain concentration on the object of meditation. In the beginning, to succeed at remaining mindful of the object, we have to monitor our state of concentration through the application of vigilance. By remaining vigilant, we keep track of whether or not we are distracted from the object of concentration. The final goal of the practice of all nine stages is to rest in a state of equanimity without wavering from our focus. If there is no vividness, vitality, or intensity of mind, then there is a flaw in our technique. Remember that here we are talking about common shamatha, which is not the same as Dzogchen meditation; we should not mix techniques.

When we reach the last of the nine stages, dullness and agitation have subsided completely. The clarity and stability aspects are balanced in a state of equanimity spontaneously, without any effort. When we have achieved that state of effortless balance and harmony, then we have achieved total concentration. This is still not quite perfect shamatha; for that we also need to cultivate mental and physical pliancy and bliss. These experiences of bliss and pliancy are not mere distractions; rather they become an ornament that reinforces and enhances our concentration.

Mental pliancy means that the mind has become serviceable; that we can place it on any object for any length of time. Once we are able to meditate single-pointedly in this way, we can use any meditation technique without too much effort – meditation with or without object, conceptual or nonconceptual meditation, or meditation on emptiness. At that stage, our single-pointed meditation does not need to rely on mindfulness and vigilance very much. A state of mental pliancy means we are well and thoroughly trained.

The experience of mental pliancy leads to the experience of physical pliancy where the meditator feels 'as light as cotton.' The reason for this feeling is that the practitioner is able to gather and control the winds simply through the power of concentration, without relying on any further technique. Considering how difficult it is to achieve even the ninth stage of shamatha, we may be less complacent about our ability to master Dzogchen.

THE ACTUAL PATH

The actual path level of the Middle Way is the direct cognition of emptiness while abiding in the union of shamatha and vipassana. The Buddha taught many samadhis as the path Middle Way. It is not necessary to go through all of them, as the essence of all of them is the union of calm abiding and special insight; all the other samadhis can be incorporated into this union.

We have already explained the significance of the wisdom of emptiness as the direct antidote to self-grasping and the illusion of a self. The method aspects of the path – renunciation, compassion, and so forth – are important but are not the direct antidote to self-grasping. The wisdom of emptiness directly eliminates and uproots self-grasping. A conceptual understanding of emptiness based on analytic meditation is not quite enough to uproot self-grasping. We need to directly cognize emptiness, and this can only be achieved while abiding in the union of calm abiding and special insight.

The purpose of combining calm-abiding and special-insight meditation is to apprehend emptiness directly without the mediation of conceptual understanding. In order to directly realize emptiness, we need to overcome two obscurations or 'bondages.' The first obscuration is the negative emotions. Our negative emotions prevent us from having control over birth, death, and the bardo. They are what propel us through birth, death, and rebirth. The antidote for the obscuration of negative emotions is settling the mind through calm abiding focusing on emptiness. The second obscuration is subtle grasping at intrinsic reality. In order to eliminate this subtle grasping, we need to engage in special insight meditation focusing on emptiness.

We can explain the practice of calm abiding and special insight focusing on emptiness in terms of the grounds and paths.

The Paths

The Mahayana path is described in terms of 'the five paths' – the path of accumulation, preparation, seeing, meditation and no more learning. The first path is the path of accumulation. Here, we are introduced to the meaning of emptiness at the conceptual level. We engage in preparatory practices and in accomplishing the extensive accumulation of merit. Meditation on emptiness, on the path of accumulation, is the practice of shamatha focusing on emptiness. Here, our understanding of emptiness is conceptual and so is not a direct experience. Our meditation may have stability and clarity, but there is not yet direct realization of emptiness. Instead we rely on a conceptual image of it. It is like meditating on a reflection of something. We may be able to see the reflection clearly, but it is still not the actual thing.

At this point, we have not begun to engage in the analysis and investigating of not finding a truly existing self. Because there is no analysis and therefore no special insight, this meditation is sometimes called 'nonconceptual reflection meditation.' 'Nonconceptual meditation' here means 'in the absence of special insight gained from analysis.' It does not mean that there are no conceptual thoughts arising. It is nonconceptual only in the sense that conceptual thought is not being deliberately used, in the form of analysis, to gain insight into the emptiness of self and phenomena. However, the path of accumulation is definitely a conceptual path because at this point we have not yet realized emptiness directly.

Through calm-abiding meditation focusing on emptiness, our clarity and stability become stronger and stronger. When stability improves to the point that we do not waver, then we can engage in special insight meditation. This means that while sustaining the single-pointed concentration of calm abiding, part of the mind is engaged in analysis while at the same time we remain focused on the conceptual image of emptiness. When we have developed this degree of unwavering stability, part of the mind – a subtle mindfulness – can engage in analysis while still aware of the focus on emptiness. We have to be careful here; this is not gross conceptual analysis. When unwavering stability together with subtle analysis is possible, we have entered the second path, the path of preparation.

On the path of preparation, the mind focuses on the conceptual image of emptiness as a kind of 'no object' or pure transparency. At the same time, a very subtle mindfulness investigates that conceptual image. Our single-pointed concentration is unwavering, but part of the mind is able to engage in investigating emptiness analytically. Even though at this point the meditator is primarily focusing by means of the stability and clarity afforded by calm abiding on a conceptual image of emptiness, there is still a very subtle part of the mind that engages in analysis. However, the mind does so in such a way that the stability of the calm abiding is never disturbed. We engage in this subtle analysis without wavering from that state, and this meditative state is likened to a clear and calm lake. When the lake is perfectly clear, we can see small fish swimming but they do not disturb the water.

You might wonder why we need to engage in analysis. Why is not it enough to sustain single-pointed concentration without analysis? The reason for subtle analysis at this level is twofold. First, the unwavering stability of single-pointed concentration allows clarity to dawn. Clarity in the form of mindfulness reinforces stability. The subtle analysis carried out by mindfulness and the insight it yields reinforce the stability of the concentration on emptiness. The second reason is that analysis makes our conceptual image of emptiness more subtle, so that it approaches a direct experience. When we engage in subtle analysis, we gradually eliminate subtle grasping at concepts and conceptual judgment. We begin this meditation with subtle grasping at the concept of emptiness, but through analysis we can make this grasping more and more subtle. As the conceptual grasping becomes more subtle, mindfulness becomes more subtle as well. Eventually there is less need for it, as both clarity and stability become more and more subtle, each reinforcing the other. Ultimately, this leads to the union of shamatha and vipasyana, in which stability is clarity, calm abiding is special insight. At this point, one is able to directly apprehend emptiness without need of relying on concepts. All dualistic notions come to an end. Subject and object are like water poured into water. When this happens, we have progressed to the path of seeing, the direct cognition of emptiness.

This progress from the path of accumulation to the path of preparation and path of seeing occurs within meditation, within our own experience. It is not like physically traversing a path. We progress based on the accumulation of wisdom in our meditation.

On the path of seeing, we directly apprehend the meaning of emptiness and then remain in that state, the union of calm abiding and special insight. We sustain this state in order to eliminate the two obscurations mentioned earlier – negative emotions and subtle grasping, the obscuration to omniscience. To eliminate the obscurations, we sustain this meditation from the path of seeing and carry it over into the fourth path, the path of meditation. The path of meditation is traversed on the ten bodhisattva grounds, or ten bhumis. On the ten grounds, the meditation is the union of calm abiding and special insight, and in the post-meditative state we engage in the six paramitas.

The Grounds

On the path of seeing, sustaining single-pointed concentration on the meaning of emptiness with calm abiding, special insight realizes the meaning of emptiness in a superior, extraordinary way. Special insight is knowledge characterized by extraordinary wisdom and insight into the meaning of emptiness. That is why it is called 'special insight.' This direct cognition of emptiness with special insight corresponds to the first of the ten bodhisattva grounds or bhumis, which is called the 'Ground of Extreme Joy.'

On the first bhumi, the direct cognition of emptiness is stabilized in meditation, and then in post-meditation the bodhisattva practices the six perfections.[20] Although all six perfections are practiced, the primary practice on the first bhumi is generosity. In this specific context, generosity primarily refers to the practice of giving our own body to other sentient beings. More generally, we speak of three types of generosity: the giving of material goods, the giving of fearlessness, and teaching the dharma. ('Fearlessness' means 'freeing beings from fear;' an example would be setting animals free that are about to be slaughtered.) The predominant practice of the bodhisattva is that of giving his or her own body to sentient beings. When bodhisattvas engage in this type of generosity, they experience an inner joy that is even more intense than the joy experienced by an arhat in the absorption of nirvana. The bodhisattvas' joy on having the opportunity to give their own body to sentient beings, or even hearing the voice of someone making such a request, is far superior to and more intense than even the joy of nirvana. That is why this bhumi is called 'Extreme Joy.' As Chandrakirti has said:[21]

> The merest thought or sound of someone crying 'Give!'
> Will bring to children of the Conqueror a joy,
> Unknown to Arhats even when they enter into peace.
> How shall we speak of when they give up everything?

Bodhisattvas experience this joy because they have eliminated all forms of stinginess and their imprints. Because they have directly realized the dharmata, the true nature of reality, there is no place for possessiveness. A bodhisattva on the first ground who engages in the generosity of his or her own body never experiences mental or physical suffering. Beginner bodhisattvas who have not attained the first bhumi do experience suffering from this type of generosity.

Chandrakirti says that the bodhisattva's generosity is inconceivable to anyone limited by bondage, but it would be unreasonable to conclude that just because we cannot imagine it ourselves, that it cannot be true. We also may have uncommon experiences that we think we cannot share because they are so unique. Our inability to explain them, however, does not mean they are not happening. In the *Entrance to the Middle Way,* Chandrakirti says that when describing the qualities of high-level bodhisattvas and buddhas, even great scholars with extensive learning have a difficult time conceiving of the bodhisattvas' qualities. When the qualities of bodhisattvas are described to Hinayana practitioners, these descriptions are met with disbelief. They say that such things could never happen. But their inability to conceive of these qualities does not mean that they are not real. Someone's believing in them or not does not impact their reality.

Nagarjuna says that if emptiness is possible, anything is possible:[22]

Where emptiness is granted,
Everything is likewise granted.
Where emptiness is unacceptable,
All is likewise unacceptable.

When we are able to establish the emptiness of phenomena, then from the ground of emptiness every phenomenon is possible. The bodhisattva directly experiences this infinite possibility as the true nature of reality, the state of suchness.

As Mahayana practitioners, we train in the practice and conduct of the bodhisattvas. Of course, it is possible that we will have doubts about our ability to attain such high realizations. However, we should be careful, because if we entertain too much doubt regarding the bodhisattva practices, there is the danger that instead of generating merit we will accrue negative karma.

The bodhisattva on the first bhumi experiences exceptional joy in the practice of generosity and no pain in offering his or her body for sentient beings, because possessiveness has been eliminated. In the past lives of the Buddha, he gave his body for sentient beings as a bodhisattva many times. At one time he took rebirth as a giant fish because there were a lot of hungry smaller fish that needed to be fed. There also is a very famous story of his offering his body to a hungry tigress. This kind of conduct is beyond our imagination. However, if we cannot conceive of such things, at a minimum we should not adopt wrong views and doubts, maintaining that they are not true or did not happen.

We have to remind ourselves of the fundamental commitment to engage in service for beings until they are enlightened. In the ancient tradition, people who are practicing Madhyamaka have to take the bodhisattva vow. The reason is that without the bodhisattva vow, their practice of Madhyamaka might focus solely on the view of emptiness and lose sight of compassion.

Those of us who practice Chöd, or 'cutting through ego,' should remind ourselves of the generosity of giving the body, of the Buddha's own generosity as a bodhisattva, and of the extraordinary generosity of Machig Labdron. Chöd practice is really an enhancement practice of the union of method and wisdom. We should not think that first we practice Chöd and then we engage in generosity, because Chod practice is the practice of generosity. We are engaging in the practice of a bodhisattva.

From the path of seeing, we progress to the path of meditation, which traverses the ten bhumis. The second bhumi, which is on the path of meditation, is called 'Stainless.' On this ground, the bodhisattva mostly practices the perfection of discipline and the keeping of vows. It is possible to have three types of vows: the external Vinaya vows of individual liberation, the internal Mahayana bodhisattva vows, and the secret tantric vows. 'Stainless' means 'free from the stains of transgressing the vows,' especially the bodhisattva vows. There is no doubt that a bodhisattva on the second bhumi will ever transgress his or her bodhisattva vows. A beginner bodhisattva who has some doubt might fall back into more limited intentions, but for a bodhisattva on the second ground there is no danger of transgression.

The third bhumi is called 'Luminous.' At this level the practice focuses on the perfection of patience, which is the antidote to anger and aversion. Again, all of these practices of the perfections belong to the conduct side in the post-meditative state. Even a bodhisattva on the path of accumulation does not experience anger as ordinary people do. On the third bhumi, the practice of patience eliminates even the subtle causes of anger. There is patience with the external, internal, and secret challenges we have to bear in order to carry out bodhisattva conduct. Remaining patient in the process of training is not easy. In order to be able to overcome all the obstacles that can arise, we need to engage in the perfection of patience.

The predominant challenge for bodhisattvas on the third bhumi is to practice patience in such a way that they never give up the practice of helping others. That is not easy. We all know the negative emotions that we encounter when we try to help others. We need to remain aware at all times so that we never fail in our commitment to helping them. It is said in the scriptures that even though countless buddhas and bodhisattvas have appeared to teach and help beings, they have never been able to wholly subdue the unruly minds of beings. Bodhisattvas have the challenge of never tiring in their unceasing activity to bring benefit to others. It is a tremendous challenge to ensure that we will never be discouraged in this commitment. This requires the armor of patience.

The fourth bhumi is called 'Radiant,' referring to an even more brilliant radiance than that of the third bhumi. Here, the fundamental practice is the perfection of diligent or joyous effort. It is said that all qualities follow upon joyous effort. In fact, the ground of all the six perfections is joyous effort. Without joyous effort, we cannot engage in the other perfections. This is true in the case of both mundane and spiritual practices. If we are not able to put forth enthusiastic effort, we do not achieve anything. This is especially the case with bodhisattvas training to benefit others.

Of course, we all want to train in the bodhisattva's conduct to help others, but when it gets difficult we are easily tired and disappointed. If we consider our own situation, we can see that it usually becomes difficult to stay joyous in making effort. It helps to recognize this, because we have stated our aspiration to train, and now we need to understand how to do so, and what hinders us from doing so.

The practice of bodhicitta is always accompanied by wisdom; it is not a form of 'idiot compassion.' Bodhicitta is accompanied by wisdom regarding the right time, the right context, the right mental disposition, the right cultural context, and so on. If we practice compassion without wisdom, there is a real danger it will be of no benefit or could even cause harm. The practice of joyous effort during the fourth bhumi is applied not for just any purpose, but for the purpose of attaining enlightenment so that we can benefit all sentient beings.

The fifth bhumi is called 'Difficult to Purify.' The reason is that on this ground the emphasis is on the practice of purifying even the subtlest grasping at intrinsic reality. The subtlest grasping is difficult to purify, so the bodhisattva needs to rely on powerful meditative absorption. Therefore, the primary practice here is the perfection of concentration.

On the fifth ground, the bodhisattva cultivates a powerful meditative absorption on the truth of cessation. Without powerful absorption, it is difficult to train in the perfection of wisdom on the sixth ground. The fundamental purpose of the fifth ground is to purify the subtle obscurations that hinder one from entering into absorption on the truth of cessation. Other obscurations are eliminated or purified earlier as a result of the bodhisattva's ability to sustain the meditation of the union of calm abiding and special insight. Here, however, the very subtlest obscurations, which hinder entry into the absorption of the truth of cessation, are purified. The foundation for the cultivation of wisdom is therefore established here.

Then we come to the sixth bhumi, which is called 'Manifest,' where the perfection of wisdom is cultivated. 'Perfection of wisdom' refers to extraordinary special insight and the actualization of the truth of cessation. We might wonder what the difference is between the direct realization of emptiness achieved with the union of calm abiding and special insight on the path of seeing, and this realization on the sixth ground. Why is this realization called 'extraordinary special insight?'

It is called extraordinary because at this point, bodhisattvas are able to enter the meditative absorption of the truth of cessation in an instant, like the snap of fingers. They are then able to arise from and enter back into the absorption. This is something that only bodhisattvas on the level of the sixth bhumi can accomplish. We might wonder what the purpose of that is. Why not maintain the absorption rather than entering into it and coming out again?

The reason bodhisattvas train in this way is that the goal of the bodhisattva is to engage in the post-meditative practices of generosity and so forth without losing the power of mind gained in meditative absorption. The goal is to be able to engage in activities without wavering from the state of absorption, so that post-meditative discipline and generosity become an ornament to enhance the meditative absorption. The bodhisattva on the fifth ground is not yet capable of unwavering absorption while engaged in post-meditative activity. This is the reason for the practice of entering and leaving absorption. Meditative absorption is not just simple mindfulness. Normally, when we practice ethical conduct, we could think of it as simple mindfulness, but here there is no wavering from absorption, and the conduct actually enhances the absorption.

The bodhisattva on the sixth ground has so many qualities. He or she is able to arise from deep meditative absorption into the illusory body in the post-meditative state, transforming the contaminated body into the uncontaminated body.

The seventh bhumi is called 'Gone Afar.' At this level, the bodhisattva has completely eliminated the obscuration of negative emotions and now begins to purify the obscuration to omniscience.

The eighth bhumi is called 'Unwavering.' This refers to the bodhisattva's ability to eliminate the subtlest obscurations. At this level, the meditative and post-meditative states have become so powerful that they inseparable. They are free from extremes and the subtlest grasping to intrinsic reality. The eighth bhumi marks the beginning of the pure bhumis, because at this point the bodhisattva has purified all of the conceptual obscurations to omniscience.

The ninth bhumi is called 'Perfect Wisdom,' because the bodhisattva perfectly understands the three vehicles and the ability to teach beings according to their capacity. The tenth bhumi is called 'Cloud of Dharma.' At this level, bodhisattvas are able to instantaneously eliminate even the subtlest grasping at intrinsic reality and the subtlest dualistic tendencies. Because of this, they are able to engage in vast activities for the benefit of beings. In the second moment of entering into the absorption, bodhisattvas at this level enter the state of complete enlightenment and the path of no more learning.

With this, we have covered the ten bodhisattva grounds; this is just to leave an auspicious imprint.

The Resultant Middle Way

The bodhisattva on the tenth ground, who has attained the meditative absorption of the final continuum, steps into the enlightened state in the second moment of the meditation. In the resultant state of the Middle Way, the nirvana described by Nagarjuna, there is no true attainment, no true birth, and no true cessation. The nirvana of the dharmakaya is free of attainment, non-attainment, abandonment, birth, and cessation.

There are two kinds of resultant states in the Middle Way, the *rupakaya* and the *dharmakaya*. The rupakaya is the form body, and the dharmakaya is the truth body, or body of suchness. We can also split the rupakaya into the *nirmanakaya* and *sambhogakaya*, so that there are three kayas. Sometimes we talk about four kayas, including the *svabhavikakaya*. For bodhisattvas on the tenth ground who are abiding in the last continuum as a sentient being before gaining enlightenment, the first thing that is actualized is the dharmakaya, the omniscience of the enlightened state. For the dharmakaya to exist, it has to be based on a body that is free of contamination. There are two such bodies: the sambhogakaya or enjoyment body, which is only visible to higher level bodhisattvas, and the nirmanakaya or emanation body, which is visible to ordinary beings.

The dharmakaya is not simply the experience of emptiness of an enlightened mind. The dharmakaya that Nagarjuna speaks of in his *Niraupamyastava* ('Song of the Incomparable Buddha') is able to see the one taste of both samsara and nirvana, of both afflictive emotions and buddhahood, or omniscience, because they are all pure.

> You have known that afflictions and purity are of a single taste,
> for reality admits of no distinctions, and is, therefore, entirely pure.[23]

Therefore, your dharmakaya is the dharmakaya of perfect purity. In the context of the state of enlightenment, there are kayas with and without remainder, as taught in the *Golden Light Sutra*. In this context, 'with remainder' and 'without remainder' are not the same as in the Hinayana context. The Hinayana arhat with remainder is still living with the residual body of the five aggregates, and the arhat without remainder has left the contaminated body behind. However, in the state of enlightenment as affirmed by the Buddha in the *Golden Light Sutra*, 'with remainder' refers to the rupakaya – the sambhogakaya and nirmanakaya – and 'without remainder' refers to the dharmakaya and svabhavikakaya.

The way in which the three kayas are actualized is further clarified by Nagarjuna. Nagarjuna says that the tenth level bodhisattva in the last continuum first actualizes the dharmakaya for his or her own sake. The dharmakaya is free from attainment and non-attainment – there is no sense of something attained and somebody attaining it. Then, from the dharmakaya, the two kayas of the rupakaya are actualized for the sake of sentient beings. These kayas are actualized without any sort of conceptual intention on the part of the enlightened person, and he or she never wavers from the state of dharmakaya. When the moon is reflected in water, it is not because the moon has any intention of being reflected. The myriad reflections appear based on causes and conditions. The dharmakaya is like the water on which the moon is reflected, and the reflected moon is like the rupakaya. This is called the 'resultant Middle Way' because the nature of this resultant state by its very nature is free from the two extremes.

6

CONCISE PRESENTATION OF THE PRACTICE

DAILY PRACTICE OF THE PATH MIDDLE WAY

How can we apply the five paths and ten grounds to our daily practice? Maintaining a joyful practice of generosity and vigilant observance of discipline is not easy. And, we may not have the time or ability to study and learn all of the detailed teachings on the paths and grounds. We can, however, practice the path Middle Way by applying and adhering to three points.

First, when we meditate, we use the uncommon union of calm abiding and special insight focused on emptiness. Second, we carry the six perfections into our practice, in their essential form. Third, we apply mindfulness and vigilance to carry the essential Mahayana practices of meditation and conduct into our daily lives. To enhance our practice of these three points, we engage in mind-training practice or *lojong*.[24]

Union of Shamatha and Vipassana

The first point is to practice the Middle Way path's union of calm abiding and special insight, in order to generate certainty regarding the primordial emptiness of our own mind. Remember that the emptiness we cultivate is not outside ourselves. It is intimately close to us, within our own mind. So we have to be able to experience the emptiness of our own mind, which is the Middle Way basis. Once we are able to generate conviction about the emptiness of our own mind, we familiarize ourselves with it in calm-abiding meditation and then with the application of special insight.

First, we generate conviction and certainty about the primordial emptiness of our own mind. This is the ground of all enlightened qualities, the treasure trove from which the qualities of the ten bhumis actually spring. We apply ourselves until we are able to recognize the primordial emptiness of our own mind and how it is the source of all higher qualities. Once we have that conviction, we sustain it in meditation. Understanding the view of the basis is not enough; we need to experience it in meditation, to gain certainty.

After we have generated conviction about the ground – the emptiness of our own mind with five features – we then simply let the mind rest in its natural state of emptiness. Just let the mind relax into a state without any particular object, like space free from clouds. Relax or let the mind go into a natural state of uncontrived mind. Here, meditation is just that. We sustain this for as long as possible. This is how we engage in calm abiding focused on emptiness. When we enter this meditation, we should not entertain the thought, 'I am here, meditating on emptiness,' as though we and emptiness were two separate things. We should not entertain dualistic notions. We should practice so that when entering into absorption, we simply experience vast emptiness.

When the empty aspect of the mind becomes obscured, then we apply mindfulness and vigilance to bring it back again. We identify the source of obscuration through mindfulness and vigilance. If it is some sort of agitation, then we loosen the focus. If it is some sort of dullness, then we exert more effort to concentrate.

We are limited to using words and concepts, which are dualistic, in order to explain how to meditate on emptiness, but in reality there is no duality or distinction between who is doing and what is done. We should not cultivate dualism of subject and object. When I talk about non-duality, you may get the impression that this meditation is the same as Dzogchen meditation, but it is not. Here we are using the mind in order to focus, so there is still a subtle dualism of concept and object. Dzogchen meditation is beyond mind, timelessly pure of any trace of mental effort.

The aim of the path Middle Way practice of calm abiding is to leave the mind in its natural state without creating an image of emptiness outside itself for the perceiving mind to experience. When we place the mind, we should not do it too intensely. That is also a form of grasping. It is not like focusing on a visual object or looking into space. Here, the focus is the experience of the mind as empty. Sustaining that absorption is the practice of calm abiding focused on emptiness.

Until we are familiar with the practice of calm abiding, it is better not to hold onto any expectations about the nature of special insight, so that we can actually experience the radiant clarity of the empty mind. Through the repeated practice of calm abiding, there comes a time when we experience the clarity of the emptiness of our mind as like the clarity of a pool of water after the sediment has settled out. This may take months or years, but when it does it becomes very easy to engage in special insight meditation using subtle mindfulness. This is also a very potent way to engage in the practice of bodhicitta from the point of view of the ground.

The subtle mindfulness of special insight does not cling to the focus on emptiness that we have in calm abiding. The scriptures say that once we experience the ground – the clarity and emptiness of mind in calm abiding – then we use this subtle mindfulness as part of the special insight practice. The scriptures also say that this subtle mindfulness actually engages in analysis, but I do not think this is the case. I think the role of subtle mindfulness, when in deep absorption on the ground of clarity and emptiness, is to enhance the clarity aspect of the mind. Stability is already there, but clarity is enhanced so that we can eliminate the subtlest dualistic perceptions. It is like removing a cataract from our eyes, that had made us unable to see clearly, restoring our clear vision. Cataracts are removed in layers, and as we remove layers of dualistic perception one by one, clarity is intensified. So the role of this subtle awareness is to remove subtle obscurations so that clarity dawns more intensely.

Essential Practice of the Six Perfections

The second point of practicing the Middle Way path is to practice the six perfections, in their essential form, in the post-meditative state. When we arise from meditation, we should practice the perfections in our daily lives. The essential way to practice generosity and giving is to dedicate the virtue accrued by our meditation and other virtuous actions of body, speech, and mind to the enlightenment of all sentient beings. This is carrying the essential form of the perfection of generosity into practice. It is not necessary to give away all of our things or to go to a cemetery to practice Chöd.

We can bring the practice of discipline into our practice within a single session as well. The essence of the practice of discipline is to guard our intention. When we dedicate the merit as part of the practice of generosity, we should also guard our intentions as part of discipline. If our intentions are wrong and we are practicing for the sake of fame or praise, or any of the eight worldly concerns, then we have the wrong intention. We should identify such intentions and refrain from them. This is the essential form of the practice of discipline.

We can practice patience together with generosity and discipline while dedicating our merit and guarding against wrong intentions. Successfully practicing generosity and discipline is not easy; it requires patience. By practicing patience, we learn to avoid giving in to habitual tendencies or obstacles. Because there are many physical and mental obstacles, we need patience. The practice of patience in turn requires the fourth perfection, joyous effort. Joyous effort supports the intention to perfect the other virtues in order to benefit beings.

When we dedicate the virtue accumulated by our practice for the sake of all beings, the fifth perfection of concentration is necessary so that we do not get distracted. If we are distracted during our practice, then there is no concentration and no power. We need to practice without wavering, remaining aware of our virtuous intention. If we are dedicating virtue in the correct manner, then we are also applying the perfection of concentration. Finally, whatever wholesome action we are doing, we remain mindful and vigilant of the sixth perfection of wisdom, seeing the illusory nature of the three spheres of agent, action and object.

In brief, when we are introduced to the basis of the Middle Way, we recognize and sustain that in our meditation. Then, we practice the six perfections simultaneously within a single session in the above manner.

Application of Mindfulness and Vigilance

The third point is the application of mindfulness and vigilance in order to carry the essence of the Mahayana teachings into our daily lives. We apply this point when we have been introduced to the wisdom of emptiness and carried the Middle Way into practice. Then, whatever kinds of external situations we might face in daily life, whatever challenges arise, it is very important to apply mindfulness and vigilance to keep an open and expansive mind, not letting it become narrow, rigid, deluded, fearful, lonely, or depressed. Even though there is conflict everywhere, by applying mindfulness we remind ourselves that ultimately these issues are like illusions from the point of view of emptiness. Then we can maintain a mind that is vast and open, powerful and stable. If we do not do that, then we will not be able to accomplish our goal.

Four-Session Yoga of the Middle Way

When we practice the Middle Way, we are building upon the introduction to the wisdom of emptiness and then carrying it into practice. At this point, the wisdom of emptiness is practiced from the point of view of our own meditative experience. Now, whatever external or internal challenges we might face in our lives, we apply mindfulness and vigilance in order to remain open and expansive and avoid slipping into narrow-mindedness and misery. How do mindfulness and vigilance accomplish this? Even though there are conflicts and problems at the apparent level of reality, we remind ourselves that appearances are illusory.

Next, I will briefly describe how to engage in this practice on a daily basis using the four-session yoga. The four-session yoga is practiced by dividing the day into four practice sessions.

In the morning when you wake up, engage in tsa lung and the preliminary practices, and then practice guru yoga. After practicing guru yoga, dissolve the guru into your own crown so that you and the guru are inseparable. Sustain this non-duality of the guru and yourself, and carry the view of emptiness into practice. Seeing your non-dual nature induces a sense of emptiness, and you carry that emptiness into your practice and sustain it in meditation.

After about an hour of this practice, engage in tonglen,[25] or 'sending and receiving,' inhaling the suffering and sickness of all beings and exhaling your positive qualities and virtue to others. Engage in this practice for about twenty minutes, and then remain in meditation on the non-dual nature of emptiness for another thirty minutes. At the end, recite the dedication prayers. This completes the first session.

In the second session, start by meditating on bodhicitta. Generate bodhicitta by recalling why you are practicing – to achieve the state of enlightenment for the benefit of other sentient beings. Then, enter into meditation without the duality of meditator and the object of meditation, which in this case is bodhicitta. There is no separation between the bodhicitta that is generated and the mind that is generating it. Settle into a non-dual meditation that sees the emptiness of both, and then remain in meditation on emptiness. Maintain that state for about an hour. Finish the second session by engaging in the essential practice of the six perfections as was discussed earlier.

In the third session, meditate on emptiness for two hours. It is okay if you need to stretch or drink water, but if possible it is better not to move and to remain in single-pointed meditation. Meditate with a great sense of emptiness, without clinging to any reference point, any thought, form, or sound. Dwell in the empty nature of all phenomena.

The Buddha taught the *Heart Sutra* from within a state of meditative absorption, so that is how we have to meditate. Here, there is no self or other, no basis of any imputation. If we do not meditate in this way, there is no point in reciting the *Heart Sutra*. When we say, 'There is no form, no sound,' we mean there is no grasping at a sense of intrinsic form or sound, even though form and sound exist conventionally. We do not want to be stuck with attachments to substantial reality. We want to move beyond that, destroy that. The power of meditative equipoise is able to destroy all such fixation.

You enter the meditation state with your eyes closed, and you begin the meditation by penetrating into the empty nature of all phenomena.

Every object of fixation, even the subtlest particle, dissolves one by one into the state of emptiness, which is like a vast expanse. You then sustain this meditation. There is no other way to meditate. If you are looking for something else, you are confused.

In the fourth session, meditate on emptiness for about an hour and then practice Chöd. If you are not practicing Chöd, then practice the six perfections.

It is also very helpful to practice the lojong or mind-training instructions on a daily basis. Begin by subduing and transforming the strongest negative emotion, whatever is predominant in your own experience. Whether it is anger, desire, jealousy, or whatever, suppress that first. This is very important.

Without mind training, it is impossible to control and subdue your mind. Instead of cultivating humility and integrity, the ego will be inflated and generate confusion. In your confusion, you will begin to look down on others and lose respect for them. When you lose respect for others, you have forgotten bodhicitta. It is very important to transform this childish behavior.

PART THREE

THE THIRD TURNING OF THE
WHEEL OF DHARMA

YOUNGE KHACHAB RINPOCHE

7

THE TATHAGATAGARBHA

In the first turning of the wheel of Dharma, we introduced the view as the selflessness of the person. The conduct practiced in the first turning is renunciation, based on understanding the conditioned nature of the skandhas, as well as the practice of the four immeasurables. In the second turning of the wheel of Dharma, the view of emptiness is the profound view of the Middle Way. We also discussed the extensive conduct of bodhisattvas, which is the practice of the six perfections. It is important to understand that in the second turning, the empty aspect of the mind is emphasized more than the clarity aspect of the mind. Now, I am going to present the third turning of the wheel of Dharma, also called the 'wheel of perfect discernment.' The third turning also teaches emptiness, but while accentuating the clarity or luminosity of the mind.

There are different positions on what constitutes the emphasis or focal point of the third turning. The Cittamatra school holds that the main doctrinal emphasis of the third turning is the doctrine of 'three natures.'[26] According to another view, held by the early masters of the Nyingma and Kagyu schools, the contents of the second and third turnings are essentially the same; there is only a difference in emphasis. Jamgon Kongtrul states that the second and third turnings are the same, though the second turning emphasizes the emptiness of mind while the third turning emphasizes the clarity of mind, and therefore also buddha nature. According to the later traditions like the Sakya and Gelug, there is a significant difference in content between the second and third turnings. The new schools hold that the third turning is principally the presentation of Cittamatra, but this is not really the case. What we will see is that the emphasis in the third turning is on buddha nature, which is directly linked to the clarity of the mind.

There are at least ten sutras that directly refer to buddha nature, or the *tathagatagarbha*. For example, the *Lankavatara Sutra* and the *Tathagatagarbha Sutra* discuss the difference between the basis and the ultimate mode of being of the basis. The basis here is the contaminated mind, the mind with stains. The ultimate mode of being of the contaminated mind is its potential to become enlightened, to be transformed into buddhahood. This potential is buddha nature. This view is quite profound and not readily understood by the disciples of the first turning. The Buddha said that with regard to the teachings on buddha nature, "The sravakas and pratyekabuddhas are not my disciples, and I am not their teacher."[27]

The Nyingma and Kagyu maintain that the teachings of the third turning of the wheel of Dharma are actually the definitive teachings, as opposed to the non-definitive teachings, which have to be interpreted according to context. The Sakya and Gelug traditions say this is not true. They hold that the teachings of the second turning are the definitive teachings. If you look at the teachings themselves, those of the third turning are more profound, and it is more suitable to view them as the definitive teachings.

WHY THE TATHAGATAGARBHA IS TAUGHT

The third turning pertains to the fundamental quest of every sentient being, which is to gain happiness and avoid suffering. In order to gain temporary and ultimate happiness, we need to look at the basis of temporary and ultimate happiness. Different religious or spiritual traditions have different presentations of this basis. The Hindu tradition might say it is *mahatma* or supreme consciousness. Others might say it is a god or creator. Materialists might say it comes from material well-being and conquering nature. From the Buddhist perspective, the source of both temporary and ultimate happiness is simply the *ultimate nature* of the contaminated or ordinary mind. This mind is the cause of both samsara and nirvana and therefore the cause of suffering and happiness, both temporary and ultimate. The ultimate nature of the contaminated mind is referred to as the 'naturally abiding buddha nature.' It is a naturally abiding potential, also referred to as a 'seed' or 'lineage.' Understanding the significance of this potential is key to understanding the cause of happiness.

The initial benefit of understanding buddha nature is that awareness of it helps us to gain freedom from suffering. If we have a basic understanding of our buddha nature, then we realize that all suffering arises from a confused mind. The source of all suffering is confused perceptions or thoughts, but there is no confusion in the ultimate nature of mind. Once we gain a more experiential understanding of buddha nature, we are able to see the possibility of freedom from all suffering; to see that if we can be free from confusion we will be free from suffering as well. This is a temporary benefit of this realization. Ultimately, whether we are tantric or Dzogchen practitioners, understanding buddha nature is very useful for our practice.

Further on I will discuss the nine metaphors that illustrate buddha nature, but I will use one of them now to introduce how buddha nature is hidden, for most of us, though it is hidden by our own ignorance. The second metaphor compares buddha nature to the honey in a busy beehive. Even though there is honey in the hive, it is hidden inside and there are many bees protecting it. If you are not skillful, you may not recognize that there is honey to be extracted, because the hive is so ugly, or you may be reluctant to try, for fear of being stung. The person who extracts the honey has to be skillful to avoid killing the bees or getting stung. The honey in this example is like buddha nature hidden by negative emotions. The meaning of this metaphor is that because buddha nature is obscured, you have to be very skilled to recognize and experience it. We have to be skillful in purifying negative emotions, so that we can experience buddha nature directly. By depending on skillful means, we can awaken and experience buddha nature.

If we want to encounter our buddha nature, we need to eliminate two types of obscurations. First is the 'innate stain,' which is very difficult to purify. This stain is the innate ignorance present in all beings that I discussed in the first turning of the wheel. The second stain, which is easier to purify, consists of the 'conceptually induced stains,' the habits, attitudes and norms that differ from person to person, culture to culture, depending on our way of life. Before we can eliminate the innate stain, we need to eliminate these conceptually induced habits and negative emotions. It is thus most practical to start by tackling the habits and cultural norms that get in the way of recognizing buddha nature.

Just as extracting honey requires tremendous experience and skill to avoid being stung, encountering the face of buddha nature depends on many causes and conditions. The first condition is the elimination of culturally induced obscurations. This is a difficult task because our culture is directly linked to our personality, our sense of who we are. When we are asked to transcend culturally induced habits, it may not even seem possible, because these habits are linked to who we think we are as a person. I am not trying to discourage people, just pointing to the fact that it is possible to leave problematic habits behind.

In India and China, there are such issues as caste, having never heard of buddha nature, or simply not caring. In Tibet, we used to know that we had buddha nature, but we did not do anything about it other than praying in the monasteries, making mandala offerings, and so on. We did not have inner realization of buddha nature. The focus was on politics, and which lamas were high lamas, so even though we all have buddha nature, in Tibet we did not care about that. Western culture also makes things difficult, especially when narrow-mindedness and self-centeredness are encouraged. Culturally induced obscurations have layers. When one layer of unskillful habits and norms is peeled away, another emerges at a subtler level. This goes on and on. It is not easy but it's very important.

Because of its profundity, buddha nature is not taught in the first turning, and only the aspect of emptiness is taught in the second turning. Only in the third turning of the wheel of Dharma does the Buddha teach the union of emptiness and clarity. The key message of the third turning is that all impurity or contamination is temporary or adventitious. Whether the impurities are innate or conceptually induced, they are all temporary in the sense that they never touch the fundamental nature of the mind. Based on this key point, some teachers say that even as ordinary beings, we all have the major and minor marks of a buddha. The Buddha said in the *Sutra Requested by King Dharaneshvara*[28] that because they have buddha nature, even ordinary people possess these characteristics at the level of the basis. This is not quite the same as, but very much like, what we say in Dzogchen – that the three kayas are spontaneously present at the level of the basis. This point is taken very literally by masters like Dolpopa, who belong to the Shentong or 'other-emptiness' school. Even though there is some controversy and debate, the key point is to understand the ultimate nature of our own contaminated mind, which is buddha nature. That is all that is required here.

In the context of the teachings and practice of the third turning, it is very important to understand the ultimate nature of the contaminated mind as empty of intrinsic existence and primordially pure. At the level of the basis for ordinary sentient beings, the contaminated mind is the cause of all suffering. At the level of the path, it becomes the cause of liberation. At the level of the result, it is transformed into the svabhavikakaya. The resultant state is pure in two ways. The first purity is the transformation of innate impurity, and the second is the transformation of temporary impurities. What this means is that even though negative emotions like hatred are something to be abandoned, the ultimate nature of hatred, etc. is *not* something to be abandoned, as it is also innately, primordially pure. We really need to appreciate this difference.At the level of the basis, buddha nature is the cause of both samsara and nirvana. This means that both arise from buddha nature. This can be explained by an analogy. The universe emerges from the ground of space. Empty space is like buddha nature. From empty space, the whole universe comes into being. The element of wind emerges from space. From wind comes fire, from fire comes water, and from water comes earth and the entirety of the diverse forms and inhabitants of the universe. This is the process of evolution. In the dissolution process, earth dissolves into water, water into fire, fire into wind, and wind into space. According to Buddhist cosmology, the entire universe dissolves back into empty space. Space is the ground from which all the forms in the universe evolve and into which they dissolve. Very much like that, buddha nature is the ground of all karma and appearances. All of our experiences arise from the ground of buddha nature and dissolve back into it.

The dissolution of the outer universe is karmically induced. It is natural; it does not happen by virtue of meditation. The dissolution of all of our experiences back into buddha nature happens by virtue of our meditation, so this applies only to practitioners. When we meditate realizing buddha nature, all of our experiences – gross conceptual thoughts and experiences of the outer world – dissolve back into the basic space of our buddha nature. When conceptual thoughts dissolve, gross and subtle afflictions dissolve, and as these dissolve, karmic action also dissolves. Eventually, even the subtlest karmic potential dissolves back into the ground of buddha nature. When the subtlest imprints of karma have dissolved into buddha nature, then we arrive at the ultimate nature of mind free from contamination. I will discuss what that means later.

THE SUTRAS AND SHASTRAS ON BUDDHA NATURE

The source of the teachings on buddha nature includes all of the lineage masters who received and transmitted these teachings, and whose own lineages can be traced back to the Buddha himself. These are not like New Age teachings where there is no lineage. The teachings on buddha nature can be traced from myself and my teachers back to the Buddha himself. Because there is a lineage, an unbroken transmission from one to another, the blessings of the lineage masters are present in the teachings and practice instructions that we receive. This means that when we practice, we receive the lineage blessings.

Since we can trace the teachings through an unbroken lineage back to the Buddha, we know that they are authentic. This gives rise to faith and conviction. Nowadays, many New Age teachers claim to have authority as spiritual teachers without any particular lineage history. Many Westerners are attracted to these kinds of teachers. Of course, if they realize buddha nature, then how can we judge them? The main point is that people who do not have realization cannot make it up on the fly. What I am teaching here comes from an unbroken lineage that extends back to the Buddha. If we intend to practice these teachings fully, then lineage is especially important. If you read a hundred books but do not have a lineage, then it is no good. If you read four lines and have a strong lineage, then you are good to go.

There are at least ten sutras given by the Buddha on buddha nature, including the *Lankavatara Sutra* and the *Tathagatagarbha Sutra*.[29] The manner of presenting buddha nature can vary from one sutra to the next, but what is presented is the same thing. There are also commentaries by lineage masters like Maitreya and Asanga that clearly explain and answer questions about buddha nature as it is taught by the Buddha. Maitreya's 'Five Treatises,' especially the *Uttaratantra*, are very clear on buddha nature.

In the *Tathagatagarbha Sutra*, the Buddha clearly states that at all times sentient beings are the embodiment of the essence of buddha nature.

> Sons of good family, the essential law (dharmata) of the dharmas is this: whether or not tathagatas appear in the world, all these sentient beings at all times contain a tathagata (tathagatagarbha).[30]

Based on what is taught in the sutras and also by Maitreya in the *Uttaratantrashastra*, we can explain how it is that all beings have buddha nature in terms of three features. First, the dharmakaya pervades all beings as *rolpa* or the capacity to appear. Second, with regard to the very essence of buddha nature, there is no difference between sentient beings and enlightened beings. Third, the ultimate nature of ordinary mind pervades all sentient beings equally. Through these three features Maitreya Buddha explains buddha nature as it was taught in the sutras.

> Because the perfect buddha's kaya is all-pervading,
> Because reality is undifferentiated,
> And because they possess the potential,
> Beings always have the buddha nature.[31]

Maitreya Buddha incorporates the basis, path, and result pertaining to buddha nature into these three features. When he says that the dharmakaya pervades all sentient beings, he describes buddha nature at the level of the resultant state. This shows that the practice of buddha nature is not without result, that ultimately it gives rise to the dharmakaya, the embodiment of the two purities we discussed earlier. The second feature, that there is no difference between sentient beings and buddhas, shows that there is a path or practice of buddha nature that gives rise to the dharmakaya because of its natural purity. The third feature, that the ultimate nature of contaminated mind pervades all sentient beings, describes the level of the basis. This means that buddha nature is present or inherent in all beings, even ordinary beings, at the level of the basis.

Asanga composed a commentary on Maitreya's *Uttaratantra* based on his own understanding of practice.[32] In it, he also describes the nature of the tathagatagarbha and how to practice it.

In Tibet, the Nyingma and Kagyu place a lot of emphasis on the teachings of buddha nature, especially those of the *Tathagatagarbha Sutra* and the *Uttaratantrashastra* of Maitreya. The Kagyu tradition regards the *Tathagatagarbha Sutra* and *Uttaratantra* as the textual basis for the authenticity of the Mahamudra teachings. In earlier times, the teachings on the tathagatagarbha were seen as extremely important, but over time their importance declined, and these days not many people pay attention to them. In the Nyingma tradition, especially in the Dzogchen semde,[33] the teachings on the tathagatagarbha are used as the basis for explaining the view of the ground. These teachings on buddha nature are used because they are extremely beneficial. Even here in the West, we know how beneficial it is to be introduced to buddha nature.

THE TEN NATURES AND NINE METAPHORS OF BUDDHA NATURE

Buddha nature can be explained in terms of ten natures and nine metaphors. The ten natures elucidate the ultimate nature of the contaminated ordinary mind. The mind with contamination and the mind free from contamination are both empty, but merely stating this is not enough to bring about recognition. Traditionally, buddha nature is explained by relying on the sutras and shastras, using reasoning to establish the authenticity of buddha nature from multiple starting points. I will explain it here in a similar but less lengthy way in terms of ten natures or aspects.[34]

The ten natures of buddha nature are:
1. The ultimate nature of the contaminated mind.
2. The cause of recognizing and actualizing buddha nature.
3. The result of actualizing buddha nature.
4. Activating buddha nature, or 'functionality.'
5. The presence of the imprint of a Mahayana practitioner.
6. Divisions of buddha nature.
7. The temporary understanding of buddha nature when the mind is contaminated.
8. Buddha nature is all-pervasive.
9. Buddha nature is unchanging.
10. Buddha nature is indivisible.

1. The ultimate nature of the contaminated mind

The usual introduction to buddha nature makes reference to the union of emptiness and clarity. Here, buddha nature is introduced as the ultimate nature of the contaminated mind – the basis upon which all negative emotions can be eliminated, and also the basis upon which all qualities of the enlightened three kayas can be actualized. Therefore, this potential is not itself composed of or a product of anything else. It is 'unproduced,' not a product of causes and conditions like the potential for success in life. It is the potential to eliminate all negative emotions and to give rise to all the qualities of enlightenment.

2. The cause of recognizing and actualizing buddha nature

The external cause of recognizing and actualizing buddha nature is finding the Mahayana teachings and a qualified Mahayana teacher. The internal cause is faith and devotion for the Mahayana, along with joyous effort, wisdom, and so forth. When we have these external and internal conditions, then we need the skillful means to purify contaminations so that we can recognize and actualize buddha nature. These external and internal factors together with skillful methods constitute the cause of actualizing buddha nature, though the practice of skillful means is especially important.

3. The result of actualizing buddha nature

The resultant enlightened state embodies the two aspects of purity. First, we purify the temporary stains, and then we are able to purify the innate stain. Having purified the two impurities, we attain the resultant state.

4. Activating buddha nature, or "functionality"

Awakening or activating buddha nature in oneself, making it functional or workable, is achieved on the basis of two aspirations. The first is genuine renunciation, based on one's understanding of the imperfection and suffering in all realms of samsara. The second is faith, or conviction and aspiration, committed to achieving liberation. When both aspirations are genuine and irreversible, together they awaken buddha nature. That is how to awaken buddha nature and make it functional.

5. The presence of the imprint of a Mahayana practitioner

The imprint of a Mahayana practitioner, or buddha nature, is present in two ways – as the qualities of the cause and as the qualities of the resultant state. 'Qualities of the cause' refers to bodhicitta and other factors such as faith and wisdom. 'Qualities of the result' refers to the qualities of the three kayas. Understanding these qualities and their presence as an imprint fortifies our intention to awaken buddha nature. We start to understand that we belong to the Mahayana lineage, and that we possess the imprint that is the potential for liberation.

6. Divisions of buddha nature

From the ultimate point of view, there are no distinctions within buddha nature, but there are differences in the level of contamination of the ordinary mind. On this basis, there are three divisions of buddha nature. First, there is the buddha nature of the contaminated mind, the ordinary being. Second, there is the buddha nature of the mind that is free from negative emotions, the arya bodhisattva. Third, there is the buddha nature of the mind that is free from both negative emotions and the obscurations to omniscience, the enlightened being. Even though from the point of view of the ultimate nature of contaminated mind there are no divisions, we can divide buddha nature into these three types of beings from the ordinary point of view. There is no differentiation within the ultimate nature of mind.

7. The temporary understanding of buddha nature when the mind is contaminated

We can also describe the three levels of buddha nature as impure buddha nature, both pure and impure buddha nature, and perfectly pure buddha nature.

The three levels of buddha nature are taught by the Buddha in the *Sutra to Shariputra*.[35] Here he said that on the first level, dharmakaya or the ultimate nature of contaminated mind is imprisoned within the cage of negative emotions. This is the buddha nature of sentient beings, who have not achieved freedom from birth and death.

The second level of buddha nature is this very same dharmakaya within beings who have given rise to bodhicitta. This is the pure and impure buddha nature of bodhisattvas. Finally, the Buddha says that this same dharmakaya, as it abides in beings who have given rise to the enlightened state and purified the two obscurations, is the dhatu of the dharmakaya, the ultimate nature of the tathagatagarbha.

8. Buddha nature is all-pervasive

'All-pervasive nature' refers to the fact that there are no distinctions or levels within natural purity. The only differences are between the kinds of beings at the level of the basis: those who have not eliminated obscurations, those who have eliminated negative emotions, and those who have eliminated both negative emotions and cognitive obscurations. These are differences between persons and not in the nature of buddha nature itself. Even though there are differences in terms of the basis, buddha nature pervades all beings like space pervades all the elements. It does not depend on effort nor on volition or attention; it is naturally so.

This is a fundamental point. Ultimately, there is no difference within buddha nature itself. Any differentiation is due to differences between sentient beings. We can use the analogy of three containers filled with water, one made of gold, one of silver, and one of copper. The water in each container reflects the outer world. Even though there is no difference in what is reflected – the world – we can talk about three distinct reflections appearing in three different containers. The division of buddha nature into categories is very much like that.

In the sutras, the buddha nature of afflicted beings is not referred to as buddhahood, but as the dhatu or sphere of sentient beings. As ordinary sentient beings, we are afflicted because of craving and self-grasping. The more intense our craving, the more buddha nature is obscured. Even in moments of intense desire, we have to say that buddha nature exists but that it is obscured by our desire. The more effectively we can apply antidotes to craving, like meditating on impermanence or selflessness, the less we will be afflicted. As the stains of desire decrease, the ultimate nature of desire becomes manifest. Even though desire is to be abandoned, the ultimate nature of the desiring mind is not to be abandoned. The ultimate nature of desire manifests because we have eliminated desire.

Desire is one example of a negative emotion. Of course, the same applies to any kind of negative emotion – desire, hatred, ignorance, jealousy, and arrogance. The ultimate nature of all negative emotions is buddha nature. Even so, the mind afflicted by emotions is not called the dhatu of buddhahood but rather the dhatu of sentient beings.

The main point is that as practitioners, we have to be able to clearly distinguish the contaminated mind from the ultimate nature of the contaminated mind. Buddha nature refers to the ultimate nature of the contaminated mind and not to the contaminated mind itself. When both obscurations have been abandoned, then buddha nature is referred to as the dharmakaya.

There are different presentations of buddha nature and its divisions based on the different traditions in Tibet, but here I am presenting it as it was explained in the sutras. The Buddha told Shariputra that 'the dhatu of sentient beings' and 'dharmakaya' refer to one and the same thing. There is no difference with regard to the ultimate nature of mind, whether a being is ordinary and contaminated or enlightened and uncontaminated, though there is a difference between ordinary and enlightened beings. This is what the Buddha meant by saying that 'the dhatu of sentient beings' and 'dharmakaya' are different words for the same thing.

This particular statement, in which the Buddha says that the dhatu of sentient beings and that of the dharmakaya are one and the same thing, is extremely profound. From the *Anunatvapurnatvanirdesa Sutra*:

> Therefore, Sariputra, the realm of beings and the dharmakaya are not different. The realm of beings is the dharmakaya and the dharmakaya is the realm of beings. Their significance is identical, only distinguished by different names.

The profundity of this statement is reflected in the presentations of the Kagyu and Nyingma traditions, but its deepest significance can only be shown in the context of Dzogchen. Nonetheless, the actual statement was made by the Buddha himself.

In the Sakya and Gelug traditions, it is difficult to take these words literally because these traditions approach them primarily from a sutric context. According to a sutric interpretation, there is a contradiction in saying that ordinary sentient beings have buddha nature. If buddha nature were already actualized in sentient beings, then how could there be any need to accumulate merit and wisdom? A literal reading of this statement would seem to be impossible.

9. Buddha nature is unchanging

Even though the contaminated mind can undergo change, the ultimate nature of the contaminated mind is unchanging. It cannot be made better or worse, more or less. By analogy, as a result of changes in the elements, the sky can be obscured by clouds or it can be clear of clouds, but the nature of the sky itself is unchanging. Applying this analogy to our practice, we cultivate the view that all temporary afflictions are changeable like clouds that can be cleared, but the ultimate nature of mind itself is unchanging. It is the same whether we are sentient beings or enlightened beings. It cannot be made more clear or more pure.

The fact that the ultimate nature of mind cannot be changed is a very positive thing. The significance of this for our practice is that if we can see that all negative emotions are temporary, then we know they do not taint the nature of mind. The possibility of purification and the possibility of actualizing the qualities of enlightenment are real, because buddha nature is unchanging.

10. Buddha nature is indivisible

The tenth and final point is the indivisible nature of the tathagatagarbha. This refers to non-duality, the inseparability of subject and object.

Nine Metaphors

Next I will discuss how these ten natures of buddha nature can be illuminated by nine metaphors. These nine metaphors illustrate how the ultimate nature of ordinary mind is obscured or hidden by different stains or contaminations. Conversely, the metaphors illustrate how it is that we can have buddha nature without being able to see it.

The first metaphor or simile is that buddha nature is hidden like the unopened blossom of a lotus that grows from the mud. Even though the lotus grows in a dirty, muddy pond, the mud does not actually taint the purity of the blossom. Likewise, even though buddha nature is hidden within the contaminated mind of an ordinary sentient being, the stains do not taint buddha nature itself. Even as ordinary sentient beings, our buddha nature is pure, though obscured by contaminations.

The second metaphor is that buddha nature is hidden like the honey inside a beehive. Even though there is honey in the hive, the hive obscures it. I mentioned this example earlier.

The third metaphor pertains to the way a grain is hidden within its husk. We cannot see the grain within the husk, but if we remove the husk the grain becomes apparent. Likewise, if we eliminate the contamination that obscures it, we will directly encounter our buddha nature. Just as we clean, wash, and cook the grain, we apply antidotes to the obscurations in order to actualize buddha nature.

The fourth metaphor compares buddha nature to gold hidden underground. Even though the gold is not visible above ground, if we dig a mine we will eventually find it. Just like the earth and rock that cover the gold, the temporary conditions of our own karma and negative emotions obscure our buddha nature. By eliminating these afflictions, we will eventually actualize it.

In the case of finding gold, first we have to understand that there is gold hidden somewhere underground. Then we have to gather the means to mine the gold. Once the gold is extracted, then we can use it to make ornaments. Likewise, when we purify that which obscures buddha nature, we can cultivate the enlightened qualities of the mind like ornaments.

The fifth metaphor compares buddha nature to a treasure hidden beneath a house. The analogy given is that of a poor man living in a house built on top of a vast treasure. The man believes he is very poor even though the ground beneath him is full of precious jewels. He spends all his time making a lot of effort to gather food without realizing there is a vast treasure in his own home. One day, a more knowledgeable person points out to him that there is a treasure under his house and that he does not need to work so hard, because he is actually quite rich. From that day forth, the person never needs to experience poverty again. Likewise, when we do not realize that we have buddha nature, we are like that poor person. When a master points out our buddha nature and instructs us on how to actualize it, then we gain a vast wealth – the qualities of a peaceful and joyful mind.

Everyone wants to have happiness and avoid suffering. We act as we do in the hope that our actions will bring about happiness, but often they give rise to more and more suffering. The reason for this is that we do not recognize our nature as buddha nature. Recognizing buddha nature is not quick and easy. It takes effort, engaging in contemplation and meditation. Even when someone points this treasure out for us, we still need to do the work of actualizing it. That process takes a lot of effort.

The sixth metaphor compares buddha nature to a type of fruit known in India that is encased within thick layers of peel and shell. One cannot gain access to the fruit without removing layer upon layer of peel and shell. It is very difficult to extract the fruit of this tree, but once we get to it we have this very delicious fruit. Likewise, to awaken our hidden buddha nature we have to eliminate layers and layers of obscurations.

The seventh metaphor compares buddha nature to a statue of the Buddha wrapped in a very dirty cloth. If we remove the cloth, a pristine statue is found inside. No one pays any attention to the bundle of rags because it is so dirty. Likewise, because it is obscured by karma and afflictions, no one pays any attention to the pristine buddha nature within. Like the dirty cloth, the contaminated aggregates of body and mind have the nature of suffering. We can see this very clearly at the time of death. When we die, the clear light nature of mind departs from the contaminated aggregates without any effort on our part. If we are not able to sustain clear light in meditation, then upon death we enter into the bardo state and continue on the cycle of rebirth.

The relentless suffering of birth, aging, sickness, and death is like a hurricane. Day after day we are bombarded by the hurricanes of our actions and negative emotions, and we do not even realize it. The prospect of external hurricanes frightens us and we make a big fuss, but we should be more concerned about the internal hurricanes with which we actually live. The internal hurricanes cannot be eliminated when the sun comes out. They are there regardless of the weather outside.

The eighth metaphor compares buddha nature to the possibility that even a woman of low caste could give birth to a universal monarch. The karma and afflictions that obscure buddha nature are likened to the burden of low caste. Just as it is possible for any woman, old or young, high or low caste, to give birth to a universal monarch, it is possible to eliminate karma and afflictions, thereby gaining control over birth and death, and give rise to the universal monarch-like buddha nature. This is really the case. Though Shakyamuni Buddha was born of an ordinary woman, the sun of his teachings still shines 2,500 years later. His power over karma and the negative emotions is greater than the power of a universal monarch.

The ninth metaphor pertains to finding a statue of the Buddha made of gold that has been buried for thousands of years. It has been there all along, and finally it is discovered.

In order to recognize buddha nature by means of these ten natures and nine metaphors, it is important to be clear about the basis of purification, that which purifies, and the result of purification. The basis of purification is the ultimate nature of the mind. The purifying factors are all of the methods and teachings given by the Buddha in order to show us how to eliminate the two obscurations and actualize our buddha nature. The result of purification is the state of buddhahood itself. We use the natures and metaphors to illuminate the basis of purification, the means of purification, and the pure result.

8

PRESENTATIONS OF BUDDHA NATURE

BUDDHA NATURE IN THE INDIAN TRADITIONS

Now we will look at the ways in which buddha nature is presented in the four Indian philosophical traditions. The two major Hinayana schools, the Vaibhashika and Sautrantika, do not mention buddha nature, but there is mention of *gotra*. Here 'gotra' refers to a potential characteristic. You can also translate 'gotra' as 'lineage,' and in this sense we can say that depending on your family lineage, you have the potential to inherit certain characteristics. Gotra includes this capacity for developing potential traits.

The Sautrantikas understand gotra as a potential within the mental consciousness that can give rise to the qualities of arhats, which were not there before. It is a mental potential that has the capacity to give rise to higher qualities. This is the Sautrantika understanding.

The Vaibhashika school also uses the term 'gotra,' but they are not very clear about it. They do discuss the cause of higher realization or direct insight into the truths, but they discuss these causes in terms of the practice of discipline and training in samadhi and wisdom, which leads to insight. Primarily, discipline is emphasized, and even sometimes itself referred to as gotra, because it gives rise to the qualities of the arya beings.

The Vaibhashikas characterize monks and nuns in terms of four traits that give rise to realization.[36] These same traits apply to all practitioners. The first trait is contentment with the simple robes of a monastic. Monks and nuns should not feel desire for thick robes or ornaments. The second trait is contentment with simple alms. Whatever food they receive is enough to be content; they do not show preferences with regard to food. The third trait is contentment with simple places to sleep; they do not need grand houses and so forth. The fourth trait is the ability to enjoy freedom from distracting conceptual thoughts and activities. All of this really comes down to a preference for outer and inner simplicity – not being attracted to busy-ness, especially the inner chaos of busy, negative thoughts and emotions.

These are the four traits that give rise to realization and the ability to actualize buddha nature. The Vaibhashikas do not use the term 'buddha nature,' but they refer to the causal factors that activate our essential nature.

The most important of the four traits is contentment and lack of desire, an uncommon causal factor that can give rise to realization. The Vaibhashikas hold that desire and lack of contentment are responsible for most types of suffering and also for the inability to manifest the gotra. We can see this for ourselves. When we crave things and are discontent, it gives rise to all kinds of suffering. Greed and discontent destroy our ability to find contentment with whatever we have, however plentiful it is. Greed and discontent are also at the root of most conflict. The teachings on lack of contentment are important and have practical application for all spiritual practitioners.

Practicing the first three traits together is a secondary cause of entering the arya path that has not yet been entered. The fourth trait, enjoying freedom from conceptual distraction, is the direct cause of entering the arya path. The Buddha told the monks and nuns that if they cultivated these four traits, then before long the state of liberation would be attained.

The third Indian philosophical tradition is the Cittamatra, or Mind-Only school. This belongs to the Mahayana, and therefore actually mentions buddha nature. The Cittamatrins developed a unique understanding of buddha nature based on the tathagatagarbha sutras and Asanga's commentary on the *Tathagatagarbha Sutra*. Some Cittamatrins, adhering to the traditional six-consciousness view of mind, do not posit the *alayavijnana* or foundational consciousness. They regard buddha nature as a seed or potential uncontaminated mind that is present in the sixth mental consciousness. They refer to this seed as 'the naturally abiding buddha nature.' For those Cittamatrins who do posit the alayavijnana (and eight types of consciousness altogether), the uncontaminated potentiality is said to reside in this foundational consciousness. They also call it the 'naturally abiding buddha nature.'

In general, the Mahayana schools differentiate between two types of buddha nature – the 'naturally abiding'[37] and the 'ornamental.'[38] Ornamental buddha nature is so named because it can be enhanced, its qualities can be increased, much like adding ornaments. According to the Cittamatra school, the naturally abiding buddha nature is an uncontaminated potential present in the mind, and it is unproduced. It has been present since beginningless time. It is not dependent on other minds or imprints. It is there naturally without having to depend on other factors.

Ornamental buddha nature has five divisions (or gotras or

'families'). These are the sravaka gotra, pratyekabuddha gotra, bodhisattva gotra, indefinite gotra, and interrupted gotra.[39] The sutras mention that the ornamental gotra can become interrupted, and when it is, enlightenment will not be gained. What this means is that for this particular being, it will take a very long time to gain enlightenment. For example, the luminosity of mind is present in someone who is born in an uninterrupted hell realm just as it is present in all sentient beings, but because of the conditions in this realm, it will take that person a very long time to achieve enlightenment. Most of us are in this category because we do not have the Hinayana traits of contentment and lack of desire, and we also do not have the Mahayana trait of having given rise to bodhicitta. Many people belong to the interrupted gotra. Do not worry though; you have a lot of friends here!

In the Cittamatra school, the relation of the naturally abiding buddha nature to ornamental buddha nature is the relation of basis to that which is based on it. The naturally abiding buddha nature is the basis, and ornamental buddha nature is based on it. The naturally abiding buddha nature is not itself the product of causes and conditions – it is spontaneously present – but it is manifested or actualized in dependence on causes and conditions like studying, contemplating, and meditating on the teachings. By engaging in these three activities, our naturally abiding buddha nature is awakened. Once we have awakened naturally abiding buddha nature, we call that which manifests 'ornamental buddha nature.' So 'naturally abiding buddha nature' and 'ornamental buddha nature' refer to the same thing in different contexts.

The Cittamatra school holds that naturally abiding buddha nature is not an imprint, because an imprint is necessarily a composite produced by causes and conditions. It is referred to instead as a potentiality or seed. It is easier to comprehend the Cittamatra view of the relation between these two types of buddha nature as the relation between basis and what depends on the basis. But one can also see naturally abiding buddha nature as ultimate reality, and ornamental buddha nature as conventional reality.

According to the Cittamatra school, the naturally abiding buddha nature is composite. The potential itself is not produced by causes and conditions, but it can be said to be composite in the sense that it becomes a cause that can be enhanced and changed by the application of conditional factors like meditation. It is like a seed that germinates and grows under the right conditions, sunlight, and so forth.

The Cittamatra view of naturally abiding buddha nature is subtle and profound but a little complicated. It is much easier to understand the Middle Way view of buddha nature as uncontaminated, uncompounded, and permanent.

The Madhyamaka or Middle Way understanding of buddha nature is based on the *Perfection of Wisdom Sutras*. The Madhyamikas hold that buddha nature is uncompounded and unproduced. The earlier discussion about the ultimate nature of contaminated mind and the ultimate nature of uncontaminated mind was from the perspective of the Madhyamaka school. For the Madhyamikas, naturally abiding buddha nature abides in these two ways – as the ultimate nature of contaminated mind and as the ultimate nature of uncontaminated mind. Ornamental buddha nature is the conventional or contaminated mind meditating on its ultimate nature. The conventional mind can be enhanced by meditating on the ultimate nature of mind, which frees it from obscurations, enhancing clarity or luminosity. Like an ornament, conventional mind can be enhanced and improved upon, in this case by meditating on the ultimate nature of the mind.

The Cittamatra and Madhyamaka schools use similar terminology, but 'basis' is understood differently. The Cittamatra school holds that naturally abiding buddha nature is the basis, and ornamental buddha nature depends on that basis, very much like crops depend on a field. For the Madhyamikas, however, the relation between basis and that which is based on it is different. Naturally abiding buddha nature is the focus or object of meditation, but the object of meditation depends on what meditates on it, the conventional mind. The basis of meditation is the conventional mind, that which meditates. The conventional mind is purified and its clarity enhanced by the meditation on naturally abiding buddha nature. Therefore, the basis and ornamental buddha nature are the same. This is how they are dependent in the Madhyamaka tradition.

This way of understanding the Madhyamaka view of buddha nature is sufficient, but if you are interested in learning more it is very clearly taught in Maitreya's *Ornament of Clear Realization*,[40] where thirteen types of buddha nature are presented. These are taught because buddha nature can also be described according to the different levels of realization on the path to enlightenment. From a practical perspective, it is helpful to understand naturally abiding buddha nature as the object of meditation by which the obscurations and afflictions of conventional mind are purified. As the intensity of the afflictions decreases, then the ultimate nature of mind becomes more and more manifest. That is how the two buddha natures depend on each other in practice.

BUDDHA NATURE IN TIBET

Now we will look at the presentation of buddha nature in Tibet by the four major Buddhist traditions – the ancient Nyingma, and the Kagyu, Sakya, and Gelug traditions.

The Nyingma presentation is found in Longchenpa's *Treasury of Philosophical Systems*, which principally relies upon the *Sutra of the Arrangement of Trees*.[41] That is the text cited to establish the unique Nyingma understanding of the tathagatagarbha. In that sutra, the Buddha describes the nature of the bodhisattva potential as empty, like space, and its characteristic as radiant clarity. This bodhisattva potential becomes the cause that gives rise to the buddhas of the three times.

The sutra describes the bodhisattva potential as 'the space of primordial purity' and as 'self-occurring wisdom.' When this bodhisattva potential is present in the mind of sentient beings, it is called 'tathagatagarbha.' When this same trait is present in the uncontaminated mind, it is called 'enlightenment,' 'bodhi,' or 'tathagata.' According to the *Ornament of Clear Realization*, this naturally occurring wisdom – the ultimate reality where clarity and emptiness coexist simultaneously – does not need to be cultivated, and nothing needs to be abandoned. If so, is this ultimate wisdom mere space-like emptiness, or are there positive qualities as well? The *Ornament of Clear Realization* speaks of naturally occurring wisdom as not simply empty like space but as containing all of the qualities of the three kayas.

The relationship of naturally occurring wisdom to samsara and nirvana is one of basis to that which is dependent. Ultimate naturally occurring wisdom is the basis from which all phenomena of samsara and nirvana arise. In the unenlightened state, the phenomena of samsara arise, and in the enlightened state, all of the qualities of enlightenment arise. This relationship of basis to that which is dependent is similar to what we find in the Mind-Only school, but this is the only resemblance between the Mind-Only and the Nyingma understandings of buddha nature.

All phenomena within samsara and the basic space of phenomena coexist like the clouds coexist with the sun. Even though the sun can never be entirely and permanently obscured, it can be temporarily obscured by clouds. Just as clouds form and block the sun, the phenomena of samsara arise from the ground of basic space and obscure it. The enlightened qualities of nirvana and the basic space of phenomena coexist like the sun and its rays.

The Nyingma tradition describes buddha nature as the dhatu of basic space (or dharmadhatu) and as primordial self-occurring wisdom. In the Nyingma tradition, it is more helpful to understand it as primordial space, because this enhances our Dzogchen meditation. The distinctive feature of the Nyingma understanding of naturally abiding buddha nature is its equivalence with the basic space of phenomena. In the Kagyu tradition, it is better to understand it as primordial wisdom because this helps with Mahamudra meditation. Many scholars and yogis have said this.

The differences between the Tibetan accounts of buddha nature have to do with naturally abiding buddha nature, not ornamental buddha nature. Ornamental buddha nature is understood in the same way in all traditions: as the clarity of the conventional mind cultivated in dependence on factors like meditation and study. Ornamental buddha nature is the enhancement of the clarity of the ordinary mind and is conditional or dependent on practice.

In the Kagyu tradition, naturally abiding buddha nature is the non-dual wisdom of the dharmadhatu, which pervades all phenomena. It is the indivisible union of the dharmadhatu and primordial wisdom. In this tradition, wisdom is regarded as buddha nature at the level of the basis. At the level of the path, by engaging in nonconceptual meditation with the view free from elaboration, you can actualize it. When the two obscurations are purified, non-dual wisdom becomes the dharmakaya, naturally abiding buddha nature at the level of the resultant state.

Nonetheless, there are two different ways of presenting naturally abiding buddha nature in the Kagyu tradition. Rangjung Dorje and Dolpopa explain it according to the Shentong, or 'other-emptiness,' school. The eighth Karmapa, Mikyo Dorje, understands it according to the Rangtong, or 'self-empty,' school. The differences between Shentong and Rangtong views are the result of differences in the manner in which naturally abiding buddha nature is identified.

It is helpful to know what the debate between these two schools is based on, but I do not think this debate is very important for the practitioner. Remember that the Kagyu understand naturally abiding buddha nature as the non-dual wisdom of the dharmadhatu. Non-dual wisdom has an emptiness aspect and a clarity aspect. Focusing on the clarity aspect directly links us to the Mahamudra practices of the completion stage, where we recognize the inherent luminosity of the mind, or the basis clear light. As it is clearly stated in the *Uttaratantra*, the foundation text of Mahamudra teachings, the clear light nature of mind is unchanging like space. Whether emptiness is empty of other or empty of self has no effect on clear light meditation practice and so does not ultimately matter.

According to Jamgon Kongtrul, in the sutric context the clarity aspect of naturally abiding buddha nature is the same as what is called the 'perfection of wisdom.' In the tantric context, the clarity aspect is variously referred to as 'primordial lord,' as 'innately born clear light,' and as 'Mahamudra.' It is also referred to as *'thig le chen po,'* the 'great drop.' It is not clear whether all Kagyupas would agree with Jamgon

Kongtrul's observation.

The Sakya tradition follows Sakya Pandita's position that naturally abiding buddha nature resides in all sentient beings and that ornamental buddha nature is only present in arya Mahayana practitioners, or in other words, only in bodhisattvas who have directly perceived emptiness. This relationship between the naturally abiding and the ornamental buddha nature is also one of basis and dependent, where naturally abiding buddha nature is the basis and ornamental buddha nature is dependent.

As I explained earlier, the Gelug tradition holds that naturally abiding buddha nature must necessarily be uncompounded, and ornamental buddha nature is compounded or produced. Similarly, when the Sakyas talk about naturally abiding buddha nature, it has to be qualified – it does not simply refer to ultimate reality. They state that the naturally abiding buddha nature is the ultimate nature of the contaminated mind.

Where the Nyingma and Kagyu traditions understand the teachings on buddha nature as teachings of the third turning, the Sakya and Gelug traditions both claim that they derive from the second turning. The Sakyapas and Gelugpas do not deny that the teachings of the third turning present buddha nature; it is obvious that they do. However, although the Gelug and Sakya do speak of a clarity aspect as well as the emptiness of naturally abiding buddha nature, they also say that ultimately, buddha nature is the emptiness aspect, and the aspect of clarity taught in the third turning is not the actual buddha nature. Both traditions hold that the definitive teachings on buddha nature are found in the second turning's presentation of emptiness. Their reasoning is that the ultimate mode of being of naturally abiding buddha nature must be permanent. In their view, the presentation in the third turning of the clarity aspect of buddha nature is not the definitive presentation. They maintain that most of the teachings of the third turning are not to be taken literally but as interpretable. When they present the subject matter of the third turning, they contextualize it as something not to be taken literally.

The Nyingma and Kagyu say that the third turning does give the definitive presentation of buddha nature. The third turning teaches luminosity or clarity as the essence of buddha nature and the ultimate nature of mind, and the Nyingma and Kagyu hold that this is to be taken literally. Proponents of the 'emptiness of other' or Shentong view take this presentation so literally that they hold that all the major and minor marks of an enlightened person are fully present as the tathagatagarbha in every sentient being.

My own view is that no tradition or philosophical school has exclusive rights over buddha nature. The Gelug and Sakya predominantly focus on emptiness because they are attached to emptiness. The Nyingma and Kagyu predominantly focus on the luminosity and clarity of the mind because they are attached to that notion of clarity. From my own perspective, what is significant is that the Buddha used words, examples, and signs as vehicles to actualize buddha nature. The actuality cannot be expressed. The main point is that when we engage in meditation based on these signs, teachings, and examples, we too can experience the tathagatagarbha.

9

CARRYING BUDDHA NATURE INTO OUR OWN PRACTICE

Buddha nature can also be discussed in terms of practice, whether it be at the level of Mahayana sutra, Tantra, Mahamudra, or Dzogchen. In the sutra context, 'buddha nature' refers to the ultimate nature of mind. This ultimate nature could be the ultimate nature of contaminated mind or the ultimate nature of an enlightened mind. To realize it, one practices the union of shamatha and vipasyana. There are many stories of Zen masters who achieved great realization by identifying buddha nature and then sustaining it in meditation.

For the tantric practitioner, it is impossible to engage in the practice without understanding buddha nature. In tantra, we talk about four continuums. The continuum at the level of the basis is buddha nature, so without understanding it we cannot have an actual tantric practice. The core practice of tantra is to see all phenomena as naturally and primordially pure. With this view as our working basis, we practice pure vision, seeing all appearances within samsara as the universe or mandala of deities. This is possible because all phenomena are primordially pure. Without understanding buddha nature, there is no way to engage in this practice of primordial purity in tantra.

Practitioners of Mahamudra rely on the innate clear light of the mind, which is the ultimate aspect of the clarity of the mind. In other words, innate clear light is buddha nature. Without understanding buddha nature, they cannot practice the ultimate clarity of the mind.

In Dzogchen, the emphasis is on the ground of basic space, and how from this basic space of emptiness, all qualities are spontaneously present. This is a very basic understanding of Dzogchen practice. Understanding this is understanding buddha nature, as having the two aspects of emptiness and clarity. Once we understand the emptiness aspect of buddha nature, then we will understand the ground of basic space and how all qualities arise from that basic space.

A SEVEN-POINT SUMMARY

I have briefly mentioned how buddha nature is practiced in the different traditions of India and Tibet. Now, it may be more helpful to have an essential presentation of the practice that is simple and powerful, and which avoids intellectual proliferation. Basically, we need to be introduced to the buddha nature that is present within us. First, we establish buddha nature at the level of the basis as something that is present within us. This is the view of the ground. Then we carry that view into practice in meditation.

Of the five traditional branches of knowledge in Buddhist education,[42] the internal science of the mind is entirely aimed at training the mind, whether from a Hinayana or Mahayana perspective. All of the Buddha's teachings share this aim. Because of this practical orientation of the Buddha's teachings, we always take refuge in the Dharma as well as the Buddha and the Sangha – the Three Jewels – at the beginning of our practice. When we take refuge in the Dharma, that refuge includes all the teachings and the qualities of the truth of cessation and the truth of the path. Of these two, first we cultivate the path.

The teachings of the Buddha are vast and profound, so for an ordinary person it is impossible to study and digest the entire collection. Out of his great compassion and skillful means, the Buddha summarized all of the teachings as the teaching of the Three Jewels. The most important of these is refuge in the Dharma. The most important part of refuge in the Dharma is our own mind. To practice Dharma means to understand the nature of our own mind and how to tame it. This is also what it means to understand our buddha nature. We take refuge in the Dharma to actualize our buddha nature.

The Buddha taught that we are our own lords and protectors, but he also said that we are our own worst enemies. The entire three realms and their inhabitants are nothing but an embodiment of our own mind. Whenever we take rebirth in any of the three realms, the form that we take and the universe that we take birth in are the result of the karma accumulated in our own mind. Underscoring the importance of mind, Shantideva said, in the *The Way of the Bodhisattva*:[43]

> And thus the outer course of things
> I myself cannot restrain.
> But let me just restrain my mind,
> And what is left to be restrained?

For the purpose of practice, it is very important to understand how everything comes from our own mind. Everything is an expression of our mind, so it is important to train our mind. When we understand that, we can begin to appreciate the significance of buddha nature. This is how we should see the sequence of our practice.

There are seven points on how to carry the teachings on buddha nature into practice. These seven points encompass all of the teachings that pertain to buddha nature. There is no scholar in India or Tibet that has anything to say that is not included in these seven points. These seven points summarize the entire collection of teachings on buddha nature.

The first point is a general presentation on buddha nature and how we are to understand and train our own mind. Generally, there are three factors that obscure the mind. Once we have identified those three obscuring factors, then we know how to free ourselves from them.

The second point explains two obscuring factors according to the sravaka perspective. We will look at how these factors are identified and eliminated. Once those are eliminated, we can understand naturally abiding buddha nature and how to awaken it with the four types of mindfulness.

The third point focuses on how the pratyekabuddhas identify grasping at external objects as the fundamental hindrance to experiencing or manifesting buddha nature. To eliminate this grasping, they apply the twelve links of dependent origination in sequential order and then reverse that cycle. We will look at how two resultant states – profound wisdom and inexpressible profound wisdom – are actualized by practicing the twelve links in reverse.

The fourth point is the Mahayana sutra understanding of the factors that obscure buddha nature and their subsequent elimination by relying on calm-abiding and special-insight meditation.

The fifth point explains how tantric practitioners identify the factors that obscure realization of the base continuum, which is buddha nature, and how they practice the tantric path of transformation which gives rise to the resultant state of the illusory body and clear light.

The sixth point explains the Mahamudra practice of buddha nature or the innate clear light mind. In this practice, the factor that obscures buddha nature (clear light mind) is conceptual thought. We will identify the innate clear light at the level of the basis and discuss the four types of yoga as the path, as well as the resultant state of great Mahamudra where body and mind are inseparable.

The seventh point gives the Dzogchen presentation of buddha nature as unobstructed awareness, or *rigpa zangthal*. The obscuring factors are very subtle meditative experiences of bliss, clarity, and nonconceptuality. We have to eliminate these in order to realize rigpa.

Three Obscuring Factors

The first point is a general presentation of the factors, or forms of ignorance, that obscure buddha nature. This will serve as a basis for understanding the approaches of the specific vehicles and schools. Generally speaking, the mind is obscured by three levels of ignorance – innate ignorance, conceptually induced ignorance, and temporary external conditions that give rise to ignorance. Simply put, while we inhabit samsara, we do not see the ultimate nature of the mind. All the events and experiences that unfold in our lives take place without awareness of the actual nature of the mind. To realize our actual buddha nature, we need to first understand and eliminate these three forms of ignorance. Then we can be introduced to the clarity and emptiness of buddha nature, which naturally abides in us.

Ignorance is by nature temporary and can be eliminated. Though we call it 'innate,' even innate ignorance can be eliminated. Innate ignorance is our deeply ingrained grasping, a deep and mistaken conviction that there is something to take hold of. This kind of grasping requires no training; it is not a product of culture or upbringing. It is something that has stayed with us, powered by habit, from one lifetime to the next. For example, when a child is born, she does not need to be taught how to suckle the mother's milk. She knows instinctively how to do that in order to survive. The inclination to sustain our self-existence is driven by deeply ingrained self-grasping. Innate self-grasping impels us to do all sorts of things for the sake of survival without anyone needing to show us how. 'Innate grasping' here does not mean that grasping is a taint innate to the mind. It refers to a conditioning or habituation so deep that it has become spontaneous and innate in that sense. This is the most significant obscuration of buddha nature. Indeed, it is the root of samsara and of all the suffering of our existence – the suffering of birth, sickness, old age, and death. All of this comes from innate grasping or innate ignorance.

Apart from uprooting innate grasping, no technique or remedy can free us from samsara. Techniques and remedies can give us temporary relief. For example, calm-abiding and mindfulness meditation can effectively free us temporarily from suffering, but such practices alone will not completely uproot innate grasping. Innate grasping is like a poisonous tree or shrub. It is not sufficient to cut the branches; we need to completely uproot it.

'Conceptually induced ignorance' refers to ignorance that develops in the form of beliefs and assumptions, regardless of whatever ideological perspective we have. Convictions and attachments to particular positions bind us to an agenda, obscuring our own nature and the real nature of things. This doesn't mean that we should avoid intellectual pursuits; of course we need to study and learn, but that study should become a means of liberation rather than a means of binding us to one theory or another.

Vasubandhu says in his *Abhidharmakosa* that the Buddha taught the skandha of discriminating thoughts because in monastic communities, discriminating thought or conceptual grasping is what binds monks to samsara most tightly. They are bound by their attachment to philosophical positions. When we are attached to our own thoughts and philosophies, they become a binding factor rather than a liberating factor. We can see this in the splintering of the Hinayana tradition into eighteen different schools. This attachment to views is conceptually induced ignorance. In Tibet, we have seen the same thing; the four major Tibetan Buddhist traditions and the Bon tradition were all strongly attached to their respective views, and that attachment led to conflict. The same thing, of course, applies to the West. People become so attached to particular traditions that they separate themselves from other centers.

Having faith and strong connections to our own tradition is very important. It is also very important to respect our sangha. What we are talking about here is the danger of strong grasping, which is like a poison. We need faith and rejoicing, loyalty and so forth, but if attachment becomes so strong that we start to disrespect other traditions, then it becomes an obscuring factor. This kind of strong grasping prevents us from seeing our buddha nature.

The third form of ignorance arises from temporary external conditions. There are two types of temporary external conditions that can obscure buddha nature, even when we know how to meditate and are motivated to practice. The first is the karmic accretions of our skandhas, which arise as physical sickness or as mental problems. Sometimes these problems preclude successful meditation, even though we may have instruction in the techniques. The second is lack of time, being too busy with work and other responsibilities. Therefore, the lack of leisure time becomes an obscuring factor for us.

To remove these obscuring factors we need to recognize and consider changing those things in our situation which prevent us from engaging in meditation and obscure our buddha nature. Our immediate situation might include temporary conditions like physical sickness or lack of health. When we have had problems, we've sought solutions that actually further complicate things. We have to recognize that our real goal is to gain freedom, and that the way to do this is to engage in meditation. The second factor is the mental challenges we face. In the West, there is a lot of loneliness, anxiety, and fear, which destroys our ability to engage in meditation. At the very least, we should find a balance of the elements so that we can gain freedom from gross physical and mental sickness. We can eliminate the gross obscuration of sickness by equalizing the elements.

In order to actualize buddha nature we have to meditate. That is the only way. For this, we need a strong mind. To have a strong mind so that we can meditate, we need a strong and healthy body. There are many techniques to increase physical and mental health and to balance the elements in a way that is conducive to meditation and the recognition of our buddha nature.

Your physical body is constituted of the five elements. Each of these five elements has its respective function to perform, in order to keep your body healthy and to give you vitality. When the elements are balanced, they naturally perform their proper function of vitality and health. Two factors in particular have a big role in maintaining or disrupting balance: food and drugs. Our food is produced with many chemicals, and we are eating many of them. They seem to interfere with the natural function of the five elements, which is to sustain and rejuvenate the body. We also use a lot of drugs, which can interfere with the balance of the five elements. Drugs interfere with the function of the channels in the brain as well as with the life-sustaining wind directly linked with our heart. We need to be careful of what we eat, and partake mindfully in the right amounts. We can benefit from having a certain amount of discipline with regard to our food.

There are also beneficial kinds of exercise, such as yoga, tai chi, and qi qong. These are all very good to practice. For the practice of prana and maintaining health, qi qong is very effective. These physical yogas enable us to balance the external elements and coarse winds. Then, to work with the subtle elements and winds, we can practice *tsa lung* ('channels and winds') as taught in the tantras. This practice balances or harmonizes the most subtle winds.

In the tantric context, tsa lung has a greater purpose than merely balancing the subtle winds. Tsa lung not only harmonizes the subtle winds, but can also purify them. It is possible to eliminate the impure aspects of the winds. As a result, not only do we become healthy but we can eliminate sickness. We live longer without sickness. It doesn't serve much purpose if we live a long life without health! Ultimately however, these practices are not merely for physical health, but are intended to be conducive to realization.

It is important to be aware of these techniques and to know that we have them available to us. There are many methods unique to the

Tibetan tradition that you cannot find in any other traditions, including the Chinese tradition. We are fortunate to have access to these teachings and methods, but we also need a teacher who can transmit the techniques that are appropriate to us. The tsa lung practices which work with the channels, winds, and subtle energy drops are foundational practices; many elaborate techniques and related practices are based on them. These techniques serve to harmonize the outer elements of the physical body and give rise to the realization of buddha nature in this lifetime.

There are powerful methods in the Buddhist tantras, not only for equalizing the elements to support our health, but also for changing the very nature of the contaminated body. When we practice deity yoga and cultivate divine pride, we develop the capacity to transform the coarse body. It is the same with the mind. Our ordinary mind thinks that we are in samsara, and the result of this is that we acquire a samsaric body. If we dwell in divine pride, then even our contaminated body is purified. The reason for this is that everything is made of mind. When you engage in the generation stage yogas, you are not merely observing some deity outside of yourself. The deity is close to you, and finally you yourself take the form of the deity. That is the purpose of the generation stage. By practicing these tantric techniques, you can eliminate sickness and increase longevity, so that you have the opportunity to practice meditation on buddha nature for a long time, and actually experience it in this lifetime.

We have addressed the physical obstacles to meditation, but we also face coarse obscurations of mind on a daily basis. These can take the form of negative thoughts or emotions, which hinder us from recognizing buddha nature. We have to learn to identify our coarse thoughts and emotions so that we can apply techniques to eliminate them.

The techniques for eliminating negative emotions can be practiced on three levels. On the first level, we analyze whatever thoughts or emotions arise with discerning wisdom, and determine whether it is positive or negative. If it is positive, then it is adopted; if not, then it is eliminated. On the second, tantric level of practice, we do not accept or reject what arises or apply antidotes. Using the path of transformation, we see everything in a pure light, whatever it may be. That is the method of the tantric technique. On the third level of practice we leave everything as it is. There is no transformation of impurity; we just look directly at the nature of that thought or emotion. Recognizing the nature itself, we leave it as it is. Those are the three levels on which eliminating negative emotions is practiced.

In actual practice, avoid holding onto expectations. Just pay attention to what you have to do right here and now. What is important here and now is to cultivate joyous effort as you train on the path. To do this, we may have to transcend some of our habits. We know how important it is to connect deeply with our buddha nature in this lifetime. For this, I think discipline is extremely important. No one is going to come and do this for you. We have to do this ourselves. Americans value freedom, but they hardly know what freedom is. We are all human beings; we have to deal with these conditions and this body, so discipline is very important. Without discipline, even though we may know a lot about how to practice, and how to eliminate emotions or purify our body, if we don't have discipline and actually apply the teachings, then this knowledge won't help. Our time is like gold; we should spend it wisely and practice with discipline.

I am not talking about monastic discipline, but real discipline – the discipline of meditation, of taking care of yourself and training your mind. If you are scared or anxious all the time, it is not going to go away by itself. We have to investigate and come to understand the teachings. Then, we need to learn the techniques to practice the teachings and then actually practice. In this way we can learn to take care of our three natures – our external karmic body, our internal channels and winds, and our 'secret' nature, our own mind. We can talk about the enlightened body, the illusory body, and the rainbow body, but at this point those are just words.

It is very important to observe self-discipline by listening to our teachers' instructions, discerning how they apply to ourselves, and then actually applying them in practice, not as a duty forced upon us, but as our own choice. This induces joyous effort, which is ultimately required to practice effectively. As Chandrakirti says, all qualities and all realizations arise from joyous effort. This is a very important point. If you look at the Buddha's story, you can see that all of his qualities resulted from his effort.

The story of the Buddha is supposed to teach us something. He meditated for six years practicing severe austerities. That is an example, but we are supposed to learn from his life story. We can see that the Buddha made a lot of effort to actualize his own buddha nature. First, he gave rise to strong renunciation by establishing that everything in the world is just drama and has nothing to do with buddha nature. Recognizing that it is temporary and thoroughly confused, he cut through grasping. This is renunciation. Then, with renunciation as his basis, he engaged in meditation. Of course, in America it is hard to generate this kind of renunciation, so we have to understand these methods in our own unique context.

We all have at least some time. Let's say once a year, perhaps during a vacation, we could engage in the path of meditation to actualize our buddha nature. Family, friends, work, comfort and enjoyment each have their place, but we should not be emotionally driven or endlessly preoccupied by them. Sometimes we think about this stuff too much. We think we have to fix something or acquire one more thing, but we never actually fix or acquire everything, so we just keep wasting time. It is very difficult for us to give rise to renunciation like the Buddha's, but we can give rise to relative renunciation using whatever time is available to us for the purpose of meditation.

Later, we will explain how to engage in a meditation practice in one session that integrates view, meditation, and conduct.

Obscurations from the Sravaka Perspective

From the sravaka perspective, the main obscuration of buddha nature is grasping at an intrinsically existing self. This grasping gives rise to all of our negative emotions, like craving and aversion. It is responsible for all of our immediate and future suffering. This self-grasping also generates grasping at external phenomena as intrinsically real. We grasp at things as 'mine:' my culture, my religion, my friend, my teacher, my stuff. This possessiveness is very strong. If we receive a compliment, then our ego is inflated; if we are criticized, then we feel hurt. This vulnerability comes from grasping, both internally and externally.

What we call 'my self' is the conventional mind. When we grasp at the conventional mind as intrinsically existing, then we obscure the actual nature of mind. The actual nature of the mind has two aspects, clarity and emptiness. However, when the actual nature is obscured by grasping, it is difficult to distinguish the clarity of the mind from the grasping at 'me' and 'mine.' If we haven't realized the emptiness and clarity of the mind, we focus outwardly and cling to dualistic notions of self and other. When we see external objects, we cling to them, becoming attached or averse to them. This outwardly projected mind doesn't see its own clear, empty nature.

These obscurations happen based on causes and conditions. The cause of the obscuration that hides buddha nature is attachment to the self as intrinsically existing. This obscuration is the basis upon which we impute a self. As humans we are attached to the psychophysical aggregates – the coarse body, our coarse feelings, and our coarse thoughts – and we impute selfhood onto them.

If we are able to cultivate and experience the clarity and emptiness of the mind, then that experience becomes a condition that supports the realization of buddha nature. This is quite difficult though because our thoughts concerned with the self are very coarse and distracting. This gross sense of self obscures the very subtle clarity of the mind. We start by learning to deal with gross self-grasping, recognizing how it arises and how we can eliminate it. Then we can begin to work on subtle self-grasping.

It is very important to understand that the actual nature of self-grasping itself is buddha nature. We shouldn't imagine that buddha nature is deeply buried within the layers and layers of gross thoughts and grasping. If every self-grasping thought has buddha nature, why don't we recognize it? If we can recognize self-grasping, why not its actual nature? The reason for this is that we are talking about the subtle luminosity or clarity of the mind. It is difficult for us to experience this because our thoughts and emotions keep us in a state of turbulence like a hurricane. The winds of karma are blowing, and we have never known any other condition than being caught in the storm. The struggle has exhausted us, and we haven't the energy to see our real nature.

So how do we become able to see our buddha nature? In the sravaka tradition, we first need to understand the process. Basically, once there is grasping at an intrinsically existing self, there is also grasping at external phenomena. All of this grasping gives rise to the full spectrum of judgments and reactions that cause our suffering. Looking more closely at the process, the objects at which we grasp are actually our own skandhas – form, feeling, judgments, motives, and agendas. Based on our experience of form and sense objects, we generate mental or physical feelings – positive, negative, or neutral. Based on those feelings, we generate discriminating judgments, which are either good or bad. Based on discriminating judgments, we generate motives and schemes, which end in suffering.

In order to interrupt this process of grasping, which obscures our buddha nature, we can rely on the four foundations of mindfulness – mindfulness of body, feelings, thoughts, and phenomena. On the basis of mindfulness of feelings, we can subdue our judgments and reactions, since it is feelings that give rise to them.

It is our gross negative thoughts that ultimately create our suffering, negative emotions, anxiety, and fear. When we manifest these mental states, it is because of discriminatory thoughts, which judge this feeling as good and that one as bad. In order to eliminate this, we need to look at our feelings and perceptions. Our feelings arise from our body, so we can look at the nature of the body and see how it is the nature of suffering. When we understand the body as the cause of suffering, then we can generate detachment from our body and the feelings we are experiencing. If we analyze the question of where the self is in the skandhas, we find that there is no self in any of them, and we sustain this non-finding in meditation. We can further enhance this selflessness in our meditation by analyzing our sensations and feelings. The gross distracted thoughts are abandoned when feelings or sensations are seen as momentary. By witnessing the momentary, fleeting nature of feelings, we are able to inhibit the gross thoughts and judgments that arise from them and create our suffering.

Once we have been introduced to selflessness or emptiness, then our gross thoughts hinder us from sustaining the meditation. The sravaka tradition uses the practice of mindfulness of sensations to eliminate thoughts, because it is our sensations that give rise to thoughts. So they look at their sensations, good or bad, scanning from the top of the head down to the tip of the toes. Wherever they are looking, they see that sensations are momentary; they come and go. Nowadays, this is often referred to as 'vipassana' and 'mindfulness' meditation, and it is very effective at eliminating negative thoughts.

This is also the reason the vipassana tradition uses the breath in meditation. If it is our feelings and sensations that give rise to negative and conflicting thoughts, then we can look at the sensations themselves to get rid of these reactive thoughts. When we focus on the breath and the wind moving in and out, then wind and sensations are directly linked with one another. So as we focus on wind, we are freed from reacting to our sensations.

This is how sravakas meditate on the four foundations of mindfulness – body, feelings, thoughts, and phenomena. When we engage in meditation on the breath, that is part of the mindfulness of the body. As we focus on the breath, inhaling and exhaling, we become more relaxed and calm. When we look at our feelings and sensations, we cannot pinpoint a truly existing feeling, because our feelings are based on our body and our body is in constant flux. Through this analysis, the sravakas come to the conclusion that there is a lack of a permanent self because everything is in constant flux. Talk about the dissolution of a self – nowhere in the skandhas is there anything that is permanent; everything is undergoing constant change. There is no permanent, independent, eternal self. Nevertheless, we think there is a self. It is important to understand that this is a very powerful method to eliminate negative emotions. This is how sravakas actually practice.

We have to be careful here how we market the teachings. For Hinayana practitioners, beyond this explanation of a lack of a unitary, permanent self, there are no teachings on buddha nature or the more profound emptiness of the Middle Way. Disciples who are the direct audience for the Hinayana teachings are presented with the teachings in this fashion. They are not the actual target audience for the teachings on buddha nature. Nonetheless, if you follow the teachings of the Hinayana tradition, then you will get closer and closer to understanding buddha nature, because the gross mind becomes more and more subtle and you remove layer upon layer of obscurations.

These teachings are very effective at purifying the contaminated gross body and feelings and preventing chasing after thoughts and feelings. Their techniques are sometimes more profound and more detailed than the Mahayana teachings for cutting through attachment to thoughts and feelings directly. That is why I am presenting these Hinayana practices, because even though they are not directly related to buddha nature, they are related in terms of your own practice, as you pass through these stages.

So this is the view of the sravakas, and how they understand the lack of an eternally existing, unitary self. In terms of conduct or practice, the sravakas emphasize the conduct of discipline. On the basis of their view and conduct, they have three abandonments on the path to arhathood – the abandonment of grasping at the notion of a truly existing self, the abandonment of engaging in inauthentic moral practices, and the abandonment of the doubtful, afflicted mind. As an example of abandoning inauthentic moral practices, some Hindus practice the discipline of punishing the body. That is an example of an inauthentic discipline, to be abandoned by the sravakas. Also, 'doubt' here refers to doubt about one's view and meditation. Lacking conviction or confidence is to be abandoned.

The four resultant states are, first, the state of the stream enterers, where one gains confidence in the Dharma and enters the path. This is the stream of rebirth that will bring you to the ocean of arhathood. Second is the once-returner, third is the path of no return, and finally there is the state of the arhat, where one has eliminated the ignorance of self-grasping.

The reason I am mentioning the Hinayana path is that they have a lot of very helpful practices related to the mindfulness of the body and feelings, including the practice of breathing. These techniques can give rise to freedom from many forms of suffering. If we examine the skandhas for a self and fail to find it, this can be a very liberating practice for us. Sometimes, if we are able to sustain this type of analytical practice on selflessness, it can really help us engage in the practice of *zangthal*, or unimpeded transparency. We can use that even when we are dealing with Dzogchen techniques, which are beyond mind.

These Hinayana practices can indirectly help us awaken our buddha nature. That does not mean that as a practitioner you need to go through the Hinayana path, but I am giving you options. Over two thousand years ago, these teachings came directly from the Buddha — and they are very powerful.

Sometimes these teachings are very important even for tantric and Dzogchen practitioners. Conduct is very important. We do not need to adopt the precepts of Hinayana conduct, but there is a lot that we can learn and use from this tradition, in our own practice of ethics and discipline. People in America have a lot of strange rules and judgments about each other's conduct. I think some of these instructions on conduct for sravakas can help. They are not intellectually difficult or complicated and can be kept simple. Even the great masters of Mahayana sutra and tantra, such as Tsongkhapa, say that conduct like that taught in Hinayana is very important. Sometimes people encounter a lot of difficulty, and that is often a product of their own habits. Tsongkhapa says that even tantric practitioners should have external conduct like the Hinayana tradition. That does not mean that we need to follow it exactly, but that conduct is important.

Even though you may be engaging in profound tantric practices, your conduct should be simple. Don't engage in too many activities. Live a simple lifestyle like the sravaka disciples. That is what Tsongkhapa emphasized. Internally we may engage in these higher practices and have realization, but externally our conduct should be as simple as a sravaka's. When we have the discipline of sustaining a simple lifestyle, then it is easier to suppress negative emotions. This makes our mind conducive to practicing without many obstacles or hindrances.

How do we apply that simple conduct of the sravakas in our own life? We all need to depend on material necessities; that is our reality. The way that we carry these teachings on simple conduct into practice is to refrain from viewing material possessions as an object of refuge. They will not give rise to freedom from suffering. So often material possessions are all that we care about. Even though we have to rely on them, we should change our attitude toward them and know their limited role in terms of our own happiness. As a practitioner, we should see our practice of dharma and our meditation as the sole factors that give rise to happiness.

Practicing this simple conduct of limiting our projects and activities is really important. I can see this in my own life. We are all saying that we want to engage in practice, but if we are lost in the pursuit of mundane goals and activities, then we have no time and leisure to actually engage in meditation. Our activities, of course, may help others as well, but when we get lost in so many projects, we will not develop genuine qualities that arise from practice. We will not have time to meditate.

Obscurations for the Pratyekabuddhas

The pratyekabuddhas are Hinayana practitioners who are considered to be of higher capacity than the sravakas. Not only do they understand the selflessness of the person, but they also understand the selflessness of the phenomenal world. The sravakas focus on the selflessness of the person and not on the selflessness of external phenomena. The pratyekabuddhas understand external phenomena to be nothing but an expression or embodiment of the mind, with no intrinsic existence. For them there is no internal self or external object, and what remains is the non-dual wisdom of one's own mind. I discussed two types of profundity earlier, and this is the first type – wisdom that is free from the duality of self and other. If we eliminate our grasping at a personal self and grasping at external phenomena, this is what remains. The pratyekabuddhas are able to sustain this in meditation, and that is why they are superior to the sravakas. As for their motivation or aspiration, they generate powerful aspirations to be born in areas where there are no buddhas. That is why they are called solitary realizers. They achieve realization in such places and then give teachings.

The unique quality of the pratyekabuddhas is the two profundities – profound wisdom and inexpressible profundity. When they engage in giving teachings to others, they maintain that if you have to use words or speech, then you are necessarily using thought, which entails volition and action. Their position is that volition and action diminish inner realization, so they give teachings without resorting to language. They teach using physical signs and mudras; that is one of their unique qualities.

Historically, when Shakyamuni Buddha appeared in India, there were many solitary realizers there. When the Buddha appeared, they decided that it was no longer their time so they miraculously traveled to other places. The accounts of the Buddha's life speak of five hundred pratyekabuddhas flying in the sky in Sarnath, who fell to the earth when the Buddha appeared. Some say they were actually commanded down by the power and majesty of the Buddha.

In terms of their practice, pratyekabuddhas prefer isolated locations where there are no people. Normally, they go to cemeteries and do their practice of contemplating death and impermanence through the twelve links of dependent origination. They proceed through these links in a forward and reverse manner to enhance their realization of non-dual wisdom, which is their primary view and wisdom-aspect practice. In terms of the method aspect of the path, they generate compassion based on the practice of the four immeasurables.

In a nutshell, the view of the pratyekabuddhas is to realize the selflessness of the person and phenomena. They then engage in two types of meditation – shamatha and vipasyana. The vipasyana or analytical meditation uses the four foundations of mindfulness – body, feelings, thoughts, and mental objects to enhance their understanding of selflessness. To stabilize their meditation on the foundation of that understanding, they then rely on nine stages of shamatha or calm-abiding practice to dwell in that realization of selflessness. Through this method, they are able to directly perceive the sixteen qualities of the four noble truths distinctly and clearly. This is how they move closer and closer to understanding buddha nature, because their mind is becoming more and more subtle through the practice. They would not use these terms to describe their practice, but we can say that is what is happening.

Their meditation is very profound. Simply by focusing on the noble truth of suffering and the ultimate nature of suffering, they are able to give rise to the realization of the rest of the four noble truths. Even though they do not have to go one by one through each truth, simply by understanding the truth of suffering, they are able to apprehend the other three truths.

This technique is very direct and experiential. It is not simply a conceptual understanding. They look at their own body, their feelings, how they react to thoughts and emotions. They really experience the reality of suffering; it is not the grand metaphysical analysis of a scholar. They are practice oriented, experiential in nature. That is very powerful.

As the teachings spread into China and Tibet, they became more and more intellectualized, and lost their vitality and experiential orientation. People began to debate and compose treatises to differentiate between traditions and schools. As a result, people lost track of experiential understanding. Everyone will say that the four noble truths are very important, but really they have lost track of the experiential aspect of the teachings. The noble truth of suffering, for example, has to be understood at the experiential level. We really need to understand these teachings as they relate to our own body and experience, not simply through an intellectual understanding.

Obscurations in the Mahayana Sutras

I will now explain buddha nature in the context of the Mahayana sutra. Mahayana sutra practitioners are the direct audience for the teachings on buddha nature. Within the context of the Mahayana sutras, 'buddha nature' refers to the ultimate nature of the contaminated mind. Even though, as its very nature, it is beyond any impurities, we have these temporary impurities that we have to purify. When these have been purified, then our buddha nature is awakened. In order to eliminate these temporary impurities, we have practices at the level of the basis and path. The basis is the union of clarity and emptiness; the path is the inseparability of method and wisdom. As a result of this union of method and wisdom, we can attain the resultant state, which is the actualization of the two kayas.

The method of introducing the nature of the contaminated mind differs between the Indian and Tibetan traditions. In a nutshell though, the contaminated mind itself is not the source of samsara or nirvana. It is the ultimate nature of the contaminated mind that is the basis of both samsara and nirvana. This is introduced in the beginning in terms of the aspects of clarity and emptiness. This introduction can be performed in accordance with three traditions. In the ancient traditions of India, China, and Tibet, the luminosity or clarity aspect of the mind was introduced first. These traditions emphasized the clarity aspect more than the empty aspect, which is very powerful in terms of tantric practice. The second tradition, that of the new schools in Tibet, emphasizes the empty aspect of the mind. Lastly, we can introduce the union of clarity and emptiness, which is the tradition of Mahamudra and Dzogchen.

The introduction is given so that we can recognize the nature of the mind. We should not be satisfied with simply being introduced. If we did not actually recognize it, then we missed the whole point. It is the same as when we are introduced to people; the purpose of being introduced is to be able to connect and relate to each other. It is the same here. We need the introduction so that we can relate to the practice.

In my own experience, being introduced to emptiness or clarity or both is not like a performance or ritual. The way I introduce the nature of the mind, and the way that we can recognize it, is as follows. First, we need to generate conventional bodhicitta based on love and compassion. Then, we should enter into meditation in which we remain in an uncontrived, natural state. If we can rest in an uncontrived, natural state without applying antidotes, then we just remain in that state regardless of what thoughts arise, not abandoning some or accepting others. We have to simply rest and recognize with mindfulness. Very powerful mindfulness is required here. Whatever thoughts arise, we recognize them with mindfulness that is free from grasping. It is like an image that appears in a mirror; the mirror does not get attached to the images that are reflected in it. So we simply recognize thoughts and appearances as they arise without grasping at them. When we can rest in such a way and there is clarity, then we recognize the experience of clarity. When thoughts do not arise, we simply recognize that with mindfulness. When there is stability, we recognize stability. We don't need to rely on any antidotes or other methods. When we can observe our mind in this way, we notice that all of the movements within the mind are momentary and unceasing. Our intention is to just look at these thoughts and appearances as they arise, with strong mindfulness. Just recognize their arising and ceasing with mindfulness. This is the introduction. This is sufficient in the beginning. Then we try to sustain this in our meditation.

The most important point thing to remember about this technique is that we should let the mind remain in an uncontrived state, without trying to do anything. Then, with powerful mindfulness, we sustain that sense of great emptiness. If we can dwell and sustain that experience of great emptiness, then clarity will dawn by itself. The sense of great emptiness refers to the empty aspect of space, the absence of any obstruction, reference point, or fixation. When we engage in this meditation, then in terms of our own recognition or mental knowing, we are not fixating on anything. The meditation is completely transparent, without any fixation. Even though there is this aspect of knowing or clarity, it is without any fixation, not stuck to or bound by anything. That is what we mean by 'empty space without reference point.' Therefore, we can call this a space-like meditative absorption.

In terms of practice, of course finding and sustaining this meditation requires a little analysis in the beginning. When we meditate on the nature of mind, there is an inherent sense of self that arises. We think of a self that is separate from awareness. We then engage in a meditation to find this sense of self, and what we find is that the self is nothing but a product of mind and mental factors. There is no substantial self to be found apart from what is constructed by mind and mental factors themselves. When we realize this, we then can meditate on this nature of emptiness or selflessness without fixation. Our concepts and thoughts are products of the movement of the mind and mental factors, which all dissolve into the aspect of the clarity of mind. We then engage in space-like meditation where, just like space, we are free of fixation, center or limit, boundary, or reference point. That is how we maintain the meditative absorption. Then, in the post-meditative state, whatever we see or experience is understood to be illusory. We do not want to arise from our space-like meditation and then see things as truly existing. We should see through them, see their illusory nature. This is the illusion-like meditation of the post-meditative state.

These three points (analytical meditation on any sense of an inherent self, maintain uncontrived meditation free of fixation, and illusoriness in post-meditation) are very important to recognize at the level of the basis. If we do not get introduced to these three sequential points at the level of the basis, then when we engage in the practice of calm abiding and special insight, we can easily lose our way. We may need to read things in a book or check back in our notes, but by then it is too late. But once we can recognize the level of the basis, it becomes very natural and easy to understand when we engage at the level of the path. That is carrying the union of calm abiding and special insight on the path.

Once we are able to recognize the level of the basis as introduced by practicing these three points, it becomes easy to understand the level of the path, and how we are to carry the union of method and wisdom into practice without separation. It becomes easy when we have the proper introduction at the level of the basis. When we talk about the union of method and wisdom, wisdom is special insight and method is bodhicitta. Our method should dawn as an ornament of engaging in the practice of special insight. This is rather difficult to explain in the sutra tradition, but in the Mahamudra and Dzogchen tradition it is thoroughly explained. When we practice insight, bodhicitta is right there as an ornament, and we do not need to engage in a separate practice. The method aspect of bodhicitta increases due to the power or inherent potential of insight, and bodhicitta is thereby naturally enhanced or intensified. If we engage in this type of practice, then we can talk about a union of method and wisdom. Without this kind of understanding, we end up engaging in them as if they were separable, one or the other.

The path is to be actualized or traversed in a state of meditative absorption. That means that once we have been introduced to the view at the level of the basis, it is important to sustain that in our meditation. Once the view has been recognized, there is no need for further intellectual analysis. If we keep on engaging in analysis, we will find that it goes in an endless loop forever. The key point is that once we have been introduced, we need to sustain that in a single-pointed meditative absorption. The benefit of practicing this key point is that if we can sustain that concentration, then it becomes like the current of a great river; it flows unceasingly until our goal is reached. We should sustain that concentration unceasingly in our own continuum, like the continuum of a river.

The aspirational prayer in the *Younge Ngondro* practice describes how we should maintain this unceasing continuum of meditation that is just like a river, until it reaches the ocean of enlightenment.

> The river of non-conceptual samadhi flows,
> from the Mt. Kailash of your accumulated virtue,
> May it effortlessly and quickly join with the
> completely pure and peaceful ocean of awakened mind.[44]

When we practice the union of calm abiding and special insight, we can achieve the resultant state of the two kayas, the dharmakaya and rupakaya. To achieve the two kayas, we engage in the practice of insight, whose natural ornaments are bodhicitta, loving kindness, and compassion. While sustaining special insight, we are practicing bodhicitta as its ornament. Bodhicitta is what is really responsible for eliminating the two obscurations and perfecting the two accumulations. The role of insight while engaging in the two accumulations is to control the mind and its negative tendencies. Within the sphere of special insight, we engage in all six perfections, and the essence of the six perfections is bodhicitta itself. So bodhicitta and all of the six perfections are practiced as an ornament or display of the practice of special insight. When we gain freedom from all forms of sickness, disease, aging, and death, the resultant state is the dharmakaya. Simultaneously, however, we achieve the rupakaya, by which we are able to benefit others through different emanations. The dharmakaya fulfills our own purpose, which is freedom from negative thoughts, emotions, birth, and death.

The enhancement practice within the context of the Mahayana sutras is the practice of *tonglen* ('giving and taking'). In order to actualize buddha nature and realize it directly, we need the support of merit. Merit refers to the capacity, power or potential of mind that enables our meditation to actually become conducive to the path. Merit is what is able to overcome resistance in our meditation; it is what allows our meditation to arise as the path. As problems arise on the path of meditation, we should engage in the practice of bodhicitta, and the most powerful way to practice this is by practicing tonglen. Actualizing bodhicitta requires great capacity of the mind, great karmic support. Just as without health and good nourishment we will not be able to digest a potent medicine, in the absence of karmic support, we will not have enough merit to digest this powerful medicine of bodhicitta. We need to have the backing of good karma, which is what we call merit.

The practice of tonglen is the cultivation of the right mental attitude. We do not need to physically give or take anything; this is a mental practice. We have a lot of mental attachment, fixation, and grasping, so when we are able to fully dedicate our body, speech, and mind to other beings, we are able to make our mind much more expansive. When we are able to dedicate in this way, then we do not have to be concerned with a fear of losing anything. It is really a mental attitude that we are trying to change.

American culture is actually very narrow-minded. People are rigid, not very expansive or inclusive. When I came here, if I had not continued with my practice of tonglen, there is a danger I could have become like that. That rigidness gives rise to a sense of fear and loneliness.

When we engage in the practice of tonglen to make our minds more expansive, we also need to be mindful of impermanence and death. We should think like this: 'I am a dharma practitioner; I am supposed to be a Mahayana practitioner. Therefore, if I cling to myself with strong grasping, if I am very rigid and narrow-minded, I still have nothing to hold onto; there is nothing permanent or eternal to grasp. Therefore, I am going to dedicate my life, my body, my speech, and my mind to other beings.' Life is impermanent, and no matter how much we may try to hold onto it, there is actually nothing there.

Even though the teachings tell us that buddha nature is timelessly inherent in all beings and that we are inherently untainted, the elimination of temporary afflictions and obscurations takes effort. For this reason, we have these many methods.

Obscurations in Tantra

In tantra, we talk about the three continuums – the continuum of the basis or ground, the continuum of method, and the continuum of the result. The tantras emphasize the clarity aspect of the nature of contaminated mind. The clarity aspect is emphasized in the view of the ground continuum. The ground continuum is introduced as self-clear, primordially clear, the innate clear light of the mind. The ground continuum is also referred to as the 'basis clear light' and is called this because it exists naturally at the level of the ground. Even though we may not have experienced the subtlest basis clear light, it does exist as the actual basis.

We have not experienced the basis clear light because we have so many obscurations and concepts, but we can still be introduced to its nature. We are like a child who has never seen the blue sky because it has been cloudy for a very long time. An older person can introduce the child to the idea that there is an empty, blue expanse beyond the clouds. Even though the child has never witnessed that space free of clouds, it could be introduced in that way. Likewise, even though we have never seen the basis clear light, we can be introduced to its nature.

In tantra, we call this the 'continuum of the ground.' In Mahayana sutra, it is called 'tathagatagarbha' or 'buddha nature.' In tantra, the ground continuum and the subtlest clear light of the mind are one and the same thing. This is introduced to us within the context of the word initiation, where we are introduced to the nature of clear light. We are introduced to the subtlest clear light as the basis of the union of bliss and emptiness. This subtlest clear light is also the basis of actualizing the illusory body. It is also the source or basis of all samsara and nirvana. This is how one is introduced to clear light in the context of the fourth, or word, initiation.

Once we are introduced to the ground, we carry it into the practice of the path. In tantra, we do not use the distinction between calm abiding and special insight. We instead rely on the method of the generation and completion stages, which we carry on the path of clear light.

When I discussed the Mahayana sutras, I indicated that the basis of purification is buddha nature or the tathagatagarbha. The thing that we are actually purifying is our subtle grasping at intrinsic reality. In the context of tantra, the basis of purification is the ground continuum, which is subtle clear light. The thing to be purified is ordinary appearances and our grasping at them. In order to do this we rely on the method of the generation and completion stages. The result of purification is the illusory body and clear light – pure body and pure mind.

In tantra, the enhancement practices involve unconventional conduct. Even though we engage in the generation and completion stages, ordinary appearances still arise. In order to cut through our attachment to these, we engage in unconventional forms of conduct. Some of this conduct may go against the law or be regarded as immoral by societal standards; nonetheless, we can engage in these practices through visualization in our own home or in remote isolated places. Practices like korde rushen,[45] for example, are methods to engage in unconventional conduct for the purpose of channeling and suppressing our attachment to ordinary thoughts and concepts.

These practices can be very powerful for people in the West, especially tantric practitioners. You Westerners have been made very conservative through your cultural upbringing. You have very rigid notions about right and wrong and the correct way of thinking. All of this is within the domain of ordinary perceptions and concepts. Sometimes our minds become very narrow because we are fixated on our cultural norms. So we can benefit from these unconventional practices because what we are doing, - the way we think, feel, and live - is already crazy. We are crazy inside, so let's go crazy outside. Then we can see our craziness.

We need to understand the best way to engage in these crazy yogic practices. There are three steps – first, we openly display our craziness. We are intoxicated and crazy because of all our negative thoughts and emotions, so we express that outwardly. We do not hide it. Second, we look at the nature of our craziness. Third, we cut through it. Destroy it. That is how we purify this negativity through unconventional yogic conduct.

This type of practice and conduct is never be done in a way that is disrespectful of others. The whole purpose is to look at our own ordinary body, speech, and mind and realize that we are bound by ordinary thoughts and perceptions. This is what really obscures our buddha nature, these ordinary gross thoughts and emotions.

That is why we see these crazy yogis carrying kapalas, malas of bone, and kangling thighbone horns. These are meant to destroy and eliminate our gross attachment to conventional thoughts and appearances, and to remind us of our own impermanence. They destroy conventional appearances by reminding us that this is our karma. This is where we will go in the end. Right now, all of this is covered by our flesh and beautiful socks, but there is a nice kangling inside. We need to recognize and know these things, to be mindful of impermanence and death.

In Mahayana sutra, the enhancement practice was tonglen. In tantra, it is the practice of yogic conduct. If we have the conditions or practices that enable us to recognize the ground continuum, then it becomes possible to realize buddha nature in this very life.

Obscurations in Mahamudra

In Mahamudra, we also talk about the basis or ground, the path, and the result. 'Base Mahamudra' refers to the innate subtlest mind, which is the ultimate nature of mind experiencing bliss, clarity, and nonconceptuality. The innate subtlest mind is the very essence of these three. This is what is introduced at the level of the base by masters, like Saraha and Naropa, who have perfected the completion stage yoga practices. We are introduced to this innate, subtlest mind through ordinary mind, because that is all that we know. While abiding in ordinary mind, we are asked to remain in an uncontrived state of ordinary mind.

In Mahamudra, there is no specific object to be abandoned or purified. In the Mahayana sutras, we are trying to purify grasping at intrinsic reality by employing antidotes. In tantra, we are trying to transform or eliminate ordinary appearances and perceptions that obscure buddha nature by practicing the two stages, the generation and completion stages. But in Mahamudra, there is no specific object to be abandoned. While we are engaging in meditation – a natural uncontrived state of sustaining ordinary mind – we make sure that we are not prevented from experiencing ordinary mind by subtle concepts, agitation, or dullness. Those three are the obscuring factors to be purified. That is not to say that concepts are intentionally purified; there is a difference here between this practice and the practice of elimination. There is no intentional elimination of thoughts.

There are four yogas that belong to the path Mahamudra – the yogas of unification, one taste, freedom from elaboration, and the yoga of non-meditation. Even though Mahamudra belongs to the tantric vehicle, Mahamudra does not recommend a lot of methods. In Mahamudra, we don't apply a lot of different methods. Rather, you should engage in a simplified practice whose main focus is meditation. You should receive one initiation, Chakrasamvara for example, and then instruction on one of the six yogas of Naropa, and then you should apply this to your practice. The main practice is meditation itself, specifically the method of sustaining the uncontrived state of ordinary mind. For that, we have the four yogas of Mahamudra, which correspond to the different levels of realization of the practitioner.

The first yoga, the yoga of unification, refers to the stage where the practitioner directly realizes the base continuum of clear light. There is a direct recognition of the basis clear light, and then one sustains that single-pointedly in meditation. The focus here is on the tathagatagarbha itself; there is no other object. You should not visualize deities or recite mantra; there is just a pure absorption on buddha nature itself. Within this first yoga, there are sequential stages of concentration, but we won't go through them yet here.

The yoga of one taste refers to the stage at which one is sustaining the basis clear light in one's meditation for a long time. Here, the aspect of clarity and the aspect of emptiness of the clear light mind, which is the tathagatagarbha, become of one taste.

The yoga of free from elaboration refers to a state in one's meditation on the ground of basis clear light that is free from all conceptual elaboration, in the form of subtle dullness and agitation. In this state, one nakedly perceives the dharmadhatu.

The fourth yoga is the yoga of non-meditation, which refers to a state where you do not need to engage in any other meditation apart from sustaining the continuum of meditation on buddha nature. You do not need to rely on other methods to realize the four kayas. Apart from maintaining the continuum of that meditative absorption, it does not require a lot of effort. Therefore, it is called the yoga of no meditation.

The resultant Mahamudra is the actualization of the non-dual Mahamudra or the state of enlightenment.

We can also use enhancement practices in Mahamudra. One of the main obstacles to the realization of Mahamudra is that we experience bliss, clarity, and nonconceptuality as a result of meditation. These are experiences, not realizations. There is a danger that we will cling to these experiences as realization, so the enhancement practice is to make sure we cultivate the ability to be careful in making a clear distinction between what are inner experiences and what is realization. Don't confuse the two.

Obscurations in Dzogchen

In the context of Dzogchen, buddha nature is not just the subtlest clear light of the mind, but rigpa, primordial awareness itself.

In the context of tantra and Mahamudra, when we are introduced to buddha nature, it is done by introducing the aspect of clarity and emptiness within the domain of the mind. Mind is the basis, and clarity and emptiness are attributes or qualities of the mind. In Dzogchen, when we talk about the tathagatagarbha or rigpa, it is as the essence of clarity and emptiness, which is to say that it is beyond mind. Rigpa is wisdom that is the inseparable union of basic space and awareness. That is what is introduced as rigpa, which is beyond mind.

Having introduced rigpa at the level of the basis, on the path we talk about four modes of resting. The resultant state is the four thogal visions.

It is not enough to simply be introduced to rigpa, the wisdom that is the union of basic space and awareness. We need to actualize it in this very lifetime. In order to actualize it, we need to rely on a method. It is not sufficient to simply maintain mind in its uncontrived natural state and eliminate the subtle dullness and agitation while doing so. We have to rely on a method that is beyond mind. That is why we rely on the four modes of resting or settling into the natural state. These four methods of resting are: settling the view naturally like a great mountain; settling the meditation naturally like resting like an ocean; settling conduct naturally by resting in appearances; and the resultant state of resting in rigpa.

'Resting like a mountain' refers to the practice of meditation. The view is the ground of meditation, and to meditate on the ground we should be like a mountain. A mountain is not moved or disturbed by external activities or internal thoughts, so our meditation should not be stirred by external or internal distractions. One should be settled without wavering in the view of the ground. The Buddha entered a mountain-like samadhi before he achieved enlightenment, and vowed not to get up until he achieved the resultant state.

We should maintain our mind in an undistracted state, but we should also settle our body and speech without movement. This results in a great settling of mind and body like a mountain, just like the arhats of the past. Practically, what this means is that we should meditate by cutting all physical activity. Even if we are not able to cut through all mental activity in the beginning, we should be able to sit without movement, without any utterance. Practice. Just like the Buddha did. We can do the same. Adopt a posture, have some discipline, and be in that, gradually increasing the time span.

The second method of resting is like an ocean. We can imagine a great ocean free from all waves, a completely calm, blue expanse with great stillness and clarity. We should rest like that great ocean, settle into rigpa itself. There is great clarity and stillness, without being obstructed by waves of thoughts or dullness.

Following the meditation stage of settling like the great ocean, in our post-meditative conduct, we rest in the nature of thoughts, perceptions, and appearances, which is the third resting. This means that in the post-meditative state, even though we are bound to have thoughts and perceptions, we are not going to cling to or have attachment to those perceptions. Instead, those thoughts and perceptions are going to enhance our experience of rigpa. This is why we call resting in the nature of appearances 'conduct.'

Fourth is resting in the resultant state of rigpa. While engaging in this method of resting, in meditation and in post-meditation, all thoughts and appearances enhance our resting, our experience of rigpa. When this happens in the course of this lifetime, we achieve the resultant state of naked intrinsic awareness itself. At that stage, we have perfected the ultimate buddha nature according to the Dzogchen tradition, which is the awakening of naked intrinsic awareness. After that, we have to engage in the practice of the four visions of thogal in order to actualize the resultant state of enlightenment.

PART FOUR

PRAJNAPARAMITA:
THE PERFECTION OF WISDOM

10

ESSENCE OF THE PRAJNAPARAMITA

Next, we will discuss the *prajnaparamita*, or perfection of wisdom teachings, in seven topics.

First, I will discuss the meaning of the term 'prajnaparamita,' second, the history of the prajnaparamita lineage, third, how the prajnaparamita is the heart of the Buddha's teachings, and fourth, the four subdivisions of the perfection of wisdom. Fifth, I will explain how the prajnaparamita scriptures contain a hidden meaning. Sixth, I will briefly present the eight topics by which the prajnaparamita teachings are usually presented by Maitreya in his *Ornament of Clear Realization*. These eight topics are elucidated through seventy meanings, and I will briefly touch on those as well. Seventh, I will present how all of the prajnaparamita teachings can be classified according to the three baskets and the three trainings.

These seven topics provide the framework for this presentation of the perfection of wisdom. The reason I have chosen these seven topics is that without such a framework, it would be impossible to approach the profound and extensive teachings on this topic. They are not only profound, but also extensive. In the monastic curriculum, the study of these teachings traditionally takes ten years. All of the perfection of wisdom teachings are presented here by means of these seven topics.

THE MEANING OF PRAJNAPARAMITA

The Sanskrit word for 'perfection of wisdom' is *prajnaparamita*. The word 'prajnaparamita' comprises two Sanskrit words: *prajna* and *paramita*. 'Prajna' refers to wisdom, and 'paramita' means transcendental, or gone beyond. The etymology of 'prajna' points to discriminating wisdom, or the ability to discriminate between what is valid and invalid, right and wrong, good and bad.

There are several ways of distinguishing between the different types of prajna. A traditional way of classifying it from the point of view of practice is to divide it into three types – prajna arising from hearing, prajna arising from contemplation, and prajna arising from meditation. Another way of categorizing prajna is to distinguish between mundane or worldly prajna and supramundane or transcendental prajna. With respect to the realization of practitioners, we distinguish between prajna that is present at the level of ordinary beings, and prajna that is present at the level of the *arya* or superior being. Prajna can also be divided into contaminated and uncontaminated prajna. For the purpose of understanding the perfection of wisdom, it is most beneficial to divide it into contaminated and uncontaminated wisdom.

Contaminated prajna is born of what is mundane or worldly, such as worldly samadhi and insight. Uncontaminated prajna comprises all the wisdom that is present in the paths of Hinayana practitioners, solitary realizers, and Mahayana practitioners. In the Hinayana, this includes the four *dhyanas* (absorptions) and the four paths.[46] In the Mahayana, this includes all of the wisdom that is present in the five paths and ten grounds.

Prajna, or discriminating wisdom, is the ability to analyze or discriminate, and it is present in all human beings. Through cultivation and practice, we enhance and extend this basic discriminating wisdom to such an extent that we are able to approach the enlightened state. When that happens, we could say that the discriminating wisdom that we started with has become transcendental, in the sense that it has transcended samsara into the realm of enlightenment. Transcending is likened to crossing an ocean; getting to the other side is likened to nirvana. To count as transcendental and not mere worldly wisdom, it must transcend samsara, meaning that the obscurations of negative emotions have been eliminated. For example, when Hinayana practitioners arrive at the state of arhathood, their wisdom transcends samsara. For the Mahayana practitioner, there is a second criterion for transcendence. Simple abandonment of negative emotions is not enough. One also seeks to remove the obscurations to omniscience, transcending the limitations of both samsara and nirvana. This is how we understand transcendental wisdom or prajnaparamita.

Since the fundamental goal of dharma practice is to gain complete freedom from suffering, including all of the suffering of each of the particular realms, we have to systematically train on the path taught by the Buddha. We cannot gain this freedom from suffering through lucky breaks, miracles, or paranormal powers. We have to train on the path as revealed by the Buddha. We have to rely on the Buddha, because only the Buddha understands causation at the subtlest level. This knowledge of subtle causation is born of the experience of achieving enlightenment, and so is only possessed by a buddha. No one but a buddha can teach with the necessary detail and subtlety on how to use the law of causality to gain freedom. That is why the Buddha is the ultimate teacher. It really comes down to the question of how one can actually gain enlightenment, which is freedom from all forms of suffering.

The Buddha taught the Dharma in accord with the aptitudes and capacities of disciples. For this reason, he gave the three turnings of the wheel of Dharma. The first turning was given for disciples at the level of the Hinayana, including the thirty-seven aspects of enlightenment such as the four bases of mindfulness, the four efforts, the five powers, the seven branches, the eightfold path, and so on. The second turning of the wheel was given for disciples at the level of the Mahayana, or bodhisattvas. The perfection of wisdom teachings belong to the second turning.

There are two dimensions to the perfection of wisdom teachings – the explicit wisdom of emptiness teachings and the hidden teachings. The wisdom of emptiness teachings, which were presented in part two of this book, constitute the explicit teachings on wisdom. We call the teachings on emptiness 'explicit' because they are directly or explicitly presented in the texts. They contain the wisdom aspect of the second turning of the wheel. There is also a second dimension that conveys a meaning that is not explicit in the text. We call these the hidden teachings. They include such teachings as those on loving kindness, compassion, and bodhicitta, which are implicit in the perfection of wisdom teachings but not stated literally.

HISTORY OF THE PRAJNAPARAMITA LINEAGE

Stories of the Buddha's life generally follow his twelve deeds or major activities. The tenth activity was gaining enlightenment, the eleventh was turning the wheel of Dharma, and the twelfth was passing into nirvana. The eleventh activity of turning the wheel of Dharma refers to all the Buddha's acts of teaching.

When he taught the perfection of wisdom, it was not just humans who were listening. In the perfection of wisdom sutras, we find different beings in different dimensions, such as gods and nagas. It is generally accepted that the prajnaparamita teachings were given to humans at Rajgir near Bodhgaya.

We should understand that just as the Buddha presented teachings according to the capacity of the audience, not all of his teachings were intended to be taken literally. There are definitive teachings, to be understood literally, and interpretable teachings that need interpretation or contextualizing. This distinction is something we should bear in mind, because the Buddha's teachings are extensive and were given to different audiences at different stages of development. Initially, the Buddha gave teachings to disciples who came from a Hindu background, and even though they were able to appreciate the Buddha's teachings on conduct, they were still attached to the Hindu concept of atman, or eternal soul. These teachings on compassion and conduct did not challenge the Hindu view very much. The teachings given to this audience therefore have to be understood as interpretable because they were given for a specific purpose in a specific context.

Another example is found in the teachings as they are understood by the Vaibashika school. The Buddha said that even though there is no permanent, independent, solitary self, nonetheless there is a substantial self that circles through samsara. In this sense, the Buddha gave the impression that there is a substantial self separate from the five aggregates, but there is no permanent, eternal, solid self as the Hindus believed. There is no permanent self, but there is a substantial self. Likewise, we see in the teachings of the Mind-Only school in the second turning that the Buddha said that emptiness inherently exists. Once we get to the third turning, the Buddha said that even emptiness does not inherently exist. So if you do not know how to contextualize teachings, then you might think there is some internal contradiction.

In the *Sutra Elucidating the Intent of the Buddha*,[47] the bodhisattva Paramarthasamudgata asks the Buddha, "In the first turning of the wheel of dharma, you taught that things exist; in the second turning, you said that they do not exist; and in the third turning, you said that we have to discern what things exist and what things do not exist. What is your intention in giving these seemingly contradictory teachings?"

In his *400 Stanzas*, Aryadeva summarizes the Buddha's answer to the bodhisattva's question.[48] Aryadeva explains that in the beginning, teachings are given in order to eliminate non-virtuous states of mind. Elimination of non-virtue gives rise to the accumulation of merit, which becomes the causal factor for rebirth in higher realms. Even though emptiness is not taught here in the beginning, this teaching has great benefits. If we engage in virtuous conduct, such as the practice of generosity, and eliminate non-virtuous thought and behavior, then we give rise to meritorious actions, and that helps us to gain rebirth in higher realms in samsara. This is a good start. In the middle, rebirth in higher samsaric realms is not enough. We aspire to gain freedom from samsara altogether. Aryadeva explains that the teachings in the middle were given in order to eliminate self-grasping. It is because of self-grasping and the subtlest imprints of self-grasping that we are propelled through samsara. By eliminating self-grasping, one is freed from samsara. In the end, the Buddha gave teachings to eliminate attachment to all views, including the peace of nirvana, and to attain the ultimate state of enlightenment.

So we should not assume that all teachings are to be taken literally. We have to understand the intent of the Buddha in particular contexts. If we are aware of that, then we can understand that some teachings are interpretable and some are definitive. For example, the *Heart Sutra* is an interpretable teaching, not to be taken literally. The *Heart Sutra* says that 'there is no form, no eye,' etc. But conventionally, there is form and there are eyes, so 'there is no eye' is not something we should take literally. When the Buddha said that there is no eye consciousness, he meant that eye consciousness does not inherently exist. We have to interpret or contextualize the statement that there is no eye consciousness. It does not literally mean there is no eye consciousness.

We can distinguish definitive from interpretable teachings on the basis of what are called the 'four reliances' – the four points to rely upon and the four points not to rely upon.[49] The Buddha tells us, 'Do not rely on the person giving teachings but on the validity of teachings.' In other words, one should not listen to a teacher just because he or she is a celebrity. This was a profound statement at the time, because prior to the Buddha's coming to India, it was typical to follow a teacher not on the grounds of having investigated the validity of the teachings, but because of the reputation of a teacher. The Buddha said that we should rely instead on the validity of teachings.

The first reliance is on teachings and not the person, and was taught by the Buddha throughout his lifetime until the time of his death. Furthermore, at the time of his passing, he told his disciples to preserve the perfection of wisdom teachings because 'wherever they are, I am there.' In his lifetime, the Buddha never emphasized his own greatness but rather the importance of examining the teachings themselves. For us, this distinction between what to rely on and what not to rely on is very important. Rely on the teachings, not the person. This does not mean that we shouldn't consult spiritual masters. It means that in order to authenticate the teachings, we examine the teachings rather than relying on the reputation of the teacher.

There is no contradiction when say that we should rely on the teachings and not the teacher. It does not mean we do not rely on the teacher. It is the same as the way that when we are sick, we consult a doctor and receive instructions and treatment, but what actually heals us is the medicine. Likewise, when we follow the instructions of the teacher, what actually heals us is our practice based on those instructions. The importance of the teacher in practice or training is not denied.

The second reliance is on the meaning, rather than the words.

When we rely on the teachings, we should not rely on the words but on the meaning of those words. If we were to rely on the words, and take things literally, then there is the danger we saw earlier. Not all teachings are meant to be taken literally and taking them literally results in misunderstanding. When we understand the meaning, however, we are able to contextualize the words based on time, stages of progress, and audience.

Another reason to rely on meaning and not words is that sometimes words convey little meaning. For example, the Vedantic teachings are very beautiful as poetry but have little substance, no depth of meaning. In contrast, if you look at some of the teachings of the mahasiddhas, the actual words are not that beautiful or poetic but are rich in meaning.

The third reliance is on the definitive meaning and not the interpretable meaning. When we rely on the meaning of the teachings, we have to remember that the meaning can be definitive or interpretable, and we should rely on the definitive, ultimate meaning.

The fourth reliance is on the definitive teachings given from the point of view of uncontaminated wisdom, not those given from the point of view of confused mind. The Buddha says we should rely on ultimate definitive teachings given from the point of view of wisdom, which is undeluded, rather than those given from the point of view of mind, which is in the domain of confusion. The Buddha presented all of his teachings through this medium of the four things to rely on and the four things not to rely on. In his teachings on the four reliances, he also taught the distinction between definitive and interpretable teachings.

When we approach taking refuge in the Buddha, we examine the worthiness of the Buddha as refuge. It is important that we do so by examining the teachings and considering their validity. We should not do so on the basis of the Buddha's personal life stories or his popular image. We might get the impression that to discover the meaning of refuge and inspire us, we should take a trip to see the beautiful statues in Thailand, but this is a misunderstanding. The way to seek refuge is to examine the teachings and come to understand them. The most important thing is to generate conviction in the teachings. This was how the Buddha's followers acted after he passed away. They preserved the Buddha's teachings and transmitted them rather than giving a lot of significance to the Buddha's life stories.

After the Buddha's passing, the teachings on the perfection of wisdom were preserved and commented upon by Maitreya. Of the five treatises of Maitreya Buddha, the *Ornament of Clear Realization*,[50] which explains the Buddha's teachings of the perfection of wisdom, is the most important one.

The Buddha's teachings comprise three lineages – the profound or wisdom lineage, the extensive or conduct lineage, and the blessing or practice lineage. The extensive lineage of conduct was transmitted from Shakyamuni Buddha to Maitreya Buddha. Maitreya's *Ornament of Clear Realization* is the principal commentary on the extensive aspect of the prajnaparamita teachings. By means of eight topics, Maitreya explained the very essence of the extensive conduct lineage of these teachings. This was passed on to Asanga, who was prophesied by the Buddha. The extensive lineage therefore descends from Shakyamuni Buddha to Maitreya to Asanga.

It is said that the perfection of wisdom teachings were in decline during Asanga's time in India, and not many people engaged in Mahayana practices. It is also said that Asanga's mother was concerned about this decline. She believed she could not do much about it because as a woman her status was low, and she thus was unable to study to become a scholar. She prayed, 'Even if I am not able to restore the Mahayana practice myself, may I give birth to someone who can do it.' In response to her fervent prayers, Asanga was born to her. When Asanga went to Nalanda, he asked for the best way to restore the Mahayana teachings. The answer he received was that he should meditate on and accomplish Maitreya Buddha. You might know the story of how Asanga accomplished Maitreya Buddha after twelve years in a cave. In the end, he was able to have a direct vision of Maitreya Buddha by generating great compassion. He received the *Ornament of Clear Realization* from Maitreya, and he also composed 'The Five Treatises.' In this way, he revived the Mahayana teachings in India.

From Asanga, the extensive teachings were transmitted to master Singhabhadra,[51] followed by Arya Vimuktisena[52] and his student Bhadanta Vimuktisena. Philosophically, they were primarily Svatantrika-Madhyamaka, but they maintained the perfection of wisdom teachings as an unbroken lineage. This transmission was brought to China and Tibet. To this day, the extensive teachings that came through Asanga are preserved in all four lineages of Tibetan Buddhism.

As I have mentioned, the perfection of wisdom teachings have a wisdom aspect and a conduct or method aspect. While from a philosophical point of view, Tibetan practitioners adhered to the Svatantrika-Madhyamaka school of the profound or wisdom lineage, they preserved the original extensive teachings on the method or conduct. These are basically all of the teachings on compassion that constitute the implicit or hidden content of the perfection of wisdom. These teachings on conduct have even been preserved in China. From a philosophical point of view, most practitioners in China follow the Mind-Only school. They might not identify themselves as Mind-Only practitioners, but if you look at their teachings, it is clear that they explain the intent of the Buddha from point of view of this school.

Philosophically, all Tibetan traditions follow the Madhyamaka tradition of Arya Nagarjuna and his spiritual sons. Shantarakshita himself belonged to the Yogacara-Svatantrika-Madhyamaka school. The ancient or Nyingma tradition followed after Shantarakshita in Tibet, and therefore it presented the profound lineage teachings of the perfection of wisdom in accordance with the Yogacara-Svatantrika-Madhyamaka. Later on, the Sakya and Gelug traditions followed Bhavaviveka who taught from the point of view of Svatantrika-Madhyamaka philosophy. Still later, others taught the perfection of wisdom from the point of view of Prasangika Madhyamaka.

This concludes the brief story of how the perfection of wisdom teachings were transmitted from the Buddha to Maitreya Buddha and preserved in India and Tibet. After Maitreya composed the *Ornament of Clear Realization*, twenty-one Indian masters produced commentaries on it, and there are an additional two hundred Tibetan commentaries.

THE HEART OF THE BUDDHA'S TEACHINGS

The perfection of wisdom is the most perfect of teachings because all of the stages of the path, and all knowledge required for an individual to gain enlightenment, are present in it. Everything that is necessary is contained within these teachings. This is not true of other teaching traditions such as the Madhyamaka, vinaya, abhidharma, and pramana or logic. Those are subsidiary or branch teachings; they do not contain the entire body of knowledge necessary for a practitioner to accomplish the state of enlightenment. By analogy, the perfection of wisdom is like the whole body while the other teachings are like limbs or hands.

This is why the Buddha tells Shariputra in the *Prajnaparamita Sutra in 8000 Stanzas,* 'in the chapter 'Completely Entrusting the Teachings,' that 'wherever perfection of wisdom teachings are, there I am.'[53] The Buddha characterized these teachings as the heart of all teachings, and the way in which to preserve these most precious teachings is not by bundling them in beautiful containers as they do in Tibet and China but by transmitting them to others. One of the attributes of the perfection of wisdom teachings is that they contain absolutely everything necessary for anyone seeking the state of complete liberation. For this reason, they are the most sublime of teachings.

The Buddha said that because of the preciousness of the

perfection of wisdom, one of its qualities is that it can only be understood by beings of the highest capacity, and is only to be given to such beings. It is prohibited to give these teachings to beings of lesser capacity, because this might result in misunderstanding and taking up wrong views.

A second reason why the perfection of wisdom is spoken of as the heart of the Buddha's teachings is that our goal is to transform contaminated wisdom into transcendental wisdom. As I mentioned earlier, we all have basic discriminating wisdom, but we want to develop and purify basic discriminating wisdom into uncontaminated transcendental wisdom. The way to do this is taught in the perfection of wisdom, and therefore it is called the heart of the teachings.

Since the perfection of wisdom is the heart of the Buddha's teachings, four of the five areas of study in the standard sutra curriculum in Tibet – logic, Madhyamaka, Abhidharma, and vinaya – are seen as ornaments of the fifth, the perfection of wisdom. The five great treatises of Buddhism correspond to these five areas of knowledge.[54]

Logic is regarded as an ornament of the perfection of wisdom because valid cognition or logic is used to ascertain its validity. The literature on valid cognition constitutes an area of intensive study in its own right, but the purpose of logic is not to engage in debate but rather to show how the validity of the perfection of wisdom teachings can be ascertained. Dignaga, the first great scholar of Buddhist logic, and his student Dharmakirti[55] developed Buddhist logic to a high standard. Their treatises start at the very beginning with the practice of taking refuge and proceed all the way to the four kayas, including both the profound wisdom aspect of the teachings, the wisdom of emptiness, and the extensive teachings on great compassion.

It is important to recognize that all of these teachings are something that can be logically or rationally ascertained. Although the three refuges were clearly taught in the sutras, by Dignaga's time there was contention and doubt about them. There were questions about the meaning of the path, especially the path of the Mahayana, and particularly concerning the perfection of wisdom. 'What is the meaning of "paramita" – "going beyond"? How can we go beyond?' Dignaga undertook to resolve these doubts. Particularly, he handled doubts concerning the Dharma as a refuge, by showing how the Dharma is established as valid cognition. Because the entire perfection of wisdom teachings are contained in the Three Jewels, especially the jewel of Dharma, Dignaga began with the foundation of refuge in the Three Jewels. It is important to understand that the aim of this endeavor was not to refute non-Buddhism, but to clarify the meaning and validity of the teachings. This is how logic or valid cognition becomes an ornament to the perfection of wisdom teachings.

Dignaga's principal text, the *Compendium on Valid Cognition*, is extremely condensed — it is only seven pages long. The Indian scholars and even Dharmakirti himself found it difficult to decipher. For this reason, Dharmakirti produced a four-chapter commentary to explain and expand upon it. The second chapter, on valid speech, establishes the authority of the Buddha and the teachings. The Mahayana is especially vast and profound, and the logical demonstrations of its validity are difficult to follow. Dharmakirti wanted to clarify and make certain the essence of what the Buddha taught. Of course, the scholars of Buddhist logic were concerned about answering the Hindu scholars and discussed endless counterexamples and paradoxes of causality and identity. Debate for its own sake, however, is not the real point. The real point is eliminating doubt about the view, about the foundation of Mahayana, and about how to cultivate the Mahayana path of prajnaparamita. How do we know that the Buddha is enlightened? If we are to follow his path and take the Dharma as a supreme refuge, then this is something we need to be able to determine for ourselves.

The teachings on valid cognition or logic are an ornament of the perfection of wisdom because one is able to generate certainty regarding the perfection of wisdom at the level of the basis, the path, and the resultant state. Certainty about the Dharma is extremely precious, and it can be cultivated by means of logical reasoning. Buddhist logic is used to eliminate aversion to entering onto the Mahayana path by generating this certainty. Having entered the path, it is used to avoid error, eliminate the dangers of doubt and uncertainty, and induce confidence in the path. It is not a means to build up the ego by winning debates; its purpose is not subordinated to the ego's ends as in other intellectual pursuits. The purpose of Buddhist logic is ultimately to destroy one's inner doubts and uncertainty about the Dharma, so that one is able to transcend ego and thereby induce transcendental wisdom, prajnaparamita.

Ultimately, logic has to dawn as the path. The teachings on logic are something that one should be able to carry as the path. Tsongkhapa composed a text called *Establishing the Path* that illustrates this point. It is important to understand that the traditional ways of understanding the function of logic are different from the contemporary practice of abstract debate and engaging in logic and reasoning for its own sake.

Another one of the five areas of knowledge in the Buddhist sutra curriculum is the Middle Way philosophy, or Madhyamaka. Middle Way philosophy becomes an ornament of the perfection of wisdom in that it develops its wisdom aspect. In the Middle Way teachings, emptiness of inherent existence is established using the 'five lines of reasoning.'[56] By progressively examining the tenets of the 'four schools' - Vaibashika, Sautrantika, Cittamatra or Mind-Only, and Middle Way or Madhyamaka - from the point of view of the more subtle principles of the five lines of reasoning, a profound view of emptiness is established. The Middle Way teachings on emptiness thus form the explicit teachings of the perfection of wisdom, giving a direct presentation of what is called the 'natural perfection of wisdom.' This is how the Middle Way teachings become an ornament of the perfection of wisdom.

Another of the five great treatises of Buddhism is the *Abhidharmakosa*, which presents the entirety of phenomena, or Buddhist phenomenology. The abhidharma teachings are meant to help us understand the five aggregates and the false notion of self, so that we can eliminate grasping at them. All of the constituents of phenomena encompassed by self-grasping, such as the skandhas, ayatanas, and dhatus, are taught in the abhidharma literature. The *Abhidharmakosa* also gives an extensive presentation of the four bases of mindfulness – body, feeling or sensation, mind or thoughts, and phenomena. By means of studying the abhidharma, ordinary discriminating wisdom is enhanced by insight into self-grasping. That is how the abhidharma becomes an ornament of the perfection of wisdom teachings.

Finally, the fourth of the five areas of study is the vinaya, the monastic code of conduct. The vinaya is taught because even when we are able to generate certainty about the dharma through reasoning, if we do not observe ethics or discipline, we will still come under the influence of the deep conditioning of habitual patterns. We will not be able to transcend these influences without discipline. The vinaya is thus taught in order to gain freedom from negative habits and conditions. Where negative habits cut us off from realization, the practice of ethical discipline is like fertile ground from which any crop can grow. Morality is therefore the ground from which we can generate the realization of the perfection of wisdom. This is true not only at the level of sutra practice, but also in tantric practice. This is how vinaya becomes an ornament of the perfection of wisdom.

The practitioner who aspires to realize the perfection of wisdom can train on the basis of the five great treatises in the following way. First of all, start by laying the ground, which is the practice of discipline. Second, practice the teachings contained in the abhidarma – how to eliminate grasping at a self by understanding the skandhas, ayatanas, and dhatus. Third, eliminate doubt through the practice of logical reasoning and generate certainty regarding the teachings. Fourth, study the Madhyamaka or Middle Way teachings and practice to attain realization of the natural great perfection, emptiness itself. Studying the view of emptiness of each of the Madhyamaka schools – Yogachara-Svatantrika Madhyamaka, Sautrantika-Svatantrika Madhyamaka, and Prasangika-Madhyamaka – we come to perfectly understand the explicit meaning of the second turning of the wheel of dharma, which is the perfection of wisdom.

Based on this study and practice, we come to see that the fundamental purpose of all the four disciplines – ethics, abhidharma, logic, and madhyamaka – is ultimately to give rise to the realization that manifests as the result of the path of perfection of wisdom, wisdom that transcends the limitations of samsara. This is the purpose of all of the treatises. The perfection of wisdom is the very essence or life force of the Buddha's teachings, because all of the other teachings are taught to actualize or realize it.

SUBDIVISIONS OF THE PERFECTION OF WISDOM

There are four subdivisions of the perfection of wisdom that may be understood as reference points. Three of the subdivisions are the actual perfection of wisdom, and one is the nominal perfection of wisdom.

The first is the natural perfection of wisdom. 'Natural perfection of wisdom' refers to the ultimate emptiness of one's own mind. Second, to understand the natural perfection of wisdom, we rely on the texts that present it. The texts that help us to understand the meaning of emptiness are together referred to as the 'textual perfection of wisdom.' These are the middle length, extremely lengthy and concise perfection of wisdom sutras. Third, we carry the teachings of the textual perfection of wisdom into practice as the 'path perfection of wisdom.' What is carried as the path by the practitioner is the path perfection of wisdom. Fourth, when we carry the path perfection of wisdom into practice, the result is the 'resultant perfection of wisdom' or the four kayas. The textual perfection of wisdom is nominal because it consists of texts and is therefore not the actual perfection of wisdom of one's own mind.

The natural perfection of wisdom is the introduction to the view of the ground, which basically comes down to establishing the ultimate emptiness of one's own mind. We discussed how the meaning of emptiness is established in Part Two of this book. In that context, emptiness refers to the nature of phenomena free of elaboration. This is an external aspect or reference point of emptiness. However, emptiness also pertains to the emptiness of one's own mind. 'Natural perfection of wisdom' refers to the emptiness of one's own mind, which is the ultimate aspect of the clarity of one's own mind. This ultimate emptiness is called the 'natural perfection of wisdom' because this empty clear light of the mind *naturally* transcends obscurations. The ultimate empty clarity of mind is naturally untainted, and so is referred to as 'natural perfection of wisdom.'

It is best to understand the natural perfection of wisdom as referring to the ultimate nature of one's own mind. In order to understand how the ultimate nature of mind is the natural perfection of wisdom, we need to understand how one's own mind is ultimately free of negative emotions and so forth. If we are able to eliminate the temporary afflictions, the nature of mind is revealed as naturally transcendental.

In the ancient Nyingma tradition in Tibet, when we talk about the ultimate nature of mind, we are mostly referring to the aspect of clarity. In the new schools such as the Gelug and Sakya, the ultimate nature of mind predominantly refers to mind's empty aspect. Which emphasis is more useful? Whether emptiness or clarity is more effective in terms of one's own practice is something we can judge for ourselves.

The ground natural perfection of wisdom is sometimes referred to as the 'great mother perfection of wisdom.' From the ground of the natural perfection of wisdom, the perfection of wisdom at the level of the path and the level of the resultant state arise like her children.

The textual perfection of wisdom is referred to as 'perfection of wisdom' because it contains the explanation of the perfection of wisdom. It is not the actual perfection of wisdom, because for it to be the actual perfection of wisdom, it would have to be within the continuum of our mind. It is therefore only perfection of wisdom in a nominal sense, but it has an important role in explaining the sequence of practices that give rise to the path and resultant perfection of wisdom.

The path perfection of wisdom is referred to as such because it is the unique or uncommon causal factor responsible for giving rise to the resultant perfection of wisdom. It is uncommon in that it is an exceptional yoga of both superior shamatha and superior vipasyana.

The resultant perfection of wisdom refers to the ultimate state of enlightenment. The ultimate state of enlightenment has two qualities: ultimate abandonment and ultimate achievement. 'Ultimate abandonment' refers to the svabhavikakaya and the dharmakaya, the ultimate state of abandonment or cessation. 'Ultimate achievement' refers to the nirmanakaya and sambhogakaya.

In the context of the perfection of wisdom teachings, the dharmakaya is usually referred to as '*jnana-dharmakaya*,' or wisdom dharmakaya. Unlike Dzogchen and Mahamudra, where 'dharmakaya' refers to the ultimate nature of mind, 'jnana-dharmakaya' refers to the positive quality of the enlightened state, the state of omniscience. The ultimate nature of omniscient mind is svabhavikakaya, the unchanging state of ultimate cessation or abandonment. The omniscient jnana-dharmakaya is a 'positive' quality of dharmakaya. The other two kayas, sambhogakaya and nirmanakaya, are emanations by means of which enlightened beings benefit other sentient beings.

THE HIDDEN MEANING OF THE PERFECTION OF WISDOM

If you look at the perfection of wisdom sutras themselves, you find that the levels of the basis, path, and resultant state are given by means of negation. At the level of the basis, the view of the ground is introduced with such statements as that 'there are no phenomena,' or 'phenomena cannot be perceived.' The whole thing is taught by negation. At the level of the path, again there is nothing but negation – phenomena cannot be grasped, phenomena do not arise, their nature is non-arising. At the level of the resultant state, it is taught that the state of enlightenment is not something that can be attained. All of the explicit teachings on emptiness given in the *Prajnaparamita Sutras* are given by means of negation. The way in which we can actualize the meaning of emptiness – the teachings on the paths and the grounds – are not explicitly stated in these sutras. The Buddha enumerated the the paths and their aspects, from mindfulness practice up to the state of omniscient mind, but instructions for the actual and enhancement practices pertaining to each level of realization, path, or ground are not given in detail. The paths and the grounds, which are the hidden aspect of the prajnaparamita teachings, are revealed by Maitreya Buddha in the *Ornament of Clear Realization*.

The reason why the Buddha gave the explicit teachings on emptiness is that there is no freedom from samsara without realizing the non-arising nature of phenomena. 'Natural perfection of wisdom' really refers to the realization of the non-arising nature of phenomena, of how there is no such thing as true arising. Without realization of the non-arising nature of phenomena, or emptiness, there is no way to gain freedom from samsaric conditioning. As long as we do not directly apprehend emptiness or the natural perfection of wisdom, there is no way to achieve liberation from samsara. We may achieve rebirth in higher realms, but without understanding the natural perfection of wisdom, there is no way to gain liberation from samsara. That is why all of the explicit teachings are on emptiness.

Realization of emptiness enables us to eliminate grasping at a self and phenomena. There are two types of grasping, whether at the level of the basis, path, or resultant state. One is innate grasping, which happens spontaneously, intuitively. The other is conceptually or intellectually induced grasping, born out of one's attachment to a particular conceptual understanding. The explicit teachings on emptiness in the perfection of wisdom sutras are given so that one can gain freedom from both. These sutras teach that there is no true thing to attach to; one should gain freedom even from grasping at the resultant state. This is why the explicit teachings are on emptiness.

'Prajna,' or 'wisdom,' refers to the natural perfection of wisdom, wisdom that realizes emptiness. The natural perfection of wisdom is nominally present in the perfection of wisdom sutras, which establish the impossibility of inherent existence. When we have actually realized emptiness, we are able to see directly that even if things appear to exist from their own side, their actual mode of abiding is like that of a mirage or dream. In order to actualize the natural perfection wisdom, we have to rely on both the explicit emptiness teachings of the sutras and the hidden method aspect of them. 'Method' refers to the teachings on bodhicitta and on the cultivation of loving kindness and compassion. So the perfection of wisdom sutras are saying that to actualize the perfection of wisdom, we not only have to rely on the wisdom aspect – the teachings on emptiness – but also on the method aspect, the practice of bodhicitta. Ultimately, the natural perfection of wisdom is actualized through the union of method and wisdom.

In the sutras, it is taught that method without wisdom is poison and wisdom without method is also poison. The sutras talk about the importance of the union of method and wisdom for correctly understanding the meaning of emptiness, the meaning of the natural perfection of wisdom.

Once one has achieved a correct understanding of the ground, then one is able to generate the path perfection of wisdom. There is a sequence to generating the perfection of wisdom at the level of the path. First one comes to understand emptiness conceptually; then one becomes able to understand emptiness directly. It is not easy to directly understand emptiness, the ground perfection of wisdom. Even a conceptual understanding is difficult. It takes a very powerful mind, great positive merit, and capacity. To cultivate a powerful mind, we engage in the method aspect of the path. One begins with the path of accumulation, extensively accumulating merit so that the mind is made powerful enough to realize emptiness directly. For example, in the path of accumulation, we study and practice bodhicitta. This is taught using the twenty-two similes of bodhicitta such as earth-like bodhicitta.[57]

Then, while still in the context of the path of accumulation, we study and practice the paths of each of the three yanas.[58] One of the reasons why the levels of Hinayana practice are taught in the Mahayana sutras is that the Mahayana practitioner needs to understand the Hinayana – the view of the ground, how the path is traversed, how the resultant state is actualized, and the realizations and grounds. Only then is the Mahayana practitioner able to benefit all sentient beings. Without that understanding, they will not be able to teach Hinayana practitioners, because there is no knowledge of their practice. One of the main reasons for studying the Hinayana is to be able to help Hinayana practitioners, and to be able to turn the wheel of dharma for all vehicles.

The root text, the *Ornament of Clear Realization*, says that those who want to benefit other sentient beings must actualize the perfection of wisdom of the path. By actualizing the path perfection of wisdom, you give rise to realization that enables you to understand the paths and teachings of all practitioners, so that you can lead them as well.

In the general sense, the sravakas and pratyekabuddhas are both Hinayana practitioners, so there is not much difference between them. They are similar in emphasizing renunciation and enlightenment for oneself, but if we look at the teachings for solitary realizers and hearers in detail, we find many differences. The views of the ground, path, and resultant state are all different, with those of pratyekabuddhas being far superior to those of sravakas. This is not usually discussed, but it is mentioned in the texts.

The nine dhyanas, or mundane absorptions, are taught in the perfection of wisdom teachings because the reality for practitioners as human beings is that we live in the desire realm. Compared to the minds that dwell in the form and formless realms, our minds are very coarse. As desire realm beings, we experience nine negative emotions that are specific to the desire realm, including innate ignorance, anger, doubt, pride, and wrong views. We see worldly morality as supreme, worldly view as valid, so we have to get rid of these. One way to get rid of them is through direct perception of the ultimate mode of reality, which is emptiness. The other way is through practicing the worldly absorptions of the form and formless realms through the practice of shamatha.[59]

By actualizing the mind of the higher realms, we can make great progress in eliminating negative emotions, though this is not easy. To do so, we have to see the desire realm as something to be abandoned and the mind of the higher realms as something to be attained. By the force of this intention, the dual force of seeing the lower realms as something to be abandoned and the higher realms as something to be achieved, our calm abiding passes sequentially through the nine absorptions of the form and formless realms. Ultimately, we reach the highest state of mind within samsara, the 'peak of existence,' the subtlest or highest mental state that we can achieve within samsara. This is an extremely subtle mind. Even though it is a worldly samadhi, all of the gross mind and mental factors have come to an end. There is no movement of mind and mental factors, because it is such a subtle state. In this way, we have the opportunity to suppress the coarse negative emotions associated with the desire realm. That is why the worldly absorptions are taught in the perfection of wisdom teachings.

Even though the peak of existence is such a subtle mind that there is no movement of mind or mental factors and all forms of negative emotion are suppressed, because we have still not directly realized emptiness, we are not yet able to eliminate innate grasping at an intrinsic reality. Because the peak of existence is only a state of meditative absorption, without the benefit of the wisdom that realizes emptiness, what happens is that once the initial force of our samadhi fades, the negative emotions return. This happens because we have not been able to eliminate grasping and attachment to intrinsic reality. Even in the subtlest state of absorption, the practitioner is still craving or attached to the bliss of absorption. We are able to stay there as long as the initial force of the samadhi is there. Once that initial force wears away, we come out of samadhi, and because we have not been able to eliminate innate grasping to inherent existence, once again all sorts of negative emotions are generated. Therefore, even this subtle state is a mundane path. To eliminate self-grasping at the root, we have to enter the transcendental or supramundane path, which actualizes the wisdom of emptiness. The prajnaparamita literature teaches all of the paths and stages of training for sravakas, pratyekhabuddhas, and Mahayana practitioners, so that we can understand all of the mundane and supramundane paths.

Once we leave the mundane path for the supramundane or transcendental path, starting with the practices of sravakas and pratyekabuddhas, we reach a point where we will not revert to mundane realms. The first level in the Hinayana vehicle is that of the stream-enterer. The stream-enterer is someone who not only has generated aversion to the desire realm, as happens in worldly absorption, but is actually eliminating some of the negative emotions. Next is the path of the once-returner, a practitioner who will take rebirth in the desire realm only once. At this point, the practitioner has eliminated most of the negative emotions of the desire realm. Then the practitioner goes to the level of the non-returner, who has been able to eliminate eight of the nine negative emotions of the desire realm. The non-returner will never take birth in the desire realm again. The practitioner then achieves the state of the arhat, who will never take rebirth in any of the samsaric realms – he or she has eliminated all negative emotions of the desire, form, and formless realms. The arhat is someone who has gained liberation from samsara altogether.

If you want to look at detailed explanations of the Hinayana and Mahayana paths, the levels of realization, and how the paths are traversed, then study the commentaries on the *Ornament of Clear Realization* by Maitreya Buddha.[60]

Earlier I mentioned the differences between Hinayana sravakas and pratyekabuddhas in terms of their view of the ground, path, and resultant state. The view of pratyekabuddhas on the ultimate mode of being is that it is free of dualism of subject and object, and there is nothing else apart from your mind. This is different from the view of sravakas, who believe in an external reality. They are dualists in that sense. Pratyekabuddhas are more profound; their view is free of dualism of subject and object.

At the level of the path, even though sravakas and pratyekabuddhas use the same terminology in referring to the stages of the path, there are differences in understanding. There is also a difference in the length of time it takes for sravakas and pratyekabuddhas to achieve the resultant state. Sravakas take countless eons to achieve enlightenment whereas pratyekabuddhas achieve their own state of cessation in one hundred eons.

The main reason that it takes so long for both is not that they get entangled with negative emotions and samsaric activities, but that they remain in absorption for a very long time. They remain in absorption for so long because they are convinced they have already gained the state of liberation, and therefore realization of the truth of cessation is slow to develop. Their understanding of perfection, or paramita, is limited to transcending samsara. Of course, even this kind of paramita is something to be appreciated and respected. If we are able to transcend samsara, we have indeed attained a high state of realization.

These days, there is a lot of excitement about the higher teachings like Mahayana, tantra, Mahamudra, and Dzogchen, but in reality most of us are still in samsara. In terms of actual realization, it would be difficult for most of us to see ourselves even as the equal of the stream-enterer of Hinayana.

According to the teachings of the perfection of wisdom, it is not sufficient simply to attain liberation from samsara. Attachment to the peace of nirvana is also a form of bondage. In order to attain complete enlightenment, we also have to train to free ourselves from this form of attachment. To enable us to do so, the Mahayana teachings of the perfection of wisdom will now be introduced – the ground perfection of wisdom from the Mahayana perspective, and the instructions for carrying this onto the path. The latter include how to engage in the five paths and the ten bhumis, including the teachings on the six perfections.

At the level of the Mahayana, the presentation of the ground has to be especially powerful so that the practitioner is able to avoid falling into the extremes of samsara and the peace of nirvana. The way in which presenting the ground perfection of wisdom is made powerful is by sequentially training in the five Mahayana paths, starting with the path of accumulation. In the beginning, all of the teachings associated with the path of accumulation are given.

The path of accumulation is divided into three levels: small, middling, and great. Even on the path of accumulation, we practice samadhi; meditation practice is always there. As we traverse from one level to the next, from small accumulation to middling accumulation, our concentration becomes stronger and stronger. Though we are able to dwell in the samadhi of the ultimate nature of reality (emptiness), there is still conceptual thought involved. The idea is to gradually eliminate the amount of conceptual thought that arises so that realization becomes direct. At the level of great accumulation, the conceptual barrier is reduced. Then we enter the path of preparation.

The path of preparation comprises four levels. The first level is called 'heat,' because we have come close to realizing emptiness directly. The second level is called 'peak,' the third 'acceptance' or 'patience,' and the fourth, the 'supreme worldly dharma.' In each of these successive stages, the clarity aspect of the ground perfection of wisdom increases, and the conceptual thought that acts as a barrier to direct realization of emptiness decreases, such that all appearances ultimately dissolve into the dharmadhatu, the ground of the nature of reality itself in which dualism disappears. This is how we attain the path of seeing. At this point, our apprehension of emptiness does not depend on the medium of images or concepts. It is direct.

Though the perfection of wisdom sutras touch on the five paths, they do not explain them in detail. The detailed explanation of the paths and levels, which make up the hidden aspect of the perfection of wisdom sutras, is found in Maitreya's *Ornament of Clear Realization*.

MAITREYA'S ORNAMENT OF CLEAR REALIZATION

Maitreya Buddha's commentary on the perfection of wisdom is called the *Ornament of Clear Realization*. He composed the 'Ornament' because the hidden teachings of the extensive aspect of the path are only briefly mentioned by the Buddha, but they are very complex. The Buddha's brief indications are difficult to decode. The 'Ornament' explains the stages of the path that are not explicitly explained in the perfection of wisdom sutras, and Maitreya composed it in order to help those who seek to achieve enlightenment. In the text, the perfection of wisdom is presented in eight chapters or eight topics.

The eight topics are divided into three categories of knowledge. The first category of knowledge contains three levels of realization or knowledge, the second contains four levels of practice, and the third contains the resultant state in the form of the dharmakaya.[61] The entire extensive path or hidden aspect of the perfection of wisdom sutras is revealed without any remainder in these eight topics.

Of the three levels of realization in the first category, the first is omniscient knowledge. The first chapter discusses the state of omniscience, or jnana-dharmakaya, complete enlightenment. Maitreya begins this way in order to show those practitioners who are inclined to the Mahayana that simple liberation from samsara is not yet complete enlightenment, and that there is a state beyond nirvana that is far superior – buddhahood. The qualities of the omniscient state are presented in order to induce aspiration in Mahayana practitioners to complete enlightenment, and not merely the peace of nirvana. The state of omniscience is referred to as 'omniscience' because it realizes conventional reality and ultimate reality simultaneously.

The state of omniscience is represented in the form of ten teachings or instructions. These instructions are necessary factors for achieving omniscience or buddhahood. They include extensive instructions on bodhicitta. Here, the nature of bodhicitta and the levels of its realization are introduced through the twenty-two similes mentioned earlier. In the sutras, it is taught that we can transform ordinary mind with its negative emotions into omniscience, the enlightened state, by the practice of these ten instructions. However, we have to wonder how such a transformation of the ordinary mind, which is contaminated with negative emotions, into the enlightened state of omniscience is even possible.

We already have the ground perfection of wisdom within us right now – our own mind with its aspects of clarity and emptiness. This is the ground aspect of the perfection of wisdom. How then can we transform this into enlightened omniscience? What keeps us from transforming this into omniscience?

Ultimately, what hinders us from transforming ground perfection of wisdom into resultant perfection of wisdom or enlightened omniscience is subtle or innate grasping at an intrinsic reality. We have to eliminate this subtle grasping. The way to do so is practice the wisdom and method aspects of the path together. Both are required. The wisdom aspect of the path eliminates the object of grasping by recognizing that grasping at an intrinsic reality is deluded. When the object of grasping is destroyed through analysis, wisdom eliminates the grasping at the object. The application of wisdom alone, however, is not sufficient. In the post-meditative state, we have to engage in the method aspect of the path, the practice of bodhicitta. Both are needed to eliminate subtle innate grasping, which is the main obstacle to omniscience.

When we are dwelling in meditative absorption on the meaning of selflessness or emptiness, grasping at an intrinsic reality does not arise within that absorption. Once we arise from that absorption, however, we realize that the habitual tendency to grasp at an intrinsic reality, and the habit of self-cherishing, which is a form of grasping at a reality, is too strong to resist in the post-meditative state. The best way to eliminate the habit of self-cherishing is to practice bodhicitta. Through bodhicitta practice, we become able to transform the very nature of self-cherishing. This is a powerful way to eliminate grasping to self, because instead of practicing self-cherishing, we practice benefiting others. The nature of that self-cherishing energy is transformed through this skillful practice in the post-meditative state. This is why the Mahayana sutras say that in order to achieve perfect buddhahood, both method and wisdom are necessary.

To recap, the first chapter of the 'Ornament' is on omniscience and the twenty-two levels of bodhicitta that illustrate how to practice bodhicitta. The topic of the second chapter is the path perfection of wisdom. The path perfection of wisdom is taught because it is the direct cause of the resultant perfection of wisdom, the omniscient state. All the teachings that are necessary to achieve the respective resultant states of all of the yanas are included. Just as the omniscient state is taught through ten representative instructions, the path perfection of wisdom is taught through eleven representative instructions, the practice of which enables one to actualize the path perfection of wisdom. For example, there is the path perfection of wisdom that knows the path of sravakas, the path perfection of wisdom that knows the path of pratyekabuddhas, the path perfection of wisdom that knows the path of Mahayana practitioners, and so on.

The topic of the third chapter is knowledge of the basis. 'Knowledge of the basis' refers to knowledge of the selflessness of the person. These first three chapters are collectively referred to as '*kyenpa sum*,' the three types of knowledge or realization.

To actualize the three types of realization, four practices are taught in chapters four through seven. In the fourth chapter, all of the different paths and levels are taught – the five paths of sravakas, the five paths of pratyekabuddhas, and the five Mahayana paths. Because all paths and levels are explained in chapter four, it is called 'the perfect union of all aspects.' This is important because it maps the entire terrain of the path. Chapter four also explains the signs of the different levels of realization, including the signs of irreversibility – signs that one has attained a state of realization from which one will not revert.

There are definite signs of attainment in the Mahayana practice of wisdom and method. 'Irreversible signs' means that once we have attained that state, we will not fall back from our bodhicitta practice or from the wisdom of realizing emptiness. From that point on, there will be intensity of both compassion and the wisdom of emptiness. The signs include physical changes, verbal expressions, and so on. At each of the successive levels of realization, for example on the path of preparation, we show clear signs that we will not fall back from that state. On achieving the path of seeing, there are signs that we will not fall back, and so on.

A sign that we have cultivated bodhicitta is that even hearing about the suffering of sentient beings will induce such empathy and compassion that tears come. The tears are not from emotion but from deep compassion. This is one of the physical signs of irreversibility, a sign that one has bodhicitta. It is said that when such a person hears that someone is happy, this gives rise to tremendous joy. Bodhicitta is not something we can see, but these are some of the signs, and many such signs are taught.

For us, the opposite is the case. When we hear of someone's suffering, we are indifferent. When we hear of someone's happiness, we become jealous. Thus, where are the signs that we are on the path of omniscience? How is it possible for us to accomplish this path?

A sign of the attainment of the bodhicitta of a bodhisattva is described in Chandrakirti's *Introduction to the Middle Way*. Merely hearing the sound of someone asking, 'Can I have your hand?' or 'Can I have your body?' – merely hearing that sound of someone needing one's service or one's body – induces a deep bliss and joy in the bodhisattva that far exceeds the bliss of sravakas and pratyekhabuddhas dwelling in nirvana for countless eons. This is the real sign that one has cultivated bodhicitta that will never be reversed. This is the exceptional quality of a Mahayana practitioner. It can never be attained by sravakas and pratyekhabuddhas.

One time, the great bodhisattva Aryadeva was invited by a Buddhist monastery to respond to the challenges of some Hindu philosophers. The tradition was that if you lose a debate, you must convert to the side of the winner. The Hindus knew that he was a bodhisattva and that one of the commitments is to give what is asked, so they sent someone disguised as a beggar to intercept Aryadeva and beg for one of his eyes. It is said that Aryadeva gave his right eye right then and there, but the beggar crushed the eye with a stone in front of Aryadeva. It is said that in that moment Aryadeva generated a tiny sense of stinginess, some attachment. Perhaps he had the thought, 'What is the use of what I've done? He didn't make use of it, and now I don't have an eye.' By virtue of that moment of attachment – a fall away from bodhicitta – he did not get his eye back and remained blind in his right eye for the rest of his life. If he had not generated that moment of attachment, then the power of truth and causation is such that even after giving away his eye, he would have regained it. This did not occur, however, as a result of generating this moment of doubt and attachment. This is just an example. Nowadays, some generous people give eyes, kidneys, blood, and so on.

These are just some examples to show the power of bodhicitta gained through practice. The more one becomes able to generate cherishing of others, the more one is able to suppress self-cherishing, and with that the mind becomes very powerful.

The primary concern of bodhisattvas is how to bring sentient beings onto the path of liberation from samsara. They are least concerned about their own suffering, or the fear that we normally have of the suffering of disease, sickness, aging, and death. Bodhisattva do not have that. Their primary concern is how to deliver other sentient beings from suffering. As Mahayana practitioners, we have to emulate this. We should not be primarily concerned with our own fears. We should be concerned with how many beings are ignorant of the path of liberation, circling in a state of darkness. We should contemplate their condition, contemplate the suffering of others and generate empathy. One result will be that we will not suffer from so much self-obsession. We will gain freedom from many of the sufferings that torment us.

We have been speaking here of the fourth chapter of the 'Ornament.' This is on completely perfected application, and as I indicated earlier is the most important chapter, as it details the entire path of Hinayana and Mahayana practitioners. Chapters five, six, and seven contain the remaining applications: application of the peak, gradual application, and instantaneous application and are much shorter than the fourth chapter. We then come to the eighth chapter, which explains the last topic, the resultant body or dharmakaya, by way of the four kayas. The resultant body or dharmakaya has four 'aspects,' so to speak – the four kayas.

The entire perfection of wisdom is presented in the *Ornament of Clear Realization* in eight chapters and seventy topics. The first three chapters, on the three levels of knowledge – omniscience, path level perfection of wisdom, and basis level perfection of wisdom – each contain ten topics or explanations, or thirty topics altogether. Next, the four applications together contain thirty-six topics. Finally, the last topic, dharmakaya, contains four topics. If you understand these, then you have understood the perfection of wisdom.

PRAJNAPARAMITA: THE ESSENCE OF THE THREE BASKETS

The three collections, or 'three *pitakas*' in Sanskrit – abhidharma pitaka, vinaya pitaka, and sutra pitaka – are categorized in this way because the subject matter of each one belongs, for the most part, to one of the three trainings. The three trainings are discipline, concentration, and prajna or wisdom. Because the perfection of wisdom teachings are predominantly on concentration and bodhicitta, they belong to the sutra pitaka. Although each of the trainings mainly focuses on one of the three – discipline, concentration, or wisdom – in fact, all of them contain a little bit of everything. For example, even though the perfection of wisdom belongs to the sutra pitaka whose real topic is concentration, it has an aspect of moral discipline and an aspect of wisdom as well.

If we look at the perfection of wisdom teachings, we see that there are aspects of all three – discipline, concentration, and wisdom. For example, when practicing the wisdom aspect, we have to observe the conduct of a bodhisattva, but the root and branch vows of a bodhisattva belong to the aspect of moral discipline, the subject of the vinaya. We have to use analysis to gain wisdom, to understand the meaning of emptiness, but we also have to practice single-pointed concentration or samadhi to sustain the meaning of emptiness in our own meditative state. We therefore see that the perfection of wisdom teachings actually contain the essence of all three trainings. It follows that the perfection of wisdom is the subject matter of all three collections as well. In this way as well, we see that the perfection of wisdom is the very essence or heart of the Buddha's teachings.

On top of this understanding of the three trainings, we have to understand how the perfection of wisdom teachings contain the mundane path comprising the nine absorptions, culminating in the peak of samsara, as well as the transcendental path, starting with the levels of realization of the sravakas and pratyekabuddhas, including stream-enterers, once-returners, non-returners, and arhats. The ten bodhisattva grounds also are included here.

With these seven topics, I have covered the entire range of possible teachings and practices you might encounter in the prajnaparamita teachings. This can be a guide for anyone who might want to study and practice them and provides a map to help navigate and contextualize the teachings. How do we carry these teachings into day-to-day practice? We turn to this next.

11

CARRYING THE PRAJNAPARAMITA TEACHINGS INTO PRACTICE

In the previous chapter, I explained the perfection of wisdom in seven topics and touched on how it is presented in the *Ornament of Clear Realization*. I will now explain how to actually carry the perfection of wisdom teachings into practice. There are many books on how to practice the Mahayana path. The best one is Tsongkhapa's *Lamrim Chenmo*, or 'Stages on the Path to Enlightenment.'

In India and Tibet, the perfection of wisdom teachings were generally transmitted in a way that was easy to understand. A classic example in India is Atisha's *Lamp of the Path to Enlightenment*. The 'Lamp' was composed for Tibetan disciples of lesser capacity. Atisha presented the stages of the path in their essential form for persons of the three capacities: lesser, middling, and great. This was extremely beneficial for Tibet, as it suited the Tibetan spiritual landscape. Based on that, we find many Tibetan masters composing lamrim or 'stages of the path' texts, which are all ways of carrying the perfection of wisdom into practice. The great master Drolungpa, for example, composed the *Great Stages of the Doctrine*, an eleventh-century commentary on Atisha's 'Lamp.' Based on this text and Atisha's 'Lamp,' Tsongkhapa composed the *Lamrim Chenmo*. Based on earlier traditions, the Kagyu also have texts belonging to the genre of lamrim literature, such as the *Stages of the Path of the Essence of Primordial Wisdom* by Chogyur Dechen Lingpa and Jamyang Khyentse Wangpo, and Gampopa's *Jewel Ornament of Liberation*. The Nyingma have Patrul Rinpoche's *Words of my Perfect Teacher*. All of these belong to the genre of lamrim literature, which set forth methods of practicing the perfection of wisdom as taught by the Buddha. All of these lamrim texts offer ways to carry the perfection of wisdom teachings into practice. The method I am presenting here is based on my own experience.

Even though all of these books are beneficial and useful if we have the time, we tend to lack leisure today in the West. We do not have the time for the in-depth study of texts that is traditionally taken. Because we do not have the time to go through the detailed explanations of the traditional texts, I am going to give instructions on how to practice the perfection of wisdom teachings in seven points.

In the Buddhist approach to study, especially if one is a Mahayana practitioner, there is no distinction between the object of academic study and that which we carry into practice. Whatever we study is necessarily a means of engaging in practice – there is no such thing as intellectual endeavor for its own sake. Study is a means of carrying the teachings into practice, leading to intuitive experiential understanding, not intellectual mastery. When we present the teachings, we have to present something to be studied followed by the means for carrying what has been studied into practice, but they are not two distinct things. We are introduced to the teachings, and then having been introduced to them, we learn how to carry them into practice.

Following are the seven points to accomplish this.

The first point introduces the ground prajnaparamita, the ground perfection of wisdom, and then how to carry that into practice.

The second point introduces the Mahayana potential and how to actually awaken one's own Mahayana potential. I point out the obscuring factors that prevent us from awakening that potential and the disadvantages of not awakening it.

The third point introduces the path perfection of wisdom and gives an explanation of the stages of the path, from the path of accumulation through the path of seeing.

The fourth point introduces the path of meditation, a unique combination or union of calm abiding and special insight.

The fifth point explains how to carry the six perfections into practice in one meditative session.

The sixth point explains how to engage in daily mind-training practice (Tib. *lojong*) as an enhancement practice.

The seventh point explains the unique Mahayana way of dedicating practice and with that, some of my own personal advice.

GROUND PERFECTION OF WISDOM

We should understand the ground perfection of wisdom as something that is present at the level of the ground as it is right now – the union of the two inseparable aspects of mind: clarity and emptiness. Though mind is clear, it is empty; though it is empty, it is clear. When we talk about the ground perfection of wisdom, we are referring to the ultimate nature of mind, the union of clarity and emptiness.

When we talk about the emptiness of mind, we refer to the nature of mind as non-arising and therefore also as unceasing. 'Emptiness of mind' means that mind does not arise, abide, or cease; it has no beginning, middle, or end. The non-arising and unceasing nature of mind is mentioned frequently in the perfection of wisdom sutras. It is represented by the *Perfection of Wisdom Sutra in a Single Letter*, the letter 'Ah.' 'Ah' represents the absence of arising and the absence of cessation, or the empty nature of mind. It therefore represents the ground perfection of wisdom.

If every phenomenon is of the nature of Ah without arising or cessation, then how do we account for the variety of appearances we actually experience, the emotions we experience, the reality of the movements of mind, the arising of thoughts, and so forth? The answer is that they are like the reflection of the moon in a pool of water. Even though we see the moon clearly, nonetheless there is no moon in the water. Watching television, we see apparent people and scenes, but if we try to touch them, we only touch the glass surface. Likewise, even though there is no true arising or cessation, and the nature of everything is empty, interdependent appearances are spontaneously present. The emptiness of mind does not entail nothingness. Emptiness does not mean things do not exist at all; it is not nihilism. Because the nature of the mind is empty, all interdependently arising appearances, both external and internal, forms, thoughts, and emotions, arise spontaneously as the clarity aspect of mind, which is unceasing. Even though mind does not actually exist, because it is empty of inherent existence, the aspect of clarity is unceasing. This apparently contradictory nature of the emptiness and clarity of mind is described in the seemingly self-contradictory saying, "All phenomena arise from their non-arising nature."

What all of the buddhas of the three times have seen can be explained in the following way. First, they have seen the empty nature of mind. Second, they have seen that all appearances, whether outer appearances or inner thoughts and feelings, arise from the empty nature of mind as display or energetic expression. Unlike the buddhas, however, ordinary people are confused because we have not realized that appearances are nothing more than the display of the empty nature of mind. We cling to appearances as intrinsically existing, grasping at them. This is how we become deluded. We take empty appearances to be intrinsically real and grasp at them. The buddhas of the three times, however, understand the empty nature of the display of appearances and how people are deluded about this display. Having understood this, they are able to dissolve all of the display of appearances into the ground, the empty nature of mind. Then, through training, they are able to actualize the resultant state. In this sense, the ground perfection of wisdom, which is basically the empty nature of our own mind, is the footprint on the path that all the buddhas of the three times have traversed. It is very important that we identify and recognize the ground perfection of wisdom in this way.

The first thing to recognize is the nature of mind, the union of emptiness and clarity, which is represented by the syllable 'Ah.' This is the ground perfection of wisdom, the ultimate nature of mind. From the point of view of its essence, which is empty, it is non-arising and unceasing. From the point of view of its nature or characteristic, it is unceasingly clear; clarity is always there. When the ground is obscured by ignorance, it is this clarity aspect that is responsible for propelling us through the world of conditioned existence, or samsara, with all of its confusions and delusions. Once we are able to identify and eliminate this confusion, this same clarity of the mind dawns as the path of pure vision. Instead of having confused, deluded vision and experience, we have pure vision and pure perception.

Having been introduced to and recognized the ground perfection of wisdom, the ultimate nature of mind, how do we carry this into practice? In the traditional perfection of wisdom teachings, the way is through training in the five paths and ten bodhisattva grounds. This takes time and effort and is very difficult to apply in our own social and environmental context. One way we can more easily carry the ground perfection of wisdom into practice is to introduce the unique Mahayana way of practicing the union of calm abiding and special insight. Once we have been introduced to this, ultimately calm abiding gives rise to special insight, or vipasyana. Vipasyana is what actually gives rise to realization. By training in special insight, we cultivate the full realization of the ground perfection of wisdom. The way in which this dawns can be likened to the way the new moon becomes a full moon.

MAHAYANA POTENTIAL

As Mahayana practitioners, we have to recognize what is called the 'Mayahana potential' or 'Mahayana lineage;' *'gotra'* in Sanskrit. The supremacy of Mahayana potential over Hinayana potential is usually explained in terms of seven factors.[62] Of course, with respect to natural buddha nature, there is no difference; there are not separate Mahayana and Hinayana buddha natures. Buddha nature is buddha nature. It is just the nature of mind, which is present in all sentient beings. Mahayana potential, however, can be distinguished from the point of view of method and from the point of view of wisdom. From the point of view of method, it can be distinguished by a fundamental difference in orientation. Instead of being concerned primarily about oneself, self-cherishing is overshadowed by the cherishing of others. From the point of view of wisdom, Mahayana realization is not limited to the emptiness or selflessness of the person it extends to the selflessness of all phenomena.

The difference between the Mahayana potential and the Hinayana potential is not a difference between types of natural buddha nature, but between different 'ornamental' buddha natures.[63] The two superior and uncommon qualities or 'ornaments' of a Mahayana practitioner – Mahayana method and Mahayana wisdom – are more profound and extensive than the qualities of practitioners of the other vehicles.

Of the seven factors that distinguish Mahayana practitioners from Hinayana practitioners, 'great focus' refers to the scope of one's intention when engaging in practice. Are you practicing for yourself, or does your intention encompass all sentient beings? One of the distinguishing qualities of Mahayana practitioners is their motivation or focus – the intention to become able to benefit all sentient beings. Another difference is in what is actually practiced. Mahayana practitioners are not satisfied with just eliminating negative emotions and gaining individual nirvana; they are willing to make tremendous effort to achieve the great non-abiding nirvana, or complete buddhahood. What is being eliminated is not just negative emotions, but the obscurations to omniscience as well. This requires a lot more practice and effort than individual nirvana. Another distinguishing quality is effort. Bodhisattvas have armor-like effort. They are able to withstand any challenge. A fourth distinguishing quality is wisdom. Mahayana wisdom is not limited to understanding the selflessness of the person; it also includes understanding the selflessness of all phenomena.

As Mahayana practitioners, we are not trying to engage in competition with Hinayana practitioners, but we must be able to understand and practice these qualities. To be a Mahayana practitioner, it is not enough to have Mahayana teachings; we must also practice. The purpose of explaining Mahayana qualities is to support their inner application, not the making of external comparisons.

To summarize, in the beginning we have to be able to recognize the ground perfection of wisdom. Then, having recognized the ground, we have to engage in practice. To engage in practice, we have to see ourselves as Mahayana practitioners. This means understanding our responsibility, how to train, and so forth. Without understanding our Mahayana potential, we cannot know these things.

Having recognized our Mahayana potential, we have to awaken it. In order to awaken it, we must be able to recognize the hindrances to awakening. The greatest hindrance of all is self-cherishing, which is poison. It does not harm us much during meditation, but in post-meditation and day-to-day activities, self-cherishing is pervasive. There is no need to explain this; we experience it all the time.

We can observe the effects of self-cherishing in our practice in three ways. First, if we are not able to encompass all sentient beings in our intention, or dedicate our virtue to all sentient beings, it is because of self-cherishing. Second, self-cherishing hinders us from engaging in practice to achieve buddhahood. Third, it hinders us from engaging in armor-like joyous effort.

Recognizing our own self-cherishing as a hindrance should not be taken as a reason to engage in self-hatred. There is a real danger of that. If having recognized our self-cherishing, we generate self-hatred, then we are only falling under the spell of self-cherishing. If we engage in self-hatred, we will not be able to eliminate self-cherishing. The point here is to identify self-cherishing as that which obscures the possibility of awakening buddha nature. In order to awaken buddha nature, we have to see what is in the way. Then, using skillful means, we can actually use self-cherishing by transforming its energy into benefiting others.

We can accomplish this by means of mind training practice. First, we look at our own nature and see the ground perfection of wisdom, which does not depend on our parents, external circumstances, or culture. The ground perfection of wisdom is inherently there. We recognize that and cultivate joy. We then generate the intention to further develop and intensify the perfection of wisdom. We identify self-cherishing as the key hindrance to progress. Then, when self-cherishing arises – as it does all the time – we try to change its very nature or energy by shifting our focus. Instead of putting ourselves there, we put other sentient beings there. Instead of thinking of our own suffering and wishing to be free of it, we think of their suffering and their wish to gain freedom from it. Whenever there is concern for the self, we transform it by changing the object of that energy and directing the concern to other sentient beings. We do this as much as possible – that is what the training takes. We talk about making the mental scope expansive, which basically means extending our focus until it is unlimited, extending infinitely to all sentient beings.

As part of mind training, it is also important to cultivate joy at having found this opportunity to meet with the teacher and the teachings, and to awaken your Mahayana potential. You should think, 'I'm going to utilize this opportunity to transform my mind as much as possible.' When we acknowledge this joy, then even though we are not able to effect change right away, it becomes a powerful motivation that gives support to the training immediately.

Our goal is to activate buddha nature through mind training, awakening our Mahayana potential. It is not sufficient to understand the factors that awaken buddha nature; we have to put them into practice. The way to do this is to increase the scope of the mind, so that it becomes expansive, encompassing all sentient beings and not merely those that directly concern us. From the point of view of method, the most important practice is the practice of compassion. Compassion here is the great compassion that encompasses all sentient beings. The most important instruction concerning Mahayana potential is to cultivate this great compassion daily. From the point of view of wisdom, the most important point is to understand the emptiness of all phenomena and not just the emptiness of self. By understanding the emptiness of all phenomena, we recognize the deluded state for what it is. Understanding the deluded state, we also understand how it gives rise to suffering. However, it is not enough to identify the deluded state; we also have to generate the mind of enlightenment, bodhicitta. It is important to understand that generating bodhicitta is not like generation stage yoga, we do not visually generate ourselves in the form of the deity. Generating bodhicitta does not involve visually imagining something – but actually skillfully transforming the mind.

The self-cherishing mind that we presently experience is very narrow and bogged down. When we talk about generating bodhicitta, we are talking about transforming this self-cherishing mind right now, in the present moment. We are not waiting for something to change in the future – we are able to change this self-cherishing mind into compassion for others right now. This basically means that you transform yourself.

So we must practice that, beginning with mindfulness. It is not easy; it takes years. But then, deep inside, the mind becomes very powerful. Whatever we see, whatever we do, we can draw on and share that, no matter the situation. Then we can say, 'I am a Mahayana practitioner.' We have to distinguish that from ego, however. We don't say, 'I have a lot of knowledge; I am a scholar' – that is delusion. If we are deluded, then when difficulties come, we fall down very easily. What I'm referring to here is very different, however, very different – a very positive, powerful mind. I hope you all understand what I am saying.

There is a great deal of discussion on different methods for awakening Mahayana potential, and the disadvantages of not awakening it. In a nutshell, I think that after you have been able to actually recognize Mahayana potential, the two practices I mentioned earlier contain what is essential for awakening it. With respect to method, cultivate great compassion on a daily basis; then cultivate bodhicitta. With respect to wisdom, the way to awaken Mahayana potential is to understand the selflessness of all appearances. Understand that in the absence of understanding selflessness, all appearances are deluded. If we do this on a daily basis, we will awaken our buddha nature. Train in the method, and train in wisdom. Through training like this on a daily basis, the time will come when we have generated such confidence that we are extremely powerful in benefiting other sentient beings. We generate the confidence to withstand any challenge. Whether circumstances are good or bad, we are able to perceive and experience them with stability and confidence, and there is no fear of difficulties, death, or the bardo state. There is inherent spontaneous joy and confidence in acting to help other sentient beings. Then we can confidently say that we have awakened our buddha nature and have entered the Mahayana path.

Chandrakirti mentions in *Introduction to the Middle Way* that the way to awaken Mahayana potential is to cultivate and practice great compassion. The homage at the beginning of this text is paid to great compassion itself, not to buddhas or bodhisattvas. Chandrakirti pays homage to great compassion itself, explaining that it is present in the beginning, the middle, and the end. In the beginning, it is like a seed; in the middle, it is like the water and fertilizer that nurture the seed; and at the end, it is like the ripened fruit.

> The Shravakas and those halfway to buddhahood are born from the Mighty Sage,
> And Buddhas take their birth from Bodhisattva heroes.
> Compassion, non-duality, the wish for buddhahood for others' sake
> Are causes of the children of the Conqueror.
> Of buddhahood's abundant crop, compassion is the seed.
> It is like moisture bringing increase and is said
> To ripen in the state of lasting happiness.
> Therefore to begin, I celebrate compassion![64]

In the beginning, to awaken buddha nature, we must have great compassion. In the middle, while training in the paths, we again must have great compassion. Simply meditating on emptiness does not become the Mahayana path. In the end, having achieved the enlightened state, great compassion is important because the nirmanakaya emanations of the enlightened person are the display, or expression, of great compassion. This is very different from the individual nirvanic peace of the Hinayana practitioner. Nirvana is profound, but there is no great compassion that expresses itself in the form of emanations in order to help sentient beings.

Cultivating and generating great compassion is not easy. Nowadays, everyone talks about loving kindness, but we do not really know what that means. To generate great compassion for sentient beings, we have to practice the techniques that lead us there; we have to cultivate love. There is a difference, however, between love and compassion. First of all, we must have a loving attitude toward sentient beings. A loving attitude is dependent on our ability to see others as connected to us and in a positive light; it is dependent on cultivating warmth. Right now, we are not able to see everyone in a positive light – we see only ourselves and some friends and family in this way. We are not able to see others as loving. Because of our inability to generate this sense of warmth, kindness, and connection, we have no way to cultivate great compassion.

Seeing others in a positive light, cultivating loving warmth, is so difficult because we are used to looking for the faults in others. If we look for faults in others, we will find them. This is why we fail to see others with a sense of loving warmth. In *Calling the Guru from Afar*, Jamgon Kongtrul describes the natural tendency to look for the faults in others and hide our own, even when they are as big as mountains. Even if someone else's faults are as small as a molehill by comparison, we have a tendency to exaggerate and publicize them.

> We conceal within ourselves a mountain of faults;
> Yet, we put down others and broadcast their shortcoming,
> though they be minute as a sesame seed.
> Though we have not the slightest good qualities, we boast
> saying how great we are.
> We have the label of Dharma practitioners, but practice
> only non-Dharma.
> Lama, think of us, behold us swiftly with compassion.

I wish to emphasize again the importance of cultivating great compassion in daily life. Cultivate loving warmth, seeing others in a positive light. Even though it is challenging, especially in the West, as Mahayana practitioners we need to apply as much effort as possible to generating this loving warmth and kindness that give rise to compassion.

American culture is not so great, and it makes it difficult to practice the Mahayana. We know the words here; we are good with the words, but that does not mean we practice them. I am pointing to the different conditions under which one practices in Asia as compared to those in America – I am not trying to denigrate the entirety of American culture. There are some negative influences that create challenges for practitioners, and pointing these out is not the same as showing disrespect to people.

First, there is tremendous ego and delusion. Second, there is rigid narrow-mindedness and an unwillingness to share anything. Third, there is no trust; people do not trust each other. These are very dangerous influences. If we want to practice compassion, we have to recognize the effects of all three of these in ourselves. If we do not change these three poisons our practice will not be successful. We can listen to the teachings and the teachings may be clear, but if there is ego, narrow-mindedness, and the inability to trust, they will bring no benefit. I say this to practitioners, not to all beings. I must give advice based on what I have seen in my life. I cannot say something is fantastic when it is not; that would be delusional. Outer conditions are good here – we are very fortunate – but inside, do we have peace in our minds? We have to recognize these poisons and change a little every day; then we can see. It is good that you all listen to instructions on bodhicitta and the five paths; this makes me very happy. However, as practitioners in this life, you need to connect through the practice and not only through words.

Recognizing our Mahayana potential and then awakening it are practices to ripen our mental continuum. After the path of ripening comes the path of liberation. The third point introduces the methods of the path, or the path perfection of wisdom.

PATH PERFECTION OF WISDOM

The first point introduced the ground perfection of wisdom and what is meant by that. Second, the Mahayana potential and how to activate it were introduced. Now, having activated our buddha nature, the Mahayana potential, we come to the third point – how to actually train on the path. Training on the path falls within the category of path perfection of wisdom. In the context of the latter, we discuss all of the five Mahayana paths, starting with the path of accumulation.

'Path perfection of wisdom' can be defined as 'a powerful, resourceful mind that is influenced by a supreme method and supreme wisdom, both of which have the potential to eliminate even the subtlest of mental obscurations.'

When we talk about traversing the path, we should not see this as something in the distance, or view the paths as things to count off, as if they were external to us. The path is intimately connected to us, and it has to do with the qualities of our own mind. On a daily basis, when we see subtle improvements, some transformation, in our own mind, then we are traversing the path. It is not something abstract. It is intimate; right here.

The traditional scriptural explanation of the path of accumulation is very elaborate. Here we are concerned with what is practical and how to train in the path of accumulation in daily life. The context of the path of accumulation is our introduction to and recognition of the ground perfection of wisdom, and our introduction to and recognition of our Mahayana potential, although we have not yet fully developed that potential. On the path of accumulation, the practitioner cultivates great compassion and the wisdom of emptiness, which activate our Mahayana potential.

On the path of accumulation, we accumulate merit. In its ordinary state, the mind is not very powerful; it is weak and scattered, in a state of delusion or confusion, which is a source of suffering. We have to change the fundamental content of mind, so that it becomes powerful and a source of happiness, thereby gaining freedom from delusions. In order to do this, we need to understand what is conducive to making the mind powerful. Because we are on the threshold of the Mahayana path of accumulation, we are looking for uncommon factors unique to the Mahayana that are conducive to entering its gate. Then, having identified these conducive factors, we have to accumulate the virtuous states of mind responsible for making the mind more powerful and a source of happiness. That is what is meant by 'accumulation.'

What we are accumulating is merit, and merit is not something we see with the eye consciousness. The term 'merit' refers to the conducive factors that make the mind more powerful and more amenable to dharma, and it is accumulated through our body, speech, and mind. We accumulate merit through the body by practicing generosity, doing chod practice, offering our body, and so forth. Through speech we accumulate merit by engaging in teaching dharma, giving advice or instructions to others that is actually beneficial. We accumulate merit through mind by cultivating right intention at all times. The intention is to accumulate merit in order to benefit sentient beings.

Our own body, speech, and mind have to be transformed through our own virtuous actions. It is wrong to think of the accumulation of merit as something outside of ourselves that leaves the body, speech, and mind unchanged.

'Accumulation of merit' means 'accumulating merit of body, speech, and mind at the level of the ground.' By engaging in virtuous wholesome activities through the three doors, we transform them into the nature of virtue. When engaging in wholesome activities, it is important to do so with the intention of bodhicitta. When we engage in these activities with this intention, we automatically accumulate merit.

As long as we know the purpose of accumulation and practice correctly, then all activities of our body, speech and mind are integral to the path of accumulation. The path is then clear. In a state of confusion, you do not know where you are going, but being on the path means that you do know where you are going. Every day, practice lojong (mind training) and Chöd or cutting through grasping by offering your body. Do not think of merit accumulation as separate from the rest of your practices and activities, thinking, 'I practice Chöd, ngondro, now I'm ready for merit accumulation.' Rather, whatever we do is the path of accumulation. I did not understand this correctly when I was young. I read all about the path of accumulation, preparation, and so on, as though it were something else. Merit is the path of accumulation; do not think that it is separate. If you practice ngondro, guru yoga, and Chöd correctly, all are the path of accumulation. The mind becomes more powerful and expansive. But, again, it is not easy to destroy negative conditioning.

We start on the path of accumulation by not waiting until next month or until we wake up one morning with enough motivation. Even when we do tsa lung, we are not doing it to benefit our own body; we are doing it with the intention to live a long life so that we can benefit a lot of beings. This is the Mahayana mind. For the Mahayana practitioner, all activity is the path of accumulation; nothing is outside of it.

The result of engaging in the path of accumulation is that the mind becomes very powerful. As the mind becomes more powerful, we need to engage in meditation to make it more subtle. Only a subtle mind can approach the realization of the true nature of reality, the ground prajnaparamita, or emptiness. If we do not enter into meditation to realize the ground perfection of wisdom, there is a danger that even though mind has become very powerful, it can fall under the sway of illusion and succumb to grasping at the illusion of an intrinsic self. Thus, once we have succeeded in making the mind powerful, it is necessary to refine our meditation in order to realize emptiness.

On the path of accumulation, we combine the practice of accumulating merit with meditation on emptiness. For those engaging in Dzogchen practice, after accumulating merit, enter into Dzogchen meditation. In this way, your accumulation of merit and accumulation of the wisdom of emptiness reinforce each other. That is the whole thing. The reason we practice method and wisdom in union is that they reinforce each other. Powerful mind reinforces meditative stability; the wisdom of emptiness reinforces virtuous activities.

In brief, practicing as a Mahayana practitioner on the path of accumulation means integrating the merit accumulated in the state of meditative absorption with merit accumulated in the context of post-meditative daily activities. In absorption, the path of accumulation involves recognizing the ground perfection of wisdom and sustaining that recognition in single-pointed calm-abiding meditation. (How to practice the union of calm abiding and special insight will be presented in more detail later.) Practicing the path of accumulation in the post-meditative state involves cultivating bodhicitta based on loving kindness and compassion. Then, based on the cultivation of loving kindness, compassion, and bodhicitta, we practice the six perfections through the application of mindfulness and vigilance. When we practice the six perfections in post-meditation influenced by loving kindness and compassion, the mind becomes more powerful, potent, and expansive. We then use that accumulation of mental power to further enhance our meditation on the ground perfection of wisdom. This is how we integrate the meditative state and the post-meditative state.

As I mentioned earlier, the path of accumulation is divided into three levels – lesser, middling, and great. The lesser path of accumulation involves studying and contemplating the Mahayana teachings, and then entering into all the practices, from the preliminary practices such as refuge, to other practices like Chöd. All of them become part of the accumulation of merit. On the lesser path of accumulation, extensive accumulation of merit actually occurs in the post-meditative state through practice of the six perfections. Then, as a sign that the mind has become more powerful, our aspiration and devotion to practice increase tremendously. There is more energy, joy, and aspiration to engage in practice, and when we can put a lot of joyous effort into practice, it is a sign that the mind has become more powerful. On the middling path of accumulation, we are able to accumulate merit without as much effort and to sustain single-pointed samadhi for longer periods of time. Then, by virtue of that, we enter into the great level of the path of accumulation. Here, the sign of accomplishment is being able to enter into long-term samadhi. The primary practice becomes absorption in samadhi, and we are able to sustain single-pointed concentration for long periods of time. At this point, the accumulation of merit in the post-meditative state becomes ancillary to meditation. The main practice is sustaining the meaning of emptiness in samadhi.

Transitioning from the great path of accumulation to the first level of the path of preparation called 'heat' occurs when we can sustain the samadhi dwelling on the meaning of ground perfection of wisdom at the level of the great path of accumulation. As this samadhi achieves stability, the clarity aspect increases. The more that clarity increases, the closer we come to actualizing the ground perfection of wisdom. What is by analogy called 'heat' is a sign that we are closer to realizing the ground perfection of wisdom or emptiness. Just as when we approach a fire we have seen from afar, we begin to be able to 'feel the heat,' as we approach the realization of emptiness, we can sense that we are closer to that realization. Thus, 'heat' is actually like an internal sign that we have come closer to actual realization. As clarity intensifies, we do not have to make as much effort to practice bodhicitta, loving kindness, and compassion. By simply reminding ourselves for a moment of these practices, we can enter into the experience of great compassion, loving kindness, and so on. As we come even closer to apprehending emptiness directly, the special insight aspect is intensified. The internal sign of this is joy at meditating in the samadhi of the the ground perfection of wisdom. This joy in sustaining meditation is a sign that we have traversed the first, or 'heat,' level of the path of preparation. At this level of the path of preparation, we do not have to engage in the extensive accumulation of merit that was necessary on the path of accumulation. The primary practice here is the special insight practice of samadhi directly apprehending emptiness.

The second level of the path of preparation is called the 'peak.' This denotes a level of realization in which our meditation dwelling on the meaning of emptiness has become greatly intensified. The union of calm abiding and special insight is developed here in such a way that engaging in analytical meditation (which is basically the special insight aspect, the wisdom aspect) does not actually disturb our single-pointed calm abiding. Rather, engaging in analytical meditation actually induces further meditative stability. One reinforces the other. This is a stage where calm abiding reinforces special insight and vice versa, so that they complement each other. At this point, we have reached the peak level of the path of preparation.

The third level on the path of preparation is called 'patience.' 'Patience' in this case, however, does not have its usual meaning, that is, the ability to withstand suffering and challenges. Here, the usage is unique, and refers to the fact that when we engage in meditative absorption on the ground perfection of wisdom, we are able to eliminate all external and internal obstacles that would otherwise disturb the stability of our meditative absorption. Patient in that sense, the patience of mindfulness, means that we are able to sustain the continuum of meditation without any disturbance. At this point, mind has become extremely powerful. It is said that from this stage onward, we have permanently shut the door to lower realms. Once we have reached that state, there is certainty that we have permanently shut the door to rebirth in the lower realms.

The fourth and final level of the path of preparation is called "supreme dharma." This represents a level of realization where our power of special insight is so intensified that we come extremely close to directly apprehending the dharmadhatu, directly apprehending the ground perfection of wisdom. At this point, however, even though there is deep meditative absorption and it feels as if dualism has actually dissolved, there is still subtle duality. Even though it seems as though we are dwelling directly in the ground perfection of wisdom, there is still no direct apprehension due to the subtle obscuration of dualism. The meaning of emptiness apprehended here is still something apprehended by way of a very subtle conceptual image. There is no direct experience like that of water being poured into water, where subject and object totally disappear. Nonetheless, we have to understand that at this stage, we have fully accomplished the meditative absorption of calm abiding. There is no dullness or agitation. There is total single-pointed absorption on the ground perfection of wisdom, but this absorption is still sustained with a subtle obscuration of concepts. Conventional conceptual mind has not yet dissolved altogether. Nonetheless, we have come very close to apprehending the ground perfection of wisdom directly, so this stage is called 'supreme dharma.'

At this point, even though most of the mind sustains single-pointed shamatha, another part of the mind engages in analysis in the act of recognizing emptiness, such that there is still a subtle dualism. The apprehension of emptiness here still uses conceptual thought, and thus it is not direct. In the state of absorption, however, the subtle concepts eventually fall apart, so that we now apprehend the ground perfection of wisdom nakedly – without concepts and without the dualism of subject and object. In the instant when we have fully traversed the path of preparation, when we see emptiness directly, we have joined the path of seeing. We have finally apprehended the ground perfection of wisdom directly, and at this point we become an arya, a noble one.

On the path of seeing, we directly apprehend emptiness without the dualism of subject and object, but when we arise from that state into the post-meditative state, we still see conventional reality. The ability to integrate the meditative and post-meditative states so that we never waver from the ground perfection of wisdom only occurs in the enlightened state. When practitioners on the path of seeing leave the meditative state and enter the post-meditative state, they see phenomena. However, even the post-meditative-state practice is experienced as illusory. In the post-meditative state, we practice compassion and loving kindness – but as an illusion: illusory compassion, illusory loving kindness, and so forth.

The experience of this meditative absorption is likened to space because the meditator sustains the absence of intrinsic existence single-pointedly without falling into conventional experience based on subject and object. The experience of the post-meditative state is likened to illusion because all appearances are experienced as illusory by the practitioner on the path of seeing.

There is no difference in the conventional appearances experienced by ourselves and these practitioners in the post-meditative state. Upon arising from meditative absorption in which they directly apprehend emptiness, practitioners on the path of seeing experience the same world of appearances as we do. The difference lies in whether or not we see appearances as things that exist from their own side, in their own right, truly independently. When we see appearances, it seems as if they have an existence independent of our seeing them. We are not able to see them as illusory. We may be able to imagine or follow some of the intellectual presentations of emptiness, but we do not experience everything as illusion-like. Even though we may have intellectual conviction, we do not have that experience. However, in the post-meditative state, for the practitioner on the path of seeing, everything actually appears as illusory. There is no need to sustain this illusion-like experience through effort. The power of the meditative absorption on emptiness is so strong that it carries over into the post-meditative state. Without effort, we experience everything as illusion-like, without any true existence. What is happening is that although there is some subtle grasping at an intrinsic reality, it is not very strong. This subtle grasping is not able to give rise to gross negative emotions for the practitioner who has had a direct experience of emptiness. Even in the post-meditative state, the three gross poisons of attachment, aversion, and ignorance are not present for the practitioner.

First, the reason we generate strong attachment, aversion, and ignorance is that we have not been able to experience the ground perfection of wisdom. Second, whenever we experience external appearances such as form and sound, we see them as intrinsically existing on their own side, and we get carried away. That is how the emotions produced by these appearances become so strong. We do not have to make any effort to give rise to attachment, aversion, or ignorance; they come spontaneously as a result of our confusion about intrinsic existence.

The difference between ourselves as ordinary beings and the practitioner who has directly apprehended the ground perfection of wisdom, and experiences appearances as illusory in the post-meditative state, lies in the power of the practitioner's mind. 'Power of the mind' refers to the fact that the practitioner has eliminated gross grasping to intrinsic reality, and gross attachment, aversion, and ignorance are no longer generated in his or her mindstream. Once we have eliminated gross grasping at things as intrinsically real, then that eliminates the experience of anything as intrinsically existing. The capacity of appearances or phenomena to appear as intrinsically existing is exhausted. As a result, our habitual ways of reacting to persons, situations, and things also come to an end. Aryas, therefore, do not generate attachment, aversion, and ignorance like ordinary people do. The external objects or phenomena themselves do not go through any change – what changes is the subtlety and profundity of the perceiving mind. To the extent that the mind becomes more profound and more subtle from meditating on the ground perfection of wisdom and apprehending it directly, appearances of external objects undergo changes. Even though the object itself does not change, the appearance of the object as something that exists independently changes because of changes in the subtlety, profundity, and clarity of the perceiving mind. As the subtlety and clarity of the mind increases, the perceived object becomes more clear, more pure, more free of confusion.

If we do not apprehend the ground perfection of wisdom directly, we can never gain freedom from conditioned samsaric existence. That is how important this direct apprehension is. Whether or not we are able to achieve this depends on our prior practice at the level of the path of accumulation and the path of preparation. It is important to understand that when we talk about the different levels of the path, we are not just telling a story. It is extremely important to understand that in order to give rise to realizations of the higher levels of the path, we must go through the lower-level practices. We can testify based on our own experience that 'traversing the stages of the path' refers to improving the power or potential of the mind. The more we train, the more we experience that there is some kind of positive transformation of our mind. The power or potential of our mind increases. Alternatively, if we do not engage in practice, if we are not mindful and conscientious, it is possible for the mind to deteriorate and its powers diminish. We have experienced this as well. Therefore when we talk about levels of realization – which really refers to stages of the path – this is something that we can see as a reality, and not just a story.

Having apprehended the ground perfection of wisdom directly, and become able to sustain space-like absorption and illusion-like post-meditation on the path of seeing, is not the end of the training. We still have to train on the path of meditation, which is the fourth of the five paths.

PATH OF MEDITATION

Transitioning from the path of seeing to the path of meditation takes place in the state of meditative absorption, not in the post-meditative state. Traversing the different levels always happens in the state of absorption. Emptiness is directly realized on the path of seeing, the attainment of the first bodhisattva ground, Great Joy, and there is nothing new to realize on the path of meditation.

The path of meditation is divided into two levels of realization – the contaminated path of meditation and the uncontaminated path of meditation. The contaminated path refers to the level where we have understood emptiness directly – free from concepts and without dualism – but when we arise in the post-meditative state, we are not able to integrate the meditative experience with the post-meditative experience such that they become inseparable. That period is referred to as the 'contaminated path of meditation.'

There is no difference in the apprehension of the ground perfection of wisdom, between the path of seeing and the path of meditation. The direct apprehension of emptiness is common to both paths, but there is a difference in the power of the mind to eliminate even subtle grasping at a reality. By virtue of having familiarized ourselves with meditation on emptiness, the mind and meditation of the practitioner on the path of meditation has become so powerful that there is no grasping even at an intrinsic reality. Even in the post-meditative state, the practitioner on the path of meditation is able to eliminate grasping at intrinsically existing appearances by seeing the illusory nature of phenomena in an even deeper sense. There is a difference of degree in the power of the mind to eliminate grasping of the subtlest kind, when the practitioner on the path of seeing is compared with the practitioner on the path of meditation.

There are definite signs that a practitioner has irreversibly reached the path of meditation. Some of the differences between the practitioner on the path of seeing and the practitioner on the path of meditation are as follows. The path of seeing is the entrance to the path of meditation at the level of the first bodhisattva bhumi. The path of meditation extends all the way to the tenth bhumi.

Another difference is that the practitioner on the path of meditation has the exceptional ability to enter into absorption and come out of it in a single instant, in the time it takes to snap your fingers. In a moment, he or she is able to come out of absorption, then enter back into it just like that. This power is unique to someone on the path of meditation; it is not present on the path of seeing. What this really means is that the practitioner on the path of meditation is able to integrate the experiences of absorption with post-meditative experience. This is not yet the cultivation of one taste, but the path of meditation involves integration of absorption and post-meditation in a way that is not possible on the path of seeing.

The ground perfection of wisdom is apprehended directly on the path of seeing, but direct apprehension of reality is not sufficient to eliminate the subtlest grasping at intrinsic reality. We have to continuously familiarize ourselves with the truth in order to further purify mind. We continue to purify our meditation, gradually eliminating subtler and subtler layers of grasping. What this means for the day-to-day practice of someone on the path of meditation, is continuous practice of meditation. Basically, we divide our day into four sessions. In the beginning session, we cultivate and meditate on loving kindness and compassion, and then we meditate on bodhicitta so that it becomes natural to the point of overflowing by virtue of our practice. After generating intense bodhicitta, we then practice guru yoga. Finally, we meditate on the ground perfection of wisdom.

At this stage, we engage in the practice corresponding to the path of meditation by sustaining the view of the ground perfection of wisdom as much as possible. Each time you arise out of meditative absorption into post-meditative mindfulness, notice whether or not appearances are illusion-like. For example, when you arise from the meditation state to cook or eat, remain mindful of whether or not appearances are illusion-like. That is now your practice. If appearances do not seem like illusions, then you should at least cultivate the conviction that they are illusion-like. This is how you engage in post-meditative practice. End the fourth session of meditation with dedication prayers.

One important thing to keep in mind is that when we engage in meditative absorption on the path of meditation, we are doing so after having realized emptiness directly on the path of seeing. Therefore, at this point, all meditation becomes transcendental meditation. There is a big difference between the mundane and the supramundane or transcendental levels of the absorptions. The transcendental absorption on the path of meditation is not simple calm-abiding absorption, but *'nyamshak'* (Tib. *mnyam bzhag*) or equipoise meditation. We enter into equipoise regarding the true nature of reality, which does not happen in the mundane absorptions.

At present, we have not achieved the path of meditation, though for the sake of presentation I am speaking as if we actually have. To get there, what is important is that we must meditate. To realize emptiness directly, we have to meditate. This involves a sequence of steps. First, we have to seek a qualified master and receive instructions. Then, we have to become familiar with the techniques of common shamatha meditation. Shamatha meditative absorption can be worldly as well as transcendental, and we need to understand the difference. It is not necessary to remain limited to sutric calm abiding until it is perfected; however, because of the danger of confusing worldly and transcendental shamatha, we have to understand it. If we do not understand common shamatha, we will not be able to distinguish worldly and transcendental absorption, and we will not be able to tell sutric from Dzogchen meditation. Then, based on common calm abiding practice, we also have to learn and practice the unique Mahayana way of absorption on the ground perfection of wisdom. To do this, we begin by meditating on bodhicitta and then, influenced by the intention of bodhicitta, enter into the unique Mahayana absorption on the ground perfection of wisdom. Once we have meditated in this way, then we can talk about what it is like to be on path of meditation.

The essential point to keep in mind here is the importance of being able to differentiate between these different techniques of meditation. For example, how are mundane shamatha practices leading to mundane absorptions different from transcendental practices and absorptions? At the level of transcendental absorptions, what is the difference between Hinayana and Mahayana meditation?

In a nutshell, once we have been directly introduced to the nature of reality, the dharmadhatu, then on the path of meditation we must continue to meditate. In the context of meditation, we will experience the different levels of this path. Apart from actually meditating, there is nothing we can do about it. The levels cannot be shown or demonstrated.

When we look at past masters like Shakyamuni Buddha, we see that their realization was the result of meditation. The Buddha meditated for many years, and his awakening was achieved in meditation while seated under the bodhi tree. If we look at the masters in India, we see that their realization was also the result of meditation. The Zen masters in China, the Tibetan masters, all of them achieved their realization by virtue of meditation. What this tells us, practically, is that after being introduced directly to the dharmadhatu, we have to sustain this direct experience unceasingly in meditation, like the continuum of a river. That is what it really means for us to practice on the path of meditation. As I mentioned earlier, when we talk about the path of accumulation, we should not think of it as something in the far distance. It really means starting here, right now. Likewise, when we talk about the path of seeing, we should not think of that as something to achieve in the distant future or in the next life. Rather, we should think of the path of seeing as achievable in this lifetime. We should think of the path of meditation as right here as well, not far off.

It is said in the sutric tradition that 'it takes countless eons' to achieve enlightenment. Generally, we take such expressions as discouraging, and compared to more profound practices like tantric practices, the sutric path does take more time. Even following the sutric tradition, however, it is not impossible to directly apprehend emptiness in this life. It is possible to have a taste by following the path of meditation. This is possible even by following sutric practices. Keep this in mind, and do not lose courage, do not feel discouraged. See if you can actually meditate on these levels of the path – the path of accumulation, the path of preparation, the path of seeing, and the path of meditation.

To work toward integrating the four paths – accumulation, preparation, seeing, and meditation – within your own practice, first practice the path of accumulation. Initially, practice Vajrasattva and guru yoga. Then, engage in lojong or mind training. Intensively cultivate loving kindness, compassion, and bodhicitta. Focus especially on cultivating great compassion. This is the essence of mind training. See if you can transform the coarse, unruly mind into the nature of great compassion. This is not stabilizing meditation but rather analytical meditation. These practices – Vajrasattva, guru yoga, and cultivating great compassion – become a profound way to engage in the accumulation of merit, which is training on the path of accumulation.

Next, we primarily focus on meditation. The path of preparation is also called the 'path of application.' It is associated with the application of effort, as meditation is difficult.

At this point, if you think to yourself, 'What should I meditate upon?' or 'What is the view here?' then you have missed the point. All of this – the view of the ground perfection of wisdom – has already been introduced.

Doubts about the view or confusion about the technique should be eliminated before attempting this level of practice, by consulting your teacher. Prior to entering meditation, ask your teacher if you have any doubts or questions. If you have doubts or questions during your actual meditation in a retreat setting, it becomes a great obstacle to meditation.

To be able to actually engage in application, you should have completed the preliminary requirements, which include clarifying doubts or confusion. At this time, you will need to continuously put effort into sustaining single-pointed meditation.

During actual meditation, you will have different experiences. Sometimes your meditation will be good; sometimes there will be dullness or fogginess. Sometimes you will fall away from meditation altogether. The right technique is to continue without any feeling of discouragement. Discouragement is eliminated by experiencing the benefits of mediation and understanding it as your own responsibility.

When you practice on a regular basis, there comes a time when aversion to meditation vanishes and you find joy and clarity in this practice. The faults of dullness and agitation fall away. Even if you have not yet apprehended reality directly, arriving at the point where the more you meditate, the more you generate joy is something very positive and wholesome. If you can see the nature of reality, that is also very good.

There will be times when you have dullness and agitation in your meditation, and it requires continuous mindfulness to stay with the practice on the meaning of emptiness. This requires the application of effort. All of this is the path of preparation practice.

As your practice deepens, you will practice corresponding to the path of seeing. You will focus your shamatha on emptiness, the nature of reality. During the post-meditative state, you can remain mindful and practice seeing everything as illusion-like. You integrate the meditative absorption experience with post-meditative experience by seeing everything as illusion-like, and then you integrate that with your dream yoga practice.

As you practice corresponding to the path of meditation, you focus on special insight rather than calm abiding. While in the state of deep concentration, subtle awareness arises as special insight itself. This is how Zen practitioners meditate as well. Without wavering from the state of absorption, you simultaneously cultivate the wisdom aspect of special insight.

Up to this point, I have taught you how to practice the four paths. This is all traditional, based on the texts. The traditional presentation is very complicated and there is a lot of explanation and commentary, but what I have given you here is new and practical – how we can practice this in our meditation in this life. I am showing you how to accomplish the path in your own practice – the path of accumulation, the path of preparation, the path of seeing, and the path of meditation.

Meditation is actually the main practice. Even when we practice the path of accumulation, we have to meditate. When we practice the path of preparation, we have to meditate. There is a difference in the qualities of meditation on these two paths, however. On the path of accumulation, we make effort to accumulate merit and cultivate a powerful mind. On the path of preparation, we cultivate insight, learning to recognize the pure and unchanging basis of perfection. We learn to recognize dullness and agitation and to sustain a deep and subtle meditation.

Here, I am not talking about the uncontrived meditation of Mahamudra and Dzogchen. I am talking about Mahayana sutra meditation. Dullness and agitation are very strong, so we have to learn to recognize them. As long as the mind is very clear and stable, that is good. Continue to sustain that in meditation – and not just in worldly absorption but in transcendental meditation. An important characteristic of insight is that it is completely transparent and empty. It is important to be able to distinguish between worldly concentration and special Mahayana meditation.

One of the key differences between mundane and transcendental absorption is that transcendental absorption takes place in the absence of the object of negation. It is a state in which the absence of object is sustained. The experience is like empty space. Even though there is the stability of absorption, there is also an experience of a great empty expanse. If that is present, then it is a transcendental absorption. If the experience of emptiness is not there, then it is a worldly absorption in which there is still grasping at the mind. This is one of the main things to understand as a meditation practitioner.

PRACTICING THE SIX PERFECTIONS IN MEDITATION

I will next explain how to carry the six perfections into practice within the context of meditation and the post-meditative state. How do we practice the six perfections in the meditative state? We begin with the practice of the first perfection, the perfection of generosity. Here, generosity is not about giving possessions or material objects away, but about getting rid of all objects of mental attachment. Attachment can come in the form of aversion, as some sort of fixation you have to destroy. For example, it can be an aversion to meditation; it can be some sort of fear or uncertainty about engaging in meditation. When you let these fixations go, that is a form of letting go. This amounts to engaging in the practice of generosity in meditation.

When we engage in meditation, we observe discipline of body and speech, which amounts to practicing the second perfection, the perfection of discipline. Eliminating dullness and agitation through mindfulness and vigilance is a true form of mental discipline.

The forces of dullness and agitation are relentless, coming at us all the time in meditation. If we continue meditating without losing hope and courage, this becomes the practice of the perfection of patience. In addition, forbearing the appearances of problems or suffering during meditation is the practice of patience. We should remind ourselves of the Buddha's own practice and how he practiced extreme austerity for six years.

The perfection of diligence or joyous effort is practiced when we sustain meditation continuously, like a river. Sustaining meditation by not only meditating when we feel like it but also when we do not feel like it requires diligence and joyous effort. Of course, if we get physically sick, that is different, but otherwise there is no excuse!

The perfection of concentration happens in the context of actual meditation. We sustain the ground perfection of wisdom that was introduced earlier in single-pointed calm abiding. When we do that without wavering, that is the real practice of samadhi.

Finally, the perfection of wisdom occurs such that without wavering from calm abiding, a very subtle part of awareness engages in analysis with respect to the nature of reality, understanding its ultimate nature as illusory. That is engaging in the perfection of wisdom.

This is how to carry the six perfections into practice in a single meditation session. Now, how do we carry the six perfections into the post-meditative state? When we arise out of meditation into the post-meditative state, we engage in daily activities such as eating, cleaning up, and spending time with friends. How do we carry six perfections into the course of these daily activities?

Practicing generosity in post-meditation means dedicating our body, wealth, and resources to other sentient beings. This does not mean we should just give everything we have away; it means we should cultivate detachment toward our resources and dedicate them to helping others. Dedicating our body, speech, mind, and wealth to sentient beings is also an important training for the mind and will increase its power. We should dedicate all resources so that they become meaningful and helpful to sentient beings.

Practicing discipline in post-meditation means getting rid of all habits that lack mindfulness or conscientiousness. We should be mindful in all actions of body, speech, and mind so that they are pacified, subdued, and pleasant to others. This should not just occur externally – internally we should cultivate genuine humility and respect.

Practicing patience in post-meditation means that when conditions give rise to anger, we remind ourselves of our training in compassion and loving kindness in order to generate patience right away. By reminding ourselves of our training, we will recognize immediately that it is inappropriate to become angry and will generate forgiveness or patience. Of course, this is not easy, but this is the way we train.

The practice of diligence or joyous effort in post-meditation means sustaining mindfulness of negative emotions and mindfully counteracting them. It is not easy to do this, especially for those emotions that are predominant due to habits and conditioning. This requires real diligence, and thus this is a context in which you can practice its perfection.

The perfection of concentration can be practiced in post-meditation whenever the mind is distracted or disturbed. We should try to catch ourselves in that moment, then rest or relax the mind for a short while. This is one way of engaging in concentration. Another way is to generate powerful mindfulness when powerful negative feelings arise, so that they are subdued or eliminated right then and there.

The practice of the perfection of wisdom in the post-meditative context of daily life does not have to mean sustaining the absorption of wisdom realizing emptiness. Wisdom in this context refers to discriminating wisdom – the ability to analyze what are the appropriate things to do as a Mahayana practitioner, what is not appropriate, what our responsibilities and standards of conduct are – all the discriminating wisdom we use in daily life is part of the perfection of wisdom.

MIND TRAINING AS AN ENHANCEMENT PRACTICE

There is, of course, a large body of literature on mind training, or 'lojong' in Tibetan. I am not going to go through the classical presentation, which is sometimes not very practical. In our context, it is most practical to first train ourselves to not lose courage and hope, so that we are able to free ourselves from being narrow-minded. We need to make our minds more expansive. We need to train in seeing how all beings are interconnected. and shed the feeling of loneliness. We should constantly remind ourselves of the vast potential that is ours as human beings, and cultivate the ground perfection of wisdom. This will counteract discouragement and give rise to hope and confidence. That is part of mind-training practice. On top of that, there is a need to actually cultivate compassion in daily life and to understand and acknowledge the law of causality. From a causal point of view, we need to recognize the kindness of other sentient beings – this is a very important practice. Seeing the kindness of other sentient beings is powerful because its absence leads to indifference, and that is dangerous for our practice.

When I say, 'Do not ignore others,' I do not mean you should become busybodies, wondering where everybody is going and what they are doing. I am referring to continuously reminding yourself of the kindness of other sentient beings.

What this really means is that we should cultivate this attitude of seeing all sentient beings as extremely kind. We should even see enemies as very kind. It is said that enemies are actually more kind than the buddhas, but that does not mean we should approach our enemies and encourage them. What I wish to stress here is that we should try to cultivate openness, expansiveness, joy, and happiness of mind. This is something we need to try to do at all times.

DEDICATE THE MERIT

We have now come to the last section, dedication. We dedicate whatever virtuous activities we have engaged in, by the doors of body, speech, and mind, to the well-being of other sentient beings. We remind ourselves that all of our actions of body, speech, and mind are done for the sake of other sentient beings without expecting anything in return. Without any expectation of power, fame, or reputation, we dedicate all virtue we have accrued to other sentient beings. Dedication is extremely important. If we do not dedicate, then even if we have accrued virtuous actions, moments of anger can destroy our virtuous dispositions.

The vital point to keep in mind when engaging in dharma practice, or any kind of wholesome practice, is in the beginning, to do so with the intention of bodhicitta; in the middle, to practice without any kind of attachment; and at the end, to dedicate all virtue accrued to other sentient beings.

At this point, what I wish to recommend is that whenever you have the time, try to do a retreat. For instance, when you have a Saturday off, try to spend the day in meditation. Divide the day into sessions of three hours each if possible, otherwise into sessions of at least two hours. If you are practicing my ngondro, in the morning session, do tsa lung and then meditate. In the second session, do Vajrasattva and guru yoga practice, and then meditate. In the third and fourth sessions, just meditate following the instructions given in the last several sections.

With these seven points, I have presented the entire Mahayana path.

PART FIVE

THE RESULTANT VEHICLES
OF THE VAJRAYANA

12

ESSENCE OF TANTRA

The practices of the Mahayana path can be grouped into two categories. The Mahayana sutra practices that we have covered so far are called "causal vehicles," because we make use of the cause that gives rise to enlightenment, and practice that cause as the path. The second category of practices of the Mahayana path, also called the 'Vajrayana,' comprises what are called 'resultant vehicles.' These are so called because the resultant state itself – the state of enlightenment – is taken as the path.

This chapter presents the tantric teachings in nine topics:

1. The meaning of 'mantra'
2. The history of tantra
3. Hindu tantra and Buddhist tantra
4. Tantra and the three baskets, and the difference between Mahayana sutra and tantra
5. The essential meaning of the ripening initiation and liberating instructions
6. The guru - the root of the tantric path
7. The three continuums
8. The generation and completion stages
9. A concise summary

Tantra is extensive and profound, but these nine topics will serve as guidelines for developing an understanding of the essential features and structure of tantra and tantric practice. The first half of this presentation is for philosophical or conceptual explanation, and the second half is for explaining the practice. In tantra, however, we cannot actually separate conceptual explanation from practice explanation and instruction.

THE MEANING OF 'MANTRA'

The resultant vehicle is sometimes called 'Tantrayana,' sometimes

'Mantrayana,' and sometimes 'Secret Mantra.' Before turning to the nine topics on tantra, I will explain the meaning of the word 'mantra.' 'Mantra' has two syllables – *man* and *tra*. *'Man'* refers to mind in Sanskrit, and *'tra'* has the connotation of 'protection.' Together they mean 'that which protects the mind.' Mantra protects the mind from ordinary appearances and our habitual tendency to grasp at ordinary appearances.

In the sense that mantra has the potential to do this, 'mantra' also refers to our potential or power. 'Potential' here refers to the possibility that all conceptual thought can be transformed into clear light, and the contaminated coarse body can be transformed into the illusory body. 'Power' refers to the power to actually transform thought into clear light and the coarse body into the illusory body through the practice of mantra. It makes sense to understand 'mantra' or 'tantra' as referring to this potential, and the transformative power that can be cultivated from it, because through the practice of mantra, we are able to actualize or realize the subtlest clear light of the mind in this very lifetime. Understanding 'mantra' as potential or power is more meaningful.

The power of mantra is unique. Where sutric practice relies on rejection and abandonment of external objects of desire, internal mental states, and other negative emotions by means of antidotes, mantra has the power to transform them. Mantra can change the very nature of that which is to be rejected on the sutric path without abandoning it. It has that power.

We should understand this potential as something that is inherent in our own mental continuum. It is not abstract or theoretical; we should not treat it as a concept to be analyzed. We should not forget that the potential being spoken of is in our own mental continuum.

THE HISTORY OF TANTRA

In tantra, desire is carried as the path and transformed into wisdom. The tantric teachings have the potential to transform desire. These teachings have always been given to disciples of the highest capacity, those who are able to carry desire as the path and transmute desire into wisdom.

These teachings did not spring from out of nowhere. They did not fall from the sky or appear miraculously. Neither are they shamanic teachings, evolving through interaction with the natural world. Shamanism is thousands and thousands of years old, and is basically about man's relationship with nature and spirits, and so forth. The teachings of the tantric vehicle are very different and can only be given by someone who has actually achieved the non-dual state of

Vajradhara, complete enlightenment. In the current era, the era of Shakyamuni, these teachings have been given by Shakyamuni Buddha himself.

Generally speaking, it is not held to be the case that Shakyamuni Buddha is the only teacher of tantra. There are other enlightened beings who have taught tantra, and other traditions that do not descend from the Buddha himself. For example, in the Nyingma tradition, there are instances of tantric teachings derived from other sources. In addition, the history of tantra in the Bonpo tradition is different from that of the Buddhist tradition, where everything comes from Shakyamuni Buddha. Generally, we speak in terms of the particular buddha that defines the teachings of a specific era. The current era is defined by the teachings of Shakyamuni Buddha, and it is generally accepted that all tantric teachings come from him. We can, however, also speak of other eras and many different buddhas that are exceptions to the generally held view.

The teachings of the buddhas across the eons have not only been given to human beings. The assemblies of beings in attendance have included nagas and gods with very long lives. The sources of tantric transmissions and teachings may vary for this reason, and tantric teachings are preserved in different forms and in different ways by different kinds of beings. Even if you look at Shakyamuni Buddha's lifetime, he made it clear that his teachings were being given in the language not only of human beings but of beings from other realms, including gods, nagas, spirits, and so forth.

We have to be open-minded if we want to understand tantric teachings, and we should not automatically doubt the authenticity of teachings that were not given by Shakyamuni Buddha in the form of a fully ordained monk. Some traditions hold this conservative standard, but not all. Among the Gelugpas and Sakyapas, the mainstream view is that any Buddhist tantric teaching must not only come from Shakyamuni Buddha, but also from Shakyamuni Buddha in the form of a fully ordained monk. If this provenance is not established, the status of the teaching is questioned. We, however, should consider the possibility that tantric teachings can belong to lineages other than Shakyamuni Buddha in this very particular form.

Differences of opinion on tantric lineages and sources can even be found during the periods when tantra flourished in Tibet. In the time of what we call the ancient Nyingma tradition during the eighth century, and again in the tenth century, after the great translator Rinchen Zangpo and others of the New Tradition transmitted the teachings, we find different accounts of the lineages.

Indian Buddhist scholars of tantra also present varying accounts.

Some Indian scholars even claim that tantric teachings were never actually given by Shakyamuni Buddha, that the historical Buddha only gave Hinayana teachings. According to them, the Buddha gave the teachings in terms of what was common, conventional, and visible, which basically amounts to the Hinayana teachings. Other Indian scholars maintain that the Buddha himself is the actual teacher of the Buddhist tantras. In their view, the Buddha gave tantric teachings while manifesting as the deity at a particular place.

The generally accepted view in Tibet is that the Buddha gave all of the sutric teachings, Hinayana as well as Mahayana sutra, in the ordinary, visible conventional world to human disciples. For example, it is accepted that he gave perfection of wisdom teachings near Rajgir on Vulture's Peak. It is further accepted that in the special case of disciples of the necessary intelligence and capacity, the Buddha arose as a deity and gave tantric teachings in that form. These disciples comprised a select few who were appropriate recipients of these tantric teachings. If these disciples were exceptionally rare, and no one else was there to witness these teachings (as they were not conventionally accessible), it would make sense that the origins of tantra are obscure.

One of the classic examples of the Buddha teaching a very select few disciples who were ready to practice tantra is the case of the Buddha's contemporary King Indrabhuti. It is said that when Buddha was passing through with his disciples, King Indrabhuti requested of the Buddha, 'I have heard that you are a great teacher, but I am a king. I have my palace, my queens, and my royal luxuries. I will not be able to abandon all of these things. Can you give me a teaching with which I can achieve enlightenment without abandoning the objects of desire? If you have such a teaching, I want you to give it to me.' It is said that the Buddha replied, 'Yes, there is such a teaching, a method that carries desire as the path.' In accordance with Indrabhuti's request, the Buddha manifested the Guhyasamaja mandala, in the form of Vajradhara in union with his consort characterized by seven types of embraces. He gave Guhyasamaja teachings to King Indrabhuti in that form. Whether that is something that actually happened or not, I don't know, but this is what is held to be true in the tantric tradition – that the Buddha arose from an ordinary monk's form as the deity and gave the teachings in that form.

The history of the Kalachakra tantra in southern India provides another example. It is said that in response to the request of Suchandra, the king of Shambala at that time, the Buddha arose in the form of Kalachakra and taught the *Kalachakra Tantra*. This is mentioned in the texts themselves. We therefore have an account that says that when the Buddha gave these teachings, he arose from the form of an ordinary monk as that deity, and gave the teachings in that form.

When we speak of the Buddha manifesting as a deity for a worthy disciple, we should not think that he is saying, 'I am going to transform into the deity for this particular individual and not for that individual.' We should not imagine that the Buddha selects certain people for whom to manifest as deities. It is not like that. It is not something that entirely and exclusively depends on the Buddha's intention or decision. Rather, it is the coming together of two factors. The first factor is the disciple who has accumulated sufficient merit and has given rise to strong imprints over countless lifetimes. Such a disciple is perfectly ready on the basis of lifetimes of practice, since for such a disciple, there is no difficulty in seeing the Buddha as the deity. Because of the disciple's readiness, it is not difficult on the Buddha's side to bring about the transformation, which is the second factor. The transformation and the teachings take place on the basis of the coming together of these two interdependent factors – the Buddha's power and the disciple's karma and devotion, along with years and years of meritorious imprints.

To give an analogy, if you have a mirror that is almost spotless but has a little bit of dirt on it, you can clean it easily. It does not take much to clean the mirror. As soon as the mirror is clean, your reflection is there. That is what happens within the context of a tantric initiation. The disciple is so well trained and purified that the transformation can take place very easily.

We need to understand this point: the Buddha manifests as a tantric deity primarily because of the disciple's own practice and readiness, the disciple's own realization, so that the disciple's pure vision is spontaneous. Then, as a result, the Buddha's manifestation of the deity is also spontaneous.

The Buddha passed into nirvana at the age of eighty-one, and we might wonder how it is possible that one monk could give countless teachings in this short span of time, sometimes in different places at the same time. When we understand the interdependence of teacher and disciple, however, it is not so difficult to see how the Buddha was able to accomplish what he did in one human lifespan of eighty-one years. Without understanding the interdependent causality I explained earlier, one would have trouble comprehending or believing many of the tantric teachings we hear about.

From the broadest perspective, as I mentioned earlier, the phenomenon of tantra and tantric teachings is not limited to the time and dimension of Shakyamuni Buddha. The conservative Tibetan Buddhist view of the history and spread of tantra is basically accepted in the Kagyu and Nyingma traditions. In general, this view is that, even though the Buddha was in the form of a fully ordained monk, he was asked by the deity Guhyapati to turn the wheel of tantric teachings. Then, the Buddha taught an audience of high bodhisattvas who are not visible to ordinary human beings, in a separate realm or land called 'the land of the tantrikas.' We imagine tantrikas in Tibet as the dreadlocked practitioners that we see pictures of, but according to the conservative Tibetan view, there is actually this hidden land where tantrikas live and practice. When Guhyapati requested Shakyamuni to turn the wheel of tantra, it was to these tantrikas, here in this land, that they were given. The teachings were then gathered by Vajrapani, who preserved and transmitted them. That is how we understand the gathering and transmission of tantric teachings according to the conservative Tibetan Buddhist view.

In *The Root Tantra of Chakrasamvara*, written by King Indrabhuti, he mentions the spread of the tantric teachings from the divine land of the tantrikas to the human realm in the land of Oddiyana. It says in the text that Vajrapani brought the teachings and empowerments to dakinis from the realm of the nagas in Oddiyana, and that is how it spread to the human realm. The transmission of the tantric teachings in the human realm has been limited in comparison to the transmission of sutric teachings. In the history of tantra, you find that tantric teachings are given, but then they are lost, only later to be retrieved and given again.

It is generally accepted that Guhyapati requested Shakyamuni Buddha to give particular tantric empowerments. In response, Shakyamuni arose in the form of the deity and gave the teachings corresponding to that deity. The teachings were preserved principally by Vajrapani, but some collections were compiled and preserved by Manjushri, Avalokiteshvara, and others. Later, they were transmitted once again. In the unique Nyingma tradition, it is said that the teachings were preserved by Manjushri and then by Avalokiteshvara, who transmitted them to Garab Dorje in the human realm. Garab Dorje then gave them to Sri Singha.

It is important to understand that the human-to-human transmission of the highest yoga tantra is very limited, whereas the transmission of the lower tantras is much more frequent. To be qualified to receive the highest yoga transmission requires the highest capacity as well as the ability to transform the bliss induced in sexual union into wisdom and carry it as the path. This is extremely difficult, and for this reason, the transmission from one qualified human teacher to another qualified human student is very limited. It might happen, for example, that a realized master receives the transmission of the highest yoga tantra teachings and engages in the practices, then achieves the illusory body, or the rainbow body, but the transmission stops because this master does not necessarily find another person capable of receiving the transmission and observing the samayas.

If we study a tantric lineage, especially of the highest yoga tantra teachings, we find that it is much more difficult to prove the unbroken transmission of the tantric lineage from master to master than it is to establish the sutra lineages of vinaya teachings. It is relatively easy to establish the unbroken transmission of sutra teachings because they are given publicly and witnessed by many ordinary human beings. By comparison, it can be very difficult to trace the transmission of the highest yoga tantra teachings.

Historical accounts also can differ with regard to the type of tantras in question. The traditional Nyingma presentation of the tantras divides them into three external and three internal tantras. The external tantras include action tantra, conduct tantra, and yoga tantra. Their transmission is universally accepted by all Buddhist tantric traditions, including the New Translation traditions. According to the Nyingma account, however, the three inner tantras of mahayoga tantra, anuyoga tantra, and atiyoga tantra were preserved in the realm of the nagas and gods where they were then introduced to the human realm. The Bonpo have a similar explanation for how teachings were preserved in the god and naga realms and introduced from there to the human realm. These explanations are seen as mystical and heterodox by some.

The account of tantric transmission given by the New Translation traditions, such as the Sakya and Kayu, says that the first tantric teachings were given by the Buddha to King Indrabhuti in the land of Oddiyana. Indrabhuti collected, preserved, and practiced all of the tantric teachings and transmitted them widely in the human realm. It is recounted that as a result of his practice he achieved rainbow body in one lifetime. He set a high standard for the whole country, and it is said that the entire population of Oddiyana engaged in the practice of tantra and achieved the illusory body and the clear light nature of mind. As a result, the entire country was emptied of inhabitants, and the land was transformed into a great lake filled with nagas. Then, it is said, Vajrapani came and transmitted the tantras to the nagas. This is the account of the New Translation school of the flourishing of the tantra.

There are some differences between traditions concerning who is considered a chief compiler of the tantras. Who collected and systematized the tantric teachings given by the Buddha? In the Nyingma tradition, it is said that the principal compiler was Vajrapani, but Manjushri and Avalokiteshvara were also important compilers. Vajrapani, Manjushri, and Avalokiteshvara are called the 'Lords of the

Three Lineages.' Manjushri is seen as the emanation of the Buddha's body, Avalokiteshvara as the emanation of the Buddha's speech, and Vajrapani as the emanation of the Buddha's mind. 'Vajrapani' ('Holder of the Vajra') and 'Guhyapati' ('Lord of Secrets') are different names for the same bodhisattva. Vajrapani is seen as the principal maker of requests for teachings, the principal recipient and collector of the teachings, and the chief preserver and compiler or systematizer.

It is helpful to understand that there are different accounts of the history of tantra – the view of Indian Buddhist scholars, the different accounts of the Ancient and New Translation schools such as the Kagyu, the point of view of the Bon tradition, and the history of tantra as understood by the Hindus. There are also differences within the various Hindu traditions. If you have the time, it would be good to read these various accounts.

The history of tantra is important in relation to the practice of tantra. It is not merely an interesting background story, or a story of kings, queens, and dynasties. It has to do with understanding what tantra is. Understanding tantra through understanding its history is directly responsible for giving rise to devotion. The more your understanding gives rise to faith or conviction in the teachings, the more effective your practice. Understanding tantric history increases your enthusiasm for the teachings. Therefore, understanding the history of tantra is directly related to your practice of tantra. That is why the historical understanding is so important.

It is also very beneficial because it is important for tantric practitioners to be aware that there are very powerful mahasiddhas. Do they exist or not exist? Sometimes it is difficult to understand the lives of Gampopa, Naropa, Marpa, Milarepa, and other such masters. Initially we are very excited, but then someone says something critical, and we start doubting the teachings. We should not doubt the mahasiddhas, however, because of their deep insight and subtlety, their unchanging realization, and their accomplishment of tantra.

These are all reasons why the history of tantra is very important. If you do not have a lot of time, you can just read a brief history of tantra. The key point is that the history is important for tantric practitioners because sometimes you are very excited, but then later you think tantra does not work. You practice for one month, two years, and experience no result, but then when you can read the history you see that tantra is not easy, and that it takes real determination. Some people think tantra is just imagination, a mental image, and that is an incorrect view. That is why I am making an effort to explain this.

Sometimes there is confusion regarding Hindu tantra and Tibetan tantra. For example, some people say Shiva's image is similar to highest yoga tantra. It is actually difficult to distinguish how they are different, and that is why I think the history of tantra is important. The reason I emphasize the importance of the different histories is that the great Indian tantric masters like Tilopa and Naropa, and the great Tibetan masters like Nubchen Sangye Yeshe, Marpa Lotsawa and others, did not confine themselves to two or three practices. They engaged in extensive study of all of the classes of tantra, their histories, rituals, and techniques. We may not have the time or the karma to do this, and perhaps it is not necessary, but we should at least comprehend the importance of tantra's history and understanding the different techniques. Even if we are not able to practice all of them, it is good to at least understand them from an intellectual point of view.

HINDU TANTRA AND BUDDHIST TANTRA

It is difficult to distinguish Hindu tantra from Buddhist tantra without understanding their histories. At a glance, there are no obvious differences. You might think that one was copied from the other – the way fire pujas are offered, the way mandalas are created, the centrality of guru devotion, the names of the deities, and the mantras used appear to be similar or even identical. Without a proper understanding of the history, you may come to the conclusion that they share the exact same history, or even that the same rituals are performed, but this is not correct.

Some people say that the tantric teachings are not Buddhist at all. Without investigating tantra's history, and based on a superficial reading, they come to the conclusion that the tantras were taught by realized individuals other than the Buddha. Similarly, some Dzogchen masters today say there is no Dzogchen lineage, that Dzogchen is not Buddhist. This is not a profound view. Saying things like 'emptiness does not belong to any religion' just indicates that one is ignorant and it is a big mistake. If you have this attitude, you will come to a point where there is no authenticity – no authentic sources, tradition, transmission, or lineage. Following this logic, you may come to a similar conclusion about cultivating bodhicitta or any of the other practices. You may think no transmission is necessary, that anyone can have bodhicitta realizations, and there is no need for a bodhicitta lineage or transmission. Bodhicitta is the heart of Mahayana practice, so such a person might also conclude that Mahayana teachings require no lineage or special teachings or even that the Hinayana teachings require no transmission and lineage, that the fundamental teachings, the four noble truths, do not require a lineage, that the truth of suffering does not require a lineage. We could easily say that everyone suffers and that we do not need a lineage for that.

There are so-called teachers like this, who claim to be presenting the teachings in a way that is suitable to modern audiences, and some people follow these teachings. You, however, should not follow them, as they are ultimately deceptive. Such conclusions are nihilistic and therefore dangerous. There is a danger that you will not be able to respect or commit to anything. People are sometimes attracted to these radical teachings, but the sense of freedom that attracts them is false. In following such teachings, one destroys a genuine systematically transmitted lineage.

This is especially true in the case of tantra. Without the blessings of the lineage and without devotion, it is impossible to have tantric realization. In order to receive the blessings of the lineage and cultivate devotion, we have to rely on tantric history, on the blessings and the transmission, which are the basis of conviction and devotion. Without devotion, it is impossible to give rise to realization.

Now, we can examine the fundamental differences between the Hindu tantras and the Buddhist tantras. The Hindu tantras derive from two traditions in the Samkhya School, one that relies on deities and one that does not. The history of the deity-practice tradition originates with the accomplishments of rishis who practice deities like Shiva, four-faced Brahma, Vishnu, and Saraswati. The masters or rishis who practiced these deities – the eight primary worldly deities like Brahma and Vishnu – achieved very powerful mundane siddhis like clairvoyance. They achieved these miraculous powers based on the practice of these worldly deities. A tantric system of practice developed out of the accomplishments of these rishis, and that is basically Hindu tantra.

If you study them carefully, you can see that these Hindu tantric practices incorporate Buddhist features later on. If you look at the original Hindu tantras, some of the practices that appear in more recent versions are not in the originals. They were developed after the rise of Buddhist tantra. Although Buddhist tantra and Hindu tantra look similar, there are fundamental differences that render them completely distinct.

One fundamental difference is that Buddhist tantra is based on the four pillars. Seeing all phenomena as empty and without self is fundamental to Buddhist tantra and is actually opposed to the view of Hindu tantra. The emptiness of phenomena and the selflessness of the person is the basis of tantra and tantric phenomena in Buddhism; there is no eternal self.

In contrast, an eternally existing self, or atman, is the very foundation of Hindu tantra. Practitioners of Hindu tantra see themselves as indivisible from the creator, as part of the universal self, which is Brahma. The basis of the practice is the view that the universal god is not separate from the atman. Buddhist tantra talks about emptiness of self, however, and this is a fundamental divergence between the two traditions.

My own position is that even though they make a fundamental mistake in their view, Hindu tantric requirements for practice and the practice techniques are excellent. In many cases, they are better than those of the Buddhists. If you look at the Hindu tantrikas, there is so much devotion. Their guru yoga is very profound, and they are diligent in maintaining secrecy. They observe the commitments, which are fundamental to accomplishing the result of practice. The secrecy, guru yoga, devotion, and observing of commitments – all of these are extremely profound in the Hindu context.

On the other hand, the Buddhist philosophical view is very profound. There is a great deal of theory and intellectual understanding of the tantric practices, but when it comes to actually doing them, we sometimes fall short. There is not much devotion, not so much secrecy, and perhaps not so much commitment. Thus, if a Hindu tantric practitioner and a Buddhist tantric practitioner were to begin a practice simultaneously, the Hindu tantrika would achieve the mundane siddhis much more quickly. That is the reality. The Hindu tantrikas achieve the mundane siddhis much more quickly because their practice of the techniques is very pure, even though the Hindu tantric view is fundamentally flawed. The difference is that they are able to generate so much devotion – devotion to the guru as well as to the teachings – and they are able to keep their commitments intact. One of the other fundamental differences is that their conviction in the efficacy of tantric practice is very strong. As soon as they come across a particular deity, a particular master, and a particular practice, they enter into the practice just like that. Until they achieve the result, they do not waiver from the path. They have that kind of conviction in the efficacy of the practice.

In contrast, many Buddhist practitioners entertain a lot of doubt. Buddhist tantra is very much like living in America and having a lot of different kinds of food to choose from. In Buddhist tantra we have so many choices. You can do this deity practice, or you can do that deity practice; you can choose this teacher or that teacher. Although a range of options can be good, a disadvantage is that it might encourage indecisiveness and lack of stability; it tends to destroy your focus. You encounter a practice, then you lose interest and go on to another, then lose interest in that and go on to another, and on and on. Practicing like this, you cannot achieve the result.

There are also differences between Hindu and Buddhist tantric meditation techniques. Finally, there are differences in conduct. There are thus differences in view, meditation, and conduct, but the main difference is in the view.

The key element of the Hindu view is that the practitioner, the deity, and the practices to accomplish the deity all have inherent existence – atman exists inherently. In contrast, Buddhist tantric practice is based on the understanding of emptiness. This is why in the beginning of any Buddhist sadhana, we say, '*Om svabhava shuddho sarva dharma svabhava shuddho ham*' – 'The nature of all phenomena is pure.' That is the ground on which the practice is based, and thus the view of Hindu tantra and the view of Buddhist tantra are fundamentally different.

There is also a fundamental difference between Hindu tantric meditation and Buddhist tantric meditation. Once the Buddhist tantric practitioner has established the emptiness of phenomena by reciting the *shunyata* mantra (the wisdom of emptiness mantra), and everything is dissolved into emptiness, then the deity, samadhi, and mantra all have to be understood as the dynamic display or expression of the subtlest innate clear light mind of the practitioner. Once everything has been dissolved into emptiness, then *everything* – deity yoga, mantra, and concentration – must be understood as the display of the subtlest clear light mind. That is the essence of Buddhist tantra, and this is not the case in Hindu tantra, as I mentioned earlier.

In Hindu meditation, there is also meditation on the deity, there is also the meditative practice of mantra recitation, and there is also devotion, but the essence of meditation is not the same as in Buddhist practice. Seeing the deity, mantra, and concentration as the dynamic display or energetic expression of the subtlest clear light of the practitioner's own mind is not there, whereas for the Buddhist practitioner, sustaining this recognition in meditation is essential.

There are also differences in conduct. Buddhist tantrikas practice both internal and external conduct. The internal conduct is bodhicitta, based on love and compassion. It is always motivated by loving kindness and compassion, always ready to engage in the service of other sentient beings. This internal conduct expresses itself as external conduct through ascetic and unconventional practices. What we call unconventional practice physically expresses itself in that way, even though the internal conduct is bodhicitta, based on loving kindness and compassion. When you engage in deity practices as a Buddhist tantric practitioner, the motivation is always bodhicitta. As soon as you lose that, you are no longer engaging in Buddhist tantra.

This is not necessarily the case for those who engage in Hindu tantric practices such as Shiva practice and so forth. The primary purpose there is to subjugate and conquer, which is very different from the intent of Buddhist tantra. The fundamental practices of the Hindu practitioner are ascetic, such as the practice of punishing one's own body. Some of these rituals of physical penitence involve beating oneself on the back with an iron hook, thereby drawing blood. Extreme forms include impaling oneself on a trident. Hindu practitioners aspire to purify negative karma by these means, and by purifying karma to see the deity face to face. Physical penance, sometimes extreme, is the approach taken to karmic purification. Although we cannot say that this is absolutely wrong, it is not a very profound practice.

Of course, not all Hindu tantrikas practice in this way, through the practice of severe physical penance. Some engage in what we call non-dual practice, where the primary practice is focusing on the meditator's mind, the sound of the mantra the meditator is reciting, and the deity the meditator is trying to accomplish like Brahma or Shiva. This non-dual view entails seeing these three things – the practitioner, the mantra, and the deity – as inseparable. This is somewhat profound, but this sense of non-duality is different from the Buddhist sense of non-duality. We use the same term, but the meaning is different.

Even though we use the same term, 'non-dual,' in Hindu tantra, Buddhist highest yoga tantra, and Dzogchen, we should be able to differentiate among the three usages. Sometimes the explanations for each seem very similar, which can lead to confusion and misunderstanding, but they are totally different.

How are they different? In Hindu tantra, 'non-duality' refers to the practitioner's seeing himself or herself and the deity as inseparable. The ground of such non-duality, however, is the imputed inherent existence of the practitioner, who is to be seen as inseparable from the deity. This understanding of non-duality differs from the Buddhist understanding.

For the Hindu tantric practitioner, non-duality consists of focusing on the sound of the mantra, on the chakras and seed syllables, and on the deity. The practitioner and the practice objects are inseparable by virtue of the single-pointedness of the focus. That is the meaning of 'non-dual' here. These days, many Hindu tantrikas, some of whom are quite learned and intelligent, have learned and make use of Dzogchen via the books by Western scholars that are now available. Real Hindu tantra, however, is not like Dzogchen and does not go very far.

In Buddhist tantra, 'non-duality' means 'inseparable.' It refers to the non-duality, or inseparability, of bliss and emptiness, which is only understood in the context of the highest yoga tantra; it is not understood in the lower yoga tantras. In Dzogchen, it refers to the non-duality or inseparability of basic space and primordial awareness.

Buddhist tantric conduct can be peaceful or wrathful. It can also take the form of ascetic, unconventional practices that can themselves take peaceful or wrathful forms. The basic understanding, however, is that even when one engages in varying types of conduct, one never waivers from the state of bodhicitta, not even for one second.

The story of Saraha is interesting here. Saraha's main practice was bodhicitta. He was never separate from his principal deity, Vajrayogini. Physically, however, he assumed the personality of a hunter and was always seen with a bow and arrow, like an ordinary hunter. He behaved so unconventionally that it is said not only his entire village but even his father lost faith in him. The Buddhist understanding is that even though one may engage in unconventional conduct, one's practice must be based on bodhicitta. One must never be separate from one's deity.

The conduct of a Buddhist tantric practitioner is unlimited and sometimes may seem strange, like the activities of Saraha. For a long time, Saraha was a very famous pandita at Nalanda and also a fully ordained monk. He was Nagarjuna's teacher and he gave many teachings at Nalanda and had many students. One day he returned to his village. He wanted to investigate more deeply the primordial nature of mind, or natural mind. He wanted to cut through ordinary judgments and concepts of good and bad, clean and unclean, and so forth, and he behaved unconventionally. He met a woman who taught him how to hunt. Singing as she instructed him in the bow, the arrow, and the target, she imparted tantric knowledge. She was Vajrayogini, and became his teacher. Outwardly, it appeared that Saraha was spending all his time hunting. His father asked him, 'Why do you do this? You had a good reputation. You were a pandita, but now you pursue horrible activities and behave crazily.' The villagers also doubted him. Then Saraha demonstrated the power of his siddhis and his father and the villagers regained confidence in him. Saraha's story is just one of many such stories we have in Tibet.

Tantric practitioners sometimes behave very strangely. That is why in India the history of tantra is not so long, as this kind of conduct was not well tolerated. In Tibet, Tsongkhapa said that you can practice any tantra internally, but should not show it outwardly. In Saraha's time, people were very devoted to the guru and had competent instruction, so there was no question about it and it was not a big deal. Yet, even in that time it was difficult. During Tsongkhapa's time in Tibet, it was very different, so he said that outside you should appear to be an ordinary being or monk, but inside be fully tantric. I think that is a very, very smart idea. Though this can have unintended consequences when the view is taken that you should not discuss tantra, as this leads to situations where the masters pass away and the instructions and lineage disappear with them.

Even though there is a positive side to keeping the very secret tantric practices secret, as Tsongkhapa advised, this conservative approach also has negative consequences. Precautions can be taken to extremes, to the point that masters are not allowed to talk about tantra at all. While they wait for the perfect student, a lot of tantric transmissions and a lot of tantric empowerments and their commentaries are lost.

Buddhist tantric conduct is very difficult to understand. It takes many forms, sometimes very peaceful, sometimes very unconventional, but the essential point is that whatever outward conduct we engage in, it is all an expression of bodhicitta. At all times, our conduct must serve to enhance bodhicitta. As soon as we lose this inner conduct, we lose the tantra. That is what happens when we are overtaken by anger and other negative emotions.

A second requirement of outer conduct is that while it is joined with the inner practice of bodhicitta, it must also be joined with a very stable and very clear practice of the deity. We must identify ourselves as the deity at all times.

In summary, Buddhist tantric conduct is very different from that of Hindu tantra. The conduct of the Hindu tantrika entails devotion and maintaining inseparability from the deity, but there is no inner practice of bodhicitta. Cultivating and enhancing bodhicitta is not a focus of Hindu tantric practice, and that is the main difference between the two.

TANTRA AND THE THREE BASKETS

Every teaching given by the Buddha belongs to one of the 'three baskets' or collections of the Tripitaka. The three baskets comprise the basket of the sutras or scriptural teachings, the basket of conduct or vinaya, and the basket of abhidharma or teachings on the treasury of knowledge. The reason that all common vehicle teachings fall into one of these baskets is that they all correspond to one of the 'three trainings.' Any sutric (causal vehicle) teaching, whether Hinayana or Mahayana, belongs to one of the three trainings – the training in discipline or morality, the training in concentration, or the training in wisdom. The teachings are collected into the three baskets on this basis.

But to which of the collections do the tantric teachings belong? The answer to that differs from tradition to tradition. In the Indian tradition, scholars and practitioners have categorized the tantric teachings as a fourth collection, apart from sutra teachings. They call it the "collection of Vidhyadhara teachings." In Tibet, the answer also differs from tradition to tradition. In the New Translation schools, they say that tantric teachings must belong to one of the three baskets. Some scholars hold that tantric teachings are not a separate class of teachings and should not be seen as a fourth collection, and some scholars and traditions hold that tantras can be found in each of the three collections.

From my own perspective, it is better to maintain that tantric teachings do not belong to any of the three baskets, and so constitute a fourth collection. The reason is that the contents of the three baskets, which are basically the three trainings, are all causal vehicle teachings, and all tantric teachings are resultant vehicle teachings. Carrying the resultant enlightened state as the path is exclusive to tantra. Nowhere in the Mahayana sutra teachings is this taught. That is why I think tantric teachings are totally separate and should be classified as the collection of the Vidhyadhara teachings.

You will find different positions on this. If you look at the reasoning of the Indian and the Tibetan scholars on why there should or should not be a separate collection, you will encounter a debate that can be confusing. Some say tantric teachings fall into one or another of the three baskets and so on, but again, as resultant vehicle teachings, I think they fundamentally differ from the causal vehicle teachings.

The question of what basket the tantric teachings belong to is related to the more fundamental question of the difference between sutra and tantra. It is universally accepted in all the Tibetan schools – the ancient Nyingma, the Sakya, the Kagyu, and the Gelug traditions – that there are fundamental differences between these two. If we investigate further and raise questions such as, 'What are the differences in terms of the view of the ground? In terms of meditation? In terms of conduct?' we will find debates regarding each of these points.

From a general perspective, one might come to the conclusion that there are no differences between sutra and tantra on view, meditation, and conduct. If you look at the Mahayana sutra view, for example, which is the view of emptiness, it seems to be the same as the view of tantra. You might think that the Mahayana sutra meditation practice of the union of calm abiding and special insight is more or less the same as tantric meditation, even though tantra uses different terms like 'generation stage' and 'completion stage.' Both sutra and tantra also emphasize bodhicitta, and you may not be able to see much of a difference. If you do not investigate deeply enough, you may come to the conclusion that there is no significant difference between the two.

Some schools and traditions hold that there is no difference between the sutric and tantric view. For example, the New Translation traditions such as the Gelugpas maintain that the view of emptiness is the same in both. I think this is fundamentally mistaken, and that it demonstrates a lack of learning, especially with respect to the extensive tantric teachings. Even though the emptiness view is fundamental, and could be likened to the life force running through both sutra and tantra, the view of the ground, meditation, and conduct is fundamentally different in Buddhist sutra and tantra. In my view, the tantric path is far superior in view, meditation, conduct, and the resultant state.

If we were to accept the New Translation school position that there is no difference between the sutric and tantric view, then since meditation is based on view, it would follow that there is no difference in meditation. If we were to accept that there is no difference in view, but claim that there is a difference between sutric meditation and tantric meditation, then we would be contradicting ourselves. If the point of finding the view through logic and analysis is not to give rise to a qualitatively distinctive meditation, then what is the point? It is much like breeding, tending, and training a very fast race horse for years and years, but when the actual race is about to begin, deciding to ride a donkey instead. It is very much like that, and it does not make sense. And of course you are going to lose the race.

The Kagyu, Sakya, Gelug, and Nyingma schools have different ways of understanding the distinctions and from my own perspective, based on my own experience, there are differences in terms of all four aspects: view, meditation, conduct, and the resultant state.

Nowadays, a lot of young Gelugpa geshes and Sakya scholars claim, as an article of faith, that there is no difference between the view of sutra and tantra; they say that the view is of emptiness and the Middle Way. Older, more learned geshes, however, hold that there are some fundamental differences and that the tantric view is far more profound. If you look at the writing of one scholar in the Sakya tradition, Panchen Sakya Chogden, he clearly says there are great differences between sutra and tantra in understanding the view. In the Nyingma and Kaygu traditions, we do not have this same debate. We say right from the beginning that there are fundamental differences when it comes to the view.

When I talk about the differences between traditions, I am not pointing them out in order to engage in inter-traditional rivalry, but to indicate the significance of the differences so that we can avoid confusion from the point of view of our own practice.

Understanding everything that goes on in these debates may not be so important, especially if one's tantric practice is quite simple, such as practicing one deity. Tantric practice is based on sound sutric foundations – whatever is done in sutra is carried into tantra. If one is a simple practitioner focusing on one practice, maybe it is not so important to understand all of the subtle differences. Although the basis or ground is very different in tantra and sutra, we tantric practitioners carry a lot of practices over from sutra.

Another reason it is important to properly understand these differences is that it is important for tantric practitioners and scholars to avoid the tendency to look down on sutra practices, even Mahayana sutra practices. If this happens, it is detrimental to one's practice. This is not merely a theoretical point or a point of etiquette. At the practical level, we must be able to integrate sutric and tantric teachings. Integration does not mean mixing sutric and tantric practices together, that the sutric practitioner should mix in some tantric practices, or the tantric practitioner should mix in some sutric practices.

The basic practice in sutra is the union of the two truths. The relative and the ultimate levels of truth are carried onto the path as the union of method and wisdom. This union is the foundation upon which we engage in the practices of the six perfections, thereby traversing the five paths and the bodhisattva grounds, which lead to the state of enlightenment. That is what we carry onto the tantric path, and that is what we mean by 'integration of sutra and tantra.' The tantric practitioner does not leave sutric practice behind, saying 'I will now enter into tantric practice.'

In sutra, the fundamental practice is the union of method and wisdom. The key practice of the method aspect is the sutric-level practice of bodhicitta. In tantra, bodhicitta is the foundation of the illusory body practice, in which the method practice becomes more subtle. In sutra, the wisdom aspect is realizing emptiness, while in tantra it is more subtle, becoming the practice of clear light. The practices become more subtle, but we do not leave the fundamental sutric practices behind by entering into the tantric path.

This does not mean that tantric practitioners should look down on anyone who begins with tantric practice right from the start. Someone who enters the Dharma path in this way does not have to be sent back to the sutric sources and practices before he or she can engage in tantric practices. It is not necessary, for example, for practitioners who begin on the tantric path to study and practice the two truths. The sutric sources can be looked at, but one does not necessarily have to. The practice of tantra can still be complete.

The fundamental practice in sutra of the union of method and wisdom is made more subtle by the exceptionally skillful means of tantra. In that sense, and only in that sense, we can talk about the union of sutra and tantra. In any other sense, there is no such union. Speaking of such a thing would be idle speculation, playing with words.

Practitioners who mix practices, sometimes thinking, 'I am practicing tantra,' and other times thinking, 'I am practicing sutra,' are simply confused about what they are doing.

My own position is that if we say there are fundamental differences between sutra and tantra, then we should understand the basis of the distinctions – the basis of the differences in view, method, meditation, and so on.

'The fundamental view of the ground' in tantra refers to the great purity of both samsara and nirvana. 'The great purity of both samsara and nirvana' really refers to the fact that all phenomena of samsara and nirvana have the three features. First, by nature all phenomena are empty. Second, all phenomena have the quality of clarity. Third, emptiness and clarity are in union. These three features of being empty, clear, and in union are how the view of the ground is introduced in tantra, but the view is never introduced like this in sutra.

Otherwise, if we say there is no difference between sutra and tantra in terms of view, because the view is the view of emptiness, then that view is also the same with respect to Hinayana. If that were the case, then we also would say there is no difference between Hinayana practice and Tantrayana practice because the view is also the view of emptiness.

This is very important.

The tantric introduction to the view differs fundamentally from the sutric introduction, and the way in which the view is introduced affects the profundity of our practice. As I mentioned earlier, tantra is swifter and more profound because of the way the view is introduced. The three features of the tantric view – those of emptiness, clarity, and the union of emptiness and clarity – encompass not only the nature of the reality of the object but the characteristic of the perceiving mind as well. Tantric introduction to the view introduces not only the object but also the apprehending mind. When I speak of 'mind' here, I am talking about consciousness. In tantra, the mental consciousness is emphasized, and there are two aspects of this cognitive state – clarity and emptiness.

In sutra, samsara is negative; it is to be abandoned, whereas nirvana is to be actualized. In tantra, we speak of the great equality of samsara and nirvana, of the purity of both. The foundation is the ground of innate clear light, which is the source of both samsara and nirvana, and the basis for their natural purity, for their being of the same taste. The ground clear light, which is the subtlest innate mind, is the source of samsara and nirvana. It is pure by nature, primordially so. Since samsara and nirvana both arise from clear light – they have the same ground, the ground of subtlest innate clear light – we cannot think of one as pure and the other impure. This is the tantric view of the ground, and in introducing it, we talk about the great purity of both samsara and nirvana. This is entirely different from the way in which view is introduced in sutra.

The view of both samsara and nirvana as one taste is not something that comes about through intellectual analysis. In fact, it is very difficult to gain any understanding of it through intellectual investigation. It is even quite difficult to come to understand it in meditation. The tantric view is subtle and profound, and it requires not only intellectual understanding but also a lot of meditation experience. It is actually cultivated by means of deep meditation experience and transcends concepts. Considering the emptiness view alone, we might think that what is taught in sutra is the same as what is taught in tantra, but we need to see that the view of the ground that is introduced in tantra is not only the emptiness of phenomena but also the nature of mind.

In sutra, the view of the ground is introduced through analysis. By applying rigorous methods of analysis, one eventually arrives at the conviction that there is no intrinsic self. First, one looks at the object, which is called the 'object of negation' because its intrinsic existence is put in question. By systematically analyzing the object of negation, one inevitably comes to the conclusion that the object does not have an intrinsic, independent existence. By conducting such analysis repeatedly on various kinds of objects, one is eventually convinced that there is no intrinsic existence, that all phenomena are empty. This conviction is said to be 'free from the four extremes.' It is the Middle Way free from elaborations. That is the introduction to the view in sutra, and it is arrived at as a logical conclusion and a mental judgment or conviction.

We should recognize the limitations of this view – it is still within the domain of the mind, the domain of the intellect. It is still an intellectually induced view. The view of the ground from the point of the view of tantra, Mahamudra, and Dzogchen is beyond the mind, beyond the intellect. In the Zen tradition and in some Mahayana sutric traditions, the same language is used, such as saying that 'view is beyond mind.' This refers only to the context of meditative absorption, however. Because one is in meditative absorption, one says one is beyond the mind. In the post-meditative state, however, the way in which the view is introduced is still in the domain of the mind.

In summary, we can understand the difference between the sutric and tantric view of the ground in this way. The sutric view is an intellectual conclusion, still in the domain of mind, whereas the tantric view is beyond the mind and is the primordially pure ground of both samsara and nirvana. If the view of the ground is different in sutra and tantra, there necessarily will be differences in meditation as well, since meditation practice simply entails continuous meditation on the view that has been introduced. One practices meditation with the view of the ground so that the view becomes subtler and subtler, and clearer and clearer.

The sutric practice of meditation amounts to familiarizing oneself with the emptiness that is the result of one's intellectual inquiry and understanding. Avoiding the conceptually induced pitfalls of this method requires making extensive use of antidotes, so the practice stays within the bounds of conceptual mind and one carries conduct as the path.

In tantra, the subtlest aspect of the clarity of the mind is introduced, which is beyond intellect, beyond concepts. Tantric meditation also differs from sutric meditation in this regard, and this feature is true of all classes of tantra. Even in the lower tantras like the action (kriya) tantra and performance (charya) tantra, the view is of the one taste of samsara and nirvana, of the equality and purity of the ground. The lower tantras do not mention the union of bliss and emptiness, but the fundamental view that samsara and nirvana are primordially pure is common to all classes.

There are also differences in how the view is introduced among the different Tibetan Buddhist traditions. For example, in the Nyingma and Kaygu traditions – the older traditions in Tibet – all of the masters say that introduction to the view of emptiness is not sufficient for tantric practitioners. Of course they need to understand the view of emptiness, since that is the fundamental ground, but to engage in tantric practice, the view of the clear light of the mind also must be introduced. For the Nyingma and Kagyu, this applies to all the classes of tantra, but particularly to the highest yoga tantra. Whether one engages in generation stage or completion stage practices, the view of clear light has to be introduced, since the practices for both stages are based on this introduction. This is a unique way of introducing the view. In Nyingma practice especially, it is emphasized that tantric practice has to be based on the nonconceptual clear light view. This is due to the Dzogchen influences on tantric practice. When we apply this, we see the real significance of using the non-conceptual clear light as the basis for practice.

The Nyingma also refer to the Dzogchen practice of introducing the primordial purity of the ground. We are taught to see every appearance, even in generation-stage practice, as appearing from the ground of primordial purity as unceasing dynamic display. This is something that is very much emphasized in Dzogchen. When we carry that into tantric practice, we see the real significance of taking a nonconceptual state as the ground for all the deity practices.

This kind of practice accounts for how in the old days, many Nyingma and Kaygu tantric practitioners achieved high siddhis and high realizations through tantric practice. This[1] is no longer so true, however, and in my personal view, some of the effectiveness of practice has been lost through engaging in too much intellectual analysis. There has been too much intellectual influence due to the popularity of debate, and too much pursuit of purely intellectual concerns. I am not saying that tantric practitioners should drop rational inquiry – there is, of course, a need for intellectual analysis. But we should be able to recognize its limit – the point at which we should depart from the intellect and enter into the non-conceptual state.

In contrast to the Nyingma and Kagyu, the New Translation schools, especially the Sakya and Gelug, do not emphasize the nature of the clear light as the ground for the practice of tantra. They say the Middle Way view of Nagarjuna is the view for any tantric practice, relying on the mind, as in sutra. They remain in the domain of the mind to the extent that the basis of their tantric view is the sutric Middle Way view.

There are also fundamental differences in which meditation techniques are used in sutra and tantra. In sutra, after rationally deducing the meaning of emptiness as the lack of a falsely imputed self (what we call the 'object of negation of self,' not just the nominal self), the certainty induced is sustained through the dual meditation technique of calm abiding and special insight. Here, special insight still plays an intellectual role. Thus, even in the meditative state, there is rigorous intellectual application combined with the single-pointed calm-abiding meditation.

In contrast, once the clear light is induced in tantric meditation, you simply engage in meditative absorption. There is no need for analytical meditation at that point. After inducing clear light, if you are still engaging in analysis, you lose the whole point of tantric meditation. That is a fundamental difference.

Just as there are differences in view and meditation between sutra and tantra, there are differences in terms of conduct. Mahayana sutric conduct involves cultivating the six perfections based on bodhicitta – perfecting generosity and so forth as the practice. Tantric conduct can involve a variety of peaceful and wrathful activities such as subjugation and so forth, as well as very unconventional ascetic practices. The latter can be misunderstood, as I explained in the life story of Saraha, but these apparently extreme or unconventional practices are also motivated by bodhicitta.

Finally, there are fundamental differences between sutra and tantra with respect to the resultant state. Although in sutra we talk about achieving the three or four kayas, if you look carefully, you will find that it is almost impossible to achieve even one kaya, let alone the four kayas, by practicing in the sutric tradition. Following logical analysis can lead people to unexpected conclusions. There are Gelug scholars who have arrived, over the course of a debate, at the conclusion that there are no means to give rise to the rupakaya through sutric practice, because it does not include the unique causal factors by which we can give rise to the rupakaya or physical form of the enlightened person. Some Indian scholars have said that it is possible through the sutric tradition to give rise to the dharmakaya but not the rupakaya. This means they have found that an enlightened person is possible – someone who has realized dharmakaya – but with no form body or rupakaya. This is rather contradictory, as the dharmakaya without the rupakaya is very much like empty space without any ornaments, without the stars or the sun or the moon.

These absurd conclusions come from being very conservative and faithful to the literal meaning of the words of the Mahayana sutra. Due to their rigid interpretation, Gelug scholars are forced to come to their strange conclusions such as the dharmakya being possible without rupakaya. My personal take on this is that we should not be too narrow-minded, conservative, or literal about sutric teachings. One could say that an approximate but not actual accomplishment of the four kayas is possible – something that is close to the rupakaya, something that is close to the dharmakaya.

The unique and exceptional causal factors that give rise to the enlightened rupakaya are not taught in sutra. Sutra divides practice into the practices of method and wisdom. Those practices belonging to the method side, including practices like generosity, observance of discipline, and so forth, allegedly become the causal factor for achieving the rupakaya. That is what the sutric teachings say. Meditation on the wisdom of emptiness becomes the factor that gives rise to the dharmakaya. Beyond these general causal factors, however, the specific uncommon factors that are directly responsible for giving rise to the kayas are not actually taught in sutra.

My own perspective is that in the sutric tradition, in addition to there being no specific causal factors that can give rise to the rupakaya, if the rupakaya is not possible, then the dharmakaya is not possible. That can be logically inferred. 'Dharmakaya' does not simply refer to the emptiness of the mind. In tantra, the dharmayaka, the inner clear light nature of the mind, is introduced at the very beginning, and then it is refined and developed by means of tantric practices in order to manifest clear light. If the dharmakaya is not introduced in sutra right at the beginning, how can it be refined? It seems to follow from this that it is even impossible to actualize the dharmakaya on the basis of sutric teachings.

If the dharmakaya is impossible, then the rupakaya is all the more impossible. Sutra says that the causal factors for achieving the rupakaya are method practices, such as generosity and compassion, but these practices are entirely mental applications. The rupakaya, the form body, however, is not just mental, but also physical and has to do with the subtlest wind. We therefore need a practice that is able to purify all of the gross and subtle winds. When the subtlest wind is purified, there is the wind that actually transforms into the illusory body. Sutric teachings do not have techniques to purify the winds, whether gross or subtle, and therefore cannot give rise to the illusory body, which then gives rise to the rupakaya.

As a tantric practitioner, my position is that it is important to understand that there are fundamental differences between sutra and tantra in terms of the view, meditation, conduct, and the resultant state. If we understand the differences between these four elements of the sutric and tantric vehicles, that alone is sufficient for practice. There is then no need to engage in further debate and further analysis.

ESSENTIAL MEANING OF THE RIPENING INITIATION AND LIBERATING INSTRUCTIONS

When I talk about the ripening initiation or empowerment, I am talking about ripening the mental continuum of the disciple. Of course, the guru has to have been ripened. If the guru's mental continuum is not ripened, then the guru will not be able to impact the ripening of the continuum of the disciple.

The ripening of the mental continuum takes place by relying on exceptional skillful methods that have to do with very subtle causal interdependence. We cannot understand this from the point of view of conventional causality, as this subtle interdependence is a very subtle kind of causality. 'Ripening of the continuum' does not refer to changing the nature of the mind, but rather refers to very skillful methods. These methods are only available in tantric initiation.

To speak of ripening the mind, or mental continuum, is not to assume that there is an object that is not ripened, that a mind that is not ripened is to be ripened through tantric initiation. In the tantric context, the unripened state of the mind refers to a lack of devotion and a lack of faith in the efficacy of the tantric teachings. When that is the state of the mind, then the mind has not been ripened.

To ripen the mind, one has to generate devotion to the guru and conviction in the efficacy of the tantric teachings. Here, we can see the primacy of the guru. The main cause for the ripening of the mind is the blessings of the guru. It is not really the initiating vase or the substances – these are just symbols. The main causal factor that determines whether one's mind is ripened or not is the guru.

This means that it is not easy to give tantric initiations. The guru plays the prominent role in the initiation and the transmission, and therefore must have some realization pertaining to the generation-stage and completion-stage yogas. At the very least, the guru must have bodhicitta and extensive learning with respect to tantra. Unless these qualities are present in the guru, it is not easy for him or her to actually bring about the empowerment.

Strictly speaking, in the ancient tradition, it is said that for the guru to give the empowerment for a particular deity yoga practice, the guru has to have received both the complete transmission and the empowerment from an unbroken lineage, and to have attained realizations based on retreat practice of that deity. Otherwise, technically speaking, the guru is not able to give and should not give the empowerment.

The definition of 'receiving the empowerment' is 'receiving the blessings of the guru.' If the guru does not have the realization and blessings, then he or she cannot transmit the blessings to someone else. The guru would be like an empty cup, and you cannot get anything from an empty cup. This is why the ancient techniques and requirements make sense in saying that not only does the guru need to have all of the lineage transmissions and the empowerments but he or she must also have the experience.

Because the purpose of the initiation is to ripen the mental continuum of the disciple, the guru's own mind must be ripened in order to be able to do that. There is no way the initiation can take place otherwise. In fact, when the guru gives the empowerment, and gives the blessing with his or her hand and so forth – the blessing on the head, for example, with the five fingers symbolizing the mastery of the five pranas, and the pranas arising in the empty form of the deity – the blessings are imparted because divine clarity and pride are there on the side of the guru. If the guru has no divine clarity and stability and blesses you, you might as well get the blessings from a dog; it would amount to the same thing.

When the initiation or blessing takes place, the guru has to arise in the form of that particular deity. Even though you see the physical human form of the teacher, the guru has actually arisen as the deity. This means that all of the winds have been subjugated and purified. The guru has no clinging to self and does not appear as an ordinary person, but rather clearly sees himself or herself in the form of the deity. During the process of the initiation, even the vase is not a mere vase. It is transformed into the initiating deity, and the water in the vase is transformed into nectar by virtue of the guru's divine pride and divine clarity. The initiation and blessing can take place when the guru is able to sustain all these aspects simultaneously.

For the initiation to take place, the disciple receiving the empowerment must also have pure vision of the guru arising in the form of the deity. It is the disciple's responsibility to be able to do this and to see the vase water as bliss in the form of nectar. For the initiation to actually take place, this pure vision of the disciple is particularly important.

In summary, two interdependent causal factors must be present. First, the guru must be able to generate divine pride and divine clarity within the view of emptiness. Second, the disciple must be able to cultivate some degree of pure vision – some ability to see the guru in the form of that particular tantric deity – and be able to sustain pure vision throughout the initiation, so as to see the water as nectar giving rise to bliss, and so forth. Only when these two factors are present can the empowerment or ripening initiation take place.

The signs that you have actually received the ripening empowerment are that you have greater devotion to the guru, you become more compassionate, and you have more conviction in the efficacy of the tantric teachings.

'Ripening' means 'transforming the mind.' As I mentioned earlier, the unripened state of mind must ripen to be transformed. Prior to initiation, you may have no devotion, no compassion toward sentient beings, and no conviction in the efficacy of the tantric teachings, but by virtue of having received the tantric initiation from a qualified guru, all of these will arise or increase. That is how the actual transformation takes place. This is something disciples must contemplate after receiving the initiation. It is your own responsibility to see whether you have actually received the initiation or not.

If you do not know what you are doing and are uncertain of whether or not you have received the initiation, thinking something like, 'I got blessed on my head with the vase, but I don't know whether I received the initiation,' then this is a waste of your time and a waste of your offering to the guru. This is something you must understand when you are going to receive an initiation.

This is the main reason why I am averse to giving initiations. Although I have my own practice and so forth, a lot of disciples really do not have these qualities and so the initiation becomes meaningless. The initiating guru has a lot of responsibilities – giving an initiation is not an easy thing to do – and the disciples also have a lot of responsibilities in coming into a tantric commitment.

When the two interdependent factors are present – a qualified master and a qualified disciple – then the disciple receives the definitive empowerment. The definitive sense of 'empowerment' entails the ability to empower your body, speech, and mind so that none fall under the sway of ordinary perception and grasping. That is true, definitive empowerment. You take hold of the power of your body, speech and mind such that you are able to transform them into the divine body, speech, and mind of the deity.

Here, I have briefly explained the meaning of the ripening initiation. There are, of course, different types of initiations belonging to each of the four classes of tantra. For example, in some lower tantras such as action tantra, there is only the vase initiation. Within the vase initiation for some deity practices, there is only the water initiation and so forth. Some initiations give only permission initiation. On the other hand, all of the higher tantric classes give the complete initiation. They give the four empowerments – the vase empowerment, the secret empowerment, the wisdom empowerment, and the word empowerment. Generally speaking, it is important for you to understand what initiation you have just received, what the deity is, what the mantra you have to recite is, and also how to engage in the meditation pertaining to the deity. These are all important once you have received the initiation.

It is not enough, however, to only ripen the mental continuum; you must also liberate it. To accomplish this, you rely on the liberating instructions, which are those given for the practice of the empowerment deity. For example, if you have received the ripening empowerment for an action-tantra deity like Avalokiteshvara or Tara, the liberating instructions explain how to engage in the meditation of that particular deity. In action tantra, there are unique tantric meditation methods that are not the same as those taught in the highest yoga tantra. For example, in action tantra there is the six-step meditation of generating the deity, or 'meditation through six-deities yoga' – the deity of emptiness, the deity of letters, the deity of mantra, and so forth. The way you engage in the meditation is to see the deity you are invoking in front of yourself; you do not actually visualize yourself as the deity in action tantra.

Since the instructions for each class of tantra are unique, the guru must give instructions on how to engage in the meditation for each and ensure that the classes are not mixed and the purity of the instructions is preserved. If you receive the empowerment for an action deity, the instructions must conform to action tantra, and likewise for yoga tantra, or highest yoga tantra.

For example, in action tantra, there is no practice of carrying the union of bliss and emptiness as the path, and the practices of union with a consort are also not taught. The practice of the union of bliss and emptiness is only taught in the highest yoga tantra and not in the lower three tantras, and such distinctions between the classes of tantra are essential.

In the lower tantras, there is the practice of yoga with signs and yoga without signs. In the action and conduct tantras, we practice mostly the yoga with signs, and there are no exceptional tantric vows, just bodhisattva vows. When the liberating instructions are given, the guru must understand these particulars and give the instructions accordingly. It is not sufficient to look up such things in commentaries or books; that does not qualify someone to give liberating instructions.

There are two major types of instructions – experiential and commentary-based. Tradition holds that tantric instructions in Mahamudra and Dzogchen must be experiential, but these are difficult to obtain. In the sutric traditions, the instructions are primarily commentary-based; the guru presents commentaries on the teachings and engages in debate and so forth. These days, instructions are mainly of the commentary type, since it is difficult to find a teacher who can give instructions from the point of view of their own experience.

Experiential instructions are given by teachers based on their own meditative experience, including exceptional instructions received from their own teachers and how they incorporated those into their own experience. Primarily, however, experiential instructions such as those for the practice of a deity are given from the point of view of the guru's own experience. These instructions include those for the conduct of your body, speech, and mind, and the signs you can expect in the course of engaging in the deity practice. Commentary-based instructions are based on the commentarial literature for a text, and they thus are not the product of the teacher's own experience. Of the two types of liberating instructions, the more profound are the experiential, but again, they are very difficult to come by.

In a nutshell, liberating instructions are for working with the mind that has been ripened. The relationship between the ripening empowerment and the liberating instructions can be illustrated by the analogy of leveling a field and throwing away the stones to prepare for planting a crop, which is like the ripening empowerment. You then have to sow the seed in order for the crop to grow. The seeds can be likened to the liberating instructions.

The role of the liberating instructions is to liberate the mental continuum, which frees it from all uncertainty, doubt and misunderstanding about your practice. If you receive the liberating instructions and you still have confusion, if you still entertain doubt, uncertainty, and misunderstanding about the meditation, then you have not actually received the instructions.

THE GURU – THE ROOT OF THE PATH

The guru is the root of the tantric path, because the foundation of all tantric practice is receiving the transformative blessings. Our mind can only be transformed by the blessings of the guru when we have devotion, and that devotion is for the guru. In this sense, the root of the path is the guru.

In the Nyingma tradition, we talk about the three roots of tantra. The root of blessings is the guru, the root of siddhis is the yidam deity, and the root of activities is the dakini. In the sutric context, the guru is to be seen as the source of all qualities to be actualized. Unlike the tantric context, the teacher in the sutric context is not regarded as the guru inseparable from the deity, the Buddha himself. The lamrim (stages of the path) commentaries begin with extensive teachings on how to find and relate to the teacher, and the role of the teacher is emphasized in sutric practice. But in tantra, the emphasis is much greater.

In his writings on the stages of the path, Tsongkhapa frequently reminds us that the source of all qualities and realizations is the teacher, the guru or lama. He explains how we should appropriately consult and relate to the guru. In the sutras, the Buddha taught extensively on the importance and role of the teacher. He told the fully ordained monks and nuns that the guru is the one that shows you the path. The guru is like the boatman that ferries you.

In tantra, the role of the guru is even more important. Here, we speak of the 'root guru.' This concept does not appear in the sutras, only in the context of tantra, and especially in the highest yoga tantra. The root guru is the person who has given you the ripening empowerment and also the liberating instructions. Most especially, the root guru is the one who has been able to introduce you to the innate clear light nature of the mind.

In tantra, we make a distinction between the root guru and other gurus with whom you have a dharma connection. The root guru is someone who has been kind to you in three ways – he or she has given you the ripening empowerment, the liberating instructions, and also the oral transmissions. That is your root guru. Other teachers are gurus with whom you have a dharma connection, and your senior teachers in tantra are called 'instructors.' Even though you do not regard them as your root guru, you should respect these senior teachers and students as your role models and instructors.

The significance of the root guru in tantra, and the way we conduct the guru-disciple relationship, is clearly illustrated in the life histories of Naropa and Tilopa, and the accounts of how Naropa related to Tilopa as his root guru. Naropa was a great scholar in India, whereas Tilopa was a mahasiddha without much learning. Nonetheless, as a disciple of Tilopa, Naropa underwent great hardship and never lost his faith or generated wrong view. In Tibet, we are also very familiar with the similar life story of Milarepa and Marpa Lotsawa. From these stories, you see clearly that the significance of the root guru and how to properly relate to him or her is not open to debate – that this is how you practice tantra.

Most of us have tantric guru-disciple relationships, and it is not always appropriate for me to talk about the proper form of that relationship. Within the present context, I happen to be the guru for some of you, and so you should learn about this by looking at the stories of authentic guru-disciple relationships. Contemplate the stories and think about how you relate to your guru. By reading the life stories of past masters and their disciples and how they maintained their relationships, try to understand what it means when we say that the root guru is the source of all blessings. If you can see that this is true, then you have understood the most important thing about how to properly relate to the guru.

Actually conducting a proper relationship with your guru, observing the samayas and guru-disciple commitments, can be difficult and challenging. In the American or Western context, where it has only been about 50 years since tantric Buddhism was introduced, it is all the more challenging because there is no established custom or tradition. Even in the Tibetan case, where we have had Buddhism for thousands of years, it is very difficult for practitioners – even for Tibetan monks – to observe samayas and understand the significance of the root guru. Some disciples refer to having a root guru, but only rarely does anyone observe the guru-disciple samayas, and this problem is very pervasive in Asian Buddhist communities as well, even though Buddhism has been there for a long time. I think the main factor responsible for this is there is not much contemplation or observation of karma or the law of causality.

The way that we become able to observe the samayas and relate to the teacher is by reminding ourselves constantly of the kindness of the guru. We can come to see this kindness by contemplating the law of karma or causality, and then within the context of karma, seeing the guru's kindness. Constantly reminding ourselves of the kindness of the teacher is the most important factor in giving rise to the right way of relating to him or her.

We can understand how contemplating causality brings about recognition of the kindness of the teacher by looking at our own life. We have a lot of respect for our parents, as we can directly see their kindness. Our mothers carried us in their womb with loving kindness for nine months, and they nurtured us and sacrificed for us so that we could have a better life. When we think of this, the wish to repay their kindness, even if only in the form of respecting them, comes naturally. Likewise, when we are sick, we depend on the doctor. When a doctor cures our illness, we have so much veneration and respect for them. We recognize that we must relate to the doctor properly, because when we see what they are doing, it inspires a real sense of veneration. A similar sense of veneration is inspired when we go to a court of law. We speak to the judge politely and respectfully, and we relate to our attorney the same way, seeing that such conduct is related to our own well-being in this lifetime. If we look at all these situations and then compare them with the spiritual teacher who is not only responsible for our happiness in this lifetime, but also for revealing and guiding us on our path to liberation over many lifetimes, we begin to see the kindness of the guru.

We have to think like this. If we respect parents, doctors, and attorneys, then we should generate even greater respect for the teacher who is showing us the path to permanent freedom from the troubles of existence.

When you remember the kindness of the guru – not as an obligation but as a fact – then devotion comes easily. You will not need to depend on anyone else for devotion, as it will arise naturally. If your recognition of the kindness of the guru is not firm, but you are instead temporarily excited by a teaching or inspired by lofty sentiments or ideas, that is not devotion.

It is important, even in the sutric context, to rely on a qualified teacher. It is also important for the teacher to relate to the student correctly. If the teacher does not do this, then it is dangerous from a karmic point of view. The teacher has a lot of responsibility and it is not easy. Both the guru and the disciples have similar responsibilities and they can be maintained if karma is correctly observed. This becomes the strongest foundation for conducting the guru-disciple relationship.

I don't know what other teachers do to fulfill their responsibilities in their guru-disciple relationships. Even though I try to maintain divine clarity and divine pride, sometimes it is difficult to sustain this. On a daily basis, I see the kindness of the students – I see them as the object of the accumulation of merit. Because of them, I do practices where I accumulate merit. I am smart, however, so I don't tell the students in case they might think they are indispensable – 'the guru is very dependent on us.'[Laughter.]

Tantric texts refer to the ten qualities of the guru and the many qualities of the suitable disciple, such as great wisdom and devotion. Honestly, today it is very difficult to find qualified gurus and qualified students with all of the requisite qualities. This is not meant to be discouraging and does not mean we should do nothing. We should always try on a daily basis to practice and to improve, so that our way of maintaining the guru-disciple relationship becomes better and better.

Especially those of you who are Western students, if you want tantric blessings and realization as a serious tantric practitioner, then you should not relate to the guru as a friend. You can enjoy social gatherings with your teacher, but for the real tantric student, regarding the guru as a friend is detrimental because it obscures the guru's real significance. Once you are able to relate to the guru properly, and consult him or her in an appropriate way, then the observance of the fourteen root vows and the eight branch vows becomes relatively easy. This is because you have done the most important thing in tantra by conducting the guru-disciple relationship correctly from the beginning.

For students in the West, it is best not to stay too close to the teacher. It is good to keep some distance and separation in order to practice guru devotion. There are, however, different cultural styles. In Tibet, when students first meet the teacher, they do not immediately have devotion, and even question the teacher. When the teacher is seen to be qualified however, they become more and more devoted.

In the West, it is the other way around. Here, we initially find the guru to be wonderful and there is so much devotion and respect, but as time goes by students lose interest and start to offer criticism. So it is best to be neither too close nor too distant, as Westerners can be very intelligent but not very stable. There are Western students who have been with a teacher for fifteen years and then have a change of mind, suddenly deciding 'Oh, he is not my kind of root teacher,' and I am very surprised by this. I urge you not to be like that and to relate in such a way that you are able to maintain guru devotion. Stability and firmness of mind are very important.

I think perhaps it is a cultural thing. In the West, you have many good qualities – there is a lot of social understanding and respect, generosity, and forgiveness – but there is a tendency to change one's mind. Maybe this is a cultural result of seeing everything in terms of individual freedom of choice. Once you enter into tantra and commit to following its rules, you lose your conventional freedom but gain a different kind of freedom.

The observance of commitment or samaya is very important in tantra – there are the fourteen root vows and the eight secondary vows – but not in the sense of counting each of these vows one by one. The most important thing is to guard your body, speech, and mind.

Guarding your samaya or commitment does not mean doing so on an independent or individual basis. Once you have received a tantric initiation from a guru, you must keep the commitments not only with the teacher but with all of your vajra brother and sisters. The observance of samaya in both of these ways is very important. Whether you achieve the siddhis or not depends on whether you observe your samayas.

Generally in the Western sanghas, you do not have the danger of failing to observe the samaya between yourself and the guru, but there is another, greater danger here in the West. I have noticed that there is more difficulty in observing the samaya between students than in keeping the samaya with the guru. This is very important in the Western context, as I think you have an ego problem. You are not able to listen to each other, but rather listen only to the teacher. When we do a ganachakra puja – the spiritual feast – there is a prayer that says we achieve enlightenment among the dakas and dakinis of the same mandala. We pray like this, and it means we are all in the same mandala.

I am not saying that it is easy to observe samaya; I find it difficult even in my own experience. We should, however, try to make an effort to do so because of its importance in giving rise to realization. Failure to observe tantric commitments among vajra brothers and sisters is due to ego, and the main antidote is sympathetic rejoicing. Whenever you rejoice in the good deeds of other students, that rejoicing counteracts your egocentric tendencies.

Another technique to ensure that we are able to keep samaya with each other is to remind ourselves constantly that we are vajra brothers and sisters. By virtue of karma we all came together within one mandala. This is a great opportunity to be in the mandala of the tantric teacher and deity, and we may never again find this opportunity. We should remember that it is the result of many lifetimes of aspirational prayers and karma that we have come together on this occasion. If we recognize and remind ourselves of this special opportunity, then it also helps us to be mindful.

In this culture we are very isolated – very far apart – even when we live in the same neighborhood. We need to make heart to heart connections, and that is a cultural problem. With no judging or criticizing we can discuss our different opinions. It is good to discuss how to function best as a sangha, and if we check that our motivation is pure, then our actions become pure. Sometimes we do not understand the meaning of samaya in daily life, and correct samaya is very important. Especially as tantric and Dzogchen practitioners, we should open our mind and connect heart to heart with people. Samaya is the source and root of siddhis. The teacher is giving direct instruction, the blood of the dakinis – giving it to students. If you don't observe samaya, the dharma protectors have three eyes and they become more difficult and very angry, which then becomes very difficult for the student. It is like eating very powerful food, if you don't have a powerful body you can't digest it. People may receive a very profound teaching – very practical and very precise - but if the people don't keep samaya they won't digest the teaching.

Therefore observance of samaya among sangha brothers and sisters is extremely important, because it is the source of all siddhis. You as students will be the lineage holders of the teachings when the teacher passes away. The lineage is maintained by the students. But if the students can't maintain good samaya, then it corrupts and dilutes the lineage teachings. You have to be very careful in tantra and Dzogchen, because sustaining the lineage is not easy.

In Tibet we have the problem of broken samaya in some of the lineages. When samaya is broken, then the lineage is broken, even though the student is smart and can be taught a lot. The blessings are not sustained. This is my responsibility, to continue and maintain the blessings.

We have to get rid of the cultural baggage that gets in the way of observing our samaya, for example, judging and putting people down. That is poisonous for a practitioner. This does not mean you cannot ask the teacher and the sangha questions or have an opinion. You can share opinions with sangha, but this does not mean being emotional or creating drama.

The observance of tantric commitments and samayas does not necessarily involve attending to the commitments literally, one by one. It means guarding your body, speech and mind. If you observe your body, speech and mind you are by necessity observing samaya. The best way to do that is to transform them into that of the deity, so that we aren't operating on the basis of our ordinary body, speech and mind. That level is a little high and a little difficult, but if we can do that, we are fulfilling all of the commitments. We should try to act from enlightened body, speech and mind. If we can't do that, then at least refrain from harming others through our body, speech and mind. Keep guard of your body, speech and mind.

THE THREE CONTINUUMS

'Tantra' means 'continuum,' or 'having the quality of being continuous.' When we speak of tantra, we speak of three continuums. The first is the ground continuum, the second is the method continuum, and the third is the resultant continuum.

The ground tantra or ground continuum refers to the ultimate nature of the mind. In the sutra vehicle, the ultimate nature of mind is called 'buddha nature' or *tathagatagarbha*. In tantra, it is the 'subtlest innate clear light of the mind.' In Dzogchen, it is called the 'primordial or intrinsic awareness of the ground.'

The method tantra or method continuum refers to the tantric path. After having been introduced to the ground continuum, we use the many skillful methods of tantra to further develop and enhance our understanding of it. This is what we mean by method tantra. It contains all of the tantric practices, and in the context of the highest yoga tantra, it comprises all of the generation stage and completion stage practices. All of these belong to the method tantra.

The essence of the method tantra is the wisdom of the union of profundity and clarity, which is the very essence of the tantric path. It becomes even more subtle in the highest yoga tantra. There, it is called "the wisdom that is the union of bliss and emptiness." The wisdom that is the union of profundity and clarity is common to all four classes of tantra, but the wisdom that is the union of bliss and emptiness is exclusive to highest yoga tantra.

The profound aspect of the wisdom that is the unity of profundity and clarity is the wisdom of emptiness I referred to earlier. This is the view of the tantric ground. The wisdom of emptiness is referred to as 'the profound wisdom.' The clarity aspect of the wisdom of the union of profundity and clarity is called 'divine clarity.' Divine clarity encompasses the complete form of the deity, including the colors, form, and implements. Sustaining that clarity, while also sustaining the view of emptiness in single-pointed meditation, is the union of profundity and clarity.

First, the practitioner meditates on emptiness, the view of the ground in tantra. While sustaining the view of the ground, the divine aspects arise out of that emptiness as the deity. The tantric practitioner arises in the form of the deity, sustaining divine clarity of themselves as the deity, including the entirety of samsara and nirvana as the mandala of the deity. By sustaining vivid clarity, the practitioner does not fall under the sway of ordinary conceptual thoughts, appearances, and perceptions, which are eliminated in that state. Every thought and perception arises as divine thought and divine vision. When this happens in single-pointed meditation, this is what is meant by the union of profundity and clarity.

This is not mentally fabricated. It actually happens, through conviction and devotion. In the absence of emptiness meditation, we can mentally fabricate a convincing image of the deity and mandala, but this is not true deity practice. The deity naturally arises from emptiness without mental fabrication. At that point in true deity meditation, there is deep single-pointed absorption in emptiness. Whatever arises in that dimension as the deity is simultaneously arising through meditation. It is not done through ordinary mental fabrication or ordinary intellectual mind. That is why it is called the wisdom that is the union of profundity and clarity. It is not ordinary thought or ordinary mind.

This wisdom or meditation is called non-dual because there is no sense of self and other in this state. The wisdom of emptiness is the certainty that everything is empty of intrinsic existence, including one's own self-identity. To the practitioner, *everything* that arises in that meditative absorption is empty. It is not like ordinary perception of forms that we see. The divine clarity aspect of that certainty is the deity – the form of the deity, the colors and everything arising from the mandala of the deity. In this sense, there is no feeling of self. There is no such thought, 'I am performing a transformation from a state of emptiness.' It is non-dual at that stage. There is no self operating here – there is no dualistic mind saying, 'Here is the aspect of clarity, and there is the aspect of emptiness.'

This is something that is general to all the tantric paths. Even in the highest yoga tantra, we use the same term – 'union of profundity and clarity,' – but the meanings of 'profundity' and 'clarity' change. In the highest yoga tantra, we have more sophisticated and profound methods, so the understanding of profundity and clarity changes. In the highest yoga tantra, there are generation and completion stage practices that are not available in the lower tantras. These practices will be discussed in the sixth section.

The third continuum is the resultant tantra. The resultant tantra refers to the three or four kayas of the enlightened state. These are also spoken of as the two kayas – dharmakaya and rupakaya. The cause of the dharmakaya, according to the lower tantras, is the profound wisdom of emptiness. Meditation on the subtle clear light of mind becomes the dharmakaya, and the practice of seeing oneself as deity and mandala becomes the form body or rupakaya. That is the account of the lower tantras. In the higher tantras, you have the subtle clear light mind, which has an aspect of subtle wind. That subtle wind becomes the form or illusory body, and the subtlest clear light mind becomes the dharmakaya. This subtlest mind and the subtlest wind are inseparable.

Understanding these three continuums – the ground, method, and resultant continuums – helps us understand the tantric teachings, which are vast and extensive. The essence of tantra is these three continuums. If you do not understand them, your understanding of tantra will be limited. Sometimes when people think about tantra, they think about activities like sexual union and fire pujas, but these are branches of tantra, not real tantra. If you understand the three continuums, there is nothing more you really need to know; you do not need to be vastly well read on the tantras. Even though it is not necessary to engage in such lengthy intellectual research, it is important that your understanding of the three continuums is correct.

The ground continuum is the first and most important to understand, and there are two steps to understanding it. First, one finds conceptual understanding through reading tantric treatises and through intellectual analysis. Conceptual understanding is not sufficient, however; one must go to the next level and find experiential understanding through practice.

Conceptual introductions to the ground continuum may define the view in terms of the subtlest clear light of the mind, with its nature as emptiness and its aspect as clarity, and both of these attributes are to be understood as in union. However, this explanation, though correct, is just touching the surface.

We have to understand the ground continuum from our own perspectives as practitioners. We have a gross mind, we have a subtle mind, and we have a subtlest mind. 'Ground continuum,' or 'ground tantra,' refers to the subtlest mind, which has the aspect of clarity. The nature of the subtlest mind is very different from the unstable gross mind, which generates lots of conceptual thoughts and grasps to things. The subtlest mind is not like that. It is very subtle, firm, stable and does not waver.

The second level of the mind, the subtle mind, is the sleep state. The sleep state is more subtle than the gross mind and has its own properties as well. Even in the sleep state, however, it is possible to give rise to concepts, thoughts, feelings, and sensations. This occurs when karmic mental imprints activated in the sleep state arise as dreams. In a dream we have feelings, sensations, and also very subtle conceptual thoughts. Not only do we have subtle conceptual thoughts, but it is also possible for us to cling to things and grasp at things. Attachment and grasping are possible even in this very subtle dream state of the mind.

Even the first level of the mind, what we call the 'gross mind,' can be made subtle through meditation. Calm-abiding meditation can calm the mind so that it becomes very clear and pure, but even then, such a mind is still prone to gross conceptual thoughts and grasping. Even a strong calm-abiding meditative state is still within the domain of conditioned phenomena, and even small changes in those conditions can make us lose the state of clarity and stillness and fall into dullness and agitation. Special insight or vipasyana techniques can be used to eliminate all dullness, even to the point that one's calm-abiding meditation eliminates the need for sleep. This is the ninth stage of calm abiding, called 'equanimity.' This state of mind is very subtle, but it is still possible for that mind to have subtle thoughts and subtle concepts.

If you get rid of dullness, you get rid of the root cause of sleepiness. When I speak of eliminating the need for sleep, I am not talking about insomnia but something very profound. It is different from a sleep disorder that prevents one from sleeping. That is a physical disorder, whereas here I am referring to a result of meditation. When we ingest heavy food, for example, that gives rise to a foggy state of mind, which in turn induces dullness, which in turn induces a sleep state.

Sleep disorders are mainly caused by an imbalance in the element of wind, which in turn causes imbalances in the other elements. When we fall into the sleep state normally, it is similar to the dissolution process. The winds dissolve into the heart center and that is when we fall asleep. In people with a sleep disorder, however, the winds do not dissolve in the heart center. The mind and the wind get so agitated that they are dispersed outwardly from the heart center and dissolution cannot take place. When this occurs, one cannot fall asleep - that is a sleep disorder.

The winds in the right and left channels are impure winds. In highest yoga tantra meditation, the winds are made to enter into the central channel, abide there, and finally dissolve there. When this happens, all gross concepts and thoughts come to an end. When one is able to channel the winds in the two side channels into the central channel, then there is no possibility of one's state being disturbed by agitation and dullness because all conceptual thoughts cease. With that, one experiences the subtlest clear light of the mind, which is now the direct experience of the ground continuum.

Generally speaking, in the sutric context, even in the profound emptiness meditation of the union of shamatha and vipasyana, this does not happen. Even on the path of seeing, where the practitioner has directly realized emptiness, he or she does not realize the subtlest clear light of mind. The mind has become very subtle - so subtle that it can purify the gross winds, enabling one to give rise to many siddhis such as clairvoyance. One can also eliminate the need for sleep by following the sutric practices and by not taking gross food, only the food of samadhi, and so forth – but even though such sutric methods are very profound, they are not enough to enable manifesting the subtlest clear light of the mind, because the winds in the side channels cannot be brought into the central channel. There are no sutric techniques that are able to accomplish this, and so the practitioner of sutric methods does not experience the ground continuum. This experience only occurs when the winds in the two side channels are made to enter the central channel, abide there, and dissolve there. This is what is responsible for the dawning of clear light, the ground continuum.

We can see that the ground continuum is even more subtle than direct apprehension of emptiness in the sutric context. This is the level of subtlety I am referring to when I talk about the experiential dawning of the ground tantra, or the clear light nature of the mind. This difference in the levels of subtlety between the sutric realization of emptiness and the ground continuum is one of the most important points of contrast between the sutric and tantric views of emptiness.

Another important point of contrast is in the degree or profundity of non-duality. When one apprehends emptiness directly in the sutric context on the path of seeing, dualism disappears and there is no grasping at things as intrinsically existing. What happens here, however, is that the mind engages emptiness as the object, so that the separation of subject and object is still there – a subtle conceptual effort is made to sustain the meditation on the meaning of emptiness. In the subtlest clear light mind, however, there is no subject and object, and no effort is made by one to sustain the other.

For the sutric practitioner on the path of seeing, there is a difference between experience in the meditative state and in the post-meditative state. In the meditative state, the experience of subject and object disappears, and there is no grasping, but in the post-meditative state, one begins to have perceptions of different appearances, even though the influence of the meditative state is very much there. One still comes back to the domain of appearances, of thoughts, of perceptions, and so forth. By pointing out what the subtlest clear light is *not*, we can gain some understanding of the very subtle nature of the subtle clear light of the mind.

Once the subtlest clear light of the mind is actualized, there is no need to further train in the meaning of emptiness, because the subtlest clear light of the mind is the very essence of emptiness. Once we get to that stage, there is no need for further analysis of emptiness or training in emptiness meditation. The subtlest mind, so realized, is used to give rise to the illusory body. Once the subtlest nature of the mind is actualized, one gains freedom over death, the intermediate state, and rebirth.

The person who is able to manifest the subtlest clear light of the mind is able to conquer the subtlest mind and the subtlest wind. This means that one is able to conquer all of the external elements and internal aggregates, especially the winds, and can then conquer and gain mastery over one's own universe. If one has control over one's subtlest mind and subtlest wind, one can consciously control and transform one's own death and the intermediate state and rebirth experiences.

If you look at the dohas or songs of realization of those who have realized the ground continuum, such as Saraha, Naropa, or Milarepa, they say we should not let ourselves be controlled by our ordinary mind and ordinary appearances. In order to see our own ordinary face, we have to rely on the instructions of our guru. They do not say that we should first train in calm abiding and practice the union of calm abiding and insight. They go straight into the heart of tantra, the subtlest clear light of the mind that is the ground continuum.

One of the unique aspects of the tantric teachings is the way in which the ground continuum is introduced. In tantric texts this is sometimes taught in a hidden way, and sometimes through analogies and examples. In the ancient Indian yogic tradition, the tradition of the mahasiddas, yogis would first receive the ripening empowerment and then they would request very short liberating instructions for that deity practice. Once they had recognized the meaning of the ground continuum during the fourth initiation, they would then make that their heart practice and engage in that one deity practice. Practicing the generation and completion stage yoga of the deity, they would actualize the subtlest clear light or ground continuum that had been introduced in the initiation. Once the ground continuum was actualized, they would engage in unconventional or ascetic yogic practices.

These ancient yogic techniques were present in Oddiyana and south India, and were brought to Tibet. We can see from history that around the time Marpa the Translator brought these traditions to Tibet, the ground continuum was introduced through spiritual songs of realization and pithy instructions. The yogis, while engaging in ascetic, crazy, or unconventional conduct, transmitted the ground continuum through dohas, and they used terms such as 'uncontrived mind,' 'natural mind,' or 'Mahamudra.' They said that to experience the ground tantra or the subtlest clear light of the mind, meditation should remain uncontrived. They said that engaging the mind in conceptual analysis, such as Madhyamikas do, makes the subtlest clear light of the mind more obscure, like muddying water.

Some of the methods of introducing the subtlest clear light mind in the Kagyu tradition, such as pointing out or introduction, involve telling the student that all phenomena come from mind. After that, the student is instructed to rest in that uncontrived state. The instruction also is given, 'Do not chase after thoughts.' Analyzing the emptiness of phenomena, as in the Middle Way philosophy, is not mentioned. Basically, the methods say you should restrain your mind from intellectual judgment and chasing after thoughts. Though they do not say they are introducing the clear light, this is basically what they intend. What they are referring to is settling the mind so that it does not chase after thoughts or appearances, or engage in judgment and scheming – thereby not contriving anything. They say that the best way to manifest the clear light mind is to apply mindfulness so that one does not chase after gross or even subtle thoughts. Leaving the mind in its natural state is the best way to realize the subtle clear light mind in this lifetime. All of the Mahamudra practices are aimed toward the realization of clear light mind.

We find two different techniques of introducing the ground continuum, which is the subtlest clear light mind. The technique in the Kagyu Mahamudra tradition is direct, and the practitioner is introduced through pith instructions. The other way is through the usual tantric teachings – by giving empowerment and liberation instructions, the practice of the generation and completion stages, and the practice of tsa lung or the channels and winds. Both of these techniques are equally valid, and so each is an option. The goal of both is to manifest the ground continuum in this very lifetime.

I will now explain how the ground continuum or subtlest clear light mind is manifested using the tantric method, particularly in highest yoga tantra. Whether or not one manifests clear light mind depends on whether one can use the vajra body and can engage the vital points of the vajra body. Being successful in this is directly related to the subtlest wind.

To experience the subtlest wind, we have to purify all of the gross impure winds and clear the blockages in the channels through which the winds flow. We have to understand the vajra body and the location of the channels and energy drops. Through meditation, we visualize the channels, the winds that course through the channels, and the drops as empty. Through this technique, we can learn to control the subtlest wind, and then the subtlest wind is used to manifest the clear light of the mind.

The other method, from the Kagyu Mahamudra tradition of directly introducing the clear light via pith instructions, bypasses the utilization of the channels and the winds. Even though this is very profound and the introduction itself is very easy, if one is not very careful there is the danger that the practitioner may remain in the domain of calm abiding, confusing that with having actualized the clear light of the mind.

The fact is that however subtle and profound our meditation may be, we have to deal with the reality of the body. As long as we have a body, we have winds, and these impure gross winds always obscure the subtlest wind and subtlest mind. If we use the tantric methods for purifying the winds, then as the winds are purified our meditation experience becomes much more profound and subtle than we could accomplish in years and years of sutric meditation. No matter how profound it may be, sutric meditation and even Mahamudra meditation conducted without utilizing the channels and chakras, is never able to transcend the obscurations of the gross winds that obscure the clear light mind. As long as we have the gross aggregates, we have the gross winds, and the winds in turn obscure the dawning of the clear light.

Everyone of course wants an uncomplicated, quick method for the dawning of the clear light mind, and the tantric method is very powerful. Direct use of the vajra body is much quicker and more effective than ten or fifteen years without its usage. The reason this method is the best is that we have to live with the reality of our ordinary aggregates. Moreover, in practicing clear light mind, we have to engage with the gross aggregates in such a way that we find their very essence, and this can only be done with tantric methods.

It can appear simpler to follow the second tradition of directly introducing the clear light, rather than doing deity practice and engaging in the practice of the channels and winds. You may assume that you understand these practices and can do without them, but that can have a detrimental effect as well. The best way for us to manifest the clear light mind or ground continuum is to receive a tantric empowerment and instructions and then engage in one deity practice, while at the same time utilizing the Dzogchen view as the ground view of the tantra, and practicing the generation and completion stages while sustaining this view.

The view of Mahamudra and Dzoghen is very profound and introduces one into a nonconceptual state of experience – you do not have to rely on the view of emptiness established by conceptual mind. If you practice in this way, everything becomes an ornament to manifest the clear light mind using the view of the ground, while using the generation and completion stage practices as the methods to enhance that.

There are many immediate and long-term benefits to practicing like this. For instance, visualizing yourself in the form of the deity has many benefits like reducing gross sickness of the body. When you arise in the form of the deity and cultivate divine pride, whenever you relate to other beings – wherever you go, whenever you speak, in all of your points of contact, including physical touching – it becomes a way of blessing sentient beings. Do not consider this as some kind of intellectual position. There is great significance in engaging in deity practice.

In summary, we have described the three continuums and elaborated on the ground continuum. In sutra, the basis or view of the ground is referred to as 'buddha nature,' and in tantra it is referred to as 'the subtlest clear light mind.' In the Nyingma tradition, the ground continuum is referred to by Longchen Rabjam as 'the union of basic space and primordial awareness.' In the Kagyu tradition, the ground continuum is referred to as 'the ordinary mind that is the union of basic space and wisdom.' The Gelugpas use 'the subtlest clear light of the mind,' and the Sakyas 'the pure nature of the mind.'

The ground continuum is called by different names in different traditions, but my own view is that even though it is explained differently in each tradition, it is the same ground continuum. The essence of the union of profundity and clarity is common to all of the traditions. The important thing is to recognize it, and after recognizing it to understand how to engage in the path.

Having introduced the ground continuum, now we carry it into practice to enhance our experience of it by means of the method continuum, which is the path. We use the term 'path' in both sutra and tantra, but it is more profound in tantra and contains more skillful methods than sutra. As I mentioned earlier, the yoga of the union of profundity and clarity is common to all four classes of tantra and is the essence of the path. In all four of the classes, we engage in the union of method and wisdom, but it is practiced differently in each. In the action tantra, for example, there is the six-step meditation of the deity. Deity yoga is practiced in six steps, meditating on the deity of emptiness, of sound, of letters, of form, of mudra, and of sign.

Essentially, 'path' in the tantric context refers to the path of deity yoga consisting of the union of profundity and clarity. In order to practice this path, we progress through the completion stage practices in six stages: isolation of the body, isolation of speech, isolation of the mind, illusory body, clear light, and the non-dual state of Vajradhara. These six stages can be seen as corresponding to the five standard paths. The phases of body isolation, speech isolation, and mind isolation correspond to the path of accumulation. The illusory body stage is the path of preparation. The clear light stage is the path of seeing. And the non-dual state is in the path of meditation and the path of no more learning. This is according to the father tantras and not according to the mother tantras.

We can also summarize the path of the four classes of tantra. In action tantra, the fundamental path is that of the union of profundity and clarity. This path involves the six deities yoga practiced in two stages, yoga with signs and yoga without signs. Yoga with signs is that of visualizing the deity and mandala, and yoga without signs is that without such visualizations. The practice of performance tantra is similar, again having the two stages. In yoga tantra, we actually practice the union of method and wisdom, and in highest yoga tantra, this union is practiced in six stages and five paths, including body isolation and so forth.

This is the fundamental structure of the entire tantric path in all the four classes of tantra, the very essence of it. If you want to study in more detail, then each of the classes of tantra has a very detailed explanation of its own unique path. If you look at the Nyingma tradition and the Sarma traditions, there are some differences in the use of terms between them, but they essentially have the same intent and meaning.

What is important to understand is that when I talk about the tantric path or skillful methods, I am referring to the method continuum. 'Method continuum' simply refers to the tantric path, which is different from the sutric path. 'Tantric path' uniquely refers to deity practice or practicing the union of profundity and clarity by maintaining the visualization of the deity while simultaneously maintaining the profound view of emptiness as well. This is basically the unique tantric path, and it should not be confused with the sutric path, where we talk about calm abiding and special insight and so forth. The unique tantric path does not have to make use of these things.

The result of practicing the yoga of the union of profundity and clarity is giving rise to the wisdom that is this union. This wisdom is the resultant continuum. The tantric path or method continuum in any of the four classes of tantra is the yoga of the union of profundity and clarity. The result of practicing this yoga is the *wisdom* of the union of profundity and clarity. This applies to all classes of tantra, and this is important to keep in mind.

In the highest yoga tantra, the goal is to actualize the wisdom that is the union of profundity and clarity, and in order to actualize this wisdom, there are the two yogas. The method comprises generation stage yoga and completion stage yoga, which gives rise to this wisdom.

GENERATION AND COMPLETION STAGES

The generation-stage yoga introduces the reality of one's own mind, followed by the reality of one's own body. In completion-stage yoga, it is the reverse – the reality of the physical body is taught first and the reality of the mind next.

The nature of mind is taught first in the generation stage because everything arises from it. One's own mind has to arise in the form of the deity. The mandala of the deity is also taught, as it is the basis for the emergence of the deity. This is followed by the transformation of the body into the deity. For example, the five aggregates are transformed into the five deities, and the senses and their contents, such as the visual field and the objects in it, are also transformed into corresponding deities. This is the way that mind and body are taught in tantra – first the nature of the mind, then the reality of one's own body.

Generation-stage yoga is actually practicing the stages of birth. If we were to give the most revealing definition of the generation stage yoga and its phases, then we would define it as 'that unique yoga that is practiced to purify the imprints of the four types of samsaric birth.'

The four types of birth are birth from the womb, birth from an egg, birth from heat or moisture, and miraculous birth or birth through penetration of consciousness into a particular physical form. The imprints in the mind, the mental potentials, left by all these forms of birth over countless previous lifetimes must be purified to prevent such samsaric rebirths, and this is accomplished through the practice of generation-stage yoga.

The generation stage has two parts – the gross generation stage and the subtle generation stage. The gross generation stage involves sustaining with clarity a generic image of the deity, without the particular details, for a period of time – not a long period of time but for a while. At this stage, mental effort is required and it thus is referred to as the gross generation stage. After training in this way for a time, there comes a point where in a moment of mental intention without much mental effort, one is able to clearly visualize and sustain the image of the deity vividly for a longer time. This is a middling-level generation stage yoga practice because we can sustain the visualization intensely and for a longer period of time. These practices are performed within the context of closed-eye formal sitting meditation, not while moving around or walking.

You have perfected the subtlest generation stage practice when you are able to maintain the visualization of the mandala within a single droplet, including the deity, the mansion, and so forth. You have gained such firmness, such certainty, and such stability that you are able to sustain a very tiny and very subtle image of the deity. In your meditation, you can enlarge it to a very grand size and then reduce it again to a very tiny drop. You train in this, reducing the size, increasing the size, going back and forth, visualizing the entire mandala within a single drop. When you have gained such stability, you have perfected the subtle generation stage practice and are very close to entering into the completion stage yoga practice. Over the course of this practice, the meditative state becomes more and more subtle. 'Subtle' here does not refer to praying to the deity, or doing the mantra recitation of the deity, but to single-pointed concentration on the deity itself.

There are four vital points that must be understood about generation-stage practice. In the New Translation Schools, they are called 'the four vital points.' In the Nyingma school, they are called 'the four essential nails.' The first of these is understanding the basis of purification, the second is understanding the object to be purified, the third is the purifying technique or the purifying method, and the fourth is the result of purification. Understanding these four points, or 'the four nails,' is central to understanding the generation stage.

The basis of purification is the ground continuum, which was introduced earlier, the subtlest clear light mind. The basis of purification is not the mind but this ground continuum. The basis is not something that has to be purified – it simply refers to the basis of practice.

The object to be purified is that which the basis is to be purified of. In the sutras, the objects to be purified are the temporary afflictions, the negative emotions, and so forth. Here in the tantric context, however, the objects to be purified are ordinary death, ordinary birth, and the intermediate state, because right now we do not have control or power over them.. That is why they have to be purified.

The method of purification is the means by which the basis of purification is purified of the object of purification. It is not limited to engaging in mantra recitation, meditating on the deity, and so forth, as these are not sufficient as methods for accomplishing the purification of ordinary birth, death, and the bardo state. The actual purifying method is the deity practice itself, not the rituals, not the mantra recitation.

Deity yoga practice has three features or properties. The first is clarity. The clarity feature requires that the deity arise in a very clear and vivid form. You have to be able to sustain the different features of the deity vividly, the individual implements, and so forth. The second feature is divine pride. Divine pride requires that one's identification with the deity be very firm and strong. The third feature is understanding the meaning of every detail of the deity's colors, form, dress, implements, and mandala, so that the iconographic representation is not just iconography or decoration, but divine qualities. By sustaining these three features, you can enter into identification with the deity.

In another method of purification taught especially in the ancient Nyingma tradition, the entire universe and all of its inhabitants – all sentient beings – arise in the form of the deity's mandala and as the deities themselves.

When we do this practice, what is purified is our own impure perception of ordinary beings as being ordinary, the ordinary universe as being ordinary. It is said, especially in the Kagyu and Nyingma traditions, that as a result of engaging in generation stage practice, all of the forms that we see arise in the form of the deity, all of the sounds we hear are transformed into the deity's mantra, and all of the thoughts we have are transformed into wisdom. That is the result of practicing the generation stage yoga.

In the New Translation schools, the method for the purification of ordinary birth, death, and the intermediate state is the practice of carrying the three kayas as the path. The dharmakaya is carried as the path to transform death, the sambhogakaya is carried as the path to transform the intermediate state, and the nirmanakaya is carried as the path to transform rebirth or birth.

In practicing generation stage yoga, it is good to practice just one deity. It is important to choose the deity, whether wrathful or peaceful, and then receive the empowerment followed by the instructions on the generation and completion stage practices. I cannot, of course, recommend one deity for everyone. Deity practice is individual and is connected with each individual's karmic connections and so forth.

When you begin your practice, you will start with the generation stage. This is very important, as you should not jump into completion stage yoga practices right away. If you do, you will not be able to do them properly, as you will not have built the proper foundation for them.

As I mentioned earlier, we have to understand the four vital points of the generation stage – the basis of purification, the objects to be purified, and so forth. Also bear in mind the different levels of the generation stage practice – the gross level and the subtle level. Bearing both the gross and subtle levels in mind, begin the practices.

If we faithfully engage in generation stage yoga practices throughout our lives, then there is no doubt we will achieve some siddhis. There will be definite signs. To gain freedom from ordinary birth, ordinary death, and the ordinary intermediate state, however, generation stage practices alone are not sufficient. We must enter into completion stage yoga practice.

When completion stage yoga instructions are given, one is first given instruction on the reality of one's own physiology, the reality of one's own subtle body. In the completion stage, the focus is on the vajra body. In other words, we engage in the practice of tsa lung, the practice of channels, winds, and drops, which makes them serviceable. We purify them and then make them serviceable or functional.

When the channels, winds, and drops have been made serviceable, we can give rise to four types of emptiness. In turn, practicing the four types of emptiness gives rise to the dawning of the clear light. Furthermore, practicing the four types of joy gives rise to the illusory body. In completion stage yoga practice, we are no longer referring just to mental visualization, but also to working with the reality of the physical body. We accomplish this by utilizing the chakras, channels, winds, and drops.

Completion stage practices are divided into two levels: completion stage yoga with signs and completion stage yoga without signs. The meaning of 'completion stage yoga with signs' is that we are working with physiological reality in the form of chakras and channels and so forth, but we still depend on the support of the generation stage visualization here. That is why it is called 'completion-stage yoga with signs.'

Completion stage practice, as I mentioned earlier, involves focusing on the vajra points, the subtle points of the vajra body. To be able to do this, we should have some understanding of the gross physical body and its relation to the subtle vajra body. To understand the reality of the vajra body, the formation of the physical body has to be explained and understood – how it evolves, how it is formed, how it remains, and how it finally dissolves. I will not go through the entire process of physical development from the time of conception through the dissolution process, but I will point to the essential aspects.[65]

The purpose of studying physiology, the actual nature of the body, and introducing its gross and subtle aspects, is not the same as that of a medical doctor trying to understand or cure physical disease. The fundamental intention here is to analyze and understand the factors responsible for giving rise to confused states of the mind. The tantras say that fundamentally, confusion and our negative emotions arise because of our physiology. There is a direct link between the body and the experiences or mental states that we have.

For example, in the tantric teachings it says that at the subtlest level, we have the experience of white luminosity and red radiance. These two are experienced because of the movement of the subtle winds. White luminosity and red radiance, in turn, are just energy drops, or bodhicitta. These bodhicitta drops are moved by the subtle winds, and when that happens, the subtlest innate clear light mind is obscured.

When the subtle winds are stirred and move the vajra body elements, giving rise to white luminosity and red radiance, we lose the clear light state. This is what gives rise to dualistic mind – the experience of subject and object.

In the clear light state, there is no subject-object dualism. When the subtle winds are stirred and we have the experience of white luminosity and red radiance, appearances arise as subject and object. All confused states of the mind, including negative emotions and so forth, arise from this fundamental subject-object dualism. It is because of this that we enter into a confused state in which we have no control over birth, death, and the intermediate state.

In the sutric context, the manner in which confused states arise is not explained from a physiological point of view. The sutric explanation traces them to the karmic imprints located in the foundational consciousness. The seventh consciousness, the afflicted emotional mind, stirs the foundational consciousness, activating the imprints, which gives rise to the six types of consciousness. That is how we come to have dualism and grasping and all the confused states.

In summary, the sutric view does not explain confusion from a physiological point of view as tantra does. It is said in tantra that at the subtlest level, it is the ovum derived from the mother and the sperm derived from the father that give rise to subject-object dualism and all the confusion that derives from it. This is explained very clearly and in great detail in the highest yoga tantra teachings. For example, this explanation can be found in the *Kalachakra Tantra* and the *Chakrasamvara Tantra*.

This is why understanding the physiology of the physical body is considered to be extremely important in completion stage practice. Tsa lung is considered very important because this is how we work with the physical body.

I next turn to the innate body. Earlier, when introducing the ground tantra, I talked about the innate subtlest *mind*, which is basically the ground continuum itself. Now, however, in the introduction to tantric physiology, the tantras speak of the innate *body*. The term 'innate body' refers to the subtlest *wind*, which abides inseparably with the subtlest mind. The subtlest wind itself cannot be made pure or impure by the channels, winds, or drops. Because it is at the subtlest level, it cannot be contaminated by winds and drops and so forth. The reality, however, is that the innate body of subtlest wind is encased within our gross contaminated body. More specifically, the innate body is encased within the channels, winds, and the variously placed bodhicitta drops within the channels, or the subtle body. In turn, the subtle body is encased within the gross body. Most importantly, the innate body or subtlest wind resides in the heart center.

Both the father and mother tantras talk about the subtlest wind and the subtlest mind, or the innate body and the innate mind, but the emphasis is different. In father tantra, the emphasis is on the subtlest wind, which is the illusory body factor. In mother tantra, the emphasis is on clear light – the innate, subtlest mind.

In father tantra, there are four types of emptiness, which give rise to pure and impure elements. This is how samsara comes into being. In mother tantra, there are four types of joy, which give rise to confused states. In mother tantra, the four joys are responsible for the arising of samsara. This is explicitly mentioned in the great commentary on the *Kalachakra Tantra*.

To understand the reality of our physical being, our real physiology, we have to understand it at the external coarse, the internal subtle, and the innermost secret levels. The external level of our physiology is that of our physical body with the aggregates, ayatanas, and dhatus. The internal physiology of our subtle body refers to the subtle body of winds, channels, and bodhicitta drops. The secret body refers to the subtlest wind, which in tantra is the cause of all things in samsara and nirvana.

In order to engage in the highest yoga tantra practice of channels and chakras, first of all you visualize your body as empty. Visualize it as translucent, like something made only of light, like an empty form with nothing inside - a body of light. Within this empty form, visualize the three main channels – the central channel and the right and left channels. The central channel goes from your secret chakra directly to the crown chakra. It is straight and dark blue in color. The right channel is red in color, and the left is white. These two channels go through the nostrils to the crown and then back and down along and beside the central channel, joining the central channel at the navel chakra. This is how you visualize the subtle body.

The channels should also be visualized as empty, translucent, and transparent, and not as solid or rigid. They are not made of a solid material like the gross body, with 'walls' that act as barriers. Visualize the channels as totally empty, translucent, like light. In the beginning, when we try to visualize this, our minds are so habituated to the perception of physical objects that we see the channels as material things, but we must learn to visualize them as light channels. The inside of the channels is totally empty, and your physical body is totally empty. If you are not able to visualize them in this way, it can negatively affect your meditation practice.

The reason we visualize the channels is so that we can focus and direct the winds into them. It is the winds and the movement of the winds that are responsible for purifying, reviving, and rejuvenating the channels. The wind is therefore the actual reason for the visualization. It is not sufficient to visualize the channels without being mindful of the winds, and becoming proficient at wind practice.

The tantras talk about 21,000 types of winds. The 21,000 winds are categorized into five primary winds and five secondary winds. The five primary winds in turn come from the innate wind – the subtlest wind. In completion-stage practice, the most important practice is gaining control of and channeling the winds into these different channels, because the winds are responsible for reviving blocked channels. The practice of the innate wind and how that manifests is especially important. This is the indestructible wind, which is regarded as the source of samsara and nirvana.

Based on this indestructible wind, we take various types of rebirth as any of the many life forms. The fact that we are able to inhale and exhale is based on this indestructible subtlest wind at the heart center. Inhaling, exhaling, and all speech are based on it. The winds are the most important factor in giving rise to meditative experiences of bliss, clarity and non-conceptuality. Such experiences are directly induced by the innate indestructible wind. This innate wind is referred to as the life force of everything in samsara and nirvana.

This innate, indestructible, or subtlest wind enters into the union of the father's sperm and the mother's ovum during the process of intercourse. It enters into the embryo and remains encased in the subtle white element of the father and the red element of the mother. It remains encased at the heart center until one dies, and then the subtlest wind escapes from that encasement.

The completion stage practices are fundamentally about making a relationship with the subtlest innate wind in order to activate and manifest it. To accomplish this, we engage in all of the tsa lung practices whereby we purify and utilize the five winds.

The primary practice of activating the subtlest wind consists of channeling the winds in the two side channels into the central channel. The winds in the side channels enter, abide, and dissolve in the central channel. When this happens, we say that the central channel is opened and becomes functional. The central channel that was closed, with no wind flowing through it, is now open with the winds beginning to course through. The coursing of the winds into the central channel activates the indestructible drop at the heart center, which contains the subtlest mind and the subtlest wind.

Within the channels are the energy drops. We call them '*thiglos*' in Tibetan and '*bindus*' in Sanskrit. The drops are like the seeds that give rise to bliss in our body. They are spread throughout the channels but predominantly abide in the heart center. They first give rise to physical bliss, which in turn gives rise to mental bliss.

In the sutric tradition, when we practice calm abiding, it is said that at the level of cultivating the mind, first one gives rise to mental bliss and this in turn gives rise to physical bliss. In the tantric context, however, one first gives rise to physical bliss.

The actual tsa lung practice is not the preliminary tsa lung we practice before meditation. If you want to receive the actual tsa lung practice, you have to receive the Vajrayogini empowerment or the Chakramsavra empowerment. Then all of the actual tsa lung practices are given, which include 'the small and high,' which is the jumping practice. All of that is taught within the context of initiation.

It is best to do purification practices like the preliminary tsa lung exercises in the morning. After practicing that, rest for five or ten minutes in meditation, then engage in Vajrasattva practice. Purify all obscurations, karma, and habitual tendencies by reciting the long and short mantra as described. After that, imagine Vajrasattva dissolving into your central channel and purifying your entire vajra body. Then rest in the non-dual state.

During the second morning session, focus on guru yoga. Afterward, rest in meditation, but not common shamatha. Our meditation here is recognizing the ground continuum, or resting in the natural state of the Great Perfection. Dzogchen is very important; if we rely on the Dzogchen view, then everything arises from that. When you are finished, everything dissolves back into the ground of awareness and you dedicate.

This is just an example of how to practice in daily life. Try to break your day into four sessions. In the evenings, try to practice chod or tsok, which are good for repaying karmic debts and making powerful offerings. Afterward, make aspiration prayers, dedicating for the benefit of all beings. You can practice in four sessions every day or especially on the weekends.

SUMMARY

Westerners are very busy with a lot of things to do, and your lives can be very complicated. In this context, tantric practice is the best method for purifying not only your body but your mind. Even in the twenty-first century, tantra is very beneficial. On the physical level, practicing tsa lung can give rise to good health and eliminate certain sicknesses, but most importantly it induces a natural meditative state.

When you engage in tantric practice, focus on one yidam. In the morning, do tsa lung and the generation-stage and completion-stage practices. Then, for your main session practice Dzogchen – that is very important.

This is the way in which you should practice. This is my own heart advice. You should treat Dzogchen as the essence, the heart, of practice. You first must receive full instructions in how to engage in Dzogchen meditation, and after having done so, you can use the tantric methods described in the generation and completion stage practices as enhancement practice to sustain the Dzogchen view. Along with these two are the ngondro or preliminary practices. These are very important and you should consider them as the fundamental practices to ripen your mental continuum.

13

ESSENCE OF MAHAMUDRA

The Dharma came to Tibet from two distinct Indian traditions: the tradition of learned scholars and the tradition of accomplished practitioners, or yogis. Both traditions can be traced back to Nalanda, and have remained unbroken up to the present day. Subsequently, Tibetan Buddhism developed into five major lineages: the old traditions, Nyingma and Kadam, and the new traditions, Kagyu, Sakya and Gelug. If we include the Bön tradition, then we can say that Tibet has six major lineages. In the context of Mahamudra, we are going to focus on the Kagyu tradition, since Mahamudra comprises the most important part of the Kagyu tradition.

To ensure correct representation of the philosophy, lineage and instructions, I will present the Mahamudra teachings within seven topics.

1. A brief history of the Kagyu tradition, including the history and transmission of the four blessing lineages.
2. The differences between Mahamura in India and Tibet.
3. The difference between Mahamudra and Dzogchen.
4. The path of method- the practice of the six yogas of Naropa.
5. The path of liberation- Mahamudra and the four yogas.
6. The uncommon Mahamudra instructions and enhancement practices for eliminating errors in meditation.
7. How to carry the profound Mahamudra instructions into practice in one meditative session.

A BRIEF HISTORY OF THE KAGYU TRADITION

The Tibetan term *'Kagyu'* consists of two parts: *'ka'* (Tib. *bka'*), which refers to the oral instructions, and *'gyu'* (Tib. *rgyud*), which means 'transmission' or 'lineage.' The term 'Kagyu' literally means 'an oral lineage,' and specifically refers to the lineage of teachings received from the vidyadharas, in an unbroken transmission. The Kagyu lineage is the oral lineage descending from Tilopa, Naropa, and Marpa through successive masters to the present day.

In brief, the Kagyu lineage began when Tilopa passed the Mahamudra teachings and tantric practices to Naropa, who transmitted them to Marpa. It was Marpa Lotsawa, the Translator, who brought the instructions of the six yogas of Naropa and the Mahamudra teachings to Tibet. There, Marpa had many disciples, and the most prominent among them was Milarepa. Milarepa had many disciples, but the most prominent among them was Gampopa, the 'Physician from Dakpo.' Gampopa's main disciples were the founders of the first branches within the Kagyu tradition. After these branches emerged, the original Kagyu tradition was referred to as 'Dakpo Kagyu.'

Tilopa is said to have received teachings from Vajradhara, and from the dakinis who were preserving the tantric teachings. Being a great yogi himself, Tilopa appeared in the world as 'one who extracts sesame oil,' while secretly, he practiced the Mahamudra teachings. His main disciple, Naropa, came from an academic background and had been one of Nalanda University's four gatekeepers, who are responsible for defending and responding to challenges to the Buddhist tradition.

When Tilopa transmitted the Mahamudra and completion stage practices to Naropa, he was conferring four blessing lineages that originated from Vajradhara. These teachings reached Tilopa through the early pioneers of Mahamudra-- Indrabhuti, Saraha and Nagarjuna. The first blessing lineage, from Vajradhara through Nagarjuna, was the lineage of the Guhyasamaja Tantra and the Catuhpitha Tantra, which taught the illusory body and the ejection of consciousness. The second blessing lineage, from Vajradhara through Kukkuripa and Charyapa, was the Mahamaya Tantra, which taught the practice of dream yoga. The third blessing lineage, from Vajradhara through Vajrapani and Dombi Heruka, included the transmission of Chakrasamvara and the mother tantras, which clearly explain the practice of clear light. The fourth blessing lineage, from Vajradhara through Vajrapani and Khelwa Sangmo, passed on the practice of tummo, or inner heat. Although all of the Mahamudra teachings descended from the 'long lineage' of Vajradhara, we are able to recognize four separate short lineages or blessing lineages that brought these teachings to Tilopa.

Tilopa did not give the teachings to Naropa very readily. Naropa had to work really hard, practicing for many years before receiving the instructions. Having received the instructions, Naropa practiced and digested them, and then started teaching them from his own experience. It was Naropa who systematized the completion stage yogas into what became known as the 'six yogas of Naropa.'

We may wonder why Tilopa put an accomplished scholar like Naropa through such hardship before bestowing the teachings on him.

The answer has to do with the role that guru devotion, and especially guru yoga, play in the tantric tradition. Without devotion, we do not receive blessings. Without blessings, we do not give rise to realization. To bring this home, guru yoga takes the central role in the tantric teachings.

If we do not understand this point, we might think that Tilopa was stingy about his teachings, but that was not case. Instead, he was teaching Naropa about guru devotion, which lies at the heart of Mahamudra and which gives rise to realization.

It is important that we understand devotion correctly. Devotion is not an emotional response or attitude toward the teacher. Devotion is based on the logic that without respecting the teacher, there is no respect for the teaching. If there is no respect for the teacher or teachings, then that is a sign of arrogance. Arrogance is a negative emotion because without respect, we will not learn or practice the teachings. Arrogance is not at all like confidence. Devotion conquers inner arrogance, which hinders us from gaining realization, and helps to purify our attachment and clinging to ordinary appearances.

Respect and devotion are the most important antidotes to negative mental states. The Tibetan term for devotion has the connotation of destroying our narrow-mindedness and pride, which prevent us from engaging in wholesome actions. By destroying these inner restrictions, we can help our mind to spontaneously engage in wholesome actions. The overflowing intention to engage in virtuous activities is devotion. Devotion is not a blind emotional state, but actually seeing the teacher's qualities. The most important quality is speech. We must see and analyze the profundity and effectiveness of the teachings, and then we generate guru devotion based on our analysis of the teachings.

By relying upon and practicing the teachings, we can eliminate all negative mental states – anger, jealousy, and so forth. Then we can give rise to spontaneous devotion by reflecting on the kindness of the teacher. This is not like blind faith. If we only have blind faith, we might do things like pray to the guru that something might fall from the sky. That is like the devotion to a god. We are not talking about devotion like that.

The significance of the stories about masters and their disciples is not to entertain, as though we have time to waste on old stories artistically told, like the 'Ramayana,' or 'Harry Potter.' It is not the same intention. The intention in the tantric context is to underscore the significance of devotion and respect, and to show how this is directly linked to your own inner realization. We talk about the Kagyu tradition as the 'accomplishment' or 'practice tradition.' If accomplishment is regarded as the most important point, then devotion is the door to practice, and these stories illustrate that devotion.

The history of Tilopa and Naropa in India, and of Marpa and Milarepa in Tibet, represent the most exemplary cases of the guru-disciple relationship. In summary, the two activities that help us understand the instructions and receive the blessings of the lineage are understanding the history, and observing the guru. We should read those stories, to understand the ways that the lineage masters entered into and maintained the guru-disciple relationship. Once we have understood the importance of this relationship, we should listen to the teacher's enlightened speech and observe his or her enlightened activities, in order to uphold our own side of the relationship with the guru. Guru devotion is the most important point in our practice.

Marpa the Translator, Naropa's student, another of the most prominent masters of the lineage, brought the Mahamudra teachings to Tibet. During his sixteen-year study in India, Marpa received Mahamudra teachings not only from Naropa, but also from Maitrepa who was an Indian Baba from the Ganges. Maitrepa, in turn, received the teachings from Saraha.

Saraha lived an unconventional life, which has been described in many translated books. A great scholar at Nalanda, Saraha left the monastery-university and became an eccentric yogi, engaging in unconventional austere practices. On the outside, he conducted himself as a hunter, carrying a bow and arrow about. On the inside, this great yogi received teachings from the wisdom dakinis. It is through his eccentric yogic practice that he received various siddhis.

It is quite clear from Marpa's history that he received teachings from many teachers in India. Sometimes we see it said of him, 'you studied with hundreds of teachers in India.' This might be an exaggeration, but we do know that he had many teachers.

It is said that Marpa was a very learned scholar of the tantras, but whether or not he was a great scholar of the sutras was not clear. With regard to his tantric texts, we know that he was an excellent scholar and practitioner, especially in the Guhyasamaja, Mahamaya and Hevajra tantras. In Tibet, he was often referred to as Hevajra himself. Even Tsongkhapa offered great praise to Marpa for the validity of his tantric teachings. Coming from Tsongkhapa, this is great praise, because Tsongkhapa was not known for praising other masters.

It is said that Marpa gave the entire transmission of his lineage, including the practice of ejecting consciousness into a dead person, to his first son, but that his son died at the age of twenty-one, which brought that practice to an end in Tibet. Even though Marpa's own son died at twenty-one, he transmitted all of the essential teachings to his spiritual son, Milarepa.

To this day, masters of all four traditions of Tibetan Buddhism greatly respect Milarepa. His life story and songs of realization can induce transformation in a practitioner's mind. They exemplify an overwhelming sense of renunciation and devotion to the teachings. As a young monk in India, after listening to Milarepa's teachings, I experienced strong renunciation towards worldly activities and devotion towards the practice and teachings. I attribute this transformation not to Milarepa's poetry but to the blessings of his teachings. We can still experience the blessings of his speech, available to us in written form. When we listen to his songs they have the power to spontaneously induce meditative states. This power signifies a master's blessings.

The strength of his blessings stems from his guru devotion, which he demonstrated through enduring the immense hardships that Marpa imposed on him. Ironically, if Marpa and Milarepa had the same type of encounters in the contemporary Western world, Marpa might have been imprisoned for abusing his student. However, reading about these stories in the scriptural context, we cannot help but give rise to inner devotion and renunciation.

In Tibet, Marpa was able to pass his entire lineage of teachings to Milarepa with few exceptions. Milarepa took to the practice and is widely accepted as the life force of Tibet. He is widely respected in the tantric community as being a role model for guru devotion, and the teacher-student relationship in general. Milarepa set the example for all tantric practitioners, irrespective of their tradition, on the importance of effort and patience.

Milarepa passed all of his teachings to Gampopa, who had begun his path as a married lay practitioner, but then became a fully-ordained monk, following the request of his dying wife. On her deathbed, Gampopa's wife struggled to take her last breath and move onto her next life. To be able to peacefully cut the ties with her life, she asked Gampopa to cut his attachments to mundane worldly concerns and dedicate his life to dharma practice. She wanted him to gain freedom from samsara; Gampopa agreed and became a fully ordained monk and studied under many Kadampa geshes.

Gampopa himself was a great scholar who trained in Tibetan medicine, becoming a famous doctor in Tibet. Although he was very learned and well-practiced in sutra, he was very interested in extending his skills and learning a technique to give rise to realization in one lifetime. When Gampopa heard about Milarepa, he went to see him. However, he was prevented from meeting Milarepa for fifteen days, because of protocol. From a commoner perspective, Gampopa's status exceeded that of Milarepa, who was just a yogi. After fifteen days all of the obstacles cleared and they were able to meet, and Gampopa studied under Milarepa. Gampopa had the Kadampa lineage, and he combined that with the teachings of Mahamudra, explaining the lamrim (stages of the path) tradition of the Kadampas by ornamenting or enhancing it with the teachings of Mahamudra. We often talk about this as the mingling of two great rivers of the Kadampa lamrim and the Mahamudra traditions.

This idea of merging the two traditions might provoke doubts about whether Mahamudra itself is sufficient. Does it also depend on gradual stages of the path as found in lamrim? A lot of people emphasize this merging of the traditions as a sign that we need to have both, but the Kadampas emphasize mind training as the heart of practice, and the heart of mind training is cultivating bodhicitta. And isn't bodhicitta included in Mahamudra? So Mahamudra is itself sufficient in that sense.

To practice Mahamudra successfully, we need to fully embrace the union of the two traditions and carry them into practice. For that, we need to take advantage of the lamrim teachings on renunciation and the four contemplations on turning the mind away from samsara,[66] which are extensively taught in the Kadam tradition. Using these teachings as a basis, we then engage in the practice of Mahamudra. This is what it means for a practitioner to unite these two traditions.

Generally, all of the Kagyu schools recognize Marpa, Milarepa, and Gampopa as the great masters and pioneers of the tradition. Their teachings have converged into a unified and coherent tradition. Gampopa had three main disciples, one of whom was referred to as a 'black hat one.' This was Dusum Khyenpa, the 'knower of the three times,' who became the first Karmapa. From the four primary branches of Kagyu, eight more minor branches emerged.[67] Currently, only three of these twelve traditions are alive and flourishing: Karma Kagyu, Drikung Kagyu, and Drukpa Kagyu. The remaining traditions remain only in name and have largely disappeared.

It is important to understand and remember the history and lineage of the tradition: all of these branches originated with Tilopa and Naropa; Marpa brought them from India to Tibet, and Milarepa accomplished and propagated them. These traditions have two practices in common: the path of method, which comprises the six yogas of Naropa, and the path of liberation, Mahamudra. Although many believe that the six yogas of Naropa are well-preserved today, my experience is different. Only tummo and phowa remain widely-practiced, without a breakage in the tradition. The remaining practices are still practiced but not widely known.

Because I am presenting these teachings to you, you need to

understand my lineage. As a young monk, I received the entire empowerment and instruction on the Kagyu treasury of tantra, and the entire empowerment for the six yogas of Naropa from the Sixteenth Karmapa Rigpa Dorje in 1975. In 1989, Bokar Rinpoche, my root guru and one of the Karmapa's main students, bestowed the entire empowerment on me and guided me through a three-year-and-seven-month retreat where I practiced the entire transmission.

Nowadays, many teachers teach the six yogas after having simply read the books, with no transmission. Even though I might not have any realization, at least I have the necessary empowerments and transmissions from my teachers. I have received authentic and valid instructions from valid teachers, and this is how a lineage is kept alive. As you are receiving these teachings from me, you do not need to doubt my lineage. Whether or not these teachings induce realization in you depends on your own practice.

This is how the Mahamudra lineage has descended to the present day in my own lineage.

MAHAMUDRA IN INDIA AND TIBET

After the Mahamudra tradition was brought into Tibet, we start noticing differences between the Indian context and the Tibetan, in how the lineage was preserved and passed on to disciples. Though the actual Mahamudra instructions have remained the same, the Tibetan transmission practices started to differ from the Indian tradition, particularly in the kind of students accepted as disciples, and how they pass on the tradition.

One of the differences between the Tibetan and Indian lineages of Mahamudra relates to the mental capacity of disciples receiving teachings. In India and China, most of the surviving tantric practices belong to the action and conduct tantras. Highest yoga tantra was only taught in the utmost secrecy to selected disciples and, for that reason, did not flourish in India.

The Indian masters closely observed the rules of tantric teachings, requiring the guru to examine a disciple's qualities for twelve years and vice versa. Because masters gave instructions only after that examination, Indian gurus gave Mahamudra transmissions to only a handful of disciples. The gurus introduced the innate clear light during the fourth empowerment of a particular tantric practice. Then, based on the ripening empowerment, the gurus gave profound and concise liberating instructions. Following that, the disciples meditated on one deity and carried that profound instruction into practice.

Historically, the Buddhist tantric teachings were transmitted in

India through two distinct branches. Within the first branch, the teachers examined the students and gave transmissions to a select few in isolated settings. These practitioners appeared humble, but developed tremendous realization. The second branch spread teachings within the royal families, who summoned the above-mentioned yogis and received instruction from them. This is why the Indian texts present the kings in the tantric form, for example Indrabhuti, who received the Kalachakra.

It was the royal-family tradition that Padmasambhava had carried to Tibet and passed on to King Trisong Detsen in the eighth century. As a result of that tradition, propagated by Padmasambhava, the highest yoga tantra teachings were flourishing by the time Marpa brought Mahamudra to Tibet. By then, Tibetan teachers had been teaching not only Mahayana, but also highest yoga tantra, to hundreds of students. Although the tradition of stringent teacher-student examination survived in Tibet for a while after Padmasambhava, the rules became more relaxed. This is why present-day Tibetan students do not have to be of the highest capacity to receive tantric teachings. As a result, in Tibet, tantra flourished extensively and became a much more common practice than India.

For these historical reasons, Mahamudra teachings became available to a wide group of individuals rather than just a select few. If students were of middling capacity, teachers introduced them to Mahamudra slowly. They first taught lamrim and emptiness according to the sutras. Then, based on the understanding of emptiness, they gave an empowerment, followed by liberating instructions. This is why the transmission of highest yoga tantra has survived in Tibet, while many of the other transmissions have been lost.

There is no difference between India and Tibet in what is introduced, which is the primordial wisdom or innate clear light, the realization of Mahamudra itself. The traditions differ in their reliance upon an empowerment to introduce the basis – the innate the primordial wisdom or innate clear light. In the dohas, the Indian and Tibetan mahasiddhas clearly talk about Mahamudra being dependent on the ripening empowerment and liberating instructions. In the Indian tradition, Mahamudra has to be understood in the context of tantric practice. The guru gives the empowerment of a particular tantra, and within that empowerment, the fourth empowerment introduces innate wisdom, which touches the heart of Mahamudra. Sakya Pandita wrote 'my own Mahamudra is wisdom born of empowerment,' meaning that Mahamudra is understood in the context of tantric practice. In contrast, latter day Kagyu masters began to discuss Mahamudra as not depending on tantric practice.

Milarepa's life story shows that he often gave Mahamudra instruction without an empowerment. When Milarepa met karmically-connected disciples, he would teach them nakedly. There is a story of him in which he instructs illiterate shephards on Mahamudra, without an empowerment.

Even though Marpa and Milarepa gave Mahamudra instruction without tantric initiation, they always did so strictly within the context of tantric practice. During Gampopa's time, the tradition was further watered down, not only giving Mahamudra instructions without the empowerment, but also beginning to teach them outside of the tantric context, by simply introducing the nature of mind and the unelaborated emptiness of object. This practice became known as 'sutric Mahamudra,' the wisdom of emptiness, and was transmitted in the context of sutra practice. So starting with Gampopa, Mahamudra developed in two distinct forms: sutric and tantric.

In summary, the fundamental differences between how the Indian and Tibetan traditions passed on the Mahamudra teachings relate to the capacity of the students and the way in which Mahamudra was introduced. Other differences also exist, but these are the major ones.

DIFFERENCES BETWEEN MAHAMUDRA AND DZOGCHEN

This discussion of differences between Mahamudra and Dzogchen by no means implies that one is higher than another. The differences between these practices stem from the profundity of the instructions and how those instructions are given.

First, the two systems differ at the level of the ground, in how they introduce the mind. In Mahamudra, the view is introduced as the innate subtlest mind of clear light. That is the view at the level of the ground. In Dzogchen, the basis is self-occurring timeless awareness, or *rangjung yeshe*. This basis is beyond mind: it transcends even the subtlest clear light, which is still within the domain of mind. In Mahamudra, the subtlest mind is referred to as the subtlest co-emergent mind. In Dzogchen, even the subtlest co-emergent mind is considered as still within the domain of mind. The ground in Dzogchen is rigpa, self-occurring intrinsic awareness that is beyond mind. So when we are introducing the view of the ground, we can see a difference between these two traditions.

There is also a difference in the method of introducing the ground. In Dzogchen, the ground is introduced directly as intrinsic awareness. Therefore, in Dzogchen, it would not suffice to introduce the ground by means of the subtlest-clear-light mind, which is still in the domain of mind. In contrast, Mahamudra introduces the mind, through three features: abiding, movement and awareness.

Secondly, the two systems differ in the meditation. Mahamudra meditation involves leaving the mind in an uncontrived state in the ground of the innate clear light of the mind. In Dzogchen, it is not sufficient to leave the mind in an uncontrived natural state. We need to transcend the mind and experience self-occurring intrinsic awareness. We then sustain this intrinsic awareness with unique Dzogchen mindfulness. Sustaining intrinsic awareness with the special application of mindfulness is different than sustaining the innate clear light mind in an uncontrived manner. Besides view and meditation, the two systems differ in the enhancement practices, or how to eliminate errors in the meditation.

Most people, even some lamas, do not realize the differences between the traditions, thinking they are one and the same. Practice in both traditions involves leaving the mind in the uncontrived natural state, but there are some considerable differences. We should not mix these two traditions, and instead we should preserve the traditions in their purity, recognizing the differences in terms of lineage, instructions, the way the ground is introduced, what is introduced and how that is maintained in meditation.

PATH OF METHOD - THE PRACTICE OF THE SIX YOGAS OF NAROPA

The fifth topic on Mahamudra concerns the practice of the six yogas of Naropa. Below, I provide a brief description of the six yogas and how to practice them.

The six yogas of Naropa belong to the path of method. The actual Mahamudra practice involving the four yogas represents the path of liberation. The six yogas of Naropa belong to the path of method because they include techniques that can give rise to the realization of Mahamudra. The state of Mahamudra, or the innate clear light, is very subtle. To realize Mahamudra, we rely on the six yogas of Naropa, which represent slightly coarser forms of practice than Mahamudra itself. The methods includes external, internal, and secret techniques. The external method refers to the ripening empowerment and liberating instructions. The internal method refers to working with the channels, winds, and drops. The secret method refers to our meditation.

The enumeration of the six yogas of Naropa varies from one tradition to another. I list them in the following way:

1. Tummo, the inner heat

2. Illusory Body
3. Dream Yoga
4. Clear Light
5. Phowa, the transference of consciousness
6. Bardo, or intermediate state

Some scholars debate whether the practice of ejecting our consciousness into a dead person's body, *drongjuk phowa*, is included within the six. Some say it is, others say it is not. We do know that this practice died with Marpa's son. Regardless of whether it belongs within the Mahamudra lineage, the practice of ejecting our consciousness exists within the Bön and Nyingma traditions.

It is important to understand that in order to give rise to the realization of Mahamudra, it is not necessary to depend on the six yogas. Disciples of the highest capacity can be introduced instantaneously, without relying on the path of method. That however is extremely rare. So it is out of compassion that we are given these methods whereby we can gradually be introduced to the realization of Mahamudra, first by receiving the ripening empowerment, and then the liberating instructions, for how to practice these six yogas.

Also, students of middling capacity do not need to practice all six yogas to induce bliss and emptiness and attain subsequent realization. It is sufficient to rely upon any one of the six. Simply by training in one, middling students are able to induce the wisdom of bliss and emptiness.

If one yoga is sufficient, why did Naropa teach six? The six yogas are suited to disciples of differing aptitudes and features. Tummo suits those with great patience and tremendous effort, like Milarepa. Dream Yoga is taught to those of higher mental capacity and who have more purified karma than tummo practitioners. Dream yoga practitioners might be a little lazy. The illusory body practice fits those who have trained in the practice of empty forms. The yoga of clear light is taught to those who have the capacity to transform the sleep state: instead of the ignorance of deep sleep, they use the sleep state to gradually awaken the clear-light nature of mind. Phowa, or the transference of consciousness, suits those who have gained control of their mind and the subtlest winds, or vayus. The yoga of the bardo is for those who are able to integrate the sleep and the waking states without any difference; they practice continuously, whether asleep or awake.

Tummo

Tummo, the yoga of inner heat, embodies the great foundation of all six of the six yogas. It serves as a highway for those who want to engage in highest yoga tantra, thus it is listed first among all six yogas. The Tibetan word 'tummo' (Tib. *gtum mo*) has a connotation of someone or something who is fierce, literally meaning 'fierce woman'.

What does 'fierce one' mean? Through the practice of inner heat, we can penetrate the central channel and thus give rise to the wisdom of bliss and emptiness. Because inner heat practice brings about the union of bliss and emptiness forcefully (we do not have any choice really), this practice is called 'fierce.' Inner heat can also forcefully burn up ignorance, along with its imprints. By meditating on inner heat at the navel, we can burn up any impure channels and winds that are causing sickness in the body. It is the activity of wrath that defines tummo, and this is why tummo is called 'the yoga of wrathful inner heat.'

As each of the six yogas has a unique function, practitioners who aspire to practice Mahamudra need tummo practice, because we rely on the channels, winds, and the subtle mind of the vajra body to give rise to clear light. Ordinary people cannot awaken the innate subtlest mind because of the relationship between their mind and wind: mind depends on the winds and the winds depend on the channels, mainly the right and left channels. As long as winds flow through these side channels, we experience ordinary thoughts. If we want to experience the basis clear light, we have to direct the winds into the central channel, and tummo practice allows us to do that. If we successfully direct our winds into the central channel, we can get rid of conceptual thoughts.

The winds naturally coarse through the right and left channels, giving rise to conceptual thoughts. So we need a practice that directs winds into the central channel, causes them to abide and then dissolve there. The practice of tummo, combined with *trulkhor*, or the yantra yoga of physical yogic enhancement practices, aids our ability to direct the winds into the central channel.

The fundamental purpose of inner heat practice is to give rise to bliss, which, in turn, gives rise to the wisdom of clarity. The inner heat opens the central channel at the navel, and the winds enter the central channel from the side channels; giving rise to the experience of bliss. This bliss differs from the bliss we experience in calm-abiding meditation or the physical bliss we experience from sensation. The bliss of inner heat is supreme bliss. Sometimes the bliss of calm-abiding can hinder realization, but the bliss of inner heat can never obstruct realization. Unlike ordinary bliss or the bliss of calm abiding, inner heat bliss is liberating by nature.

At the level of the basis, 'inner heat' refers to the very refined red and white body elements derived from our father and mother, which become the substantial cause of our physical body. The red and white elements constitute the inner heat of the basis. In the tantric context, the white and red elements are the substantial cause of the body, or the conventional drop. The health of the conventional drops depends on the health of our physical body, and how well we take care of it, such as through yoga, exercise, diet, and so forth.

It is insufficient to simply know about the conventional drop; we need to understand how it relates to the greater tantric practice, and how to incorporate it into inner heat practice. We need to know where the conventional drop abides and how to use it. Therefore it is insufficient to simply focus on the Ah-stroke at the navel. We also need to engage in the practices of trulkhor, pranayama and vase breathing.

The full details about inner heat are explained in the context of a retreat, with an opportunity to practice these instructions. If we do not have an opportunity to practice these teachings in retreat, we should at least know how inner heat relates to the dawning of the realization of Mahamudra.

Illusory Body

The yoga of the illusory body belongs to the father tantras, like the *Guhyasamaja Tantra*. This practice focuses on the subtle winds, which become the substantial cause of the illusory body. The yoga of the illusory body requires training in empty forms, which involves seeing all appearances as illusory. After lengthy practice, we become familiar with seeing appearances as illusions, which allows us to engage in the practice of the illusory body itself.

When we talk about seeing all appearances as illusory, or empty forms, it does not mean that all appearances of the mind do not exist. Here, we train ourselves to recognize that whatever appears to mind does not inherently exist from the side of the object. In other words, all appearances exist as illusions and not some kind of substantial or intrinsic reality. Therefore, everything appears as empty forms, and through this practice we see our own mind as illusory, which allows us to gain control of wind. Once we gain control of wind, we also gain control over mind, therefore we can easily engage in the actual illusory body practice. This practice eventually enables us to transform our own subtlest wind and mind into the form of the divine body.

The divine-body practice here differs from that in the generation-stage yogas, where the self-manifestation as a deity relies on imagination. In fact, in the practices that involve the generation stage only, we are not able to fully manifest as deities; for that, we need the completion stage. It is in the completion stage that we are able to actually arise in the deity form, which is difficult to perfect. Through prior training in seeing all appearances as empty, one gains control of the winds and mind and through that practice it is very easy to engage in the completion stage, in which you arise in the form of the illusory body by transforming the subtlest mind and subtlest wind. The divine illusory body is nothing but the union of clarity and emptiness: even though it arises clearly, it is empty of inherent existence. Therefore, the yoga of illusory body is the union of clarity and emptiness.

The *Kalachakra tantra* talks about 'the great Mahamudra of empty forms,' which means seeing all forms as empty. There is no discrimination between forms as good or bad, clean or unclean. From the empty-form point of view, there is no difference between a piece of chocolate and a piece of manure: both are established in the nature of being empty forms, arising but not truly existing.

Once we are able to train in this practice of empty forms, it is easy to practice the illusory body. Therefore, for a practitioner of the illusory body it is very important to see our own ordinary body as clear and empty. Our own ordinary gross body is the union of clarity and emptiness, not made of gross physical flesh and bone.

Our conceptual inclination to discriminate between pure and impure becomes an obstacle for tantric practice. From the point of view of ultimate reality, there is no difference between pure and impure. Conceptual discrimination becomes a hindrance to our practice. The instructions tell us to visualize ourselves in the form of translucent light, not physical lungs, heart and flesh. The intention is to visualize all forms as empty forms, translucent and free of any obstructions. If we are not able to engage in the practice of empty forms, then it is impossible to engage in illusory body practice.

We can find the detailed instructions on the practice of the illusory body in the Kagyu highest yoga tantras as well as in the traditions of the Nyingma, Sakya and Gelug. It is explained clearly in the *Guhyasamaja Tantra*. Each tradition uses slightly different terminology and has a different lineage, but the heart of the practice is basically the same.

In summary, the basis of the illusory body is the subtlest wind, as opposed to the subtlest mind. We aim to gain control over the subtlest wind through the practice of empty forms, where we see all forms as empty, like a reflection of the moon in water. Once we have gained control of our subtlest wind, then we engage in the completion stage practice, visualizing the body as appearing yet empty. This clear-yet-empty visualization includes the channels, winds and drops. Beginners may struggle even to imagine something that appears but has no substance. This concept is not something we can conjure up, and once we have an image, it is difficult to sustain. Once we have gained experience with the empty-form yoga, we are able to self-manifest as divine beings in the union of clarity and emptiness. Our own illusory form is able arise as the deity's form, the union of clarity and emptiness, which signifies the realization of Mahamudra. This is how the practice of the illusory body leads us to that realization.

Dream Yoga

Having taught dream yoga extensively during numerous retreats, I will briefly summarize the essence of the practice here. The dream state has been often mentioned in the Buddhist scriptures. For example, the sutras often rely on the example of a dream to explain the illusory nature of phenomena.

We spend a considerable portion of our lives sleeping, and dream yoga allows us to avoid wasting the dream state as abiding in ignorance. The dream yoga technique involves using the dream state to give rise to the illusory body. Dream yoga also has the distinctive feature of being able to induce clear light, but the unique feature of dream yoga is giving rise to the illusory body in the dream state. The teacher introduces the clear light in a way that enables the dream yoga practitioner to carry the deep sleep state as the practice for the dawning of clear light.

Although it may sound simple, dream yoga is regarded as the most difficult of the six yogas. It is easy to fall into ordinary sleep, and during the sleep state, it is very difficult to maintain the awareness required to practice key activities of dream yoga: the recognition and transformation of the sleep state.

Dream yoga training leverages the practice of clear light. We practice the yoga of clear light in meditation during the day, and then sustain this experience while going to sleep. If we leave the mind in an uncontrived state as we enter the sleep state, and maintain that clear light with mindfulness, the practice of clear light can overflow into the dream state.

This is a little more difficult than it sounds, because our mind goes through the phases of the dissolution of the elements as we fall asleep. During this process, coarse thoughts and the sense faculties dissolve into the alaya-vijnana, the foundational consciousness. At this point, it is very easy to slip into the sleep state without awareness. Therefore, we rely on effort and special techniques to practice dream yoga. For example, we visualize Vajrayogini, the chakras, or seed syllables and then sustain the visualization while falling asleep. If you struggle maintaining awareness in your sleep state, you can have a partner watch you falling asleep and give you a nudge if you slip into deep sleep.

By practicing dream yoga, we dissolve our mind into the state of clear light – total clarity and awareness. With that vivid clarity, we experience all things in the dream state as illusory. During the daytime, we can see all forms as empty, and during our sleep, we continue our practice by seeing the illusory nature of all appearances in the dream state. The purpose of dream yoga is to carry our practice of illusory body and clear light from daytime into our sleep state. Once we accomplish dream yoga, there is no need to engage in the bardo practices.

Clear Light

The yoga of clear light goes to the heart of Mahamudra. Here, I will provide only a brief explanation of the practice. The basis clear light is the very intense aspect of the clarity of the nature of mind that is beyond the gross-level mind that we ordinarily experience. After our teacher has introduced us to the basis clear light, we sustain it in meditation as path clear light. When we experience the basis clear light and transform it into the path clear light, then we can rely on other methods, like dream yoga. The practice of clear light and dream yoga really complement each other.

Phowa

Phowa – the transference of consciousness – is a practice that can greatly help us at the time of death. Ordinarily, we do not know how long we will live, and cannot predict the time of death. During our daily lives, we are busy setting goals and accomplishing projects, but at death, we need to leave them behind. Tibetans compare dying to pulling a hair from butter. While in the butter, the hair seems to be a part of it. However, once we have pulled the hair out, it hangs there all by itself. Likewise, at the time of death, our body and mind separate. If we cannot maintain our mindfulness while dying, our mind gets caught up in an uncontrollable state of negative emotions, leaving us to wander through the different realms in the bardo. As a result, our rebirth happens due to the karmic forces and not our own choice. Relying on phowa, we can control our rebirth.

Phowa is a technique that is used so that our mind does not to fall prey to karma and negative emotions at the time of death, by transferring our consciousness to pure realms, like Sukhavati. There are two types of phowa: the general transference of consciousness, and the particular transference of ejecting the consciousness into another body. General phowa falls into one of three categories: dharmakaya, sambhogakaya, and niramanakaya transference. With dharmakaya phowa we recognize the great Mahamudra of the nature of our own mind, transferring our consciousness through the crown chakra directly into the heart of the guru. Simply by relying on the guru's instructions, we can transfer our consciousness into pure realms, thus avoiding the frightening visions of the bardo.

Many traditions have their own phowa techniques. Some rely on Vajrayogini, others on Vajrasattva. We can also find the practice of phowa within the chöd practice. Most tantric practices tend to rely on Vajrayogini. During this practice, we manifest as the deity, and visualize either a drop or a seed syllable in the central channel. Then, sounding syllables specific to the practice, we visualize the syllable at the navel ascending through each of the chakras to the crown chakra. While practicing the technique, we do not eject the consciousness through the crown chakra, we maintain it there and then descend back to the navel chakra. This is how we train. During the actual practice, we proceed with ejecting our consciousness instead of keeping it in the central channel.

Bardo

The last of the six yogas is the yoga of the bardo or intermediate state. The bardo, which literally means 'in-between state', is most commonly identified with the state between this life and the next. Because our body and mind have separated during this time, our mind wanders in the intermediate state and it is important that we do not come under the influence of negative emotions and karma, which can negatively influence our next rebirth.

There are four types of bardo states that are common to all of our lifecycles: the natural bardo, bardo of birth, bardo of death and the bardo of becoming. During each of these bardos it is important to recognize them as an intermediate state.

The natural bardo takes place from the time of our birth until death. During this period whatever we experience is like an illusion in the context of the natural bardo of our life. This time is extremely important because during this period of time we have the opportunity to encounter a teacher, receive instructions and practice what we have been taught. It is during this time that we have the possibility to put an end to the bardo of death and the bardo of becoming. We should understand that the significance of the natural bardo is the opportunity that is presented to us in terms of practice.

To train in the bardo is to rely on a teacher who is an expert on tantric practices and is familiar with the practices of the bardo. These bardo teachings are more profound in the Kagyu and Nyingma traditions within Tibetan Buddhism. The teacher who is introducing you to the bardo has to be experienced in the dissolution process of the elements and consciousness, which culminates in the three subtlest conceptual states and the three appearances. Through these teachings the teacher can introduce you to the bardo state, which has to be done in the context of a particular deity. When you are well trained in the natural bardo of this life, as you experience the bardo of death you will have confidence as a result of your familiarity with the dissolution process. If you have practiced Mahamudra or Dzogchen, then you are able to integrate your practice of clear light with the dissolution process. These practices of the bardo and clear light complement each other very well, by inducing a deeper state of the clear light experience. Longchenpa mentions that the most profound practice is the chonyid bardo, or the bardo of the natural reality pertaining to each of the bardos.

The significance of being introduced to the bardo of natural reality, or the chonyid bardo, is that as we go through the dissolution process at the time of death, our mind and body are separated, and there is a time when the subtlest mind travels on the subtlest wind. During that time, it is difficult to recall the bardo teachings and easy to get lost in confusion, so if we have been introduced to the bardo of natural reality we can understand the ultimate reality of the bardo. Having been introduced to the fact that all experiences belong to the experience of the bardo, and that all phenomena are experienced within the bardo, we can understand that all of samsara and nirvana as nothing more than confused appearances of the mind. As the mind becomes more and more subtle, all conceptual thoughts dissolve and eventually we recognize the bardo of natural reality. Through this dissolution of concepts and negative emotions, we are eventually led to the direct experience of the ultimate bardo. It is similar to returning to our hometown: we know all of the roads and everything inside and outside of our home. Just like that, the chonyid bardo is like returning to our home.

The relationship between the six yogas of Naropa and how to carry them into practice

Besides knowing the essence of each practice, it is important to understand how they relate to one another and how to carry them into practice. As I mentioned previously, the scriptures clearly state that we do not need to practice all six of these yogas; instead, it is sufficient to rely on any one of them. Having said that, if you wish to practice all of them, you will need to follow a specific sequence.

Our first practice is tummo, the yoga of inner heat. Right now, we have this ordinary physical body, which is contaminated. In order to purify this contaminated body, we first receive the empowerment from a qualified tantric teacher to engage in the generation and completion stage practices. In the practice of tummo, we purify the winds and channels. Tummo opens up our central channel, allowing the winds to enter and abide within the central channel. While practicing tummo, we adopt specific postures and rely on a specific type of breathing. However, the real tummo practice is the focus on the Ah-stroke in the navel chakra. The physical yogas serve merely as an enhancement to this practice. Tummo purifies not only the winds and channels, but also our contaminated physical body: it eliminates all kinds of sickness and disease, increases overall health and vitality, and prolongs life.

Although the physical exercises of tummo are not the main part of the practice, they play the important role of enhancing the main practice. The physical exercises of the practice, called 'trulkhor' or 'yantra yoga,' include different physical techniques coming from the different traditions. Naropa taught six techniques, Milarepa taught his own unique technique called the 'six great hearths,' and Karma Pakshi[68] taught 37 yogas. In highest yoga tantra, the fundamental purpose of yantra yoga is not just to invoke physical heat, but to ignite the fire in the navel and open the central channel, subsequently directing the flow of energy from the side channels into the central channel. Once the winds enter the central channel, this gives rise to the experience of bliss and emptiness. In summary, in the context of highest yoga tantra, the ultimate purpose of tummo is twofold: first, to purify the contaminated body and transform it into the illusory body, and second, to induce the wisdom of bliss and emptiness.

As for how to practice, engage in tummo during the day, and then at night, engage in dream yoga. The purpose of dream yoga is to be able to recognize the clear light of the dream state and to train in recognizing appearances of the dream state as like the experience of the bardo. There is a prayer that expresses the intent to accomplish this:

> All appearances are like illusions, like dreams.
> I am going to know that this is the way they are.
> In particular, I shall dream tonight and recognize my dreams
> to be dreams.[69]

There is a direct relationship between the mind in the dream state and the subtle winds on which the mind rides. The subtle winds belong to the subtle body, or mental body. At the subtlest level, wind and mind are inseparable. Therefore, in the dream state, we can use this wind as the substantial cause to arise in the illusory body. Being able to arise in the illusory body in the dream state helps us practice the yoga of the illusory body during the waking state. This is the relationship between dream yoga and the yoga of illusory body.

Within the illusory body practice, we rely on a deity and experiencing our own body, speech, and mind as inseparable from the deity's body, speech, and mind. The body, speech and mind of oneself and the deity are both illusory by nature, with the only the difference that ours are impure and the deity's are pure. The ultimate goal of illusory body practice is to transform our ordinary body, speech, and mind into the deity's body, speech, and mind. Dream yoga and yoga of illusory body complement each other to accomplish this goal. With dream yoga, we can use the subtlest wind to arise in the illusory body during the sleep state. Similarly, during the daytime, we can rely on deity yoga to practice the illusory body, through the exceptional methods of completion stage yoga.

In the context of the six yogas of Naropa, as well as the tantric context in general, 'yoga of clear light' refers to the clear light of death, which we experience during the dissolution process. If we are able to recognize clear light at the time of death, we have no need for a separate yoga of the bardo or phowa. Our ability to recognize clear light at death depends on the quality of our meditation. Mahamudra and Dzogchen traditions have the most profound meditation instructions for recognizing the clear light.

We can practice the yoga of clear light during the dream state to transform the experience of deep sleep into the experience of clear light. As your dream yoga practice becomes very subtle, you can recognize the clear light of the dying process. Clear light at the time of death is subtler than the clear light of the sleep state. However, if we are proficient at the clear light of sleep, we are prepared for the clear light of death.

At the time of death, the practice of clear light makes the mind more and more subtle and we can gain control of the subtlest mind and wind. Then we can engage in the practice of phowa. At that point, we have total control over the subtlest mind and wind, and can transfer our consciousness into the heart of the guru. Those who have directly realized the transference of consciousness have no need to rely on the regular practices performed for or by the dying. Usually, when someone is dying, we read special texts into their ear, guiding the person through the experience of the bardo. However, those who are able to directly perceive the ultimate reality of the bardo, have no need for that kind of help. Neither do they need to practice conventional bardo yoga. They can transfer their consciousness on their own.

This concludes the very essential and brief description of the six yogas of Naropa. I hope it inspires further study and practice in you.

THE PATH OF LIBERATION - MAHAMUDRA

In Mahamudra, the ultimate attainment of the completion stage encompasses the union of the illusory body with clear light. The unique methods of the six yogas of Naropa help us achieve the illusory body, and the Mahamudra meditative techniques help us actualize innate clear light. The set of instructions that bring about the ultimate attainment of clear light is called the 'path of liberation.'

By virtue of engaging in the completion stage yogas, we experience a very subtle form of clear light. To actualize this, we need to perfect the generation stage yogas and practice the completion stage extensively, so that our mind becomes even subtler than the mind we experience in the dream state. This subtlest mind retains no conceptual thoughts or mental contrivance.

Our ultimate goal is to experience the subtlest mind, which is not easy to do. You must engage in sequential stages of practice to achieve this state. First, you experience the subtle level of mind as the clarity aspect of the gross mind. What prevents you at first from experiencing the clarity of the gross mind is your craving and attachment to ordinary appearances. Therefore, to refine your mind, you have to get rid of ordinary appearances and attachment to them.

To help us along in this sequential process, Mahamudra teachers first introduce the mind, namely the clarity and awareness of the mind. In contrast with sutra, tantra does not distinguish between the conventional and ultimate nature of mind while introducing the mind. Instead, tantric masters simply introduce us to the ultimate features, or functions, of the mind: clarity and awareness. Without any distinction between the conventional and ultimate forms, the introduction of the nature of mind focuses on mind's origin, or where it comes from, its abiding, or how it stays, and its cessation, or where it goes. This analysis of the origin, abiding and cessation of conventional mind is how the nature of mind is introduced.

Even though we can explain the subtlest clear light nature of mind, it is difficult to experience. Therefore, while introducing the gross mind that changes, the teachers introduce its fundamental nature by showing us that all phenomena in samsara and nirvana are nothing but expressions of this mind. Indeed, all phenomena in samsara and nirvana are nothing but the display, or expression, of mind. This includes all impure and even pure objects, like the mandala deities.

However, even though we can understand this intellectually, it is very difficult to get to the point where we can experience that directly. The two practice traditions, Kagyu and Nyingma, first introduce the subtle mind by introducing the gross ever-changing mind through its function: origin, abiding, and cessation.

Within the path of liberation, we free ourselves from ordinary appearances and attachment to those appearances. However, not every instruction that helps us gain liberation from ordinary appearances is a Mahamudra instruction. In Mahamudra, we become liberated by understanding the ultimate reality of the mind. This is why Mahamudra introduces the mind as being immaterial: not having any shape, color or any other material characteristics. In order to directly understand, or see, the ultimate reality of the mind, we have to examine our mind in terms of its origin, abiding and cessation.

When we are introduced to the mind, we tend to have no difficulty recognizing that we have a mind, or that the mind has tremendous power. However, this is not enough; we need to see that all appearances are the dynamic expression of the mind. According to the Kagyu tradition, the best way to recognize mind in its ultimate reality is through meditation. When we experience different diverse appearances, such as suffering or happiness, we need to investigate whether they exist from their own side, independent of our mind, or as dynamic expressions of the mind. This practice helps us realize that appearances are nothing but the radiance of our own mind, and this recognition needs to happen not through conventional intellectual thinking, but through direct meditative experience.

For that, we practice uncontrived meditation: we simply leave our mind in an uncontrived state. The analogy here is to muddy water: if we leave it alone it will settle on its own after a while and become clear. The importance of stillness is illustrated through the analogy of an ocean. In the presence of turbulent waves, we cannot see anything in the ocean, but when the ocean is still, then we can see even the subtle movement of small fish. Likewise, when we leave the mind uncontrived in the natural state, we begin to experience the natural clarity of the mind.

However, this mode of resting or stilling the mind is still not the actual Mahamudra meditation. Through years of practice, we familiarize ourselves with the technique, after which we can enter the actual meditation. When we come out of the meditative state, in the post meditation state, we experience all phenomena as being like an illusion. At that stage, we experience the illusory expressions of the mind directly, without reliance on analysis.

In Mahamudra, we introduce the nature of the mind as the union of clarity and emptiness, regardless of its state: coarse or subtle, virtuous or non-virtuous. Every mind has this quality of being the union of clarity and emptiness. This means that any experience of our awareness has an aspect of clarity to it. Every mental perception, every momentary mental state, has its own function, and that is the aspect of clarity. If we look at that our mental state in the present moment, we can see the aspect of clarity in the functioning of appearances. However, if we try to pinpoint the mind, analyzing where it comes from, abides, and ceases, we do not find anything. In that way, mind is transparent, empty, ineffable and has no reference point. Every mind has this nature of being the union of clarity and emptiness.

Why do we need a teacher to recognize the nature of mind and why do we need to recognize its ultimate reality? The reason is that we all experience suffering because of confused appearances, that arise due to our clinging to the idea that things exist from their own side, as external objects. Due to our clinging to the view that things substantially exist outside our mind, we divide things into positive and negative and generate expectation and fear. We desire good things and fear negative things. Our ignorance of the mind's true nature, which blocks us from realizing the mind's ultimate reality, and our dualistic thinking, which results in attachment and aversion, act as a dual force that binds us in the state of delusion. Our fundamental goal is to clear the confusion, eliminate confused appearances, which will eliminate suffering and the cause of suffering. Recognizing the ultimate reality of our mind, through uncontrived meditation, can help us achieve this goal. However, to practice correctly and understand what we are doing, we need the help of a qualified teacher who can introduce the nature of mind and explain how to practice correctly.

Once we recognize the nature of mind as the union of clarity and emptiness, we can engage in the generation and completion stage yogas as an enhancement. If we lose the fundamental recognition of the nature of mind, by losing the technique of uncontrived meditation, our practice of the completion stage yogas would amount to little more than a physical yoga, because we have lost the heart practice and are touching only the branch practices. In this case, the inner-heat practices would equate to some sort of a physical yoga.

The four yogas of Mahamudra practice

In the word 'Mahamudra,' 'mudra' means 'seal,' and has different meanings in different contexts. For example, we can talk about the hand mudras displayed by different Buddhas. The highest-yoga tantras include four mudras: the activity mudra (*karmamudrā*), the samaya mudra (*samayamudrā*), the dharma mudra (*dharmamudrā*), and the great mudra (*mahāmudrā*). In Mahamudra, 'mudra' refers to the four stages of meditation: the yoga of single-pointedness, the yoga of non-elaboration, the yoga of one taste, and the yoga non-meditation.

The first stage of Mahamudra is the yoga of single-pointedness, which has two phases: the method of resting and the actual meditation. Here the term 'single-pointedness' does not mean focusing the mind on an object single-pointedly, as it does in the sutras. This technique requires settling the mind and leaving it in an uncontrived state. More specifically, this means that we are not chasing thoughts. Whatever thoughts arise, we do not chase after them. We simply let the mind settle in its own natural clarity. Through this initial practice of settling or resting the mind, we enter the actual meditation and experience stability and clarity of the mind simultaneously. More specifically, we experience a deep level of stability in the clarity of the mind, though the mind itself does not remain stable. The mind moves, and we experience the movement of mind from the state of stability. This is the actual Mahamudra meditation: to maintain stability and to recognize movement from the point of view of that stability.

During the actual single-pointedness meditation, after having settled the mind, we experience its great clarity and stillness, like a stainless sky. It is vast, like an empty sky without clouds. When we can sustain such clarity and stillness for some time, the mind becomes very stable. Out of this stability, when minor thoughts arise, with our mindfulness, we recognize them as the mind's movement. The meditation itself involves sustaining this stability while recognizing the mental movements.

As we progress in this manner, we are able to recognize the movement of the mind from within the state of stability. At this point, mental movement is not able to disturb stability; this fundamental stability is called 'mind holding onto its own ground.' In this state, the movement and stability of the mind complement and reinforce each other. For beginners in meditation, stability and movement destroy each other. At first, when we experience stability, we do not experience movement, and when we experience movement, we lose our stability. But in this yoga of single-pointedness, stability and movement complement each other.

As this integration takes place, we do not entertain concepts about it, thinking 'Now I am integrating movement.' Any conceptualizing about the experience is a movement away from the experience itself. When we can engage in this yoga non-conceptually, that is the start of the first yoga of single-pointedness. Through this practice, we experience an increase in the clarity of the mind, and as clarity increases, our mindfulness becomes more and more subtle. Based on the level of progression of the two realizations, the yoga of single-pointedness can be divided into small, middling, and great single-pointedness.

During the next stage of Mahamudra meditation, the yoga of non-fabrication, we gain confidence in liberation amidst confusion. The confusion we face here differs from our usual coarse confusion that pertains to external objects. This subtle form of confusion arises from the subtle movement of mind and mental factors. The subtle movements themselves do not create confusion. Subtle confusion arises when we are trying to control the movement, by accepting or rejecting it in any way. This reaction creates a subtle clinging to the intrinsic reality of mind, which results in subtle confusion.

To free ourselves from subtle confusion, we need to relax our grasping, or our attempts to control the movement of the mind, and let it flow naturally. Once we do that, the confusion will disappear on its own. Here, we use the analogy of a snake uncoiling itself. Though a snake might be coiled up, it will uncoil naturally in its own time. Likewise, when appearances arise in our mind, if we let them be, they will liberate themselves on their own accord. Once this natural self-liberation of subtle movement occurs, we gain confidence in liberation amidst confusion.

Some scholars believe that this confidence results from experience: once we gain certain experience, we will gain confidence. In my own practice, experience and confidence are the same: once we have a direct experience of the natural self-liberation of subtle mental movements, we instantaneously gain confidence in that, simply from that experience.

A second kind of confidence that we achieve in the yoga of non-fabrication is the confidence that we are able to eliminate our confusion. In the experience of liberation, we are able to eliminate or destroy confusion. 'Liberation' here refers to experiencing the clarity and emptiness of mind. As soon as we have liberated ourselves from subtle confusion, we then abide in the state of empty clarity. As we abide in empty clarity, as soon as subtle confusion arises in the form of subtle thoughts and mental factors, leading to subtle grasping at an intrinsic reality, our own mental clarity and emptiness eliminate that grasping. In the midst of our experience of liberation, we are able to destroy subtle confusion. By means of this second yoga, the yoga of non-fabrication, we gain these two related kinds of confidence.

The third stage of Mahamudra, the yoga of one taste, refers to the practice of leaving the mind in an uncontrived state amidst different thoughts and appearances. When we understand the ultimate reality of our own mind, and maintain that in an uncontrived state, we understand how diverse appearances arise from mind and so do not get caught up in diverse appearances and thoughts. When we experience this, it means that we are practicing the yoga of one taste.

During this stage of meditation, we experience two aspects of one taste. First, when we leave the mind in an uncontrived state amidst diverse thoughts and appearances, we realize that the clarity of mind does not become diminished by these diverse appearances and thoughts. Second, we realize that every appearance of this diversity appears from mind. We perceive all appearances as like a reflection in a mirror, without any sense of grasping at a truly existing reality. We perceive all appearances as mere illusion. Even though appearances arise, we see them as mere illusion, without mind's dualistic grasping. This is the state of meditative equipoise.

'One taste' refers to the realization that diverse appearances and mind are of one taste. They are in union, not things apart. Appearances do not obscure the clarity of the mind, and the clarity of mind does not obstruct the diversity of experiences in the forms of thoughts and so forth.

The final stage in Mahamudra, the yoga of non-meditation, is a state where we no longer distinguish between meditation and non-meditation. In the post-meditation state, through sustaining subtle mindfulness, we never waver from the experience of dharmakaya. In that state of equipoise, the display of mind unceasingly arises in the form of compassion. Both of these things happen spontaneously without any effort, which is why it is called 'the yoga of non-meditation.'

In my own experience, the first yoga of single-pointedness is the state of meditative absorption in which we have been able to recognize the mind as the union of clarity and emptiness after it has been introduced by the teacher. We then remain in an uncontrived state, without wavering for one second. We do that through the application of unique mindfulness, never becoming distracted from the nature of mind, which is the nature of emptiness and clarity. This is the yoga of single-pointedness.

Within the second stage, the yoga of non-fabrication, we continuously sustain that unique mindfulness without wavering, and experience the nature of mind as like a clear, empty morning sky pervaded by moonlight. Resting in a state free of all conceptual elaboration and fabrications, we experience a great and profound sense of emptiness and clarity. In the post-meditation state, we continue to integrate the appearances of mind and mind, so that they blend into a state of one taste, which is the third stage, the yoga of one taste.

As we continue to sustain the yoga of one taste in the post-meditation state, blending mind and appearances, their unity becomes perfected, and subject-object dualism disappears. The appropriate analogy for this experience is water poured into water. When we achieve the yoga of non-meditation, all experiences are blended with the four yogas at all times, so we that always experience clear light, whether in meditation or post-meditation states. When we experience clear light continuously, while awake or asleep, there is no ordinary effort to enter into meditation, which is why this practice is called 'the yoga of non-meditation.'

UNCOMMON MAHAMUDRA INSTRUCTION AND ENHANCEMENT PRACTICES FOR ELIMINATING ERRORS IN MEDITATION

In Mahamudra meditation, we start by leaving the mind in an uncontrived state. Sometimes this practice can induce a state of dullness or spacing out, where the mind gets lost in emptiness without clarity. This aspect of spacing out is a flaw in meditation. While we may have a sense of relaxing the mind in an uncontrived state, we need to experience intense clarity as well. If we have an experience of intense clarity, that itself is the mindfulness, and sustaining that clarity of mind is the unique Mahamudra mindfulness that we have been discussing.

To sustain the clarity of the mind, we rely on enhancement practices. One enhancement is the practice of calm abiding with the application of mental vigilance and mindfulness.

Another enhancement practice involves repeatedly coming out of meditation and then reentering it-- we enter the meditative state and then come out of it, again and again. If we continuously maintain a deep state of calm abiding without destroying it, the meditative absorption can bind us. To enhance our Mahamudra practice, we need to give rise to the liberating factor by repeatedly entering and coming out of the meditative absorption. We can use the example of a waterfall. The higher the waterfall, the purer the water becomes as it crashes on the rocks below. The more we come in and out of absorption, the more valid the liberating aspect of meditation becomes.

A saying in the Indian Mahamudra lineage states:

Although people know how to enter absorption,
few actually know how to get out of it and destroy it.
Similarly, we find Dza Patrul Rinpoche saying:
Even though yogis know how to meditate,
they do not know how to liberate themselves.

This means that even though yogis have the knowledge of how to engage in meditative absorption, many of them do not have the skill to get out of and reenter it. The significance of this point is difficult to understand. In the sutric context, simply maintaining the state of single-pointed concentration is not enough to lead to liberation, we need to also engage in special insight. Similarly, it is not enough to simply sustain the absorption of emptiness and clarity; we have to develop the capacity of a liberating force, or superior wisdom, that is able to come in and out of absorption.

The third enhancement practice for eliminating the errors of meditation involves engaging the mind in the training of bodhicitta in the post-meditative state.

HOW TO CARRY THE PRACTICE OF MAHAMUDRA INTO ONE MEDITATIVE SESSION

To carry Mahamudra into one meditation session, we have to integrate the preliminary practices, the actual practice, and the dedication. Since we have received these instructions from a qualified teacher, we need to engage in the practice. Traditionally, this involves preliminary practices, or ngondro.

The preliminary practices can be divided into two types: common and uncommon. The uncommon practices include taking refuge in the three roots through prostrations, purification of negative karma through Vajrasattva practice, accumulation of merit through mandala offerings, and swiftly receiving the two blessings through guru yoga. Among many excellent descriptions of these practices, I specifically recommend *Words of My Perfect Teacher* by Patrul Rinpoche, if you want further explanation of these.

The common preliminaries refer to the four practices of turning the mind to the Dharma. In this context, I would like to discuss a famous prayer by one of the core figures in the Mahamudra lineage, the *Four Dharmas of Gampopa*:

> Grant your blessings that my mind may turn towards the Dharma.
> Grant your blessings that Dharma may progress as the path.
> Grant your blessings that the path may clarify confusion.
> Grant your blessing that confusion may dawn as wisdom.

These points are very profound. As Mahamudra and Dzogchen practitioners, we should not look down on these teachings as being preliminary because they provide a foundation upon which we can build our actual practice. The founder of the Drikung Kagyu, Jigten Sumgon, mentioned that the preliminary practices are actually more profound than the actual practice, because we depend on this foundation for the actual practice.

Mind Transforms into Dharma

The measure of our mind transforming into the nature of Dharma is when we are no longer attached to the activities and concerns of ordinary life, and our recognition of impermanence and death increases.

Dharma arises as the Path

The Dharma arises as the path when our actions are propelled by the altruistic motivation of bodhicitta.

Path eliminates Confusion

Our path eliminates confusion whenever our wholesome activities bring benefit to others, and we perform these activities without any attachment to intrinsic reality. We see the empty aspect of our body, speech and mind and dwell in the impermanence of our actions. This way we are able to eliminate confusion on the path.

Confusion dawns as Wisdom

'Confusion' here refers to appearances. When we can see all appearances and experiences as illusory, and free ourselves of attachment to their having intrinsic reality, then we are able to use appearances in such a way that they dawn as wisdom. Viewed this way, all appearances are nothing but an expression of the mind, and mind itself is the expression of the ground of Mahamudra, which is clear light. When we are able to view all appearances in such way, we can say that the confused appearances have dawned as wisdom.

We should rely on these four Dharmas of Gampopa as our daily preliminary. We do not necessarily need to practice them during a formal meditation session, instead we should contemplate them throughout our daily lives.

As Mahamudra and Dzogchen practitioners, we face many obstacles to our dharma practice. We receive these precious and profound teachings, but we live in a degenerate age, with very little virtuous karma. Many of us lack the positive karma to enjoy these teachings, and so we face various obstacles. An analogy to our inability to fully comprehend the precious teachings can be found in someone who lives with a disease of the digestive system, and so cannot digest even very healthy and pure food. Therefore, to build positive karma, which will help us understand the teachings, we practice preliminaries. To eliminate obstacles to our practice, we have to make our minds powerful through the purification of karma and the accumulation of merit and wisdom, which we do through the uncommon preliminaries.

Guru yoga is especially important for Mahamudra and Dzogchen practitioners. It is even more important than deity yoga practice. Once Naropa asked Marpa, 'if you had the opportunity to see your guru or the deity, which would you prefer?' Marpa chose the vision of the deity, because he thought he could see the teacher any time. Naropa responded by saying that his choice was inauspicious, because the guru is the source of the blessings and instructions of the lineage. Without the guru, we would not be able to practice deity yoga. Naropa predicted that because of Marpa's inauspicious choice, even though Marpa's teaching lineage would flourish, his family lineage would disappear like a rainbow in the clouds, which is exactly what happened.

In the Western context, guru yoga is difficult to practice, because there is no established tradition. All gurus appear as very ordinary people. Without a great deal of pure vision, which Westerners tend to struggle with, it is easy to see the faults in the guru. At the very minimum, we should see the guru's kindness in giving teachings to us. In this way we should develop deep respect and reverence towards the teacher by reflecting on the qualities of their body, speech, and mind. The guru's speech (which can be oral or written, like this book) is very important, because this is how we tend to receive teachings in the beginning of our spiritual journey. If we focus on the qualities of the teacher's speech, then it is easy to generate devotion on a rational basis. For example, although we have never seen the Buddha, by reading his teachings, or speech, we can generate real devotion towards him. This is because of the quality of his teachings. Training in this way by contemplating the qualities of guru's speech, we can generate and increase our guru devotion, and engage in guru yoga. Correct practice of guru yoga reduces the obstacles to our practice and induces realization swiftly. This is how Marpa taught the significance of guru yoga to Milarepa.

CLOSING ADVICE

After we have been introduced to mind, the union of clarity and emptiness, we sustain that union through the application of unique mindfulness and mental vigilance. By means of this practice, we traverse the four yogas of Mahamudra, one at a time. Following the actual practice, we dedicate our merit, so that the virtue that we have accrued in our body, speech, and mind induces the realized state of Mahamudra in this very lifetime.

In our practice, it is important to recognize the mind. Mahamudra, as given to us by the great mahasiddhas, is very difficult to understand if you do not have any experience looking at the mind. We need to be able to identify and recognize mind: where it comes from in the beginning, where it abides in the interim, and where it goes at the end. Once we are able to recognize the nature of mind, then the actual meditation involves sustaining uncontrived meditation. Once we are able to recognize the nature of mind, then our practice involves engaging in meditation repeatedly for a long time. Earlier, when we discussed uncommon Mahamudra instructions, we mentioned how to engage in this type of meditation and referred to the unique Mahamudra mindfulness. If we apply this special technique, then we can easily engage in Dzogchen practice and recognize intrinsic awareness.

We should read Milarepa's life story again and again. It is full of blessings and can inspire our practice. We should read the biographies of other masters of the past, in order to be inspired by their Dharma practice. Each of them faced challenges in their practice, just like we experience challenges on our own path.

This concludes my heart advice on the path of liberation. I urge you to make your mind very strong, open, powerful, and expansive, to no longer be constrained by cultural habits and limitations, and to be able to engage in a pure Dharma practice. As practitioners, you should analyze whether your mind has been integrated with the Dharma or not. That is your responsibility; no one else can do that for you. You must examine your mind and determine whether it has been integrated with the Dharma.

When we talk about transforming the mind, we are not talking about instantly perceiving emptiness or giving rise to bodhicitta or realization. Transformation takes place gradually. We start by counteracting our negative habits and transcending them. These are signs that we are progressing on the path.

NOTES

[1] *Dharmacakrapravartana*, "Setting in Motion the Wheel of Dharma Sutra"

[2] The early Buddhist philosophy of the first turning, which is more attuned than the second and third turnings to a materialistic understanding of our being, provides a relatively 'scientific' or systematic analysis of contaminated and pure phenomena. This analysis is used to methodically refine our understanding of the four noble truths and thereby purify the mind in meditation. It is traditionally mastered by studying the *abhidharma* literature. These terms are explained below for our purposes here, which call for more meditation and insight than conceptual elaboration.

[3] Fifteen moments are realized on the path of seeing and one on the path of meditation. The sixteen moments are explained in detail in the *Ornament of Clear Realization* Maitreya.

[4] The form and formless realms (there are four of each) experience little or no attachment to material form and are thus very refined. (Sometimes the form realms are called the "refined form" realms.) In meditation, as we move from the desire to the form to the formless realm absorptions, coarse defiled mental factors are abandoned. However, all three realms are samsaric, as confusion remains even at the highest level of the formless realm.

[5] There are eight worldly (defiled) dhyanas or samadhis, four in the form realm and four in the formless realm. The ninth defiled absorption is the absorption of non-thought, which is reached from the fourth dhyana and can be mistaken for liberation. The worldly dhyanas are enumerated and explained in the *abhidharma* literature.

[6] Stanza 69 of Nagarjuna, 'Letter to a Friend' (Tib. *bshes-pa'i springs-yig*, Skt. *suhrllekha*), as translated by Alexander Berzin, March 2006, and published in the Berzin Archives.

[7] Asanga (Maitreya), *Abhisamaya-alamkara*, fourth century, designated by Tsongkhapa as the root text of the lamrim tradition.

[8] Such as Saraha, Tilopa and Naropa.

[9] Philosophical schools such as the Cittamatra, Prasangika Madhyamaka, and Svatantrika Madhyamaka, which we will discuss here.

[10] The other five treatises on emptiness and Buddhist reasoning by Nagarjuna are: *Vigrahavyavartani* ('End of Disputes'), *Vaidalyaprakarana* ('Pulverizing the Categories'), *Vyavaharasiddhi* (Proof of Convention), *Yuktisastika* (60 Verses on Reasoning), and *Sunyatasaptati* (70 Verses on Emptiness).

[11] 'Four-Hundred-Verse Treatise on the Actions of a Bodhisattva's Yoga' (Tib. *Byang-chub sems-dpa'i rnal-'byor spyod-pa bzhi-brgya-pa'i bstan-bcos kyi tshig-le'ur byas-pa*, Skt. *Bodhisattvayogacarya-catushataka-shastra-karika*).

[12] Skt. *Pitaputrasamagama Sutra*, Tib. *Yab dang sras mjal ba'i mdo*.

[13] 'Analysis in the treatises does not come from fascination with polemics. Suchness is shown for the sake of [attaining] liberation. If suchness is fully explained, and [the views] of opposing scriptures will come apart, this is not [our] fault.' – Chandrakirti, 'Introduction to the Middle Way: Chandrakirti's *Madhyamakavatara*,' with commentary by Dzongsar Khyentse Rinpoche, Khyentse Foundation, 2003. Chapter VI, sloka 118.

[14] 'Frameworks of Buddhist Philosophy,' Book Six, Part 3 of Jamgon Kongtrul's 'Treasury of Knowledge,' Chapters 8 and 11 of Section II

[15] Shakyamuni, *Lalitavistara Sutra* XXV, 1. In the Pali sutras, this story is told in the *Ayacana Sutra*.

[16] Chandrakirti, 'Introduction to the Middle Way' (Skt. *Madhyamakaavatara*). Shambhala Publications, 2005. p.68

[17] Nagarjuna, ' Root Stanzas of the Middle Way' (Skt. *Mulamadhyamakakarika*). Ch. 24 v11.

[18] The eighteen types of emptiness are taught as a concise teaching of the *Prajnaparamita Sutras* in the short 'The Perfection of Wisdom for Kausika Sutra.' Translated by Edward Conze in 'Perfect Wisdom: The Short Prajnaparamita Texts' (Buddhist Publishing Group, 1993.) The fourth type of emptiness, the 'emptiness of emptiness,' is called *sunyatasunyata* in Sanskrit.

[19] Chandrakirti, 'Introduction to the Middle Way.' Ch 6, v226.

[20] The six perfections of generosity, discipline, patience, diligence, meditation and wisdom.

[21] Chandrakirti, ' Entrance to the Middle Way.' Ch 1, v14.

[22] Nagarjuna, ' Root Stanzas of the Middle Way,' Ch 24, v14.

[23] Nagarjuna, *Niraupamyastava*, translated by Joshua Norager as 'Song of the Incomparable Buddha.' (Smashwords Edition ebook, 2011) Stanza 6.

[24] Lojong (from the Tibetan *blos sbyong* or "mind training") is a practice for generating bodhicitta attributed to the tenth-century New school lineage master Atisha and subsequently developed into the "seven points of mind training" by Geshe Chekawa Yeshe Dorje (1101-1175). A classic guide to lojong is Jamgon Kongtrul's *The Great Path of Awakening*, which presents the traditional series of seven points comprising fifty-nine guidelines along

with instructions for practicing the guidelines.

[25] Tonglen (from the Tibetan 'gtong len,' or giving and taking) is the main practice for cultivating relative bodhicitta, described in the second of the seven points of mind training. See *Great Path of Awakening*, p.14ff.

[26] The three natures are: imputed, dependent, and ultimate

[27] 'Sutra Expounding Neither Decrease Nor Increase' (*Anunatvapurnatvanirdesa Sutra*), 'Shariputra, should any monk, nun, upasakas, and upasikas give rise to one or other of these opinions, increase [or eternalism] and decrease [or nihilism], Buddha Tathagata is not their teacher [sastr]. They are not my disciples [sravaka].'

[28] Part of the *Tathagatamahakarunanirdesa Sutra*

[29] The lists vary; the first 5 are in all lists: 1. *Tathagatagarbha Sutra*, 2. *Srimaladevi Simhanada Sutra*, 3. *Anunatva Apurnatva Nirdesa* ('Expounding Non-decrease and Non-increase),' 4. *Angulimaliya Sutra*, 5. (*Mahayana*) *Mahaparinirvana Sutra*, 6. *Aryadharanishvararaja* ('Sutra Requested by Daraneshvara'), 7. *Lankavatara Sutra* ('Sutra of the Descent into Lanka'), 8. *Jnanalokalamkara Sutra*, 9. *Mahabheriharaka Sutra* ('Great Drum Sutra'), 10. 'Sutra of Entering the Nonconceptual.' Some lists also refer to the *Samdhinirmocana Sutra* ('Sutra Which Decisively Reveals the Intention,' often classified as Yogacara) and the *Ratnagotravibhaga* (or *Uttaratantra Shastra*), a commentary by Maitreya on the first five sutras above.

[30] From the section, 'Simile of a tathagata in a lotus,' in 'A Buddha Within: The Tathagatagarbhasutra,' Michael Zimmerman, trans., IRIAB, 2002. p.106

[31] 'Sublime Continuum,' I, 27

[32] *Uttaratantrashastravyakhya*, or *Ratnagotravibhagavyakhya*, a commentary by Asanga on the *Uttaratantrashastra* by Maitreya

[33] Tib. *sems sde* or 'mind section' – along with the 'space' and 'instruction' sections, one of the three sections into which Dzogchen teachings were divided by Manjushrimitra

[34] The ten 'aspects' or meanings of 'tathagatagarbha' are mentioned individually in various sutras; they are listed and explained in Maitreya's *Uttaratantrashastra*, Chapter 1, Section 8.

[35] *Anunatvapurnatvanirdesa Sutra*

[36] See *Aryavamsa Sutra* ('Discourse on the Traditions of the Noble Ones') *Anguttara Nikaya*, Vol. II, p. 27.

[37] Tib. *rang bzhin gyi gnas rigs*

[38] Tib. *rgyas 'gyur gyi rigs*

[39] These families of beings are described in the *Lankavatara* and *Samdhinirmocana Sutras*

[40] One of the five treatises of Maitreya, a principal commentary on the *Prajnaparamita Sutras* literature.

[41] The Tibetan title, '*sdong po bkod pa'i mdo*,' or the Skt. *Gandavyuhasutra*,

is sometimes translated as 'Flower Array Sutra.' The *Gandavyuhasutra* is the final book of the *Avatamsakasutra*, and tells the story of a bodhisattva with 52 teachers

[42] Grammar or linguistics, logic, medicine, the arts, and 'inner science'

[43] Skt. *Bodhisattvacaryaavataara,* Shambala Classics, 2006. p.63. Verse 14 of chapter 5, on vigilence or alertness.

[44] From the 'Opening the Door to the Path of Liberation,' Younge Khachab Rinpoche.

[45] Korde rushen (Tib. *khor 'das ru shan*) is a Dzogchen preliminary practice for distinguishing or exchanging samsara and nirvana

[46] The four paths are: stream enterers, once-returners, non-returners, and no more learning

[47] *Samdhinirmocana,* Ch. 7

[48] 'Four Hundred Verse Treatise on the Actions of a Bodhisattva,' Ch.8

[49] The 'four reliances' are given in several Mahayana sources, including chapter 8 of the Mahayana *Mahaparinirvana Sutra* and stanza 53 of Nagarjuna's *Dharmasangraha.*

[50] *Abhisamayalankara.* The full title is translated as 'The Treatise of Quintessential Instructions of the Perfection of Wisdom: Ornament of Clear Realization.'

[51] Tibetan name Senge Zangpo (Tib. *seng ge bzang po*), an eighth-century Indian pandita, also called Haribhadra, disciple of Santarakshita and important commentator on Maitreya/Asanga's 'Ornament of Clear Realization.'

[52] Tib. *'phags pa grol sde,'* Tibetan name of Vimuktisena, disciple of Vasubhandu, author of the first (sixth century) commentary on the 'Ornament of Clear Realization.'

[53] *Astahasrika Prajnamaramita Sutra*, chapter 32, section 2. As translated by Edward Conze, 'As long as this perfection of wisdom shall be observed in the world, one can be sure that for so long does the Tathagata abide in it.'

[54] Dignaga (Tib. *phyogs kyi glang po*), *Pramanasamuccaya,* or 'Compendium of Pramana (Valid Cognition)' The five great treatises are Maitreya's 'Ornament of Clear Realization,' Dharmakirti's *Pramanavarttika* (commentary on the *Pramanasamuccaya*) , Chandrakirti's *Madhyamakavatara,* Vasubandhu's *Abhidharmakosa*, and Gunaprabha's *Vinayasutra.*

[55] Dignaga wrote the 'Compendium on Valid Cognition, and Dharmakirti wrote the *Pramanavarttika*, which is one of the five great treatises

[56] 1) neither one nor many, 2) vajra slivers (analysis of causality), 3) refuting the arising of either an existent or a nonexistent (analysis of result), 4) refuting the four possibilities of arising (both cause and result), and 5) dependent "origination (the "king of reasons')

⁵⁷ The twenty-two similes are mentioned in chapter 1 of Maitreya's Ornament of Clear Realization and elaborated upon in commentaries. They correspond to aspects of bodhicitta practice, from the aspirations of ordinary beings through the full enlightenment of buddhahood. The similes are: 1) earth-like, 2) gold-like, 3) moon-like, 4) fire-like, 5) treasure-like, 6) jewel-mine-like, 7) ocean-like, 8) vajra-like, 9) mountain-like, 10) medicine-like, 11) guide-like, 12) wishing-jewel-like, 13) sun-like, 14) song-like, 15) king-like, 16) treasury-like, 17) great-highway-like, 18) excellent-horse-like, 19) spring-of-water-like, 20) sweet-sounding-music-like, 21) river-like, and 22) cloud-like.

⁵⁸ Knowledge, practice, and completion of all paths is a part of Mahayana training on the implicit meaning of the perfection of wisdom. From the *Perfection of Wisdom Sutra in 18,000 Lines*, "Bodhisattvas should practice all paths – whether the path of a sravaka, a pratyekabuddha, or a buddha – and should know all paths. They should also perform the deeds of these paths and bring all of them to completion."

⁵⁹ The (refined) form and formless realms, although higher than the desire realm, are still in samsara, hence mundane.

⁶⁰ An overview of prajnaparamita literature is given in Karl Brunnholzl, 'Gone Beyond: The Prajnaparamita Sutras, the Ornament of Clear Realization and Its Commentaries in the Kagyu Tradition.'

⁶¹ The eight topics are 1) knowledge of all aspects, the omniscient wisdom of buddhas, 2) knowledge of paths, the wisdom of bodhisattvas, 3) knowledge of basis, the wisdom of hearers and pratyekabuddhas, 4) (practice of) full awakening to all aspects, 5) (practice of) culmination clear realization, 6) (practice of) serial clear realization, 7) (practice of) clear realization in a single instant, and 8) resultant truth body.

⁶² These seven factors are: great focus, great practice, great wisdom, great effort, great skill, great accomplishment, and great Buddha activity.

⁶³ For an explanation of ornamental buddha nature, see chapter 8, first section on buddha nature in the Indian traditions.

⁶⁴ Chandrakirti, 'Introduction to the Middle Way.' Shambhala Publications, 2005. Ch 1, v1-2.

⁶⁵ For an extensive presentation of the development and conception process see 'Profound Inner Meaning' by the Third Karmapa Rangjung Dorje.

⁶⁶ These four contemplations are on precious human life, impermanence, karma and the suffering of samsara.

⁶⁷ The four primary branches are the Karma Kagyu, Barom Kagyu, Tshalpa Kagyu and Phagdru Kagyu. The eight secondary branches are the Drikung, Drukpa, Lingre, Shuksep, Taklung, Trophu, Yazang, and Yelpa, which all stemmed from Phagmo Drupa, who was one of Gampopa disciples.

⁶⁸ The second Karmapa, Karma Pakshi.

[69] Roberts, Peter Alan, 'Mahamudra and Related Instructions.' p. 353

ABOUT YOUNGE KHACHAB RINPOCHE

Younge Khachab Rinpoche is a highly accomplished Dzogchen master and non-sectarian, or Rime, scholar. Seventh in the line of Khachab reincarnations, he is a direct descendent of the famed terton, Yongey Mingyur Dorje, and holds the family lineage for this cycle of termas. Rinpoche's family has been closely associated with the Karmapas since the 17th century.

At the age of thirteen, Rinpoche was ordained by the 16th Gyalwa Karmapa and began his study within the Karma Kagyu Lineage. However, at age fifteen, he left for Ganden Jangtse, the Gelug University in South India to begin his distinguished academic pursuit, obtaining the title of Geshe in Madhyamaka philosophy under the direction of Ganden Trichen Jamphel Shenphen.

In 1989, following his father's advice, he went to the seat of the Karma Kagyu in Rumtek monastery in Sikkim to complete the traditional three-year-seven month retreat in Mahamudra and the Six-Yogas of Naropa under the guidance of his root lama Bokar Rinpoche.

After the retreat he received an invitation to teach at Thagten Nyingje Ling monastery in Nepal, where he stayed for several years.

Rinpoche became a Khenpo at the Kagyu Thagten Nyingje Ling Monastery and is revered as the first Khenpo at the montastery. During this time he received further Mahamudra clarifications with the Drikung Drubwang Rinpoche and stayed in retreat for four months under his personal direction. Afterwards, inspired by the great realized masters who followed the Rime path, Rinpoche went on to pursue the Nyingma and Bön practice of Dzogchen.

Rinpoche has received teachings and transmissions from many great Nyingma masters, including H.H. Dilgo Khyentse, H.H. Dudjom Rinpoche, H.H. Penor Rinpoche, H.H. Chobgyed Trichen Rinpoche, and Khenchen Phyentse, a heart disciple of the Dzogchen master Khenpo Munsel. He studied the Bön Dzogchen tradition with Lopon Tenzin Namdak Rinpoche. His Dzogchen root guru was the hidden Nyingma yogi Dingri Khenchen who lived his whole life in isolated retreat.

Younge Khachab Rinpoche is considered to be a highly qualified Tantra and Dzogchen teacher. His training has incorporated the view and meditations of the four main schools in Tibetan Buddhism. He believes in the transmission of the uncompromised, pure teachings of the oral and textual lineages. He represents the Rime philosophical tradition, incorporating the best the four schools have to offer.

Younge Khachab Rinpoche is acknowledged as a traditional master of the Mahamudra and Dzogchen practices. He received all signs of accomplishment in the Six Yogas of Naropa, particularly Tsa Lung and Dream Yoga. He is fully able to transmit all stages of the Vajrayana path. He has studied widely with the top masters in the Kagyu, Nyingma, Gelug, Sakya and Bön traditions and he is known in India and Nepal for his vast knowledge of the Rime tradition.

Rinpoche's style of teaching is direct, warm and engaging, extensive yet practical. He is accessible to his students and takes a personal interest in his student's progress. Rinpoche currently makes his home in Madison, Wisconsin.

For more information visit youngedrodulling.org

CPSIA information can be obtained
at www.ICGtesting.com
Printed in the USA
FSHW011253221019
63276FS